Advance Praise for Killing Journalism

Jim Lehrer, former anchor, PBS NewsHour

KILLING JOURNALISM is a veteran journalist/critic's forceful take on the crisis mode that currently swamps and shadows the work of American journalism. Joe Strupp offers some ways out along with his warts-and-faults critique. The valuable end result is a book for anyone who cares about the past, present and future of a free press in our democratic society.

Ken Auletta, Media Writer, *The New Yorker*

Joe Strupp has written a vital book. His lens is wide, spanning the many business challenges, ethical minefields, and disruptions that assail the Fourth Estate. His reporting is careful and judicious. And his writing is as clear as a church bell. Yes, Strupp's book should be taught in journalism schools. But it deserves a broader audience. It should be read by citizens alarmed both by false claims of "fake news," and by how the press too often heedlessly grants ammunition to its critics.

Margaret Sullivan, *Washington Post* media columnist, former *New York Times* public editor

Joe Strupp provides a much-needed voice of sanity as he surveys today's media landscape, and all that's gone wrong. His knowledge and experience might even help us fix it – or at least understand the scope of the problem.

Marc Berman, Editor in Chief, *Programming Insider*

Joe Strupp is a professional media journalist with an observing eye, a passion for reporting, and the knowledge and connections to make a positive difference. We worked together when Joe was a media reporter for *Editor & Publisher*, and my experience with Joe remains a personal highlight.

D1472021

KILLING JOURNALISM

KILLING JOURNALISM

*How Greed, Laziness
(and Donald Trump) Are Destroying News,
and How We Can Save It*

JOE STRUPP

Willow Street Press   New York

For Claire, Cloey, and Cole.

CONTENTS

INTRODUCTION	3
TRUMPED	10
FEWER JOURNALISTS, LESS JOURNALISM	40
WHEN NEWS WAS NEWS	73
FAIR AND BALANCED? NOT QUITE	108
FALSE EQUIVALENCY IS FALSE NEWS	160
FALSE AND DEADLY?	188
WEB WOES	208
OVERKILLED AND UNDERREPORTED	244
FEAR FACTOR	276
AFFORDING THE FIRST AMENDMENT	284
WHO IS WATCHING?	317
WHO IS NO LONGER WATCHING?	339
NON-PROFIT IS THE FUTURE	359
ACKNOWLEDGMENTS	378
ABOUT THE AUTHOR	380
SOURCES	383

INTRODUCTION

I had already covered many conservative political events when I attended my first and only Values Voter Summit in Washington, D.C., in September 2015. After five years at progressive media watchdog outlet *Media Matters for America*, exposing right-wing lies and inaccuracies was nothing new.

But nothing I had done prepared me for the Values Voter Summit, the annual political event sponsored by the anti-gay and anti-choice Family Research Council. I didn't ordinarily cover this hate fest because, unlike even the Conservative Political Action Conference (CPAC), it included such raw discrimination and anger that most of the top right-wing media names avoided it.

But this year was different. My bosses at *Media Matters* wanted to check it out because then-presidential candidate Donald Trump was set to appear. A year later, Trump became the first major party presidential nominee to address the group.

At the time, it surprised me that Trump, even with bigoted and sexist views of his own, would lower himself to this level. The Family Research Council's long history of hate speech and discrimination lead the Southern Poverty Law Center to designate them as a hate group.

"The FRC often makes false claims about the LGBT community based on discredited research and junk science," the SPLC declares on its website. "The intention is to denigrate LGBT people as the

3

organization battles against same-sex marriage, hate crime laws, anti-bullying programs and the repeal of the military's 'Don't Ask, Don't Tell' policy."

The Human Rights Campaign has also stated: "FRC's Values Voters Summit, an influential watering hole for many anti-LGBTQ politicians with national ambitions, provides a platform for candidates to spew anti-LGBTQ vitriol … at past Values Voters Summits, speakers have compared same-sex couples getting married to drug use and people marrying children and dogs."

On this particular week, the Summit was planning to honor infamous Kentucky Clerk Kim Davis, who had been jailed for refusing to issue a marriage license to a gay couple that year in defiance of state law and the U.S. Supreme Court. She declined to be interviewed by anyone other than right-wing media at the event and, when I approached her to ask a question, her husband elbowed me in the ribs.

With that kind of atmosphere at play, it seemed surprising that anyone who wanted to be elected president would attend and be tied in with such a mean-spirited group. But with Marco Rubio and Ted Cruz also on the schedule, perhaps it was not so surprising Trump would also show up.

It turned out to be a crucial foreshadowing of what would become the most hate-filled presidential campaign in modern U.S. history. Trump would spend much of the next two years vehemently attacking women, the LGBT community, immigrants, Muslims, and many others.

Just a few months earlier, Trump had formally entered the presidential race and at the time of the summit, he had a falling out with Fox News. At the first GOP presidential debate a month earlier, Megyn Kelly asked Trump about his abusive comments against women, to which Trump responded by falsely claiming he had not made such comments about anyone other than Rosie O'Donnell. Soon after, he created a media firestorm when he said of Kelly, "you could see there was blood coming out of her eyes, blood coming out of her, wherever." Despite his later denials, many took that as Trump insinuating Kelly was on her period.

I was curious to see if we could ask Trump about it as he entered the room. At that time, he loved sucking up the public accolades when he appeared at a location, so he often nixed the backstage doors for a full-crowd entrance.

Sure enough, as *Media Matters'* then-president Bradley Beychok and I awaited his arrival, Trump bounded in to the entryway and headed toward the ballroom.

While his entourage moved him through the crowd, Bradley asked him if Fox had been fair to him. He responded: "We'll see." Then I asked when he would return to Fox. His answer: "We'll see, we'll see. They have to treat me fairly and I'm sure they will. I'm sure they will."

Of course, he was right, he returned and his relationship with Fox News only grew more devoted and intertwined as he ascended to the presidency.

What stuck with me was the vile nature of the entire Values Voter event and how Trump, and other candidates, would pander to this discriminatory and hateful group. It showed early on what kind of crowd he preferred, and how outlets like Fox News and others on the right would support him despite these questionable leanings. This kind of right-wing news favoritism of Trump and other divisive candidates has proven to be less about ideology and more about taking advantage of a growing, angry population.

Yes, the mainstream news media has their own share of issues, but slanting the story to the left, making facts up and unfairly attacking the president are not usually among them, despite what Trump and his allies would have you believe.

The problems the news media faces are actually much more serious.

The traditional news media that had long been the place for the public to demand information about important events, people of power, uncovering of wrongdoing, investigation of government, and stories of interest and intrigue has become nothing less than a shadow of its former self.

More interested in profits and ratings/circulation/web traffic than the people it serves or the responsibilities the profession requires, the only industry that enjoys U.S. Constitutional protection has given up on its job of fully and fairly informing the public.

And the most recent and perhaps egregious example of this was the fawning, lazy and dangerous coverage of Trump during the 2016 campaign. And now that Trump is in office, he is succeeding in discounting the press, having convinced millions that they are not to be trusted, mostly based on false statements and impressions.

As my former colleagues at *Media Matters for America* and I have chronicled, news coverage of Trump – and much of the 2016 presidential campaign – centered on the outrageous comments and claims of "The Donald" that have brought record ratings to many news outlets.

Worse yet, news outlets altered the practice of responsible journalism in many cases by failing to challenge Trump on certain claims and proposals, while letting him appear at length with little or no context. Even allowing him to call into news shows in a way that no other candidate has or would have been allowed in the past.

During my 30 years in journalism, I have seen how the cutbacks in staffing and resources forced newsrooms, from newspapers to television, to greatly contract their scope of coverage.

Journalism reporting jobs have shrunk from nearly 53,000 in 2005 to 42,920 in 2015, according to the U.S. Department of Labor. This evidence is clear in the news product. Newspapers are much smaller and are providing fewer real news stories, while broadcast and cable outlets do less reporting and more stories and programs based on hype and speculation. Opinion makers dominate night time cable audiences in place of real news gathering or investigation.

News outlets will say the cutbacks in revenue and advertising force them to take the easy approach. But it's more than that. Many have found that giving audiences easy, cheap coverage on something is enough to keep, or even increase, ratings. The demand for eyeballs has overtaken the demand for in-depth coverage or wide-ranging reporting.

Overhyping stories has become more common than not. Just in the last few years news organizations devoted hours and pages of coverage to Ebola scares that grossly inflated domestic dangers, mundane and overdone coverage of weather events, and inane celebrity non-stories centered on people like the Kardashians or Kanye West.

At the same time, many so-called "conservative" journalists and news outlets have been able to expand the myth that mainstream journalism is left-leaning, and even slanted toward misreporting to favor progressives. This is not only untrue, but dangerous to believe.

By swaying public opinion of many to mistrust traditional news outlets, these conservative "journalists" also open the door for themselves and allow their self-admitted slanted coverage to be accepted.

The truth is, what some claim to be left-leaning bias is actually an open view of the world and of news, facts, and viewpoints. To truly offer a fair account of a news story or issue, a reporter must be open-minded, be able to seek understanding of all sides and even fringe beliefs. Issues involving gay rights, gender identity, gun ownership, drugs, sex, politics, and the environment need to be seen through a non-judgmental lens. If that is seen as liberal, so be it.

That's just part of the problem. The main issue at work is how news coverage has given in to greed with demands for profits, and laziness by allowing coverage to target the easy, "sexy" story. Political coverage focuses much more on the horse race of candidates rather than the issues. It often allows spokespeople for both sides to battle on air instead of journalists and political experts with no dog in the fight explaining and reviewing such issues.

My first news assignments came as a staffer at *The Tempest*, our high school newspaper in Summit, New Jersey. After four years at Brooklyn College, where I was involved with the campus newspapers and radio station, I worked for the now-defunct *Daily Journal* of Elizabeth, N.J.

Curiosity took me west after two years and I spent time at three California papers – *The Argus* in Fremont; *The San Francisco Independent* and *The Press-Enterprise* of Riverside.

But my interest in news soon went beyond the stories to the process, ethics and issues of covering them. That's when I headed back east to join *Editor & Publisher*, the one-time "bible" of the newspaper business, where I focused on newsroom conflicts, reporter rights, and the ever-growing staff cutbacks. After 11 years, it folded in 2009, later popping up in a much more streamlined format.

Luckily, *Media Matters for America* came along and tapped me as an investigative reporter. A dream job that allowed me to learn more about right-wing and false journalism – often one in the same – than I ever expected, and a chance to identify such misreporting.

During my 18 years at *Editor & Publisher* and *Media Matters*, I saw in too many places the real problems with today's news and media, and how it has fallen in both quantity and quality.

There have been many media-related books that either claim the media is too far right or too far left and detail the problems with the industry and its changing tide. But I believe not enough attention has been paid to the real problems that I cite – the greed and laziness, and the fact that many people now accept that news is poorly done and focused on the lowest common denominator in terms of audience and programming.

But it doesn't have to be. There are answer to these issues, among them the rise of non-profit news outlets that focus on reporting and facts without a worry about advertising or readership. But that will only take us to part of the solution: there is a clear need to get back to direct reporting with real investigation and basic journalism, as well as the need for removal of the greed-based and easy approach aspects that now exploit the business all too often.

TRUMPED

I first reported on Donald Trump back in 1990 as a reporter for *The Daily Journal* in Elizabeth, N.J.

My rookie job out of college, the small daily paper – which closed two years later – was a perfect training ground for hungry, cheap-living reporters who wanted to learn about local news, digging up sources, cops, crime and politics.

A Jersey boy since age seven, I was fresh out of Brooklyn College when I signed on with the scrappy daily whose alum included Carl Bernstein and whose first owner was none other than Alexander Hamilton.

Before becoming the subject of a Broadway hit, Hamilton was the creator of a few papers, including the *New York Post*. *The Daily Journal* had been the oldest daily paper in the state and one of the longest-printing in the nation when it shut down in early 1992.

But it was still going that day in June 1990 when I stumbled across the local diner that would become nationally known within 24 hours thanks to Trump. At the time, The Donald was going through one of several financial upheavals.

Among his troubles that month were a group of bondholders who filed a class-action lawsuit related to more than $600 million worth of bonds in Trump's Atlantic City casinos. Other mounting debt-related problems forced him into the first of four corporate bankruptcies just a year later.

So, when I walked into the EATS coffee shop on June 18, 1990, across from *The Daily Journal* building on North Broad Street to get my usual morning cup of java, I was not completely surprised that Trump's financial situation was a topic of discussion.

The 1980s is where he had rocketed to fame as the flashy, outspoken and tabloid-favorite New York real estate developer. The *Post*'s Page Six loved him and he loved the attention. In reality, he was never among the top city real estate magnates. He was just very good at getting attention, sparking controversy and mostly putting his name on everything he owned.

His first book, *The Art of the Deal*, was a bestseller. But co-author Tony Schwartz, who worked with him on the book, became one of his fiercest critics during Trump's 2016 presidential run, later writing in 2017, "When he feels aggrieved, he reacts impulsively and defensively, constructing a self-justifying story that doesn't depend on facts and always directs the blame to others."

But back then, Trump still had a largely positive image and his plight was a source of concern for some. Among them was the owner of the coffee shop, Ed Marcini, who had put out an empty mayonnaise jar with a sign that read – Donald Trump Fund.

"Donald is into free enterprise and he's in trouble, so we feel bad for him," Marcini told me that day. "We are trying to help him."

Partly tongue-in-cheek, but partly serious, Marcini wanted to raise some cash for the over-leveraged businessman.

After my story ran on Page One the following day, the news went wild with camera crews, phone interview requests and radio talk shows seeking out Marcini for comment. When I visited later, tripods lined the front of the counter and Marcini was bouncing from short-order cook to on-camera interviewee all day. It all culminated that night on NBC *Nightly News* when the story was used as part of a package on Trump's financial woes.

It was clear then the drawing power Trump had, even in apparent defeat. Few likely expected him to run for president. But when he later did, it was not a complete surprise as he had transformed his local developer fame into television success and tabloid fodder. First as producer of the Miss Universe and Miss America pageants, and later with *The Apprentice*. And all along the way Trump was able to push the image of himself as some kind of business success. New York media, and those elsewhere, ate it up. But the facts later revealed he was no business genius. That first bankruptcy was followed up by numerous others in the following decades.

Wayne Barrett, who wrote a 1992 book on Trump and covered him for *The Village Voice* for decades, told me in 2016 that issues such as Trump's "mob associations – probably 25 named in my book," hadn't been covered, adding that "nobody would finance him since 1991, no bank would finance him on a significant finance deal."

But the tabloid coverage of his personal life, outspoken views and Manhattan party scene participation overshadowed most of his reality. Trump became an expert at using the media that also used him for ratings, readership and headlines, to promote himself.

Eventually Trump became the outspoken, dapper and still youthful New York developer. His willingness to be interviewed, photographed and involved in any number of public events and issues gave him a step up on most other, more-successful business leaders who coveted the gains and power from their real successes more than publicity.

Trump also began early to put his name on everything, in many cases projects he had no part in creating other than being paid to share his famous moniker on buildings, products and a bogus university.

In the growing "me" decade of the 1980s, and later personalized identity elements of the 1990s and beyond, Trump's publicity approach was gold for him. And again, the press took it all in. When he hosted *The Apprentice*, he was not the first person to yell "You're Fired!" on television. But he did it on a major network reality show as that genre was exploding and the connection stuck.

The Donald took that fame and built it further, amassing wealth through selling his name for others to use. Many of the buildings you see with "TRUMP" in big, often gold, letters are not even owned by him. He was merely paid for their use. If that isn't a sign of celebrity, what is?

When he apparently became bored with just making money off his name and found less and less financial opportunity due to economic woes in the early 2000s – and fewer people willing to do business with him – he began creeping into politics.

As early as 1980 Trump had been asked about running for office when Rona Barrett inquired if he would ever seek the presidency. At that time, he said no. Although when Barret asked what he would do if he lost his fortune then, he said, "Maybe I'd run for president." And the question kept coming up in later years.

Trump would always humor the press and help promote whatever project he was involved with by allowing speculation of a presidential campaign, but never formally entered the race. He made clear his disagreements with George W. Bush's policies in the early 2000s and always hinted a run was possible, but again fell short of tossing his hat into the ring.

Then came 2008 and the historic election of Barack Obama, whose eligibility some began questioning early in the race. At issue: Obama's birth certificate. Some wondered if he was actually a naturalized citizen eligible to run given his father's Kenyan background and his birth in Hawaii.

This bogus claim about the new African-American leader was not only racist on its face, but baseless as well. But while some used it to sow doubt about Obama's eligibility, many in the news media went along with it and allowed it to become at least for a while, an issue. There was no reason to question where the president had been born other than the fact he had an unusual name, a different color, and a foreign-born father.

The eligibility of his GOP opponent, John McCain, could have been a subject of more uncertainty since McCain had been born in the Panama Canal Zone, which is technically a foreign location, but considered U.S. property due to a treaty at the time.

Obama's citizenship issue appeared to have died down in mid-2008 when his campaign released the so-called "short-form" of the document, and later the "long-form."

But it didn't go away completely and as Obama prepared to run for re-election in 2012, Trump drew major attention when he renewed the false debate in early 2011 at the Conservative Political Action Conference (CPAC).

During my eight years at *Media Matters for America*, I attended at least eight CPACs dating back to 2010. Trump attended most of those events and anyone who understands politics knows CPAC has become the heartbeat for hard-right viewpoints.

The events are true "red meat" for hardline conservatives and Trump knew just what to say to fire up the crowds. I recall vividly the 2011 CPAC appearance by the future president, who breathed new life into the virtually dead issue of Obama's legitimacy just in time for the upcoming 2012 presidential campaign.

During his address, Trump hinted at his own 2012 candidacy, which never came to pass. But more importantly, he again questioned Obama's background and sparked continued questioning of Obama's legitimacy that went on for several more months in 2011.

"The people who went to school with him, they never saw him, they don't know who he is," Trump said in the CPAC speech, raising the doubt about his background in Hawaii. Five more times that year, he specifically called on Obama to release his full birth certificate, according to CNN.com.

"Why doesn't he show his birth certificate? There's something on that birth certificate that he doesn't like," Trump said during a lively appearance on *The View* on March 23, 2011, just a month following the speech.

A week later, on *The Laura Ingraham Show*, he added, "He doesn't have a birth certificate, or if he does, there's something on that certificate that is very bad for him. Now, somebody told me – and I have no idea if this is bad for him or not, but perhaps it would be – that where it says 'religion,' it might have 'Muslim.' And if you're a Muslim, you don't change your religion, by the way."

In that instance, Trump not only fed the false myth about Obama's citizenship, but added a hint that he was Muslim, another fake claim espoused by many against the former president.

And while many in the press were glad to counter Trump's claims by reporting that there was no proof of any false birth certificate or justified reason to question the short-form version that had been released, they would also let Trump repeat the lie and baseless claim again and again. And many on the right, including Fox News's own Sean Hannity, Lou Dobbs and Jeanine Pirro, all demanded Obama release the longer version in 2011.

A demand like this was never made of any previous president. Like the old news joke, asking the mayor if he ever beat his wife. He says, "no." Headline: "Mayor Denies Beating Wife." In this case, it was the press asking Obama if he was born in another country." He says: "no." Headline: "Obama Denies Foreign Birth."

Several books were also written claiming Obama's birth certificate was either a fraud or not properly produced. One of the more well-known was by Jerome Corsi, a conspiracy theorist linked to far-right radio host and Sandy Hook Truther Alex Jones. *Where's the Birth Certificate? The Case That Barack Obama is Not Eligible to Be President* debuted at Number 6 on *The New York Times* Best Sellers list on June 5, 2011.

First, it falsely claimed that McCain's citizenship had been strongly questioned in 2008, which was untrue. It later stated, "no legal authority has ever verified Barack Obama's eligibility to be president, that glaring inconsistencies and blackouts in his life narrative have caused widespread doubts among the American populace and that, in fact, a compelling body of evidence exists that Obama is not a natural-born citizen."

He did not point out that no other president had ever had his "eligibility verified."

Months later, when Obama finally released the long-form birth certificate, Corsi told me in an interview he still wasn't convinced.

"I think the birth certificate released by the White House is a fraudulent document," he insisted.

But none of those outlets and their push against the legitimacy of Obama would have come about had Trump not first raised the issue months earlier. It clearly had an effect as a 2011 poll found more than half of Republican voters who were planning to vote in the 2012 presidential primary believed Obama had been born outside the United States.

Trump had proved not only his ability to rouse GOP voters with outrageous claims, partly based on a racist and an anti-Muslim approach, but also a willingness to perpetuate a lie and use it to boost his own popularity. Although he finally admitted in 2016 during his own campaign that Obama was born in the U.S., Trump would again repeat the birther claim in years to come.

When he finally ran for president in 2016, announcing in mid-2015, the birther issue was put on the back burner as Trump raised a slew of new issues – and untruths – that would be wielded throughout his run for the White House. And many of those were either not questioned by many in the press, or in some cases backed up and repeated by some of the same outlets that let his birther claims be spread about.

At first, many in the press discounted his candidacy. The *Huffington Post* went so far as to famously announce that its entertainment department, not the news section, would be covering Trump. Others did more to cover him, but with a lack of seriousness and a willingness to let his comments be reported without question or fact-checking.

Cable TV may have made the biggest blunder by broadcasting many of his events and rallies, where he would spew false claims and incorrect assertions without any real oversight. There were times when MSNBC or CNN would offer live feeds of his entire appearance, much broader than any of his opponents, and with no real editing.

"While there are journalists who have aggressively challenged Trump … much of the coverage, including broadcasting his rallies and events live in their entirety, has been uncritical and even unfiltered," *Buzzfeed*'s Kyle Blaine wrote in March 2016. "Some of it conducted by interviewers unwilling or unable to provide much more than a platform for the candidate."

A June 2016 study of primary coverage from the Shorenstein Center on Media, Politics and Public Policy at Harvard University found that Trump received 34% of Republican presidential news coverage in the last six months of 2015, with Jeb Bush second at just 18%. A *New York Times* study in March 2016 found that Trump had received what amounted to nearly $2 billion in "free media" via such coverage, with the next closest Republican being Ted Cruz at $313 million and Hillary Clinton receiving $746 million.

"Like all candidates, he benefits from what is known as earned media: news and commentary about his campaign on television, in newspapers and magazines, and on social media," the *Times* reported. "Earned media typically dwarfs paid media in a campaign. The big difference between Mr. Trump and other candidates is that he is far better than any other candidate – maybe than any candidate ever – at earning media."

In addition to the free coverage and air time, Trump was not truly scrutinized in the early months of his campaign as news outlets still saw him as a side story and with no chance of being nominated. He was treated as a celebrity and someone whose comments – from anti-Muslim attacks to outrageous views of women – were ratings gold. Networks and cable TV shows knew that he would draw interest no matter what he said, but they remained unconvinced that his entire profile needed to be reviewed.

Some traditional investigative outlets such as *The New York Times* and the *Washington Post* dug into Trump's past early on. The *Post* on May 14, 2016, published a lengthy look at Trump's previous mistreatment of women, while the *Post*'s David Farenthold earned a Pulitzer Prize for a string of articles that began as early as March 2016 exposing Trump's misleading charitable giving claims.

But those were few and far between. For most media brands, letting Trump be Trump – lies, offensive comments and all – was enough.

Among the biggest and perhaps most surprising offenders were Joe Scarborough and Mika Brzezinski on MSNBC's *Morning Joe*. The pair, and future married couple, went all out for Trump in the beginning of 2016, to the point where *Fortune* magazine called it an "overly friendly relationship with the former reality-TV host," later noting, "at one point in February, the Republican candidate thanked the hosts for their support. 'You guys have been supporters, and I really appreciate it,' he said."

Fortune cited a CNN report in February that revealed Scarborough's friendship with Trump had become an "increasing source of discomfort" at NBC. Jonah Goldberg of *National Review* wrote about how *Morning Joe*'s "Trump worship" had made the show unwatchable. Goldberg said the hosts "have taken to insufferable gloating about their prescience and condescending snootiness aimed at anyone or anything that might disrupt the Trump narrative they've bought into and helped to create."

But Trump then turned on the couple in mid-2016, at one point raising widespread reaction when he tweeted that Brzezinski was "off the wall, a neurotic and not very bright mess!" The show has since made it a mission to ridicule Trump and attack many of his actions, apparently hoping people will forget how they buddied up to him not too long ago.

During the time I spent at *Media Matters for America*, from 2010 to 2018, we followed Trump's campaign and its coverage closely and saw an unprecedented number of false statements and outright lies for a major presidential candidate. But many of these statements were not initially challenged, in many cases because they were from live events or interviews with either pro-Trump outlets or unqualified interviewers.

But one of the most notable was former NBC *Today Show* anchor Matt Lauer's strange hosting of one-on-one interviews with Trump and Democratic nominee Hillary Clinton in September 2016. Instead of having them debate or at least having a joint event where voters could compare the two on similar issues, they were interviewed separately.

The host – who would eventually be fired from NBC for alleged improper treatment and sexual harassment of women – was later criticized for failing to challenge Trump on his claims that he had always opposed the Iraq war. Although such a claim had been proven false on many occasions. Lauer let it slide.

Media Matters later wrote: "Challenging mendacity in the presidential debates is paramount for a number of reasons, first and foremost being that Trump's entire campaign has been grounded in lies and conspiracy theories ... As *Huffington Post* senior media reporter Michael Calderone explained, failure to fact-check lies in the debates 'leaves the viewing public with a 'he said, she said' situation when the journalist picked to be onstage could say, decisively, who is right.' This, in turn, enables misinformation – an injustice to voters – and normalizes this behavior – a threat to democratic and journalistic processes."

PolitiFact, the Pulitzer-Prize-winning website that built a side industry exposing Trump's inaccuracies, has rated 69% of Trump's statements since he began running for office to be either false or mostly false. It found that just five percent are true.

In a July 2016 posting, *PolitiFact* detailed what it dubbed "17 Times Donald Trump Said One Thing and Then Denied It," with examples ranging from denying he said John McCain was not a hero because he was captured to claiming he never called women, 'fat pigs,' 'dogs,' 'slobs,' and 'disgusting animals,' which became a major moment in the first 2016 GOP primary debate moderated by Megyn Kelly.

On March 13, 2016, *Politico* posted a lengthy report on its fact-checking of Trump for one week in the middle of primary season, revealing it had scrutinized about four and a half hours of speeches, comments and statements during that time.

Their findings: "More than five dozen statements [are] deemed mischaracterizations, exaggerations, or simply false – the kind of stuff that would have been stripped from one of our stories, or made the whole thing worthy of the spike. It equates to roughly one misstatement every five minutes on average."

The story added, "From warning of the death of Christianity in America to claiming that he is taking no money from donors, the

Manhattan billionaire and reality-show celebrity said something far from truthful many times over to the thousands of people packed into his raucous rallies. His remarks represent an extraordinary mix of inaccurate claims about domestic and foreign policy and personal and professional boasts that rarely measure up when checked against primary sources."

Reporters are used to politicians who exaggerate and, yes, lie on occasion. But Trump's blatant dishonesty and continued pattern of making up facts, or denying those that are true, was unparalleled in a presidential election, at least from a front-runner and eventual major party nominee.

At first, many reporters were unsure how to handle the outright dishonesty given its unique status. Such a phenomenon forced many news outlets to fact-check even the most basic statements because it was unknown when or where he would falsify a fact.

It eventually reached a point where CNN and MSNBC would clearly state via lower-screen graphics that Trump had just stated an incorrect claim. One example was in August 2016 when during a speech, CNN posted a chyron graphic on screen stating: "TRUMP CALLS OBAMA FOUNDER OF ISIS (HE'S NOT)." Two months earlier, during its broadcast of a Trump speech clip from Sacramento, CNN did it again, declaring on screen during the clip, "TRUMP: I NEVER SAID JAPAN SHOULD HAVE NUKES (HE DID)."

The unusual approach drew both support from Trump opponents and some journalists, while others claimed it focused such corrections more on Trump than rival Hillary Clinton.

When the 2016 presidential debates took place in the fall, fact-checking was a regular part of the coverage, with live, real-time corrections of the candidate's comments – targeting both Trump and Clinton. The *Washington Post*, *The New York Times*, NPR, Bloomberg as well as *PolitiFact*, Factcheck.org, and *Politico* provided unprecedented detailed scrutiny of the candidates' debate claims.

"It's really remarkable to see how big news operations have come around to challenging false and deceitful claims directly. It's about time," Brooks Jackson, the director emeritus of Factcheck.org told CNN in 2016.

One final major story before the 2016 election was the now infamous Access Hollywood tape when Trump was caught in a private discussion from 2005 with host Bully Bush bragging about abusing women, at one point saying he could "grab them by the pussy."

The story was accurate, with clear audio evidence of Trump's comments and no apparent excuse for the behavior. Ironically, Bush was later fired from NBC, where he was then working for the *Today Show* and rumors flew that Trump might drop out of the race.

But no exit occurred and, of course, Trump went on to win the election.

Some critics have said the scrutiny of Trump's past, actions, comments and claims came too late. Aside from the specific cases mentioned and the ongoing investigations by the likes of the *Washington Post*, *The New York Times* and others, most news outlets and mainstream media did not jump into real diligent investigations of Trump until his GOP nomination was assured, in the early summer of 2016.

And even when they did, few gave his checkered and misleading business record the true scrutiny it deserved. Great reporting in the *Post*, the *Times*, *Newsweek* and elsewhere did not transfer to bigger audiences on cable or broadcast television, where much of the election discourse occurred.

From the moment Trump announced his presidential run in mid-2015, *60 Minutes* did no major reporting on his business career. A September 2015 interview with Scott Pelley had a brief mention of

Trump's net worth and future tax plans, but little real information on the failures and false claims he has made about his supposed empire.

Most of Pelley's report was asking questions and allowing Trump to make claims about how he would fix heath care, taxes and, of course, build the Mexican-funded border wall. But *60 Minutes* confirmed no other reports were done during his campaign.

It would be too easy to simply blame a lazy and late-to-the-party press for Trump's surprise victory. After all, he did not win the popular vote, so it is not as if Clinton did not have more support in the electorate.

Trump also made gains by reaching many middle-income and low-income working-class voters with a populist message on low wages, government waste and the all-around anti-Washington view that struck a nerve with most of his supporters who saw him as an outspoken non-'political machine' outsider. Add to that his blatant anti-immigrant and anti-Muslim messages – most of which included serious falsehoods about both groups – and many voters who felt left out by the liberal-backed, Washington establishment leaders that Clinton represented believed he would serve their needs.

Clinton didn't do herself many favors either. Much has been written about the infighting in her campaign and her inability to secure electoral wins in Wisconsin, Pennsylvania, and other states that polls show could have been won over with more appearances and more attention.

"Her approach, guided by [Campaign Manager Robbie] Mook and informed by the demands of winning the primary, was to build a coalition focused on core strengths: African Americans, Latinos, college-educated whites, and women," authors Jonathan Allen and Amie Parnes wrote in their 2017 campaign memoir *Shattered: Inside Hillary Clinton's Doomed Campaign*. "But the more she catered to them, the more she pushed away other segments of the electorate."

The book later noted, "Whether she was perceived as hostile to working- and middle-class whites or just indifferent, it wasn't a big leap from 'she doesn't care about my job' to 'she'd rather give my job to a minority or a foreigner than fight for me to keep it.' She and her aides were focused on the wrong issue set for working-class white Michigan voters, and, even when she talked about the economy – rather than her e-mail scandal, mass shootings, or the water crisis in Flint – it wasn't at all clear to them that she was on their side."

But did the press focus unfairly on two Clinton issues that dominated the campaign: Benghazi and emails? From the moment it was disclosed that Clinton had a private email server created that had been used to conduct some State Department business, the attacks flew. And the overwhelming news reports followed.

"When Clinton says she couldn't get out from under email coverage, in a lot of ways, she is totally spot on," *U.S. News & World Report* assistant editor for opinion Pat Garofalo wrote in 2017. "It was a ceaseless drumbeat that overshadowed anything else about her historic effort to win the Oval Office. Any attempt to talk about issues was drowned out by the cacophony of stories about emails, emails, emails."

Garofalo cited an August 2017 study by the Berkman Klein Center at Harvard University on media coverage of the election that found coverage of Clinton's emails vastly surpassed all other issues, including Trump's own scandals related to treatment of women, failure to reveal his income tax returns, Trump University and his foundation.

"…When reporting on Hillary Clinton, coverage primarily focused on the various scandals related to the Clinton Foundation and emails," the study stated. "When focused on Trump, major substantive issues, primarily immigration, were prominent. Indeed, immigration emerged as a central issue in the campaign and served as a defining issue for the Trump campaign."

It also didn't help her that FBI Director James Comey revealed days before the election that he had re-opened the investigation into her emails. Even though it was later revealed nothing illegal had been found, it brought the issue back into the daily news feed and reminded many voters about the already sensitive issue just as they were about to cast their ballots.

As for Benghazi, which was the Libyan city where four Americans were killed in a 2012 terrorist attack, coverage seeking to blame Clinton as Secretary of State seemed non-stop through the campaign, despite little to no evidence of any wrongdoing on her part.

The press was aided in its over-focus by the Republican-led Congress, which held 33 hearings, four public hearings and spent about $7 million to investigate the incident, according to *Vanity Fair*. In the end, it offered little more than a slap on the wrist and no new information linking Clinton to anything that caused the four deaths.

There were also plenty of press missteps. One was a 2013 *60 Minutes'* report on the incident based on a book by a former security consultant who claimed to be an eyewitness to the attack, but whose story was later discredited. That caused his book to be pulled from the shelves and CBS News reporter Lara Logan to be placed on leave while an internal investigation occurred.

A 2014 *Media Matters* study found that Fox News also took the reins on the Benghazi story, revealing, "Fox News' evening lineup ran nearly 1,100 segments on the Benghazi attacks and their aftermath in the first 20 months following the attacks. Nearly 500 segments focused on a set of Obama administration talking points used in September 2012 interviews; more than 100 linked the attacks to a potential Hillary Clinton 2016 presidential run; and dozens of segments compared the attacks and the administration response to the Watergate or Iran-Contra scandals.

The network hosted Republican members of Congress to discuss Benghazi nearly 30 times more frequently than Democrats."

As with the email story, no real wrongdoing has ever been found connecting Clinton to Benghazi, but the amount of coverage both received was clearly higher than most other issues.

Still, news coverage of two Clinton-related "scandals" was not the most impactful media-related cause of Trump's victory. Two other key things helped bring him to the White House and eroded many of his supporters' already weak trust in mainstream news.

First, Trump launched an early harsh attack on traditional news outlets as "fake news" even before he formally ran for office. He hammered away at them like no previous presidential candidate, not even the well-known press paranoid Richard Nixon.

Then he was aided by a string of far-right media voices who would defend his work, attack the mainstream media, and produce what really amounted to fake news – from claims that Hillary Clinton was linked to a child sex ring out of a Washington, D.C., pizza place to lies about the Clinton Foundation (more on them later).

Early on, Trump would point to reporters in the crowd and turn his supporters against them. His efforts both intimidated reporters and drilled in millions of Americans' heads that reporters could not be trusted. He, of course, offered no basis for such mistrust. And with his own practice of false statements, one would think his claims about the media would be hard to accept.

But it worked. At least for his so-called base, the 30% of voters who seemed to support him no matter what.

"This whole thing of reporters being demonized. This movement led by the president that journalists as a group are liars is painful," James Rainey, an NBC.com reporter and former media writer for the *Los Angeles Times*, told me in an interview. "People who are trying to do the right thing and are bludgeoned. It is such a fundamental myth that is being created."

Katy Tur of NBC News became something of a poster child for Trump media targets when he pointed her out several times at campaign rallies and blamed her for what he claimed was media underreporting of his crowds. This was, of course, false. But Tur later said on air and in her book, *Unbelievable: My Front-Row Seat to the Craziest Campaign in American History*, that it caused real concern for her safety and for other journalists on the campaign trail.

"Imagine someone calling you a liar," she recalled in the book. "Now amplify the experience by a thousand if a presidential candidate calls you a liar. And tack on another factor of ten if that presidential candidate is named Donald J. Trump. Waves of insults and threats poured into my phone – the device buzzing like a shock collar."

But more than making journalists uncomfortable, the Trump press attacks and claims of "fake news" by respected outlets such as CNN, *The New York Times* and others, helped sow distrust in the mainstream media among his base. He could just label something fake or not true, and millions of his followers believed

"To me he's been like an accelerant," said one board member of the White House Correspondents Association who requested anonymity. "He has provided presidential credibility to the totally incorrect premise that a good news story is one that reinforces your beliefs and that is a totally toxic thing."

Andy Alexander, a former *Washington Post* ombudsman and one-time D.C. bureau chief for Cox Media, said the Trump press slams have also affected media trust globally: "The Trump effect internationally has had a tremendous impact on treatment of the press around the world. He has successfully exploited mistrust in all institutions, including the media."

An October 2017 poll sponsored in part by *Politico* found that 46 percent of respondents believed that the media make up stories about Trump, with only 37 percent of voters believing there is not such fabrication and 17 percent undecided.

"More than three-quarters of Republican voters, 76 percent, think the news media invent stories about Trump and his administration, compared with only 11 percent who don't think so," *Politico* reported on the poll. "Among Democrats, one-in-five think the media make up stories, but a 65 percent majority think they do not. Forty-four percent of independent voters think the media make up stories about Trump, and 31 percent think they do not."

A more recent survey from the Knight Foundation and Gallup found that 51 percent of Republicans labeled most newspaper, TV and radio news as "misinformation," compared to just 23 percent of Democrats. Meanwhile, 54 percent of those identifying as conservative offered that view, with just 24 percent who called themselves liberal.

But it wasn't just Trump denying factual stories and making false counter claims that helped him spread untruths, he had an entire army of far-right extremist media folks pushing lies and seeking to undermine real reporting.

I hesitate to call these folks journalists as many regularly break the Society of Professional Journalists Code of Ethics and have more interest in pushing an attention-getting claim than seeking out the truth without fear or favor.

Two of the key people who had close ties to Trump were Steve Bannon, the former head of *Breitbart News*, and Roger Stone, a former Nixon White House employee, conservative lobbyist, commentator and author of several books filled with outrageous claims and misinformation.

During the election, I was tasked to attend several Stone events, where he spoke to supporters and touted his books. The major book he was hawking during the campaign was *The Clintons' War on Women*. Among its misleading entries was a claim that Hillary Clinton was somehow to blame for the 1993 Branch Davidian massacre in which members of the cult died in a fire; revisited sketchy claims of Bill Clinton raping or assaulting women; and false allegations that Hillary Clinton threatened these women and, as Stone wrote, "The Clintons' activities have not only included Bill's physical rape of women, but also Hillary's degradation and psychological rape of women whom Bill has assaulted. Hillary, it will be seen, looks likely to authorize the heavy-handed private detectives who terrorize Bill's victims into silence."

The book then goes on to cite "sources" such as fellow flawed conservative voices *World Net Daily*, *Washington Free Beacon* and *Breitbart News*.

Stone's own background includes other previous books that accuse Lyndon Johnson of planning the assassination of JFK; George H.W. Bush of being involved in the shooting of Ronald Reagan; and allege Richard Nixon was wrongly vilified and actually "the victim."

Then there are Stone's offensive and racist actions, including many attacks on the media, which I noted in a *Media Matters* story in 2016 that stated, Stone "wrote (among many other things) that commentator Roland Martin is a 'stupid negro' and a 'fat negro,' *New York Times* columnist Gail Collins is an 'elitist c*nt,' MSNBC host Rachel Maddow is "Rachel the muff-diver," CNN's Ana Navarro is 'borderline retarded' and an 'Entitled Diva Bitch,' and Fox's Allen West is an 'arrogant know-it-all negro.' He mocked writer Charles Krauthammer for being paralyzed, and tweeted 'DIE BITCH' at former *New York Times* executive editor Jill Abramson."

When I would see Stone at events and ask him questions, he was always pleasant, but would deny most of the claims against him and always point me out to the rabid, pro-Trump audience: "We have a friend from *Media Matters* here with us." When the crowd would boo and yell toward me, with some chanting, "throw him out," Stone would act the fair-minded host and declare: "Now, now, the press has a right to be here."

Dirty looks and glares would be cast my way for the rest of the event. Having dealt with hardline New Jersey politicians and threats on my safety during days at *The Daily Journal* in the late 1980s – where the son of a former mayor tried to attack me at a rally – some angry obscenities were nothing for me to fear.

What was more interesting was to see these crowds eat up Stone's lies and false stories about Clinton and what Trump would do as president, just as Trump fans elsewhere were doing in reaction to Trump's own words.

Stone could dish out the falsities from his books and other writings and they took it as fact. When I would ask a question during the Q&A portion, he often dismissed it, claiming, "you are not a real journalist."

Stone's efforts were a prime example, on a smaller scale, of the willingness of Trump supporters to believe what they wanted and ignore clear evidence of the opposite.

Bannon's case was similar, and he had his website, *Breitbart News*, to dish out the reckless claims as well. The creation of the late Andrew Breitbart, a conservative commentator who died unexpectedly in 2012, *Breitbart News* had its share of misleading and inaccurate assertions.

Breitbart himself always seemed at least approachable and willing to discuss differences. I nearly ambushed him with a video camera at CPAC in 2011, firing questions at him. He stayed calm and answered them directly. We later shook hands when the quick interview ended.

Bannon, however, raised the vitriol to a nastier form when Trump was the subject. He co-produced and co-wrote a 2016 documentary based on the discredited book, *Clinton Cash* by Peter Schweizer.

A *Media Matters* analysis of the book found more than 20 "errors, fabrications and distortions," stating, "Media outlets tore apart Schweizer's allegation that Hillary Clinton played a 'central role' in approving a Russian uranium deal for Clinton Foundation donors. He made multiple errors in a section alleging Bill Clinton's speaking fees influenced State Department grants in Haiti. He cited as fact a press release that was revealed as a hoax some years before.

"He took a former U.S. ambassador's words 'badly out of context,' drawing condemnation from the individual. He erred in his conspiracy about Hillary Clinton's vote on an India nuclear deal. He excluded multiple pieces of exculpatory evidence that undermine his claims. He hypocritically attacked the Clintons for engaging in the same behavior that Schweizer's former boss, George W. Bush, did. And he alleged Clinton conspiracies that, in the words of third parties who reviewed his work, have 'no evidence,' are 'circumstantial,' and have 'no smoking gun.'"

At a screening of *Clinton Cash* I attended, where Fox News anchors were also in the crowd, Bannon criticized mainstream outlets for not reporting on the claims in the book and film. Perhaps because they were not true.

As I wrote at the time, "The film had many of the same factual problems [as the book]. For example, a key accusation lobbed at the Clinton Foundation in the film, is the claim that only '10 percent' of its donations actually go to charity.

Schweizer repeatedly relied on this talking point while on the *Clinton Cash* book tour, claiming that other than the 10 percent the Clinton

Foundation gives to "other charitable organizations, the rest they keep for themselves."

But the '10 percent' statistic is deceptive – even Fox News labeled it 'incredibly misleading.' Fox News network correspondent Eric Shawn explained in a 2015 report that the Clinton Foundation doesn't 'give grants to other charities. They do most of it themselves.' He also cited IRS figures indicating the foundation has a 'rate of spending of about 80 percent' and 'experts for charity say that's very good.'"

That is just a smattering of the pro-Trump media outlets that helped push Trump's false claims, and even provide some new ones. (I will address conservative media more directly later in this book.)

Since Election Day, when many believed Trump would back off on his continued false statement and anti-press claims – and perhaps become "more presidential" – the lies have only continued. The president has also taken to Twitter like never before, often firing direct shots at media outlets and specific reporters and commentators, and falsely claiming they were inaccurate.

One Twitter tirade occurred on Sunday, Aug. 5, 2018, after CNN reported a stinging story about infighting and the president's concerns about his son being brought into the FBI investigation of Russian influence in U.S. elections. Trump fired off six angry tweets that morning, including one that stated: "The Fake News hates me saying that they are the Enemy of the People only because they know it's TRUE. I am providing a great service by explaining this to the American People. They purposely cause great division & distrust. They can also cause War! They are very dangerous & sick!"

Sadly, this is more the rule than the exception with Trump. Worse is when the public believes him over clear, factual reporting.

"I think journalists of all kinds feel that there has been an increasing pressure on their physical safety, and certainly that the journalists operate in a less permissive environment than ever," David Frum, a conservative columnist and former Bush speechwriter, told me in an interview. "And they have to wade through a lot of active disinformation."

In late 2018, White House Correspondents Association President Olivier Knox told me that at least three of his press room colleagues had hired security details to protect them following threats.

Frum later noted, "the people who say they distrust the media would be incredibly incredulous without the media they wish to believe. So people say, 'I don't believe the media,' but they don't include Fox or *Breitbart* with the media."

Ken Auletta, the veteran media writer for *The New Yorker*, agreed Trump's actions had hurt press credibility unfairly.

"I think what he does with fake news … is much more harmful to the press," Auletta told me in an interview. "I think the press should be held to account, but this is much more damaging to a free press, and the public attitude towards the importance of a free press, is what Donald Trump has done.

"That's the larger truth, and that is when you go around as he does, the President of the United States, basically, if someone criticizes him, they are perpetrators of false news … If you start pumping that shit out, that poison out to people, a lot of people are forced to believe that, and that's really harmful and scary."

In February 2017, less than a month after Trump took office, *Media Matters* began a database to collect examples of Trump attacking the press. It eventually reached hundreds of items. Some are as simple as Trump Tweeting on Feb. 6, 2017, that, "any negative polls are fake news. Just like the CNN, ABC, NBC polls in the election." Others included stronger attacks, such as his repeated threat to strengthen libel laws to limit journalistic power.

The press seems to be one of several areas where Trump seeks to plant seeds of doubt in the credibility of long-standing institutions. As he tries to rip down the media, he also claimed the FBI investigation of his possible Russian ties was bogus, with similar attacks on the CIA, the Justice Department and several other intelligence areas and government agencies.

While journalists are fearing for their safety and lost credibility, have many of the same news people crossed a line in exposing Trump's actions?

I'm not saying they have become the fake news Trump alleges. But the growing focus on every element of Trump's activities, even minor things that would not otherwise be noticed, has sparked concern among some veteran reporters.

"It discourages me when the [New York] *Times* is putting out lists of things Trump has said that were factually wrong," said Daniel Okrent, the longtime author and former *Times* public editor. "Put it on the editorial page, that's fine, we need some news media in this country that can be trusted by people irrespective of their view. To hand a weapon to the right-wing critics of the *Times* hurts the *Times*. If the right-wing can use these things to discredit the *Times*, then the *Times* can't hold its position as a trusted source."

Auletta said that with many on the right skewing the truth and others on the left targeting Trump, no direct reporting can get through.

"Therefore, there's no coming together on a common set of facts," Auletta told me in an interview. "And, with so many different choices, Fox News versus MSNBC for instance, you could choose your facts. And, if you watch Fox, Trump doesn't have a problem, and the problem is the FBI, or Mueller. And, if you watch CNN or MSNBC, more so MSNBC than CNN, but CNN as well, Trump has huge problems. So, when I watch Fox, I get too little Trump. When I watch MSNBC and CNN, I get too much Trump.

"Which gets to a second problem. Attitudinizing. I find extraordinary the amount of attitudinizing, maybe Fox started it, but it's now aided by what CNN and MSNBC does. I think MSNBC was doing it before, but CNN, now, does it extraordinarily. So, if I'm a Trump voter and I watch CNN, I watch Jake Tapper, right, I think he's amazingly gifted and does great interviews. But Jake is full of opinion and full of attitudes about Trump ... opinion, a kind of a sneer. 'And then Trump, who said he wouldn't do this, did this today. The guy has trouble with the truth.' It's just too much opinion. I happen to agree with the opinion, but that's not what an anchor is supposed to be doing."

It's not surprising that some journalists want to focus on and expose everything Trump does that is considered dangerous or problematic. For many, he is such a bad president that they believe it is okay to step over the line, even in a minor fashion.

But does that hurt credibility in another way? And with so much focus on everything Trump does, what other news is lost or ignored?

"Trump is sucking the air out of other stories," Michael Harrison, the longtime editor of *Talkers* magazine said.

Auletta agreed, stating, "There's no Middle East, there's no Africa, there's no Korea, and I think that's a mistake. And, I think we're walking, where the press walks into a trap, reconfirming the worst things that critics of the press say about it."

Dana Priest, the Pulitzer Prize-winning reporter for the *Washington Post*, also showed concern. "I think I see it far more than I ever have," she said in an interview. "There is anti-Trump language that gets into a lot of news stories that shouldn't be there. It is not that subtle. Adjectives, the way things are phrased. They scream at him every day, that everything is the worst thing that ever happened. It feeds into the distrust. Not giving facts, just giving snide comments one way or another. I think we've lost our way on television, mainly on the talking head shows."

MSNBC, which I have long admired and still support, has seen some of the biggest changes in this regard. The night time shows were always very opinionated and progressive. But now they seem to focus only on Trump-related scandals.

And the daytime has shifted even more. In the past, one could turn on MSNBC and get a list of events of the day. Now it is the Trump events of the day. And rarely very specific things such as the litany of environmental regulations he has eliminated or other executive orders and policy changes that might not be as sexy as the last Stormy Daniels-type scandal.

Billmoyers.com, the website overseen by the legendary journalist and television news host, cited Trump's conflicts of interest as the most overlooked story of 2017.

"...TV, the most popular medium from which Americans get their news, remains relentlessly focused on the sexier topics of the day," Journalist Bill Adler wrote on Moyers' site. "That's often just what Trump tweeted. Sometimes, as when he's tweeting provocations to North Korea, that's an important news story. Other times, as when we're being distracted by the president's insults to the appearance of a talk show host, it's not. In any case, the complicated connections between the personal financial interests of Trump, his White House staffers, family and associates and the policies being promulgated at the White House remains under-illuminated."

Adler then pointed to a Public Citizen post that "few journalists picked up on" that showed "even standard Republican deregulation of labor and the environment raises new ethical questions when Trump's own business stands to profit from it.

"Moreover, we have discovered, too late, that many of the safeguards rely upon public officials' voluntary compliance. Trump violated norms, but no laws, by not releasing his tax returns. His staffers and cabinet appointees may have broken laws by promoting Trump brands and campaigning on behalf of elected officials, but no one in the Trump administration seems interested in enforcing those laws. The press should be not only examining these problems, but their potential solutions."

But as with many issues, getting eyeballs and readers are the focus for too many news outlets, and they know Trump sells.

"Trump is very good for the news business and there is a lot of money to be made to cover the White House, remain accessible and not ask the tough questions," said Eric Boehlert, the progressive journalist and author, and my former *Media Matters* colleague. "There are steps you can take that do not cross the line. They are worried about access. They should have walked out a long time ago."

And then there was Stormy Daniels. The adult film star who claimed that she had a one-time affair with Trump in 2007 and sparked a media frenzy in March 2018. She went on *60 Minutes* and detailed her one-night stand, and her allegations of being threatened to keep quiet about it before the 2016 election.

The national news that had not given such attention to more serious Trump actions such as potential ties to Russian election infiltration, handling of the North Korean nuclear threat, and continued dismantling of environmental regulations, was all too glad to replay Daniels' tawdry tales and speculate on how it might bring the president down.

Some, however, see Trump's election, and even his attacks, as a positive in many ways.

For one thing, news consumption has been on the rise since he first joined the race, and has grown ever since, according to experts. Ratings are growing, along with circulation for many print outlets.

"What has helped these newscasts in the past year is our president," said Marc Berman, a longtime TV analyst and founder of *Programming Insider.* "It has been so much in the news, so much turmoil, people are watching to see what's going on."

In May 2017, *The New York Times* reported record new subscribers with 308,000 new digital subscribers in the first quarter of 2017. "*Times* editors and executives have cited curiosity and concern about the Trump administration as one of the reasons for the subscriber gains in late 2016 and early 2017," CNN reported at the time.

But *Times* Executive Editor Dean Baquet pointed out that covering Trump raised a new dilemma; how to handle a president who lies so often. In the 2018 Showtime documentary *The Fourth Estate*, which followed the *Times'* coverage during Trump's first year, Baquet stated in a meeting with colleagues, "This White House publicly fabricates more than any previous White House, at least in my time. If we do this, we are doing this because we are saying this White House merits this. The word lie is a very powerful word...and I don't want to use it all the time."

Another apparent positive result has been some news outlets ramping up their investigative reporting, and others scrutinizing facts more strongly, knowing that Trump and his supporters will pounce on any minor error.

"He has created an impetus to the news to be better than it ever was. He puts reporters in position to be better, not to make mistakes, to fact check," *Talkers'* Harrison said. "News on all sides has become more self-conscious and I think in the long run news will be better than it has ever been because of Trump. I have seen journalists be very, very careful because they can't get away with mistakes anymore. Journalists will become more self-conscious and aware of the burden that it has."

But White House reporters point out that the chaotic nature of Trump's West Wing leaves many unable to tell the entire story.

"One of the trends in Trump coverage is that we have talked to 625 advisors in and out of the White House and we still can't tell you what he is going to do," said one White House correspondent who requested anonymity. "You have this daily churn of palace intrigue stories and what is he going to do about major problem X or major issue X and because the interest in this is boundless, we keep shoveling this without much thought to why."

FEWER JOURNALISTS, LESS JOURNALISM

From my first job in 1988 to my most recent position in 2018, financial struggles and personnel layoffs have been a part of the process. In most cases, I was spared. Although the last two times I left positions were at least partially driven by money. I'm not alone.

The combination of reduced ad revenue, expanded competition and the resulting desperation for profits by media ownership has resulted in both a sharp drop in the number of people reporting news and a dangerous reduction in actual news quality.

The drive for the most viewers, listeners, and readers over public service and accurate, important information is dumbing down the audience. Ad revenue reductions due to web competition and splintered revenue options, along with the takeover of most news outlets by public companies and big corporations who demand higher profits, have cut resources to a fraction of what they were just a few decades ago.

This mix has led to my view that today's news is not slanted toward liberals as many believe, but is greedy and lazy. Stories are not pursued enough to dig into all the facts and newsrooms are run by companies seeking as much profit as possible with less cost.

The numbers are clear, there are fewer working journalists in the United States than there were just a few years ago, a lot fewer. The Pew

Research Center's annual *State of the News Media* report revealed in 2017 that the number of newspaper jobs, in and out of the newsroom, had dropped from 66,490 in 2005 to 41,400 in 2015 – a 37 percent dive in only 10 years.

"It is a long-standing trend that jobs have been declining for a while," said Michael Barthel, a research associate focused on U.S. news media at the Pew Research Center. "Publishers talk about cutting costs and the way to do that is cutting head counts, and also declining ad revenue, which is still the majority revenue for newspapers."

U.S. Labor Department statistics show there were 38,790 jobs in news for reporters and correspondents in mid-2017, earning a median annual salary of $51,550. In 2005, there were 52,920 reporters and correspondent jobs in the United States. That's a loss of more than 14,000 jobs in just over a decade.

And the cutbacks continued in just the last year with a July 2018 Pew report finding that 36 percent of the largest newspapers in the U.S. had experienced layoffs between January 2017 and April 2018. "Larger newspapers – those with circulations of at least 250,000 – were more likely than smaller-circulation newspapers to have experienced layoffs," the study found. "Nine of the 16 newspapers with circulations of 250,000 or more (56%) had layoffs. By comparison, that was true of 16 of the 44 newspapers with circulations between 100,000 and 249,999 (36%) and 15 of the 50 newspapers with circulations between 50,000 and 99,999 (30%)."

Among the most notable was the *New York Daily News*, which cut half its newsroom staff in July 2018, with the paper admitting it will have to focus on breaking news and reduce other essential work. Tronc, the publishing arm of the former Tribune Company that owns the *Daily News,* also laid off several dozen staffers at its *Los Angeles Times* as well as a dozen more at the flagship *Chicago Tribune* in 2018. (It has since been renamed Tribune Publishing Company.)

Even with those declines, newspapers and their growing online versions still have the most journalists. But with such a dramatic drop in staff, they are having to do more with less.

The advent of the web and related handheld devices put an end to deadlines in most cases and force most outlets to push the story out as soon as possible.

So instead of covering as many stories as possible each day and having until 5 or 6 or 8 p.m. to put the story together, fewer reporters are having to do more work. And that leaves less time and manpower to cover all of the news that's out there.

"If they're not able to cover the things they used to cover before, like health for example, which is such an important story right now, that has an effect," said Leonard Downie, Jr., the former executive editor of the *Washington Post*, who led the paper to more Pulitzer Prizes during his tenure than any previous editor. "Is the newspaper in Toledo or Memphis or wherever, do they have a health reporter? Do they have an education reporter? Do they have enough education reporters? If they have even one, covering all those aspects of life that are important to their reader's lives and I just don't know how well they're doing that right now. I don't know how many of those stories are gone because the reporters are gone."

Rick Edmonds, a business media expert at The Poynter Institute, agreed. "You see a whole lot less science reporting and some medical reporting," he told me in an interview. "Back in the day *The Dallas Morning News* or a paper like that would have a half dozen people covering it. That is hardly the case anymore."

The cutback in personnel can be traced to several things – but a major culprit is the loss of ad revenue for traditional news outlets coupled with increased corporate ownership demanding higher and higher profit margins.

For years, the attacks on mainstream media have been about alleged bias. The "liberal *New York Times*" and CNN (or Clinton News Network, as some claimed) took all the attention. Dating back to pre-Nixon days, such false swipes masked the true nature of news media's key problems – fewer journalists and greedier owners.

A 2016 story at Billmoyers.com focused on the 1996 Telecommunications Act, which made mergers of big media companies easier. It stated, in part, "The goal of this new law is to let anyone enter any communications business – to let any communications business compete in any market against any other. The Telecommunications Act of 1996 has the potential to change the way we work, live and learn. It will affect telephone service – local and long distance, cable programming and other video services, broadcast services and services provided to schools."

Prior to that law, and the FCC's resulting willingness to allow mergers that were previously barred, giant buyouts were few and far between.

But as author Michael Corcoran wrote in the Moyer's web piece, "Twenty years later the devastating impact of the legislation is undeniable: About 90 percent of the country's major media companies are owned by six corporations. Bill Clinton's legacy in empowering the consolidation of corporate media is right up there with the North American Free Trade Agreement (NAFTA) and welfare reform, as being among the most tragic and destructive policies of his administration."

Corcoran pointed to a *Business Insider* 2012 report that indicated those six corporations to be G.E., Disney, News Corporation, Viacom, TimeWarner and CBS. They have changed slightly with buyouts since then, making the top six companies as of 2016 to be Comcast, Disney,

News Corp., TimeWarner, Sony and the lesser known National Amusements.

That's a far cry from 1983 when 90% of U.S. media was owned by 50 companies. And in many cases, local newspapers were family-owned or controlled by smaller, local groups that sought lower profit margins. In many shops, the local publishers were happy with eight to ten percent profit margins and ad revenue was positive without the Internet. Lucrative public notices and classified ads and strong local competition also kept news coverage vibrant.

More news outlets – especially newspapers – in each market meant better coverage, and a different take on numerous stories.

But today, with so much of the news media being owned by large corporations – who have to seek higher net returns and please shareholders – the bottom line is squeezed, and journalists are squeezed out. The number of independent news outlets in each market has shrunk dramatically.

In many cases, cities that had two or more daily papers, now have one, while some smaller municipalities have no regular daily options for news.

During my 11 years at *Editor & Publisher*, I had to chronicle the annual cutbacks in newspaper jobs and the shutdown of long-time newspapers. When I wrote a yearly "Top Ten Newspaper Stories of the Year" piece, the financial hits and losses were often number one.

Among the former two-paper towns that are down to a lone daily news print outlet in the past 20 years are Milwaukee, Seattle, Phoenix, San Diego, San Antonio, Sacramento, San Francisco, Albuquerque, and Denver. Papers in other towns such as Cleveland, New Orleans and Detroit deliver print products only a few days per week.

"If you lose a local and community newspaper there are a couple of parts to that – nobody else is going to fill in that blank, a national newspaper isn't going to come in and cover the school board," said David Chaver, President & Chief Executive Officer of the News Media Alliance and American Press Institute. "People's interest will be filled by other things and truly fake news. There is not going to be any fact-checking organization that is going to be able to check in on every state."

Poytner's Edmonds echoed that view.

"This has caused a lot of attrition in staff of local papers," he said. "There are differences between very small papers and the big metros, but different kinds of coverage have disappeared, or been vastly reduced."

And even when print papers remain and expand online, the consolidation of ownership reduces the actual bodies covering each major story and eliminates coverage of smaller ones. Much has been written about the impact on low-income and poor readers who either cannot afford a computer, laptop, or other electronic web device or do not have access at libraries.

In New Jersey, for example, nearly all the remaining daily papers are owned by two companies – Gannett and Advance Media, including the largest, *The Star-Ledger* of Newark. Advance runs that flagship as well as *The Trenton Times,* the *South Jersey Times* and a slew of weekly newspapers.

Sadly, the consolidations and cutbacks in New Jersey are the rule rather than the exception. One can point to any news market and find either mergers, staff cuts or both, that simply mean less news covered by fewer people. And with the online push, the quality of the work suffers as reporters and editors are forced to push news on the web continuously, often affecting depth and accuracy.

And that affects newspaper readership as well.

Newspaper circulation reached a high of 60 million nationwide for the first time in 1964 and kept it there for more than 20 years, according to reports from Pew's *State of the News Media*. But once it fell below this in the early 1990s, it kept tumbling to 50 million in 2007, then 40 million in 2013 with estimates that daily readership, both online and in print, has fallen to an estimated 34 million daily in 2016.

"Circulation continues to decline while revenue is steady or going up slightly," Pew's Barthel said. "That is due at least in part to charging more." He also pointed out that while much of the readership has transferred to the web, "most people spend a very short time on a story and often don't return to the same source in online news readership."

Readership online is not stable and offers few steady readers to any one site. Most online readers are linked to a specific story or two, click on to that article, then go elsewhere, research reveals.

Pew's data finds that the average newspaper website reader spends less than three minutes on a specific site, hardly time to read even what used to be the print front page, let alone what is inside or beyond a 500-word story. So good luck in getting them to notice ads in that short time span.

More people are going to news websites for their daily fix which means more readers, but more people also spending less time with news. The number of unique users on the highest trafficked news websites was up from 18 million in 2014 to 22 million in 2016, according to Pew, although much of that was due to the 2016 presidential election.

As a consequence, nationwide newspaper ad revenue dropped from $25 billion in 2012 to $18 billion in 2016, while circulation revenue stayed pretty steady at about $10 billion for the past 20 years.

But as Barthel noted, much of that is due to higher newsstand and subscription costs like *The New York Times* monthly rate running at $60 for New York area readers as well as a Sunday newsstand newspaper at $5. Few readers want to fork over cash when they see so much "free" news online.

But, of course, news isn't free. Someone has to pay the people who go out and find the news, write it, photograph or video it, organize it and present it.

The news delivery online is very different than the traditional print product, or even a 30-minute or hour-long newscast, both of which present a menu of stories from different areas and give the news consumer a rundown of what is deemed most important and easily accessible.

Like most long-time newshounds, I enjoy opening a newspaper and going page to page with a cup of coffee, scanning headlines and seeing what the entire paper has to offer. Granted, this can take more time than checking a Twitter feed or Facebook and clicking on stories that seem interesting. But it's much more informative.

And with more and more people opting for the quick news feed, the actual information being conveyed is diminished.

On the web pop-up ads continue to mount and drive many away from a page or make it more cumbersome to the reader. Many readers come to a story via links from Facebook, Twitter and other aggregate sites, so they can choose what they want and never see numerous other important stories.

"The other great challenge of the Internet is what is the product we are creating? How do we deliver it? And what is the value? The traditional newspaper product was a buffet of information," said News Media Alliance President and CEO David Chavern. "In a digital world people get parts of the buffet in different places. There are a lot of places to read about sports, a lot of places to read about entertainment, a lot of places to read about national news."

So even with more people coming to the web and, theoretically, having more options for news, the practice that occurs of limiting personal readership to certain sites, and even specific stories, the amount of news and information for any single person is reduced.

So how did we get here?

To say that news coverage cutbacks are a completely new phenomenon would be misleading. Sixty or seventy years ago, before television and cable burst on the scene, many cities had at least three daily newspapers, each with strong local voices. New York City in the 1950s boasted more than 10 daily papers but lost four of them after the bitter 1962-63 newspaper strike that took with it the famed *New York Herald-Tribune.*

San Francisco, Washington, D.C., Los Angeles, Chicago, and others could count numerous daily print products during the middle of the 20th Century. But when television hit, and the first bits of new technology made some jobs unnecessary, the pink slips flew.

Still, the more recent and more dramatic drop in reporters and coverage can be traced back to the Internet, which officially reached a major newspaper in 1995 when *the Mercury News* – fittingly located in Silicon Valley – launched the first online edition.

The Mercury News and those newspapers that followed online did not give the web the deserved credit and impact at the time. They did not demand payment for online stories or defend themselves against the ad competition.

By the 21st Century, most newspapers and a large number of broadcast and cable outlets, had websites where some – but not the majority – of the news was placed.

The print products did not utilize the online options for both display ads and classified advertising as many consumers migrated to the web for quicker, easier online ad searches, job hunting and buying and selling of products.

Enter Craigslist, Monster.com and other online ad sites, which stole the classified market away from the newspapers that had traditionally dominated in print. In large part, the takeover was due to the fact that newspapers did not properly see the web options and the growing change by readers to online news and ads.

"It really began around 2000," Edmonds said. "The impact of Craigslist and Monster and various other places that run classifieds that have withered away [from print]. The survivors are obits, paid obits, legal notices and they have been pretty successful in preserving them."

But look for legal, or public, notices to move away from newspapers, as many states pass legislation that allows online outlets to run them, and other government entities themselves.

Traditional news outlets also failed to charge for web content initially, believing they could only compete with other, weaker news sites by giving content away. They failed to realize that having valid news content – that others did not – would have drawn a least some payment.

"We've gone through this incredible technological revolution. It is changing the way people get information the way they process it and it is absolutely devastating the economics of the traditional structure of the American news industry," said Clark Hoyt, a former *New York Times* public editor and long-time Washington, D.C. journalist and bureau chief. "The newspaper industry that I grew up in and had the great bulk of my career in was supported in small part by subscription, but overwhelmingly by advertising. As advertising has departed print in search of its audience that is leaving print, the financial supports of print have been knocked out."

And the non-news web dominance in advertising has only continued to grow in to the 21st Century, experts say. While Craigslist and Monster.com struck the first blows, Facebook, Google and other web giants have provided the heavy artillery against traditional news outlets.

As of late 2017, 60% of digital display ad revenue now goes to Facebook, Google, Twitter, Yahoo and Verizon, according to Pew.

"It's for everything, not just news sites," Barthel explained. "But it does show the dominance of the platforms in capturing ad revenue."

While non-digital advertising revenue has stayed pretty steady at around $123 billion since 2011, the digital advertising side has exploded from $31 billion to $71 billion in the same span of time. That includes newspaper digital ads, which are growing, but the bulk of which are going to non-news sites.

And the economics that have cut back revenue for many news outlets, and subsequently staffing, have also pushed these same newsrooms to do more with less. Either having fewer people juggle more duties or cutting some of those duties altogether.

NPR Media Reporter David Folkenflik calls it "disturbing trends," adding that with "severe corporate cutbacks for funding in newsrooms, you are seeing it in many corporate chain newspapers. You are seeing there is not an answer here for a lot of mid-sized newspapers. You are seeing that with journalists seeking to be their own brands and people working harder for their news organizations, encouraged, goaded, sometimes forced to work more platforms with fewer colleagues."

Some news outlets have given up covering certain areas they used to. Few local papers can be at every city council or school board meeting. They just don't have the bodies. That leaves very vital local news either untouched or poorly reported.

The Star-Ledger was once able to keep tabs on nearly all of New Jersey's 500-plus municipalities, but no more. In most cases, you won't see their reporter in a small town except in the event of a big tragedy or murder or an out-of-the-ordinary occasion.

Beat reporters covering topics like the local county courts, the water board, state transportation commission or regional waste authorities are disappearing nationwide, affecting what people find out about these relevant public services.

"The newsrooms are a fraction of the size so the small elements that go into civic life do not get covered," said Tom Fiedler, former executive editor of The *Miami Herald* and current dean of the College of Communication at Boston University. "There are all of the little elements of local government now functioning in the dark."

Among them are crime and courts, which often see reductions at several levels – the county courthouse, police department, and civil actions. That said, major cases such as Bill Cosby's sexual assault trial or a major murder or kidnapping case – often involving upscale white victims over poor or other minority subjects – get the attention.

A recent study by the Center on Media Crime and Justice at the John Jay College of Criminal Justice in New York found a clear correlation between the loss of reporters and beat journalists in this area and a loss of regular reporting.

The 2018 report stated, in part, "it is important to note that the manpower available to report on justice and many other major topics has dropped sharply in recent years," later adding, "crime and justice always have been staples of local reporting, and that hasn't changed. There is bound to be less of that reporting as the number of people doing it on a regular basis is much diminished in many U.S. cities."

The same report indicated that national coverage of some issues had increased, pointing to the flurry of sexual harassment and sexual assault cases that arose and included major celebrities such as Harvey Weinstein, Bill Cosby, and Charlie Rose, among others. The interest was great enough for *Time* magazine to make these assault survivors its Person of the Year.

There was also heightened coverage of mass shootings, with the 2018 Parkland, Fla., killings of 17 people at a local high school sparking national protests and calls for legislation, while police shootings of citizens received more scrutiny as well, again on a national level.

Then there was the growing opioid crisis, another legal area that saw a boost due to the apparent increase in overdoses and usage.

"These and other stories are indications that the media have covered the opioid crisis both as a public health emergency and as a criminal justice challenge. This contrasts with the treatment of the crack cocaine surge of the 1980s, which was mostly reported on the topic as a law enforcement issue," the report said, later adding, "Media coverage also highlighted the business aspect of the opioid crisis. 'Mexican heroin is flooding the US, and the Sinaloa cartel is steering the flow,' was the headline to a *Business Insider* piece last fall, referring to the band of traffickers formerly headed by Joaquin El Chapo Guzman."

But on the local level, the cutbacks have continued to hamper specific police and courts coverage in readers' hometowns and through local news sources.

One example of a serious cutback is the Charleston (W.V.) *Gazette-Mail*, which won a Pulitzer Prize for investigative reporting in 2017 for a series of stories on – what a surprise – opioid addiction. Statehouse reporter Eric Eyre was credited by the Pulitzer board "for courageous reporting, performed in the face of powerful opposition, to expose the flood of opioids flowing into depressed West Virginia counties with the highest overdose death rates in the country."

But about 10 months later the paper declared bankruptcy, announcing plans for a new buyer to take over, but with an unclear future.

Eyre's work also occurred as statehouse journalists are decreasing in numbers rapidly. A 2014 Pew study found that the number of full-time newspaper reporters assigned to cover state capitols had dropped by 35% during the previous 10 years.

"One of the best ways to hold government accountable is by having a skilled beat reporter, like Eyre, in the statehouse," Margaret Sullivan, a media writer at the *Washington Post* and former *New York Times* public editor, wrote in a piece about newsroom cutbacks. "He told me that his opioids series grew out of his long-term knowledge about the state attorney general's connections to the pharmaceutical industry."

It's that kind of institutional knowledge, local contacts and sources, and downright shoe-leather reporting that makes local beat reporting and regional coverage so vital. And when it is lost, readers suffer because so little is known about daily life issues.

A 2017 *Columbia Journalism Review* piece pointed to local reporting as the impetus for the Congressional defeat of legislation that would have overturned most of Obamacare.

"As editorial boards delivered blunt critiques, many newsrooms delivered sharp stories that brought the impact of the Republican health proposal home," CJR stated. "In Montana, Lee Enterprises newspapers like the Billings *Gazette* and *The Missoulian* published stories that examined how the loss of Medicaid coverage would affect Native Americans; nearly 10,000 of them had signed up for coverage under Montana's Medicaid expansion …

In Louisiana, the *Times-Picayune* brought home the point that many older people would pay more for insurance under the AHCA. Last year, Jefferson Parish – a Republican stronghold – had the state's greatest number of residents enrolled in Obamacare policies."

Healthcare reporting is also suffering at the hands of the newsroom cutbacks. A 2009 survey of members of the Association of Health Care Journalists by the Kaiser Family Foundation found that 40 percent of healthcare journalists surveyed said the number of health reporters at their news outlets had dropped since they started, with just 16 percent saying it had increased.

Meanwhile, 39 percent of respondents said, "it was at least somewhat likely that their own position would be eliminated in the next few years."

"Editors rank the loss of talent and experience in their newsrooms as the factor that has hurt them the most," the survey added. "As one veteran reporter noted in an interview for this report, 'It takes time to develop expertise to cover healthcare with authority. When you downsize something has to give. What gives is both quality and quantity.'"

A 2011 FCC report, titled "The Information Needs of Communities," pointed out examples of good, solid local reporting, but found overall that such cutbacks were hurting local journalism and local residents.

"In many communities, we now face a shortage of local, professional, accountability reporting. This is likely to lead to the kinds of problems that are, not surprisingly, associated with a lack of accountability – more government waste, more local corruption, less effective schools, and other serious community problems," the report stated, in part. "The independent watchdog function that the Founding Fathers envisioned for journalism – going so far as to call it crucial to a healthy democracy – is in some cases at risk at the local level. As technology offered consumers new choices, it upended traditional news industry business models, resulting in massive job losses."

It later added that, "This has created gaps in coverage that even the fast-growing digital world has yet to fill. It is difficult to know what positive changes might be just around the corner, but at this moment the media deficits in many communities are consequential."

That is true for most any local news subject. Even when positions are added or expanded, time on the beat is crucial.

In my first news jobs at small papers in New Jersey and California, experienced editors taught me that it can take up to a year to get engrossed in a beat, know the players, issues, history, and gain the trust of both public officials and sources, as well as readers.

With today's job cuts, constant changing of beats, and doubling or tripling up such assignments for a single reporter, getting to know a specific area or beat is much harder.

Local reporters often feed larger regional and big city news outlets with stories that the big papers and broadcast outlets do minimal reporting about.

I recall being in San Francisco in the 1990s, where I worked at two different smaller papers, and began most days reading the larger and newsier, *San Francisco Chronicle*. Then I would turn on the local television news and see their headlines practically repeat what was on the *Chronicle*'s front page.

As the *Chronicle* and many other newspapers have shrunk, their impact as a source for broadcast and cable news content has also been felt.

"Newspaper beat reporters sifting through dull government agency filings regularly turned up hints of what would become juicy stories, played out over days and weeks in newsprint, then copied and amplified on local radio and TV news," former *Denver Post* TV Critic Joann Ostrow wrote in that paper in April 2018. "The amplification process now extends to the blogosphere and social media, too. It's loud out there, but the source material is minimized. Instead of hundreds of print reporters competing for the latest story, fanning out across the city and around the state to reflect the current reality, we now have a vastly diminished newsroom relocated outside Denver.

"The number of stories that go uncovered climbs as the number of watchdogs shrinks. The talent and institutional memory that walks out the door each time another round of layoffs and buyouts is announced is staggering."

That leaves significant news on school issues, taxes, local government and events to often less-experienced and more-opinionated bloggers and local sites. In many cases, a simple Facebook page is good to spread the word about an upcoming town event or meeting.

But they also open the door to rumors, half-truths and downright inaccurate information. In my New Jersey town, a local Facebook page has more than 11,000 members and is a great repository for events and opinion. But all it takes is one ill-informed post – often about a controversial issue – and the false claims and innuendos abound.

Someone once posted on that page a claim that a homeless African-American man was wrongly arrested outside a Starbucks in a nearby downtown, with video and still images that appeared to show the unnecessary action by law enforcement. The person who posted it wrote that he had not bothered anyone and had been being wrongly removed from an outdoor bench.

A local public official saw the posting and looked into it. It turned out the man had been harassing people at the location and was refusing to leave when asked to stop. He was reportedly arrested for that and resisting arrest.

That is just one example of many in which local social media, be it Facebook or Twitter, allows rumors and false perceptions to spread due to the speed of the Internet rumor mill, as well as the reduction of actual local news outlets.

That's not to say there has been no effort to supplement the lost local reporting from newsroom reductions and cutbacks. Many local online blogs and websites have become a staple at state and regional journalism awards each year.

From *New Brunswick Today* in New Jersey winning a state Society of Professional Journalism local news prize in 2017 for localizing the immigration debate to Berkeleyside, a Berkeley, Ca., website that has won a handful of awards for issues ranging from homelessness to land use to local government.

A 2014 Pew study of the growing, local news sites found that they accounted for 2,000 of the 5,000 new digital news jobs up until that time and "represent a growing and increasingly important part of a shifting media ecosystem." The review focused on more than 400 such sites at that time, noting more than half had been created in just a two-year span between 2008 and 2010.

Those are the years when about 11,000 newspaper newsroom jobs were lost as the economic recession took its toll. While the pace of small digital startups has slowed notably in recent years, 16% (65) of them were created between 2011 and the first few months of 2014. At the same time, several dozen of the outlets in the Pew Research accounting (28, or 7%) predate the year 2000.

They are not going away with groups recently created like LION (Local Independent Online News Publishers). The group, launched in 2012, vows on its website to "champion ... the local online news industry, in the firm belief that independent publishers are establishing the template for successful local digital news organizations – just as independent publishers did for print newspapers in the 19th century."

While others with a national name and audience, such as *Patch*, claim to cover many communities, some organizations just stick their toes in the water of towns for brief and minimal coverage at best.

Take *Patch*'s New Jersey operation. I was in discussions with them for a position in 2017 and they revealed that most local reporting editors have a stable of up to eight communities they must cover – making it virtually impossible to do a thorough job.

In early 2018, *The Ringer*'s Kate Knibbs called *Patch* "one of the most notorious recent failures in hyperlocal reporting," adding "In 2010, [*Patch* owner] AOL claimed that it would be the largest hirer of full-time journalists in America that year, and by 2014 *Patch* employed more than 540 people at more than 900 neighborhood and town sites, covering local politics and events, and linking out to breaking news. But the *Patch* sites were roundly criticized for their inconsistent quality— "Often the sites are like digital Yellow Pages," the *New Yorker* noted in 2011. "The company is now finally profitable, but prestige has not followed profitability; the collection of sites is a decent resource for quick-hit news, like police blotter items, but nothing more."

That "nothing more" leads to what is becoming known as "news deserts," or geographic areas with watered-down or non-existent news sources.

The Saving Community Journalism project out of the University of North Carolina, a student research effort that combined a book and website on the topic, cited the impact in a report titled, "The Emerging Threat of News Deserts." It focused on areas where news cutbacks have occurred and had negative fallout.

"In states and some larger cities, niche online news organizations have sprung up to fill gaps left by the downsizing of metropolitan newspapers. But for residents in smaller cities and towns, from Goldsboro, North Carolina, to Minot, North Dakota, the internet offers little substantive coverage of events and issues of everyday interest and importance," the report states. "Unless local newspapers in those communities reconstruct themselves and sustain their coverage online, who will pay attention to the actions of the city council, the success of local schools, or the safety of the town's water supply?"

The findings go on to point out that with larger companies owning more local news products, they are either consolidating them or closing them all together, creating the "desert" of news.

"The largest investment companies bring a different philosophy and day-to-day operational strategy," the report added. "While the websites of the investment-owned newspapers still stress their civic mission and their aspirations to provide reliable and meaningful information to their communities, the public statements by executives of the large investment firms emphasize business and return on investment."

It later noted, "The turnover in staff that often occurs with the buying and flipping of properties erodes the connection of a local newspaper to the community. But at least there is still a newspaper. When no buyer can be found, investment entities are willing to close local newspapers."

The report added that the largest investment firms have closed or merged at least 85 newspapers, including 22 dailies since 2004. New Media/GateHouse had closed or merged at least 40 papers and CNHI, 24. Since 2011, when Digital First, Civitas and BH Media were formed, these three investment firms have closed or merged 22 of their newspapers, including six dailies.

During the 2000s while at *Editor & Publisher*, I attended the annual American Society of News Editors (ASNE) Conference each year, where jobs and cutbacks were always a major issue. In 2006, former *Los Angeles Times* and *Baltimore Sun* editor John Carroll gave one of the event's most memorable speeches related to the reduction in local and beat news coverage.

Labeled "Last Call at the ASNE Saloon," Carroll's speech took on the crisis of coverage, noting how newsrooms were having to reduce the extent of local reporting and put its readers in jeopardy. Carroll, who was one of the great newspapermen of the last half century, painted a picture of missed stories and failed watchdogging that is evidently coming to fruition.

"If, at some point in America's newspaper-free future, the police decide that the guilt or innocence of murder suspects can be determined perfectly well by beating them until somebody confesses, who will sound the alarm, as the *Philadelphia Inquirer* did in 1977?" he asked in the speech.

"Or, if those federal scientists who tell our doctors what drugs and what dosages are best for us are secretly allowed to take salaries and stock options from drug companies, how will we know it, if the *Los Angeles Times* is not there to tell us, as it did in 2003? Or, if some future president secretly decides to nullify the law and spy on American citizens without warrants, who – if *The New York Times* falls by the wayside – will sound the warning?"

He went on to warn, "More routinely, who will make the checks at City Hall? Who, in cities and towns across America, will go down to the courthouse every day, or to the police station? Who will inspect the tens of thousands of politicians who seek to govern? Who – amid America's great din of flackery and cant – will tell us in plain language what's actually going on?"

Carroll, who had left the *Los Angeles Times* a year before that speech, died in 2015, leaving a legacy of great work not only in Los Angeles – where he led the paper to 13 Pulitzer Prizes in just five years – but as the top newsman for the *Sun* and the *Lexington Herald-Leader.*

That speech and warning about losing the local news beat stayed with many editors in the years that followed as the vibrant reporting dwindled in so many places.

Boston University's Fiedler recalled Carroll's words and cited a more recent example that proved the point.

"He was talking obviously to newspaper editors on that, the things we stop covering are the things that are the esoterica of civic life," Fiedler said. "It would be the local zoning board or the planning board or maybe the utility commission … the county courts, the magistrate's courts and gradually those beats just literally shriveled and ultimately died. Or it ended up where instead of having one person covering county court and then you had another person covering federal court and so forth, you ended up with one person charged with covering all of that. What he was saying it's what isn't covered that is really the grist of being of civic life. Those are the things that we don't know what we don't know ultimately it breeds corruption."

Fiedler then pointed to the Bell, Ca., scandal of 2010, in which the small California community of about 37,000 people was exposed for massive salaries paid to top officials and other wasteful spending in the millions.

Among the crooked practices was a town manager salary approaching $800,000 and city council members making nearly $100,000 for part-time positions. At one point, the District Attorney called it "corruption on steroids."

But while the *Los Angeles Times* eventually won a Pulitzer Prize for its exposure of the scandal, Fiedler points out that it was allowed to go on as long as it did because the community had no regular beat coverage by any mainstream news outlet.

"Many, many years before, the *Times* and other daily news outlets had stopped covering that town and because they weren't, all the corruption festered and blew up into such a magnitude that ultimately when the *L.A. Times* did decide to cover it, it was worthy of a Pulitzer," Fiedler said. "If you think about it in the long term, it never should have happened. Because in the prior days or in days when journalism was that broad blanket the situation never would have gotten out of control. I point that out because every major metro area in the country is facing that very same situation."

It's not just local news that suffers. A 2018 *Politico* investigation found that the lack of news in some areas contributed to Donald Trump's 2016 presidential election victory.

"An extensive review of subscription data and election results shows that Trump outperformed the previous Republican nominee, Mitt Romney, in counties with the lowest numbers of news subscribers, but didn't do nearly as well in areas with heavier circulation," the *Politico* piece begins.

It later added, "*Politico*'s analysis shows how [Trump] succeeded in avoiding mainstream outlets and turned that into a winning strategy: Voters in so-called news deserts – places with minimal newspaper subscriptions, print or online – went for him in higher-than-expected numbers. In tight races with Clinton in states like Wisconsin, North Carolina and Pennsylvania, the decline in local media could have made a decisive difference."

But the print cutbacks and weak online replacements are only part of the dumbing down story.

Local and national television and cable TV news has been spiraling downward for years. Perhaps not in the profitability or ratings area (as the major networks and cable news sites remain money-makers and major new sources for most folks), but in the quality, range and professionalism of their work.

As the splintering of audiences has hit crisis levels for many broadcast and cable outlets with new channels coming along almost weekly, many have lowered themselves to replace traditional news reporting with talking head opinion shows. They are mostly at night and have less and less real reporting, which is replaced by so-called analysis and panel discussions.

This is being done on the news medium voters say provides them with the most helpful political news, at least in the 2016 election, according to a Pew report.

The report, part of the *State of the News Media* findings, found that 24 percent of respondents described cable news as "most helpful" in their effort to get election information in 2016. Social media, which has its own biases and inaccuracy problems, was next with 14 percent, followed by local news at the same 14 percent.

In a related survey, Pew found that 54 percent said cable news was their most common source on a weekly basis for 2016 presidential election news, topped only by local news at 57 percent.

So, when that form of news is increasingly providing opinion and panel discussions over concrete reporting and informational journalism, the public is not well-served.

"I think CNN has, at once, been home to some incredibly irresponsible and diversionary punditry and debate, really pundit debate," said David Folkenflik, NPR media reporter. "And it's also been home to some of the best TV interviews and the toughest accountability reporting that you've seen on television." Later he added, "Sometimes it's just for theater. You know, you question a lot of choices about why they put on guests, why they hire pundits. I think it compromises a lot of what's there."

Average nightly primetime viewership on the big three cable outlets – CNN, MSNBC and Fox – hit a previous high of 4.2 million viewers back in 2008, the last open presidential race, but then started a downward trend to 3.3 million two years later and then 2.8 million in 2014.

But the 2016 race jump-started things with just over 3 million viewers in 2015 and a whopping 4.7 million in 2016, likely due in part to the increased analysis and decreased outright reporting. Daytime cable viewership on those three channels also increased from a 1.5 million average in 2007 – and a steady up and down around 2 million in the years that followed – to a blockbuster 2.7 million in 2016.

The cash boost followed closely with those three cable outlets seeing a steady combined revenue increase from $1.7 billion in 2007 to $3.1 billion in 2011 to $4.7 billion in 2016.

People like tuning into loudmouth debate and opinion. It goes with the increased findings that many prefer to get news and views they agree with – which would mean right-wing audiences to Fox News and left-wing audiences to MSNBC.

CNN? Well, a smattering of more emotional and opinionated efforts has come from the likes of Jake Tapper, Chris Cuomo and Erin Burnett, but on both sides. CNN has been accused more so of allowing argumentative debate and emotional jousting than favoring either side, although both liberals and conservatives would accuse them of serving the other side.

"These days, the people of Punditstan are a critical part of the cable news-industrial complex," Paul Farhi of the *Washington Post* wrote in a critical 2016 piece on the demise of reporting and growth of talking cable heads. "The leading news networks – CNN, Fox, MSNBC – don't report the news as much as they talk and speculate endlessly about it. For at least the past year, as well as for the next six months, the only thing they're talking about is the presidential campaign, a story perfectly tailored for 24-hour cable with its built-in conflict, historic importance and, yes, ever-changing 'narratives' (plus, who in America doesn't have something to say about Trump and Clinton?). That means just one thing: Right now, we're at peak punditry."

And a low of reporting.

When I was a CNN intern in the winter of 1988 in Washington, D.C., the news channel, just eight years old at the time, was essentially one long newscast. From *Daybreak*, the early morning show that was on when I arrived each morning at 5 a.m., through to the younger *Larry King Live*, at 9 p.m., traditional news dominated the screen where you could get big helpings of the day's top stories.

Back then, the D.C bureau was just a few floors at 111 Massachusetts Ave. and Fox and MSNBC were not even in the blueprint stage.

Today, CNN boasts its own campus of sorts down the road, a few blocks from the capital on First Street. But for all its expansion, modern technology and flashy home, viewers get less news each day than when interns in the 80s were working the studio cameras, lugging equipment and turning the old-fashioned teleprompter feed pages by hand.

They are not the only ones. MSNBC has become the anti-Trump show during most of the day and night. There is nothing wrong with news outlets reporting on what our president is doing wrongly, offensively or deceptively. Trump lies so often, and has since before he began running for president, that it's the duty of the press to expose him and report on his actions.

I'm all for that, as it relates to any public official from any party at any level. But it's gotten to where all MSNBC does for much of the time is report on Trump. He is not the only story. When they over-cover him, they undercover more pressing issues, from crime to health, education, the environment and finances.

A typical evening of CNN, MSNBC or Fox has so-called "personalities," from Anderson Cooper to Rachel Maddow to Sean Hannity either focused on one or two stories, giving pundits and other loudmouths a place to spew – often inaccurately – and with way too much opinion in most cases.

Tom Fenton, the author of *Bad News: The Decline of Reporting, the Business of News, and the Danger to Us All* and a former CBS News correspondent from 1966 until 2004, saw the problem developing more than a decade ago when he predicted it in his book and in a 2005 piece for CJR warning how such news cutbacks can help terrorism.

"I think that the basic problem is the dilution of actual reporting. Spin and bias proliferate in a news vacuum," he wrote of the trend of over-reporting. "In spite of the fact that there seem to be many more outlets for so-called news, I don't think the sum total of actual on-the-ground, first-hand reporting, especially investigative reporting, has increased. In fact, you can make the argument that it has decreased – it certainly has in international newsgathering. There are far fewer reporters on the ground, far fewer eyes and ears than there were ten or fifteen years ago."

He later added, "The news business shouldn't be a bottom-line oriented business. I won't argue that this business should lose money. I think they should at the very least break even. But there's always been a balance between the responsibility to the public – what news is supposed to deliver, because it has a public function – and the responsibility to the stockholders and to the bottom line. And this has gotten seriously out of balance."

And then there is Fox, which is an entirely different animal in that it purports to be "fair and balanced," but is obviously not. It is a propaganda outlet for the Republican Party, and more so, for Trump. But it is worth noting Fox's part in the news reporting reduction and pundit increase.

The news channel has never really distinguished itself as a reporting outlet that breaks important stories or digs into real journalism.

It's daytime and early evening programs, with the likes of Bret Baier and Shepard Smith, do provide a brand of basic news similar to its cable news competitors.

But when it gets past 7 p.m., it's Tucker Carlson, Sean Hannity and Laura Ingraham, three non-journalists whose mission seems to be to counter any valid news they disagree with, especially as it relates to Donald Trump.

Even when other news outlets are reporting on a story of the day, Fox News' evening shift will often largely ignore it. Especially if it reflects poorly on Trump, or any issue of import to Fox and its far-right audience.

One example is the early 2018 resignation of Trump aide Rob Porter, who was accused of abusing two of his ex-wives. It was the "story of the day" on Feb. 7, 2018, according to *The Daily Beast*, which detailed the Fox non-coverage.

"...from 7 p.m. onward, all of Fox News ignored the story," *the Daily Beast* wrote. "Not a single Porter mention on *The Story with Martha McCallum, Tucker Carlson Tonight,* or *The Ingraham Angle*." It later noted, "By contrast, according to a survey of television monitoring service TVEyes, Porter was the subject of at least 10 segments on CNN during its primetime hours, and of at least six segments on MSNBC."

Then there is local television news, which has had a news reporting problem for decades, but appears to be worse in recent years as it, too, deals with competition and less-patient audiences.

Thirty or forty years ago when there was little or no cable TV in most places, and the standard local news options were network affiliates and independent channels, most local news was received from the morning news briefs, some Noon news casts and the 5 p.m., 6 p.m. and 11 p.m. local shows. These half-hour and hour-long programs mixed weather, always in demand, with the best fires, floods and other lively video, as well as some government news from the nearest big city.

Smaller nearby towns only made it if there was a deadly tragedy, strange occurrence, sexually-related crime, or unique event. The phrase, "if it bleeds, it leads," still fits perfectly.

Not everything, however, was dire and deadly. Many shows mixed in consumer guidance, how-to segments on buying a car, a house or other big-ticket item, as well as the favorite green grocer or restaurant review.

But in-depth reporting and complete coverage of local basic entities – school boards, crime trends or the impact of taxes – were few and far between.

"Local TV news has thrived by developing a franchise around a handful of topics that have the widest appeal," a 2011 Pew survey reported, later adding, "Local television still has a hold on some of the most sought-after local topics, and ones that people seek out most often. But these are also topics for which convenience and timeliness are key features, and television might easily be replaced by mobile platforms that are even more accessible than TV."

That diminishing audience is clear in a more recent Pew study within its *2017 State of the News Media* research, which said in part, "Local television news programming has shed audience over the past decade, including this past year in most timeslots studied. Even with these viewership losses, local TV news still garners more viewers on average than cable and network news programs. However, for election news in particular – a big part of last year's news agenda – cable news brands were named as the main news source by a greater portion of voters than local TV news programming. Financially, local TV companies have generated increasing revenue, though in a cyclical pattern tied to election years."

As with its print and cable counterparts, local TV news has also begun grasping for the easy and often salacious-seeking audience – which also require less staffing and time than traditional reporting – to win back some of that departing viewership.

During my time in California in the 1990s, I saw this clearly portrayed with the oft-seen stolen-car chase. On many evenings, TV news helicopters got wind of a stolen car and hit the air and the airwaves, with live video feed of the pursuit, sometimes taking more than an hour away from the regular programming or the newscast to watch police chase the thief.

This might be worthwhile if it involved a bigger crime, such as an escaped killer or kidnapped victim in the backseat. But in many cases, it was simply a car theft that happened every day in most big cities and would rarely find space in the back page of a daily newspaper.

The local affiliates – and sometimes networks and cable news – know that people love watching any kind of chase or conflict. This is visible in the popularity of reality shows, most of which involved conflict and, real or false, human drama.

Much of the car chase coverage dates to the infamous O.J. Simpson "Bronco chase" of June 1994, when Simpson, still wanted for the murder of his wife, Nicole, and her friend Ronald Goldman, sought to escape capture in his friend's Ford Bronco. It was eventually spotted on a Los Angeles freeway and when TV helicopters caught up to him, the chase broke into every major, and many local, newscasts.

Millions of viewers flocked to their televisions on that Friday night to watch the chase that eventually ended with Simpson surrendering. The bizarre event became surreal when, at one point, an NBC affiliate, which was showing an NBA Finals game – put up a split screen with half of it on the New York Knicks and Houston Rockets and the other half on the chase.

More than creating a bizarre television moment, it also opened the floodgates for local affiliates to jump on air with any strange or eye-grabbing event, newsworthy or not. The discovery that people are glued to broadcasts of dramatic events, strange occurrences or conflict-involved reality no matter how relevant sparked local news outlets to put aside many of the traditional rules or ethics for news.

Along with the "anything goes" view of live events came the overkill of other local news. Weather, especially during hurricanes, heavy rains or blizzards, is on overdrive for local television. In much of the northeast, for instance, a storm that might bring half a foot of snow also brings non-stop coverage on the local channels, even if there is no real news other than the constant snow that could be updated with a short hourly news brief.

Instead, local affiliates send many reporters out in the snow to interview disrupted residents, show accidents, talk with children who are playing or hype the event in many other ways that fill time.

Why? They know people will watch, many of whom are stuck due to the storm and are willing to keep monitoring the TV, even if no real news comes forth.

Finally, there are the local stations that will report on, and often lead with, a national story that has no local connection. When the story of the day nationally was the Las Vegas shooting or a Florida Hurricane or the latest White House intrigue, it's often high up on the local TV news agenda – displacing more valuable news that has more impact on the local viewer.

"Local TV news shines in crisis. But it must be better and more relevant day in and day out," a 2018 Knight Foundation report stated. "Some newsroom leaders are embracing enterprise and investigative strategies and trying to develop innovative approaches to daily newscasts, but those efforts are not yet permeating the industry."

Another recent study from the Nieman Foundation at Harvard University offers a similar view: "The deterioration of the local news media poses dangers. Local stations are less likely today to offer robust coverage of city hall and state government. Reducing local news coverage may leave citizens less knowledgeable about issues of civic importance in their own communities."

The same report notes that even with such changes and cutbacks, local TV news remains a major source for most Americans, especially as newspapers and other local news entities are shrinking. It also stressed that changes need to occur, including reaching the growing web audience of younger news consumers and embracing new media options along with the traditional broadcast programs.

"At a time when local TV news is often written off as formulaic, with sensationalism triumphing over substance, advertising stagnant, and viewership declining, a host of stations is experimenting with new ways to attract audiences," the report stated, citing WRAL-TV in Raleigh, N.C., and its coverage of the Rev. Billy Graham's death in February 2018. "In addition to reporting the news of Graham's death, the station produced a 30-minute special, 'Remembering Billy Graham.' It aired the day of his funeral, which was livestreamed on the WRAL website, Facebook, and their mobile news app as well as broadcast live on television, pre-empting the noon newscast."

The Nieman study also warned there is not enough innovation: "While TV stations are well-positioned to create high-quality, internet-native videos that might attract younger audiences who don't watch television, too few are doing so. While 63 percent of stations say they are trying to attract younger demographics, according to a 2017 RTDNA survey, the majority defined those efforts as simply using social media. Only about 14 percent said they are looking at what they classified as 'younger-oriented content on digital platforms.'"

Then there is the consolidation question. With more national and monopolistic owners on the local level – in TV and radio – less independent journalism takes place.

A 2017 Pew study finds five of the largest media companies own most local TV news outlets, stating, "In 2004, the five largest companies in local TV – Sinclair, Nexstar, Gray, Tegna and Tribune – owned, operated or serviced 179 full-power stations, according to a Pew Research Center analysis of Securities and Exchange Commission filings data. That number grew to 378 in 2014 and to 443 in 2016. If approved by regulators, Sinclair's proposed acquisition of Tribune would have brought its total to 208, by far the largest among the media companies." That purchase was initially approved, but later blocked by the FCC when questions arose about Sinclair's misrepresentation of some internal holdings.

The company has also come under fire for dictating more and more of what its local stations broadcast, much of it with a pro-Trump tilt that has sparked protests both in and out of their newsrooms. One incident that drew sharp rebukes was Sinclair's 2018 directive that anchors at dozens of its local stations recite a warning against alleged "biased and fake news," a clear boosting of Trump's long-held false claims against mainstream media.

In reporting on the action, NPR stated online, "It was the latest show of the vast reach of a company that owns local TV stations across the country and has long been criticized for pushing conservative coverage and commentary onto local airwaves. Sinclair required local anchors to record promos where they denounce 'the troubling trend of irresponsible, one-sided news stories plaguing our country' and say that 'some members of the media use their platforms to push their own personal bias and agenda to control exactly what people think.'"

WHEN NEWS WAS NEWS

Along with the newsroom cutbacks, corporate takeovers and consolidation of news outlets, false claims that "fake news" is real and real news is fake creates the growing misunderstanding of what journalists do.

For years, we have been painted with the broad brush of being liberal-biased reporters who only want to skew news to the left and push our own political or social views.

Most recently, as true partisans take advantage of the web and growing cable outlet options for their platforms – on both sides of the political spectrum – the misrepresentation has grown more and more. Add to that our president's constant haranguing that any news he doesn't like is untrue, and that long-respected and fundamentally honest reporting outlets are lying and it's no wonder trust in the press is down.

A 2017 Gallup/Knight Foundation Survey on Trust, Media and Democracy found that 43 percent of those surveyed have a negative view of the news media, compared to 33 percent who have a positive view, with 23 percent neutral.

It also found that the 66 percent who believe most in news, up from just 42 percent in 1984, have difficulty separating fact from opinion. Fewer than half, 44 percent, can name a news outlet they believe is objective, while 40 percent of Republicans "consider accurate news stories that cast a politician or political group in a negative light to always be 'fake news.'"

"Not only is more information readily available, but so is more misinformation, and many consumers may not be able to easily discern the difference between the two," the report stated. "Amid the changing informational landscape, media trust in the U.S. has been eroding, making it harder for the news media to fulfill their democratic responsibilities of informing the public and holding government leaders accountable."

I agree with much of the criticism as it relates to properly covering news, staffing newsrooms, providing a balance, and doing in-depth investigations. These are valid problems that the industry needs to improve.

I strongly disagree, however, with the claims by folks on the right and the left, that reporters are out there to misinform and slant coverage. There are people purporting to be journalists, liberal and conservative, who seek only to sway opinion and views of events toward their beliefs. But they are in the minority.

During my 30 years as a reporter, with 19 of them covering news and media, I've met hundreds of reporters and editors, most of whom are out to get the facts, the interesting story and break the big scoop. And yes, they often want to bring down corrupt politicians – but in most cases because they deserve it not because they favor or oppose any specific public official or powerful leader.

That can include pushiness, rudeness, egotism and what seems like a drive for "negative news." But in most cases what some consider "negative," is important information. My rules for deciding if something is news have often been one of three things – is it interesting, important or unusual?

I don't see news as negative or positive, I see it as news, often falling in to one or both of those criteria.

When I teach college students, I put those three basics up front. After that, it is up to individual judgment for each story. You also must have an innate curiosity to find out what is happening. A friend of mine in the business used to say, "Journalism is the bug that bites you and sucks the blood out of you."

In college, one of my favorite professors, Bruce Porter, used to assign students to interview a short-order cook and write a profile of their life. The idea being that if you could be interested enough in this person to write a compelling story, you could be interested in anything. If not, then, well, get out.

Again, there are some who do not see it that way and get into the business to direct coverage a certain way – that's not journalism, but luckily it is also not the rule, but the exception.

The rule is: find out the facts, the news and the who, what, where, when and why. Then report it, "without fear or favor."

"I always wanted to change the world, the stories I have been attracted to have been those that go unnoticed," said Dana Priest, the two-time Pulitzer Prize-winning reporter for the *Washington Post*, whose 2007 expose on Walter Reed Army Hospital drew national attention and calls for improvements. "I've always been motivated by the idea that if you show people an inconvenient truth and the facts of it, they will make changes. I think a lot of people [in journalism] were motivated by that. Holding government accountable."

She later added, "That's still, I find, among my generation and I think I see it coming back among young people. There is a swing toward click bait stories, that is evolving. But I think you see a little bit swinging back away from that."

James Rainey, a former *Los Angeles Times* media writer and currently with NBC News online, said he also wanted to "change the world," with an eye on an interesting, meaningful work, not slanted coverage.

"It just seemed like an interesting way to be in a lot of other worlds and have a job where you aren't pinned down to one thing every day," said Rainey. "I was also able to travel and talk to people who were interesting."

He said assumptions that most reporters are out to mislead is anathema to a journalist's views.

"This whole thing of reporters being demonized. This movement led by the president that journalists as a group are liars is painful. People who are trying to do the right thing and are bludgeoned. It is such a fundamental myth that is being created."

He cited the 2015 film *Spotlight*, which chronicled the 2002 *Boston Globe* investigation of the Catholic Church scandal and broke the first stories about priest abuse that sparked subsequent discoveries worldwide. That reporting won the paper the 2003 Pulitzer Prize for Public Service, the most prominent Pulitzer, while the movie won the Academy Award for Best Picture.

"It showed what journalism should be," Rainey said about the *Globe*'s work. "It felt so much like what people I work with do."

Critics contend if most reporters are liberal, which could be true, they automatically steer coverage that way. But that ignores the drive most of us have to be professional, accurate and fair.

That is like assuming a doctor or lawyer or plumber who might be liberal would treat his or her conservative customers worse than liberal customers – or vice-versa.

In recent history those making such claims – mostly conservatives – are generally doing so in the face of truth about them or their leaders they don't want revealed. Much of it beginning with Watergate, which sparked anti-press backlash by Nixon supporters who attacked the press for reporting that turned out to be true.

In Trump's case it has grown like a wildfire in which he baselessly attacks news outlets almost daily when they report something he does not like. No proof of inaccuracy or slanted coverage is ever included, just his slanderous tweets of "fake news."

During the Lewinsky scandal, Bill Clinton and his supporters also went after the press, some of the same news outlets now accused of being so liberal. In fact, it was *The New York Times* – accused of being too 'lefty' – that first reported in March 1992 on the Clinton Whitewater deal that sparked a special prosecutor investigation that later ended with the Lewinsky scandal findings.

The *Times* editorial page became one of the lead critics of Clinton and the affair, editorializing on several occasions about Clinton's poor behavior and disruption of his presidency.

Years later, the *Times* broke the story of New York's Democratic Governor Eliot Spitzer's ties to prostitutes, which eventually forced his resignation.

And back in 1987 The *Miami Herald*, no bastion of conservatism, exposed former Senator Gary Hart's infidelities after he dared the press to follow him amid rumors of womanizing. Hart dropped out of the 1988 presidential race within a week.

In each case, the supposed liberal press dug deep to expose the misdeeds and questionable acts of liberal politicians. They continue to do so today.

To better understand journalism and the news, it's worth digging into a little history. First: the newspaper.

No product in the history of the United States had the same impact on or relationship with its consumers as the daily newspaper. For centuries, this chronicle of each 24-hour time capsule, truly dubbed the

"Daily Miracle," brought news from far and wide to your front door, for a nominal fee and with the expectation that you could find most everything you needed.

More than that, the intimacy of the hold-in-your hand pages, gave readers a one-on-one relationship unmatched by any broadcast, cable or computer connection.

Reliable information and strong writing also came through the newsprint in a way that no other product could match. Newspapers and their operators fell into the dual role of a profit-making company as well as a public servant. Some have argued that papers should be non-profits, while others saw them as a way to both make money – often via a family unit – and influence public thought. The agenda-setting power of daily newspapers – from *The New York Times* to the *Dayton Daily News* – was unmatched.

With mobile devices, websites and a growing array of hand-held gadgets, the daily newspaper as we knew it is gone. But that does not mean its purpose cannot thrive in the technological age.

The first recorded history of a newspaper in America is credited to *Publick Occurrences Both Forreign and Domestick* by printer Richard Pierce and edited by Benjamin Harris in Boston on September 25th, 1690.

On September 26th it ceased publication as it was published without permission of British colonial authorities. Pierce was arrested, and all copies were destroyed. There is no record of Pierce ever returning to the newspaper business.

Still, the mark had been made for newspapers in the United States. For the next 300-plus years, newspapers remained the nation's most prominent, factual and expansive news source. Even with the rise of online journalism and social media platforms, newspapers still resonate today, benefitting from a legacy of trust and a wealth of resources to draw upon. Newspaper reporting often sets the agenda and tone for online and public discourse.

That was evident in 2008 when Barack Obama won the presidential election as the first African-American president and readers flocked to newsstands and newspaper offices, to grab editions declaring his victory.

From the *Washington Post* to the *Los Angeles Times*, newspapers reported record single-copy sales from Nov. 4, 2008. Most readers said they wanted a piece of history – so much so that Craigslist had ads offering copies of *The New York Times* and the *Washington Post* at $25 each.

The *Washington Post* printed 30,000 extra copies on Election Night that year. "It sold out almost instantly," Steve Hills, president and general manager of Washington Post Media, told *The New York Times.*

The next day the *Post* printed 150,000 copies of a special edition, charging $1.50, a dollar more than usual. "As the day wore on, it raised that to 250,000, then 350,000," the *Times* reported. "I've been here for 21 years and I've never seen anything like this," Hills told them.

That was repeated around the country, with newspapers reporting readers lined up around the block for souvenir editions.

"We sold 16,000 copies from our lobby, where we're not set up to sell any," Jennifer Morrow, a spokeswoman for *The Atlanta Journal-Constitution*, told the *Times.*

Another historical element of newspapers includes hundreds of movies that often use headlines to declare plotlines, surprises and events occurring over time on the big screen.

"Between newspapers and the Associated Press, they are still crucially important," said Michael Schudson, a professor at the Columbia University Graduate School of Journalism and author of *Discovering the News*. "Most people get their news from television, but television takes its cue from the wire services and the leading newspapers."

He adds, "The vast majority of people to this day are figuring out what the public agenda is from the work of newspapers, both print and online versions. In the past, it differs depending on what era."

Schudson points out that newspapers have always evolved and the current migration to online or mobile devices may well be another change, but not a death knell.

"One of the things that is hard to make sense of is that until about the 1820s, newspapers didn't do any reporting, they wrote editorials, they reprinted stories from the London papers, they printed documents that the government handed out, but they didn't hire reporters," he says. "Did they set the agenda? Well how else did people find out what else was going on in the nation's capital, there weren't other alternatives."

He also debunks the non-partisan claims of some of today's media, noting, "The press was quite partisan, you read the paper that you agreed with, like conservatives watching Fox News, the same thing. From the 1790s to the early 20th century. The newspapers were kind of subdivisions of the political parties."

Schudson adds that newspapers still give the most, and most believable coverage: "Most credible, most in-depth and the major daily newspapers in each city even with all the shredding of newsrooms over the last 15 years, they still have more reporters than all of the television stations in a community."

As for politics, newspaper endorsements remain a key piece of influence in both local and national elections. To this day, campaigns continue to promote their candidate or ballot measure cause by using a newspaper's endorsement as a sign of someone with interest and influence backing their effort.

As recently as September 12, 2013, *The New York Times* Op Ed page was the center of news when Russian President Vladimir Putin chose the space to offer his argument in the form of a column to Americans to be cautious in the then-debate over Syria and chemical weapons.

It has always been the newspaper as the agenda-setter, the community forum and often, the keeper of the public trust.

"Newspapers are what helped bring a community together, a community and a nation," declared Dale Cressman, a newspaper historian and associate chair of undergraduate studies at the Department of Communications at Brigham Young University. "Newspaper buildings created civic locations not only for news, but for celebrations and events."

He cited the famed New Year's Eve ball drop at Times Square in New York City, which was named for *The New York Times*, whose headquarters was at the center of the event.

"People would actually go to newspapers' offices and see headlines stream across the top of the building and learn the news that way. Newspapers were also the first buildings in New York City allowed to surpass the height of churches," Cressman said.

He added that, "The penny press was the first mass media," referring to the one-cent copies of newspapers hawked by street carriers. It was also the early, bigger-than-life editors who drove much of the news-setting agenda. They were the Rush Limbaughs, Rachel Maddows and Stephen Colberts of their day.

He cited Joseph Pulitzer, publisher of the *New York World* and *St. Louis Post-Dispatch*; William Randolph Hearst, the flamboyant owner of the *New York Journal* and *San Francisco Examiner*, and Horace Greeley, famed for his advice, "Go west, young man" in an editorial appearing in the *New York Tribune*.

"The [newspapers] were reflections of the editors, in the day of the larger-than-life editors – Pulitzer, Hearst, Greeley. In a way they were community leaders," Cressman said. "Joseph Pulitzer was embarrassed that people could not pay for the platform on which to place the Statue of Liberty, so he asked readers to send in pennies and that raised much of the money."

He noted Pulitzer would send his newspaper wagons to poorer neighborhoods with ice to help keep milk fresh. He would also have strawberry festivals for children in Madison Square Garden. "They were forces in the community," Cressman said.

Then there are these famed newspaper moments in history:

- o **1948** – President Harry S. Truman holding the infamous copy of the *Chicago Daily Tribune* declaring "DEWEY DEFEATS TRUMAN."

- o **1972** – The Pentagon Papers, a classified history of the Vietnam War, were obtained by *The New York Times* and the *Washington Post*. When the Supreme Court ruled against prior restraint, they were published and credited as the best, complete story of the war.

- o **1871-1872** – Cartoonist Thomas Nast's crusade against the corruption of Boss Tweed helped bring down the political power broker.

- o **1898** – William Randolph Hearst and Joseph Pulitzer are all but credited with sparking the Spanish-American War. Both publishers hyped the conflict following the sinking of the U.S.S. Maine, despite little evidence that Spain attacked the vessel.

"They were the only game in town," declares Douglas Brinkley, the respected historian and Rice University history professor. "It used to be that they were more politically partisan, be a federalist paper, or a Democrat or Republican paper. The age that we think of this ombudsman balance journalism is more of a recent creation of the 20th Century."

Brinkley also cited Ida Tarbel and other muckrakers of the early 20th Century who took on big business-like Standard Oil, and the more recent journalist, Seymour Hersh, who exposed the Vietnam War killings in My Lai, a village where hundreds of unarmed civilians were murdered by U.S. Soldiers. (Hersh won the 1970 Pulitzer Prize for International Reporting for his work).

Many also credit the press with forging coverage of the 1950's and 1960's civil rights movement. It was the African-American press of the time that really led the way early on, according to historians.

"The black press was covering black people for a black audience the white people weren't reading them and if they had they would have realized there was a lot of outrage out there and anger and a lot of African Americans who were doing remarkable things," said Hank Klibanoff, a former *Atlanta Journal-Constitution* top editor and co-author of *The Race Beat*, the 2006 Pulitzer Prize-winning account of civil rights reporting. "Black reporters had to do more than just run the stories, they had to become advocates and they remained advocacy newspapers."

One often unknown example is how the African-American press lobbied for Jackie Robinson, who became the first black baseball player for the Major Leagues in 1947.

"I was bowled over by what I didn't know about the role of the black press in getting Jackie Robinson in front of Branch Rickey," said Klibanoff, who cited writer Wendell Smith, a Hall of Fame reporter for the *Pittsburgh Courier.* "In the movie, *42,* they had him covering Jackie

Robinson, in reality you had the black reporters pushing him in front of the Dodgers owner."

He also cited the *Baltimore Afro-American* and its sports scribe Sam Lacy. "That becomes the first running race story that the white press began following the black press on," Klibanoff says. "A story that was not a crime story."

He said the Lacys and Smiths of the black press made a difference because they were among the first to know about the push for baseball integration.

"They knew from covering the Negro baseball leagues who was really good, and they got Jimmy Cannon in on this, why is baseball ignoring this huge talent out there?" Klibanoff said.

Later, the African-American press were among the first to report on lynchings in the south and other horrid tales of racist-fueled physical abuse.

"They got there first and they cared, they remained advocacy oriented and they were committed to telling not only the ugly sordid side of racial discrimination of America, but telling the story of black achievements," Klibanoff said. "So, on the ugly side, telling the story of lynching became really important to them. We do tell the story of Vincent Tubbs and how he couldn't drive down to Texas and couldn't fly because that was expensive and a black man driving in the south would not do well.

"The white press would cover the lynching with these photographs, but not with the sense of horror at the coverage. Beyond that it was just black reporters had access to what became movement leaders over time."

More recently, the *Washington Post* and the *Chicago Sun-Times* took an extra step to seek some truth, with both criticism and risk, and came out ahead in terms of helping a greater public good and keeping their journalistic values strong.

The *Post* had been known for several consequential moments in newspaper history, from breaking its Pulitzer Prize-winning coverage of Watergate in the early 1970's to suffering a major black eye with the Janet Cooke scandal in 1980 and 1981, when the paper had to return a Pulitzer after revealing that Cooke, a young reporter, had fabricated a story about a nine-year-old heroin addict.

But perhaps its most impactful and controversial moment came in 1996 with the Unabomber manifesto. For nearly two decades, from 1978 to 1995, the so-called Unabomber, later identified as Ted Kaczynski, had sent 16 mail bombs to people with notes about his opposition to growing technology. It was a national terrorist action that injured 23 people and killed three.

At one point, in 1995, he sent a letter to the *Post* and *The New York Times* promising to stop if the *Post* or the *Times* published his 35,000-word "manifesto," titled, Industrial Society and its Future.

Leonard Downie, Jr., then executive editor of the *Post*, recalls it being a "very dramatic moment for us, I still have a copy the FBI made of the copy he sent to us."

"Our mailroom, like all mailrooms, had become security conscious," Downie, now retired, recalls about receiving the Unabomber's initial letter. "They discovered it, they didn't touch it, we called the FBI and they, the FBI in their hazmat suits, took away the original."

Downie said the paper was asked by the FBI to publish the manifesto in the hopes that it would raise public interest, with the potential that someone may recognize the person's writing style or beliefs.

"The FBI contacted both *The New York Times* and the *Washington Post* to ask us to publish the manifesto in whole," said Downie, who recalled going to a meeting at FBI headquarters with *Washington Post* Company chair Donald Graham and *Post* Publisher Bo Jones.

Also at the meeting were their *Times* counterparts, Publisher Arthur Sulzberger Jr. and Executive Editor Joe Lelyveld, as well as FBI Director Louis Freed and Attorney General Janet Reno.

"They showed us models they had reconstructed of what they thought the bombs looked like, which was kind of impressive actually, and a profiler told us who they thought the Unabomber might be like and they were completely wrong about that," Downie recalled. "They thought it was some leftist guy living in the Bay Area and they figured he would want to keep up with news about what he was doing and if we published the manifesto he would want to see it, and so they wanted us to publish it so that they could distribute it, the *Times* or *Post*, distribute it around the country, and then hopefully he would go in and buy it and they'd have somebody there watching and they would grab him and they thought it would be in the Bay Area."

In the end, the *Times* and the *Post* split the costs, and both published the manifesto as an insert in their papers on September 19, 1995.

"There was a lot of discussion on this and a lot of soul-searching," Downie recalls, noting the criticism that arose from those who claimed it was giving into a terrorist's wishes. "After a lot of discussion what was decided was that the *Post* with the *Times* and the *Post* dividing the cost, the *Post* would publish the manifesto.

"It was left up to us as a kind of moral and journalistic decision. The Justice Department asked us, but they also realized Janet Reno was very good about this. That she, A, couldn't force us to do this, and B, did not want to argue us into doing it if we thought it was a bad idea. But the FBI laid out the rationale for why they thought it was a good idea and, of course, they were mistaken about how they thought it would work out, but nevertheless it worked out."

Kaczynski's brother, David, saw the publication of the manifesto and contacted the FBI. The *Post* later reported that David Kaczynski had been suspicious of his brother for several months upon hearing about his letters related to the bombings.

Kaczynski was eventually arrested on April 3, 1996, in a Montana cabin where he lived. He later pleaded guilty to three murder charges and was given a sentence of life without parole.

"I thought it was newsworthy, to see this was a guy who was blowing people up and kept on doing it forever and I thought it was newsworthy for people to see exactly what he was saying," Downie remembers about the decision to print the massive manifesto. "I didn't personally, necessarily believe if we published it, he would stop sending bombs."

But Downie calls the paper's actions "clearly, very significant," also adding that, "we didn't know what would happen, I thought it was newsworthy and did not see strong reasons not to publish it, it was a joint decision by Don and me because of the nature of the decision."

Another, perhaps lesser known, case of a daily newspaper's impact is that of The Mirage and the *Chicago Sun-Times*, which bought a local tavern, operated it secretly, and chronicled the massive graft from officials that followed.

"I still get calls from students doing term papers who call and ask if it could be done today," says Zay N. Smith, a former *Sun-Times* reporter and one of the creators of the project. "It was a public service, newspapers in that day often go off complaints and we had received for years complaints from small businesses that everyone had their hand out, but no one could go on the record. The best way to find out and document what's going on is to become a victim."

That is what the *Sun-Times* did in 1977 when it bought the neighborhood bar, dubbed it, appropriately, The Mirage, and opened its doors. The goal was to find out how corrupt local city officials, inspectors, and business people might be in efforts to either shake-down local business owners or accept kickbacks and bribes to do business.

For six months, the bar operated under the tightest of newsroom secrecy and the reporters, with the help the journalistic, non-profit Better Government Association, chronicled all activities, from demands for bribes to inspectors to local vendors skimming off the top.

"We became a victim and a small business, the tavern was chosen because it is more colorful to write about, but it also goes under so many licensing approvals and inspections," Smith recalls. "We never put anything forward, we would not initiate anything. We just opened the door and the rest happened."

Smith, who was among those who served as bartenders, joined with fellow scribe Pamela Zekman, who went on to become a local anchorwoman, in what would become a major 25-part series for the paper in early 1978, and eventually a book by the duo.

"If I recall, the saloon cost $18,000 and it lost a lot of money, tied up two reporters for a year and two photographers for months," Smith says.

As it operated, the bar reached out to accountants to find out exactly what was legal or not in the day-to-day activities, which ended when the saloon closed on Halloween 1977. But in the time it operated, even Smith and Zekman were surprised at how much corruption was attempted.

"We would run behind the back bar a lot and write notes and we would phone in to the BGA a lot," Smith says. "It did have a certain chilling effect, going undercover. Would a Mirage find something today? I would be fascinated to see."

In the end, more than a dozen city officials were fired or suspended because of the series, the book later reported, while a federal investigation ended up with indictments for bribery against 31 electrical inspectors. Permanent internal review departments were created for city employees, code inspectors and fire prevention bureau staffers.

The *Sun-Times* re-ran the series online in 2013 to mark its 35th anniversary.

"A lot of inspectors went down, the feds were doing a probe unbeknownst to us and they came back to us and said it helped them get going," Smith says. When asked if it could be done today, he stated, "Newspaper don't have the dough that they had."

Brinkley said those examples of in-depth reporting helped mold the image of newspapers into a greater public service in the 1900's, but he agreed the lack of the printed product does diminish its unique value.

From the moment that Pierce's one-day experiment occurred, newspapers became both the agenda-driving outlet for news and commentary, the fiercest protectors of the First Amendment and most dogged pursuers of news and information.

And readers took advantage.

In 1940, the first statistical year for the Newspaper Association of America, there were more than 1,800 newspapers with a combined circulation of about 41 million

The number of newspapers dipped in the decade after that to 1,772 in 1950, but readership rose as circulation jumped to more than 53 million.

The good times remained as the newspaper population stayed in the 1,700 range through 1983 and circulation skyrocketed to its high of 63 million a year later.

"Let's remember that as soon as TV became ubiquitous, 1952, 53, the penetration of daily newspapers in urban households was more than one per household," recalls Mark Fitzgerald of Chicago, who was at the newspaper trade journal *Editor & Publisher* for 27 years, including the last year as top editor. "Families were commonly getting two papers, which is most unheard of now."

Certainly, television cut into market share in a big way starting in the 1940s. The long-standing traditional evening newspaper readership crumbled because most people were working 9-to-5 and television was providing more up-to-date coverage at dinnertime.

"It is a complex chain of events that occurred in this country and not really in other countries, a kind of monopoly of complacency," said Bill Kovarik, author of *Revolutions in Communication: Media History from Gutenberg to the Digital Age*. "Newspapers really coasted through the first half of the 20th century."

Kovarik notes that newspaper owners perceived the threat to their existence long ago. He points to collusion as far back as 1922 between Associated Press and publishers by which AP would limit news service to television and radio.

"It was a battle," Kovarik said. "The publishers and AP colluded to keep radio out and forced CBS and NBC not to run news. They wouldn't allow them to use Associated Press content."

This was altered slightly in 1933 with the so-called Biltmore Agreement. It was named for New York's Biltmore Hotel, where a pact was hammered out allowing broadcasters limited use of AP copy to two five-minute programs each day provided that the stations carried the tagline: "See your daily newspaper for further details." In exchange, newspapers printed radio schedules for free.

But the agreement was short-lived: Publishers began to realize they could own radio stations, which they used to promote their newspapers and cross-sell newspaper and radio advertising.

When television exploded on the scene, it took some of the audience, Kovarik said. But he said television and radio still could not provide the kind of display and classified advertising that newspapers did.

"TV comes along and there's a huge drop in movie-going and in newspaper circulation. You could say television killed the afternoon daily," he explains. "But the newspaper was a monopoly, it was the only place you could advertise a job or a car or a house. That is a major piece."

Newspapers were just the first place that quality journalism was found. Even with their recent problems, the history of television and radio news should be praised.

The first radio station has long been believed to be KDKA in Pittsburgh, which went on the air Nov. 2, 1920. It is credited with reporting the first radio news on Election Night that year, broadcasting returns of the Harding-Cox presidential election that led to Warren Harding's victory.

Other historians credit WWJ Radio in Detroit with the first broadcast and first regular radio news on Aug. 31 of that same year, according to *Wired*.

In an early signal of the eventual media consolidation that would take over the nation, WWJ was created by Scripps, then owners of *The Detroit News*.

"Scripps was motivated to invent news radio, but didn't exactly know how," *Wired* states. "And the company even wanted to hedge this bet, just in case radio turned out to be a passing fad with which they didn't want their good name associated. So, in what would become a cliché of the internet age, they hired a teenager to build and explain it to them."

By the end of 1921, eight radio stations were operating in the U.S., according to Encyclopedia Britannica.

In 1925, WGN Radio in Chicago covered the infamous Scopes monkey trial, which put the teaching of evolution over creationism on trial for the first time. By 1925, NBC launched the first radio network with 25 stations, followed by CBS in 1928.

In 1930, NBC created the first regular network newscast, a 15-minute report by Lowell Thomas across all its stations. These marked the first national newscasts in which multiple regions were given the same nationwide news from one broadcast source.

The 1932 Lindbergh baby kidnapping and murder was another major early radio news story, and the later trial of convicted kidnapper Bruno Richard Hauptman, who was put to death in 1936.

At one point, NBC Radio played a role in communicating with the kidnappers when the baby's parents, Charles and Anne Morrow Lindbergh, used NBC Radio to broadcast a plea to the kidnapper. The Lindberghs promised to keep confidential any agreements to bring the baby back, according to historian Douglas Linder.

World War II gave radio news a major boost as NBC and CBS sent correspondents overseas. NBC created a European operation in 1937. For CBS, it was Edward R. Murrow's now famous dispatches from London that put him and radio coverage of the war on the map.

One of Murrow's most dramatic and historic broadcasts came from the London Blitzkrieg on Sept. 22, 1940 during Germany's air raids over the British city. With sirens and other warning sounds, from a rooftop, Murrow describes the scene of the city where people are rushing to shelters as the sounds of anti-aircraft fire are heard.

Another vivid radio reporting moment came in 1937 when the German airship Hindenburg crashed at Lakehurst, N.J., and WLS Radio reporter Herb Morrison told the story live on the air, his voice cracking with emotion. As it burst into flames, Morrison described the horror, declaring, "this is terrible, this is one of the worst catastrophes in the world ... oh the humanity."

For television, 1940 brought the first regular news program when Lowell Thomas' daily NBC Radio report went on air with visual images of Thomas. By 1941, WCBS-TV in New York was broadcasting its first regular television newscast twice a day.

When the Japanese attacked Pearl Harbor on Dec. 7, 1941, it became the first national crisis to give television the scoop as WNBT – NBC's New York affiliate – stopped its showing of the comedy film *Millionaire Playboy* to report on the event that drew the U.S. into World War II.

On May 3, 1948, Douglas Edwards began anchoring *CBS Television News*, a regular 15-minute nightly newscast on the CBS Television Network, including WCBS-TV.

During the 1950's, Murrow's *See It Now* on CBS, marked the first in-depth news broadcasts focused on specific subjects, including a famous episode on March 9, 1954 that delved into the communist witch hunts of Sen. Joseph McCarthy, eventually leading to McCarthy's censure in the U.S. Senate.

In 1952, both national party nominating conventions were first broadcast on television, while 1960 was the first televised presidential debate, between John Kennedy and Richard Nixon.

Television news also played a major role in civil rights coverage early on, including the 1957 court-ordered integration of Little Rock High School in Arkansas.

In their 2006 Pulitzer Prize-winning book, *The Race Beat*, authors and veteran journalists Gene Roberts and Hank Klibanoff detail how TV news kept the nation informed during the National Guard and U.S. military intervention of the newly desegregated southern city school campus:

"On the 101st Airborne's first full day in Little Rock, news directors for the three networks got clearance to break into daily programming virtually at will. CBS broke in 11 times. NBC eight times. ABC joined later in the day. Far away, in the Pentagon, Army Secretary Wilber M. Brucker was handed an update on the troops in Little Rock. 'But what's happening there right now?' he snapped. 'Why not turn on the television set?' an officer suggested. A television was brought into the room, plugged in, and turned on, and images of soldiers at stiff parade rest emerged on the screen …. That an army secretary and his chief of staff were able to examine their soldiers in action from nine hundred miles away, live, was a powerful sensation, one the American people would share in the coming years."

In the years to come, television news would continue to break new ground as it covered the civil rights marches and violence, from Birmingham to Memphis and beyond.

"The civil rights movement would have been like a bird without wings if it hadn't been for the news media," former Congressman John Lewis (D-Ga.), who led the 1965 "Bloody Sunday" march in Selma, Alabama, said at a 1987 symposium according to the *Los Angeles Times*, which added, "He said that civil rights workers looked upon the media as 'sympathetic referees' in their struggle to topple the South's system of racial segregation."

Aniko Bodroghkozy, an associate professor in the Department of Media Studies at the University of Virginia and author of the 2012 book, *Equal Time: Television and the Civil Rights Movement*, said in an interview with media expert Henry Jenkins that television coverage of Martin Luther King's famed 1963 March on Washington and "I Have a Dream" speech gave the event much of its publicity in a way past coverage had not.

"All three networks carried significant amounts of live coverage of the March on Washington which occurred, by the way, on a Wednesday," Bodroghkozy said. "Nowadays it's no spectacular feat to get masses of people to Washington for a march, but they always happen on the weekend. Try to get a quarter of a million people to the national Mall on a weekday!

"Along with the live coverage during the day, CBS that evening provided a primetime news program that both recapped the events of the day and provided background about the March. For people interested in the March, CBS's primetime coverage is probably where they first got their sense of what happened. Now this is the pre-sound bite era. The news special provided long excerpts for quite a number of the speeches that preceded King's."

The other major story of the 1960s also came to the small screen when the Vietnam War heated up, marking the first war that entered millions of living rooms with color images of brutality.

"Vietnam was the first truly televised war; the war and the medium through which millions of Americans experienced it were inextricable," former NBC News Saigon bureau chief Ronald Steinman wrote in a 2017 *New York Times* piece. "To understand the war, one needs to understand how NBC – and our colleagues at CBS and ABC – shaped how that story was told. Those of us in broadcast news understood our role clearly. We went all out. NBC News had bureaus around the world, but in size and scope, there was nothing like the one in Saigon."

It was the televised aspect of the war that brought such condemnation, opposition, and the eventual nationwide protests, veteran journalists say.

One historic report was CBS News correspondent and future *60 Minutes* reporter Morley Safer's 1965 report from the village of Cam Ne that dramatically showed Marines setting fire to civilian thatched roofs with flamethrowers, guns and Zippo lighters – a symbolic image of corporate America and technology taking down fearful Vietnam villagers.

"It seemed a heartless and pointless kind of operation," Safer said in a 1990 C-SPAN interview related to promotion of his book, *Flashbacks: On Returning to Vietnam*. "And the visual images, as I think I said in the piece at the time, demonstrated the kind of frustration of that kind of war, where here you had American assault units – that's what Marines are trained to do. That's what they're best at, from the kind of romantic ideal of splashing ashore in the second World War. But, you know, these are our tough guys, go in under fire. And here they were part of something euphemistically called a pacification operation, a dreadful word that the French first claimed in Algeria, I believe, in describing that war...."

Safer's report, which revealed the event that destroyed 150 homes and killed at least one baby, was among the first to draw condemnation from the pro-war Johnson Administration and military officials who threatened to force Safer out as a war correspondent and expose him as a communist, he claims. It would also not be the last time the press was targeted for reporting on the truth of this war or future conflicts.

As Safer later stated in the interview, "The broadcast inflamed the White House, inflamed the Marine Corps. Lyndon Johnson was enraged by it. A lot of pressure on CBS to have me withdrawn from Vietnam, or the release withdrawn. CBS refused to do so, and the White House ultimately said, 'Well, unless you pull him out' – ultimately being over a matter of days – 'we're going to go public with the fact that, at the very least, he is a Communist sympathizer and probably is even a KGB agent and we've got the goods on him,' which was just a silly bluff."

It was a stark example of what many journalists endure to report a truth people in power do not want exposed. Safer's reporting, and that of others down the line, likely changed the treatment of Vietnam and foreign policy. It was not done for personal gain or political views. It was simply reporting the facts, the extent of the cover-up and the lies about Vietnam.

It was the images that TV delivered in clear, offensive form that gave viewers a realism of this war that they did not have earlier. The fact that it was such a controversial and lie-strewn event made the TV reporting that much more impactful.

Safer's fellow Vietnam correspondent David Halberstam, who reported on the war for *The New York Times,* described Safer's report in a later interview, as a "jarring image of our troops, instead of giving out chewing gum to kids, turning the firepower really, on a village, that raised in a very elemental way the question of whether we were on the right side."

Historian Daniel Hallin, a professor of political science at the University of California, Berkeley, contends that most images were just people involved with battles, with little real bloodshed on camera. But stresses that such images when presented were impactful.

"There were, to be sure, occasions when television did deliver images of violence and suffering," Hallin wrote in an online essay at The Museum of Broadcasting, saying of Cam Ne, "This story could never have passed the censorship of World War II or Korea, and it generated an angry reaction from Lyndon Johnson."

He also noted other examples, stating, "In 1968, during the Tet offensive, viewers of NBC news saw Col. Nguyen Ngoc Loan blow out the brains of his captive in a Saigon street. And in 1972, during the North Vietnamese spring offensive, the audience witnessed the aftermath of errant napalm strike, in which South Vietnamese planes mistook their own fleeing civilians for North Vietnamese troops."

When the war protests turned deadly at Kent State University on May 4, 1970, with four unarmed students murdered by National Guardsmen, TV film of the killings did even more to show the violence of the war, both home and abroad.

"Kent State created a ripple effect," author Edward Wakin wrote in his book, *How TV Changed America's Mind.* "Coverage of demonstrations, student strikes and takeovers and burnings of buildings made more and more Americans ask: 'Was Vietnam worth these young lives at home as well as on the battlefield?' The controversy tore the country apart."

Then there was CBS Anchorman Walter Cronkite, dubbed "the most trusted man in America." Many credit – or blame – Cronkite for administering the final blow on the Vietnam War in his famed editorializing during his broadcast on Feb. 27, 1968, in which he essentially said the war was doomed:

> *To say that we are closer to victory today is to believe, in the face of the evidence, the optimists who have been wrong in the past. To suggest we are on the edge of defeat is to yield to unreasonable pessimism. To say that we are mired in stalemate seems the only realistic, yet unsatisfactory, conclusion.*
>
> *On the off chance that military and political analysts are right, in the next few months we must test the enemy's intentions, in case this is indeed his last big gasp before negotiations. But it is increasingly clear to this reporter that the only rational way out then will be to negotiate, not as victors, but as an honorable people who lived up to their pledge to defend democracy, and did the best they could.*

Walter Cronkite, Feb. 27, 1968

President Lyndon Johnson, watching live in the White House, is reported to have said to an aide, "If I've lost Cronkite, I've lost Middle America." Just over a month later, on March 31, 1968, Johnson announced he would not seek re-election, a decision most historians tie directly to the Vietnam War debacle.

"Cronkite's report was significant. It contributed greatly to the shift in public opinion against the war," veteran war correspondent and author Mark Bowden wrote in a 2018 *New York Times* piece about Vietnam. "But there was no immediate, radical turn. Most polls would continue to show narrowing but clear public support for the war for years to come. Richard Nixon was elected later that year, and vigorously prosecuted the war for six years more. If Cronkite was wrong, if the war was in fact being won and winnable, there were ample resources, time and commitment to prove it. In fact, Cronkite was right. The war was not being won, nor would it be."

Then when Watergate hit, the TV floodgates poured open with live hearings in both the House and the Senate. Later, the impeachment debate and some of the first punditry arrived as press, politicos and others argued this very real, and unchartered territory of presidential abuse, political lying, and the now famous "constitutional crisis."

Print news, which broke the story via the *Washington Post*'s Pulitzer Prize-winning reporting, led the initial charge. But as the story grew and TV did its own digging, the Nixon crimes received more widespread attention and daily scrutiny than they ever could have from print alone.

Cronkite brought more attention to the issue just a month before the 1972 election with a two-part "explainer" feature on the *CBS Evening News* that put the story in perspective for many viewers and resembled something of a college lecture.

"A furious White House threatened to punish CBS by revoking its station licenses," A PBS story on the events stated. "But CBS stuck by its story and watched as Nixon self-destructed over the next two years. Cronkite reported with quiet admiration the thoughtful proceedings of the House Judiciary Committee on the Impeachment of President Nixon. And he reported Nixon's resignation with sadness. There was no gloating, nor hard feelings. He was a professional doing his job, which he never doubted was serving the public."

Since the Senate Watergate hearings were held in the summer of 1973, they made for even more interesting TV to many, prompting *Variety* at the time to refer to them as "the hottest daytime soap opera" and later report that "the proceedings scored high ratings and were full of bombshell revelations."

"Over 85% of Americans watched some portion of the hearings, which lasted for weeks," Reporter Mark Jones of WETA Public Television in Washington, D.C., wrote in a retrospective. "And, chances are, most of them watched on public television. In an age before CNN and the 24-hour television news cycle, your local PBS station ... WETA broadcast all 250 hours of testimony and fed it to public television stations around the country. Many stations ran the coverage live and then rebroadcast it again at night. (After the first week of testimony, the three commercial networks returned to their normal programming and rotated daily coverage of the hearings.)"

The PBS coverage, led by Jim Lehrer and Robert MacNeil, eventually led to the creation of *The MacNeil/Lehrer NewsHour*, which still broadcasts today as *PBS NewsHour*.

"Watergate's most significant impact on journalism has probably been less on the White House beat than on investigative reporting as a whole," Veteran investigative reporter and broadcast journalism professor Mark Feldstein wrote in *American Journalism Review* in 2004. "The nonprofit organization Investigative Reporters and Editors (IRE), founded the year after Nixon's resignation, has grown from a handful of journalists to 5,000 members who regularly receive training in investigative techniques, from filing Freedom of Information Act requests and using computer databases to working undercover and preventing libel suits. Magazines like *Mother Jones* and television programs like *"60 Minutes"* – as well as other nonprofit groups and foundations that support investigative reporting – have put down roots in the past 30 years."

While IRE formed in 1975, it made a real mark a year later after the tragic death of Don Bolles, an *Arizona Republic* reporter, who was blown up in his car as he investigated local organized crime allegations. Bolles, 47, received a tip from a would-be source who asked to meet him on

June 2, 1976, at a hotel lobby in Phoenix. He arrived, entered the building and waited, but left when no one appeared.

When he started his car, a bomb apparently placed there while Bolles was inside exploded. He died more than a week later, just a few days before he was set to speak at the first IRE conference.

But that did not end his investigation. Members of IRE and other reporters from around the country soon arrived in Arizona to finish Bolles' work in what became known as the Arizona Project.

"In the months that followed that call in the summer of 1976, nearly 40 reporters and editors from 23 newspapers as varied as *Newsday* and *The Milwaukee Journal* interviewed politicians, mobsters, prostitutes and businessmen, crossed and re-crossed the Mexican border and filled six large file drawers and 40,000 cross-index files with notes," The Republic revealed years later. "It was the biggest investigation in Arizona history."

It resulted in 40 stories over 23 days that "aimed the spotlight on organized crime in Arizona and blamed the mafia's infiltration on greedy public officials and a justice system that they called a 'social club' of judges, prosecutors and bar associations."

The series was re-printed by several newspapers, including *The Indianapolis Star, Tulsa Tribune, The Miami Herald, The Boston Globe* and *Newsday* and it won a special award from the Sigma Delta Chi Foundation.

Since then, IRE remains a repository of information, guidance, tools, and support for investigative reporters, including many that more recently uncovered Donald Trump's activities, predators of sexual assault and sexual harassment, and ongoing government abuse.

During my time at *Editor & Publisher*, one of my favorite assignments was covering the annual Pulitzer announcements each year in early April.

When the biggest awards in journalism were announced inside the third-floor World Room at the Columbia University Graduate School of

Journalism each spring, I was like a kid in a candy store awaiting the unveiling of the year's best journalism.

At *Editor & Publisher*, we also had a string of finding out the finalists' names in advance for several years – a scoop that upset the decision-makers at Columbia – but one that still gets some people reaching out to me for the information.

Since we were lucky enough to get leaked finalist names for several years, it became something of a guessing game to see how many were correct. Most of the time we were on top of it, until the Pulitzer folks got wise and put the clamps on the leaks.

Known by many as "The Cabal," the leaks were the work of a group of Pulitzer jurors, members of these committees that filter through the thousands of Pulitzer entries and provide three finalists for the 17-member Pulitzer Board to consider.

For years the group, led in part by former *Washington Post* ombudsman and D.C. news veteran Deborah Howell – among others – would hit the phones after the finalists were chosen and a printed list would eventually evolve. It circulated and found its way to me back in 2004.

After determining it was valid, Editor Greg Mitchell and I posted it online at *Editor & Publisher* and found it was correct once the announcements occurred. "The Cabal" and its leaks continued for several years, but later died out due to tighter controls and new jurors.

Still, it has become clear that the Pulitzer Board itself is known to advise friends and colleagues if a win is coming. Past editors and winners have told me how they were informed hours – even days – before the big announcement, in some cases even receiving champagne from the top brass at their papers ahead of time.

In 2017, *The New York Times* accidently let the word out online when it prematurely advised readers that its winners would be discussing their prizes later in the day.

It was interesting that in 2018, nine of the 17 Pulitzer Board members worked for news organizations that likely had entries in the competition. The past practice has required that they leave the room when categories in which they were finalists are discussed and voted upon.

That has even extended to journalism and media companies that own many outlets. With so much consolidation, such conflicts have grown.

For instance, *Houston Chronicle* Editor Nancy Barnes, a long-time respected editor, is on the Pulitzer board. But since her paper is owned by Hearst, which owns 24 daily papers and 25 U.S. magazines, she cannot be involved in the board deliberations if any of them are finalists.

The same went for board member Aminda Marques Gonzalez, executive editor of The *Miami Herald*, whose owner is McClatchy, owner of more than two dozen daily papers. Those include the *News & Observer of Raleigh*, *The Kansas City Star*, *The Charlotte Observer* and *The Sacramento Bee*.

The board reads and decides what to award – or not award. One of the beauties of the prizes is that the board has final say and can award prizes to winners who were not finalists, move entries around among the 14 journalism categories, give no, or sometimes two, awards in a category.

Then there are always the "little engines that could." In 2017, the tiny *Storm Lake Times* in Iowa won for editorial writing with in-depth opinion on local agricultural issues.

The idea that the Pulitzer could be won by any newspaper, of any size or readership, remains one of its most attractive elements. To this day, *The New York Times* – which garnered three more prizes in 2018 – can be challenged by the likes of a *Point Reyes Light* or *Grand Forks Herald* in the competition that gives no weight or sympathy to staff size or revenue.

You win if you speak truth to power, dig up the real story, or challenge the status quo.

In my time at *Editor & Publisher*, I was lucky to write about many notable Pulitzer winners – ranging from *The Village Voice*'s Mark Schoofs, who won the *Voice*'s first Pulitzer in 2000 for a lengthy series on AIDS in Africa (for which he caught malaria during his time overseas) to *The Eagle-Tribune* of Lawrence, MA., honored in 2003, when it went all out on the story of four local boys who drowned in a river boating tragedy.

One of the biggest, however, was *The Boston Globe*'s Spotlight team revelations about the Catholic Church. Although far from a small newspaper, The *Globe* had additional challenges as it took on one of the city's sacred institutions. That coverage won the 2003 Public Service Pulitzer, considered to be the most prestigious of the awards, and the only one without a cash prize.

Granted, some of the larger news outlets such as *The New York Times*, *Washington Post*, Associated Press or *Los Angeles Times* will sometimes take on an issue knowing it may have some Pulitzer 'juice.' In those cases, the big media companies can invest more time and money into a project.

The prizes usually go to one of two types of projects or stories. First, breaking news and the ability of a news outlet to "flood the zone," as former *New York Times* Executive Editor Howell Raines used to say. These winners usually blanket a flood, fire or other tragedy with coverage from all sides, and often for several days.

Second is the big investigative project, which usually includes a series of stories with data, interviews, and deep research on any subject. With today's expansion into web images, video, graphics and audio, these entries have an almost endless supply of side material to back up their reporting.

The most deserving winners are often the small papers that take on a big local story and knock it out of the park, and often with limited resources and myriad challenges.

One of those that got my attention in recent years was *The Sun-Herald* of Biloxi, Miss., and its then-editor Stan Tiner, one of the smartest, fairest and nicest editors I had the good fortune to know and interview during my time covering media.

When Hurricane Katrina struck on Aug. 29, 2005, most of the nation's attention went to New Orleans where the city suffered horrendous damage from the wind and rain, and subsequent levee breaks that flooded major portions of the metropolis.

The *Times-Picayune* of New Orleans won part of a well-deserved Pulitzer Prize for Public Service the following spring for its coverage that included regular online updates as the printing presses were unable to operate at one point, along with dogged reporting by journalists who, in many cases, were themselves forced to evacuate.

Just as impressive, and perhaps more so given their smaller staff and resources, was Tiner's crew in Biloxi, which shared the Public Service prize that year and had the distinction of producing a printed paper every day during the crisis – a feat even the *Times-Picayune* could not match.

"As reporters, photographers and editors assessed the damage, we quickly recognized that the scale of this event was epic and that it would be necessary to reorganize our approach to newsgathering in response to the new reality," Tiner later wrote in a piece for Nieman Reports. "So we exploded our newsgathering departmental and beat structures. All of the silos were leveled, and the *Sun-Herald* newsroom became a blended team with an intense Katrina focus. There were no more business reporters, sports reporters, or features writers. Everyone was a news reporter – and newspaper delivery person, I might add, as every employee's honorable duty was to distribute papers to people wherever they were encountered on our daily rounds."

I first met Tiner in 1999 when I joined *Editor & Publisher* and he was running the *News-Register* in Mobile, AL. I made the rounds at editors' conferences and did a handful of reaction stories on issues that included seeking comment from newsroom leaders about various news ethics challenges. Tiner was often first on my list of those to seek out.

With a deep southern drawl that smacked of a character from Hee-Haw or The Grand 'Ole Opry, this former Marine and strong fan of his Southern roots initially sounded more like a cotton farmer or moonshiner than a journalist.

But after speaking to him for only a few minutes, it was clear he was a real newsman with compassion, drive and smarts that rival any big city editor. He also belied the sometimes-automatic stereotype of those below the Mason-Dixon line as less than progressive on race and other issues. Far from racially insensitive, Tiner not only offered a sense of fairness to all readers, and news subjects, but in a place where such equality does not always go over so well.

After bringing journalistic and financial improvements to the *News-Register*, Tiner moved across the south to Oklahoma City in April 1999 to take charge of *the Daily Oklahoman*, a much larger daily paper in a capital city.

The paper at the time was a mess, having been dubbed "The Worst Paper in America," by the *Columbia Journalism Review* a year earlier, in part because of its "reportorial attacks on Democrats, rosy view of industry and editorial savaging of homosexuals," according to *The New York Times*.

Enter Tiner, who oversaw a redesign, went into controversial topics such as atheism in the bible belt, and increased the efforts on feature work.

Within nine months, Tiner was out. He was let go by the billionaire owners, The Gaylord Family, who did not appreciate Tiner's December 1999 multi-part series on the 25th Anniversary of the death of Karen Silkwood.

Silkwood was the employee of a nearby power plant owned by Kerr-McGee, a powerful Oklahoma company. She had been gathering evidence of safety and security violations at the plant when she was killed in a 1974 car accident while on her way to meet with a reporter.

Her story was the subject of a 1983 film starring Meryl Streep and Kurt Russell that drew wide attention to the safety plight of plant employees and brought scorn on Kerr-McGee at the time.

The first part of *the Oklahoman* series ran on Dec. 16, 1999, and focused on the federal trial against Kerr-McGee, in which the company was found liable for $1.38 million for plutonium contamination of Silkwood.

But the second and third parts never ran, having been spiked by *Oklahoman* ownership against the wishes of Tiner, who fought hard for them to be run. He could have laid down and given way to the owners, but he knew it was the wrong thing to do and would give the paper a black eye.

So, because he disagreed with such an unethical decision, they fired him, and the paper eventually ran an editorial praising Kerr-McGee as "one of the best corporate citizens in Oklahoma."

In all my time as a media reporter, and a journalist overall, that could rank as the most disgusting action by a major mainstream news outlet.

But Tiner, who retired in 2015, went on to have the last laugh, giving Biloxi its first Pulitzer Prize and continuing a news career worthy of notice.

The same goes for Murrow, Downie, Priest, Safer and hundreds of thousands of other journalists dating back to Richard Pierce and *Publick Occurrences*. Today's reporters and editors – and their audiences – need to remember what reporters did in the past and what the job still is today, and how to keep it going in the face of so many obstacles.

FAIR AND BALANCED?
NOT QUITE

The first time Sean Hannity ran away from me was at the *Talkers* radio conference in 2012. The event is run by *Talkers* magazine – considered the bible of the talk radio business – and it is a great cross-section of the business of talk radio, with no partisan view or agenda.

Michael Harrison, the magazine's leader and a true radio pro, makes sure that the conference – and his magazine/website – keep clear of political views.

That fair and direct approach is what keeps the audience, and the talk radio big names, coming back again and again.

When Harrison invited Hannity to speak years earlier, the conservative mouthpiece's initial speech was mostly business-related. Hannity actually made a good point at that appearance about how radio stations were not getting their deserved audience credit for online listeners.

He urged station managers and radio executives to demand more detailed accountability for their online data and to get as much information as possible to show valuable advertisers the high number of listeners and why ad fees should be as high as possible. And he was right.

But at the 2012 event, Hannity took square aim at my former employer, *Media Matters for America*, which at the time had launched one of its occasional advertiser boycotts against Rush Limbaugh.

Limbaugh was under fire for his offensive comments against Georgetown Law School student Sandra Fluke, after Fluke testified before a congressional committee holding hearings on health care funding, including for contraception.

He called Fluke a "slut" and a "prostitute," claiming she wanted to be "paid for having sex" with free contraception. "She's having so much sex she can't afford the contraception," Limbaugh said. "She wants you and me and the taxpayers to pay her to have sex. What does that make us? We're the pimps. The johns, that's right. We would be the johns – no! We're not the johns. Well – yeah, that's right. Pimp's not the right word."

During my eight years at *Media Matters*, I was never formally part of the boycott efforts, which made me glad as I am first and foremost a reporter.

A year later, *Media Matters* reported, "…Cumulus Media, a radio company that carries Limbaugh's show in 38 markets, reported millions of dollars in lost revenue and attributed the losses in part to the Limbaugh advertiser fallout. Dial Global, a radio syndication company, reported roughly $100 million in losses for 2012 and publicly cited Limbaugh as a significant contributing factor."

During his 2012 speech, Hannity said, "We get to a situation where we don't like what so-and-so says on the radio, and we call for boycotts, and we have these special interest groups monitoring and taping every minute of every show, and they're trying to silence one group of people – well then, at some point it's going to be the other group of people … Most recently Rush Limbaugh, here it is, this icon that saved AM radio, that has been saying controversial things since the first time he did a caller abortion on the air – now under fire."

Afterwards, as he talked to some conference attendees, I walked up and introduced myself, then asked a question about why he was attacking the boycott organizers.

Quicker than you can say, "cowardly exit," Hannity sprinted away with one of his people blocking me from following him. As I got past him and caught up to Hannity, asking over and over if he meant *Media Matters* in his attack and why he objected to a boycott, he sped up and ignored me until he left the building, with his guard/henchman/flunky, blocking the door again.

A similar scene occurred at a *Talkers* event years later when, during the opening breakfast that Hannity often sponsored, I walked up to him and again asked if I could ask a question; he ducked away into another room, door locked, as before.

Hannity's unwillingness to be questioned about his actions, and his more recent conflict-of-interest ties to Donald Trump's troubled personal lawyer, Michael Cohen, are not a surprise given his background of bias, lies and misleading broadcasts.

"The problem for Fox News is that while Hannity has risen to become the top ratings-earner of the nightly lineup, he is also a figure prone to barreling headfirst into the murky territory between opinion and out-and-out conspiracy theorism," *The New York Times* wrote in a 2017 profile. "And Fox executives frequently have been forced to juggle advertiser discontent with the need to ensure that Hannity, does not leave for a rival network, like Sinclair Broadcast Group, a right-leaning owner of local TV stations."

While not every conservative broadcaster or news person operates in Hannity's cowardly way, he is an example of the negative influence of so-called "conservative journalism" that has taken over much of the media landscape that's done damage to news reporting and audience understanding of fact versus fiction.

The rise of so-called "conservative" news is the biggest media increase and influence in the last 20 years, dating back to Fox News' launch in 1996.

Although right-wing reporting has been ongoing since the *National Review* launched in 1955, more slanted reporting from Fox and others has misled readers and viewers into thinking the "mainstream" media is liberal and slanted more than it is.

This allows conservative journalists to twist their own coverage that is often inaccurate or simply wrong and blame the traditional media for it.

"Conservative media is big," declared *Talkers* chief Harrison. "The biggest distortion of conservative media is that it is somehow smaller than liberal media, but that is not true. Conservative media has successfully made it appear that its constituents are being lied to by some bigger media. A lot of it began with William F. Buckley and it has been growing for years. I laugh when they present themselves as the underdog and they are all as corporate as hell. There would be no need for *Media Matters* if conservative media were not powerful. There is not enough independence on either side."

Much of the recent anti-press mudslinging by right-wing media and leadership dates back to Richard Nixon, whose 1974 fall from grace followed his own paranoid approach to many issues – including the press. He had a famed "enemies list," which included nearly 60 media names, such as *Los Angeles Times* managing editor Ed Guthman, CBS newsman Daniel Schorr, Washington columnists Mary McGrory and Jack Anderson, and *New York Times* reporter Tom Wicker.

"It was a theme that Nixon would repeat often. The president was convinced that 'the press and TV don't change their attitude and approach unless you hurt them,'" Veteran journalist Robert Parry wrote in a 1995 piece for Fair and Accuracy in Reporting (FAIR), a prominent media watchdog organization. Parry, a former *Newsweek* and Associated Press scribe was citing a portion of former Nixon Chief of Staff H.R. Haldeman's diary, which added that "Nixon was never one to miss a chance to 'screw' his 'enemies' in the media," which included a "brutal vicious attack on" them.

Of course, it was Nixon's vice-president, Spiro Agnew – later forced out due to tax evasion charges – who coined the term, "nattering nabobs of negativism." (Actually, Nixon speechwriter William Safire wrote the line for Agnew).

Safire's link to this piece of history is somewhat ironic given that he later became a respected *New York Times* columnist. But back then, he was among the right-wing voices seeking to diminish the power of the press, and even scare them into backing off. First with the *Times* and *Washington Post* 1971 coverage of the Pentagon Papers, the secret history of the Vietnam War that the White House sought to stop in a dangerous threat to press freedom.

Then, a year later, with the *Post* coverage of the Watergate scandal; which was later revealed to include secret surveillance of reporters and threats of government reprisals against the newspaper.

In *All the Presidents Men*, their account of the *Post*'s Watergate coverage, Bob Woodward and Carl Bernstein cite several instances of government backlash against the paper at the time, including efforts to stop FCC approval of some *Post* television ownership.

"Soon, challenges against the *Post*'s ownership of two television stations in Florida were filed with the Federal Communications Commission," the book states. "The price of *Post* stock on the American Exchange dropped by almost 50 percent. Among the challengers – forming the organizations of 'citizens' who proposed to become the new FCC licensees – were several persons long associated with the President."

While Nixon and friends did not have the long list of right-wing media supporters that Trump and others enjoy today, there were enough backing of Nixon and attacking the press to gain support.

"Consider how conservative radio host Clarence Manion framed the role of the media in the early days of the Watergate hearings," Nicole Hemmer, author of *Messengers of the Right: Conservative Media and the Transformation of American Politics*, wrote in a 2017 piece for Vox.com. "In an interview with Dan Lyons, an anticommunist Catholic writer, Manion directly attacked the freedom of the press. That noble-sounding phrase, he argued, was something journalists hid behind to appear uniquely vulnerable to government overreach; in fact, the media held the cards.

"'The result,' he told his listeners, 'is that a gullible public is caught in the talons of a power that ironically disguises itself as freedom.' Lyons echoed the charge, arguing that Watergate had indeed exposed a dangerous concentration of power – but in the press, not the executive branch."

She said even radio icon Paul Harvey, a news legend and "Rest of the Story" creator, went after the press coverage of Nixon: "Paul Harvey, the radio personality, repeated the attack in his nationally syndicated broadcast. How, he wondered, could the American people accept an all-powerful media capable of turning 'a prosecution into a persecution'?"

Hemmer later noted that conservative book publisher Henry Regnery "greeted the accusations by observing: 'I can see no grounds for impeachment, or even to get worked up about.'" As for the *National Review*, its editors wrote in 1973, "the target is really not Nixon himself or this or that aide, but, rather, the 'new majority' threatening to break the liberal hold on political power."

When Nixon was forced out, due in large part to Republican leaders urging him to quit before impeachment, many on the right blamed the press. Some of those included staunch Nixon supporters in the media who reappeared later in powerful conservative roles that continue to influence public opinion.

Among them was Roger Ailes, the former *Mike Douglas Show* producer and future Fox News leader. He basically recreated Nixon from the former dark and moody vice-president who had lost a presidential bid in 1960 and a California governor's race two years later to a sharp TV personality in time for the 1968 presidential election.

Ailes used his TV experience and the country's anti-Vietnam mood coupled with civil rights movement and free love fatigue, to tap into a growing conservative mood at a time when the Democratic party was in chaos. With Lyndon Johnson not seeking reelection, Eugene McCarthy leading the youth revolt, and despair from the assassinations of both Martin Luther King Jr. and Robert F. Kennedy, the liberal party seemed unable to pull the country back to stability.

"Ailes would help to recreate Nixon and Nixon, in turn, recreated Ailes," Journalist Gabriel Sherman wrote in his 2014 Ailes biography, *The Loudest Voice in the Room*, later noting, "He imbibed Nixon's world view, learning how to connect with the many Americans who felt left behind by the upheavals of the 1960s, an insight Ailes would deploy for political advantage, and, later at Fox News, for record ratings and profits."

Ailes knew that Nixon's past difficulties had been with television. He knew the growing use of the media images and staged events would help Nixon not only overcome his inherent lack of on-air charm and charisma, but also take advantage of the growing use of the "idiot box." American TV use had jumped from at least one television in 45 million America homes in 1960, when Nixon lost the presidential election, to 56 million by 1968 when he won. That's a nearly 25 percent increase in just eight years.

The key was also in how Ailes helped Nixon use that huge, new audience. While Democrats had to deal with protests, street unrest, an unpopular war and a political convention marred by walkouts, fights, and arrests, Ailes fashioned Nixon's image on the air with staged "town halls" and presidential panel events that presented him as the competent, calming alternative to the Democratic Party's chaos.

In his groundbreaking book about the 1968 campaign, *The Selling of the President,* Joe McGinnis detailed how the panels and audiences for the town halls were chosen down to the smallest detail, and questions geared for each local community.

"There was to be a studio audience – three hundred people – recruited by the local Republican organization," McGinnis wrote in the 1969 memoir. "Just enough Negroes so the press could not write 'all-white' stories but not enough so it would look like a ballpark. The audience, of course, would applaud every answer Richard Nixon gave, boosting his confidence and giving the impression to a viewer that Nixon certainly did have charisma, and whatever other qualities he wanted his president to have."

Ailes even gave Nixon a sense of humor when the often dour-looking politician appeared on *Laugh-In* and uttered the show's famous phrase, "Sock it to me."

It was a strategy of a different kind that Ailes would push through Fox News and Donald Trump decades later that focused on anger and outrage at immigrants, the poor, unions, and big government, which resulted in Trump's offensive and bullying comments, and his promises to close the border, clamp down on foreign trade imbalances and get tough with enemy nations.

But in 1968, Ailes knew that a would-be leader offering a steady hand, promises of peace and civility, and a new outlook – not to mention his misleading secret plan to end the Vietnam War – would draw voters in.

"Nixon was fortification, reaffirmation of much that needed to be reaffirmed," McGinnis wrote about the appeal to voters. "They needed him now, these Republicans, much more than they had in 1960."

And it showed as Nixon won the nomination and beat Democrat Hubert Humphrey in the general election with 301 electoral votes to Humphrey's 191.

Still, even with this 1968 victory, Nixon remained an anti-press paranoid because he and his campaign went too far to secure his 1972 re-election.

Despite winning big in 1972, the president would be forced out just two years later, a move that sparked an anti-mainstream media resentment by his supporters in the conservative media that has only grown since.

Many right-wing voices and commentators were angered when Nixon left, and Gerald Ford lost re-election two years later to Jimmy Carter – an unknown Georgia Democratic governor – that the efforts to undermine credible news outlets and ramp up the conservative opposition to the left reached new heights.

There was a hint of the conservative powerhouse to come when Ronald Reagan, a lesser-known former California governor when he challenged Ford in 1976, made a first splash with a primary challenge that raised attention and took him all the way to the GOP convention that year. Many believe that internal battle hurt Ford's chances and aided in his eventual loss to Carter.

But when Carter proved too weak, or perhaps too honest, to prevail as president, the conservative media saw their chance and rallied behind Reagan again as he rode to victory in 1980 and launched a 12-year GOP hold on the White House. That included Reagan's landslide re-election in 1984 over Walter Mondale, and his vice-president, George H.W. Bush, securing victory over Michael Dukakis in 1988.

Part of Reagan's success in the 1980s included the rise of the conservative religious right, which latched on to him early on through groups like Jerry Falwell's Moral Majority and Pat Robertson's Christian Coalition, later boosted by Ralph Reed. Much of their focus was on so-called "family values" and a strong anti-abortion message.

Robertson, through his *700 Club* television show and Falwell via both radio and TV outlets, drove their political message home in a way that had not been done before in the Republican Party. While Carter received support in his first campaign as a "born-again" Christian, the political and media power of the evangelicals proved stronger.

"The Christian Right's leaders received disproportionate media attention, not least because they served up a steady dish of spectacles," according to author Steven P. Miller's *The Age of Evangelicalism: The Born-Again Years*. "In the minds of many, they were the public expression of born-again Christianity. Politics, of course, hardly captured the full power of evangelicalism within American culture. But it influenced all impressions of that power."

Miller later added, "Falwell was a persistent and savvy media presence. He demonstrated how the Christian Right could shape public discussions even without achieving clear policy victories. With the help of speechwriter Cal Thomas, Falwell evinced a knack for quips that were simultaneously provocative and disarming."

The same year Reagan was elected, 1980, also saw the launch of CNN. MTV hit the cable airwaves in 1981, and *USA Today* launched a year after that. Those three outlets would completely transform much of the country's news and media diet.

In all three cases, a new national media option arose and began to present information and content like never before. CNN started out with basic news from morning to night with traditional anchors and reporters, but with the ability to update at any moment.

Even at the start, however, CNN Founder Ted Turner knew that its limited resources would require some commentary and talk, mostly at night to start, to both save money and draw in viewers. He credits co-founder Reese Schonfeld with seeking the opinion-makers.

"He realized that we couldn't do it all with breaking news and felt we should hire a group of well-known people specifically to provide editorial commentary," Turner wrote in his 2008 biography, *Call Me Ted*. "I thought that was a good idea as long as we did our best to get people from across the political spectrum and we always identify their views as their own, not CNN's."

Thus, cable TV opinion talk was born. And it had an immediate competitive effect. "As cable news rose in popularity, network television pushed the boundaries of acceptability in order to remain competitive," according to Oscar W. Anderson, author of *Media in the 20th Century*.

USA Today, meanwhile, aimed to be a quick-read paper with short stories, graphics and data to the growing business traveler market. The paper was even sold in machines designed to resemble television sets. The mix of images on Page One looked a lot like today's news website home pages.

But the biggest blow for conservative media at that time was talk radio, which exploded in the 1980s with a strong right-wing voice and an audience that has since grown only larger, and angrier.

"Angry people are easier to get as an audience and as a voter," Michael Harrison of *Talkers* explained. "It happens to do with the nature of what liberal meant and conservative meant."

Harrison's point is well-taken. Among the reasons conservatives have taken over most of political talk radio is the angry, outlandish voice of most on the right and the lack of many liberals' interest in radio over other forms, such as the web, books, printed publications and film.

While liberals do have a place for their views on the likes of NPR and some liberal hosted shows, it's still the Hannitys, Limbaughs, Mark Levins and Hugh Hewitts that garner the biggest audiences.

Look at the demise of Air America, the liberal-themed talk radio network that launched in 2004 with names that included Al Franken and Janeane Garofalo, as well as a young, lesser-known Rachel Maddow. It hoped to tap into people not in line with Rush Limbaugh or Michael Savage, but after just six years the air went out of Air America.

"Conservative or regressive radio has an easier time of it, because what it does is tap into your lesser nature," Garofalo told *Vanity Fair* in 2009 when asked why it failed. "It's really easy to do that. That's why it has the success it has: because it allows assholes to think they're doing good things, to think they're patriots. …Working for radio that speaks truth to power, that asks people to be better, to be good citizens, to participate in democracy, is not as easy as what regressive radio does, which is ask people to do nothing."

The rise of talk radio in the 1980s, most of it conservative, can be linked to three main things, according to author David Foster Wallace, who detailed the issue in a lengthy 2005 piece in *The Atlantic*.

He cited the need for AM radio to change as FM and its stereo and better signals lured music listeners away; the Reagan Administration's repeal of the Fairness Doctrine, which had required equal time for differing views; and the syndication and national spread of Limbaugh's show.

"Limbaugh is the third great progenitor of today's political talk radio partly because he's a host of extraordinary, once-in-a-generation talent and charisma – bright, loquacious, witty, complexly authoritative – whose show's blend of news, entertainment, and partisan analysis became the model for legions of imitators," Wallace wrote. "But he was also the first great promulgator of the Mainstream Media's Liberal Bias idea. This turned out to be a brilliantly effective rhetorical move, since the MMLB concept functioned simultaneously as a standard around which Rush's audience could rally, as an articulation of the need for right-wing (i.e., unbiased) media, and as a mechanism by which any criticism or refutation of conservative ideas could be dismissed (either as biased or as the product of indoctrination by biased media). Boiled way down, the MMLB thesis is able both to exploit and to perpetuate many conservatives' dissatisfaction with extant media sources – and it's this dissatisfaction that cements political talk radio's large and loyal audience."

That was the first real use of fears and claims about "fake news," which Trump and his supporters have advanced to an even greater level.

With Reagan in office, followed by George H.W. Bush, conservative media gained attention and an audience as the country's power structure backed them up. When Reagan took on the "evil empire" of the U.S.S.R., the right-wing had its celebrations and took credit for sparking the Soviet Union's demise.

The 80s also brought success and profit for many conservatives in big business as Wall Street was riding high, Reagan deregulation eased burdens on corporations and social issues such as abortion, gay rights and government assistance saw declines.

"The economy was skyrocketing," Alexander noted in *Media in the 20th Century*. "The baby boomers had come of age and their children had an even more voracious appetite for the consumption of products advertised in the media."

The U.S. also got its first taste of Rupert Murdoch's broadcast approach in the 1980s when the Fox Network launched in 1986 and soon linked to more than 200 affiliates. While the Fox News Channel would not be created for another 10 years, this intrusion into the three-network market was major. Fox had its first hit with the raunchy *Married with Children*, as well as the first real tabloid news and entertainment show of its time, *A Current Affair*.

"The format exploded because of a combination of Limbaugh's success upon entering national syndication in 1988, and technological and regulatory developments, including cheaper satellite technology and the development of mobile phones," a 2014 *Politico* retrospective on talk radio stated. "Limbaugh, with his rants about 'feminazis' and environmentalist wackos, parodies and updates complete with theme music, tapped into the widespread feeling among conservatives that the 'mainstream media' neglected their need – and looked down upon them … By 1993, his audience had reached 17 million – begot the development of entirely conservative and political talk stations, and as those stations succeeded, an increasing number of stations adopted the format."

Harrison of *Talkers* points out that many liberals give conservative talk its audience because they want to know what their opponents are saying, unlike most conservative listeners who have less interest in their liberal counterparts.

But nearing the end of the 1980s, Reagan's political power started to diminish. First, in 1987, when he nominated Robert Bork to the U.S. Supreme Court. Opposition to Bork's civil rights record and involvement in the Nixon Administration led to a Senate defeat. His next nominee, Douglas Ginsburg, was forced to drop out after it was found he had used marijuana in the past.

He eventually was successful on the third try with Justice Anthony Kennedy. But the defeats were part of several late-second term problems that caused Reagan trouble.

The biggest scandal was the Iran-Contra affair, in which the Reagan Administration illegally traded arms to Iran for hostages and funds that were than funneled to rebels in Nicaragua.

The rebel Contras were an issue close to Reagan as they were fighting the communist Sandinistas that controlled Nicaragua. But the secret deal violated the Boland Amendment, passed in the early 1980s to limit such international dealings.

Several federal investigations found wrongdoing by Lt. Col. Oliver North, a National Security council member, and others, but never directly linked Reagan to the activities. Still, they raised questions about the actions for Reagan's administration and cast a cloud that lasted for much of his second term.

When George H.W. Bush ran for president in 1988, Iran-Contra was brought up again and again by the mainstream press as they sought to know what involvement Bush might have had.

In one famous incident, Bush went on the attack against Dan Rather of CBS News in January 1988 during a live interview in which Rather asked about the scandal. Bush criticized the move as a "rehash" on the Iran-Contra issue and then complained that Rather was focusing on it too much.

The then-candidate Bush complained that the introductory video report prior to the interview had been unfair and that he had been misled into believing it would be a profile, not with so much discussion on the Iran-Contra scandal.

During that report, Rather revealed also that Bush had adopted the practice of requiring reporters to submit questions in writing about Iran-Contra rather than face journalists one on one. He also noted that recent polling had found many Americans still believed he was hiding something, and that Bush had declined to comment on the issue for the report agreeing only to the live interview.

As the interview continued and Rather pressed him, Bush turned the tables on Rather and raised an earlier incident from September 1987 in which Rather walked off the set of the news program after a tennis match was broadcast too long and delayed Rather's show. That left the show with six minutes of dead air.

"I don't think it's fair to judge a whole career, it's not fair to judge my whole career by a rehash on Iran," Bush said in the interview. "How would you like it if I judged your career by those seven minutes when you walked off the set in New York? Would you like that?"

Rather than simply answer a question that had been a major issue in the campaign, Bush sought to go after the interviewer.

Newsweek, in its book about the campaign, *The Quest for the Presidency, 1988*, revealed that it was Roger Ailes who prepped Bush to use the Rather walk-off incident if needed to deflect from Iran-Contra issues. He had also negotiated it to be a live interview so that Bush could change course and the CBS producers could not edit it out. Bush was also on a live feed from his office rather than in the studio.

"The word was around that the subject would be Iran-Contra and that CBS was going to open up half the show for it, Rather's piece first, then the interview," the *Newsweek* book stated, later adding, "As it happened, Ailes had thought about what to fight with: a notorious incident several months earlier when Rather, on location in Miami, had got sore at having his newscast held up by a tennis match and had walked off his set to call New York to bitch about it … It was the ultimate embarrassment for a network, as Ailes reminded Bush; Rather would deny afterward that that had been his intent, but he caught heat for it … 'Look,' Ailes said, 'he's trying to judge your whole vice-presidency by this stuff. That's like judging his whole career in broadcasting by six minutes when he acted like an asshole.'"

In another account, *Attack the Messenger, How Politicians Turn You Against the Media*, journalist Craig Crawford wrote that Ailes stood behind the camera pointed at Bush with a cue card that reminded him to raise the walk-off incident at the right time.

"Ailes stood next to the camera operator, some thirty feet away from Bush," Crawford wrote. "At the moment he wanted Bush to go on the attack, he held up a poster with a handwritten message. 'NOW ASK,' the homemade cue card began. It went on to prompt Bush to refer to an incident when Rather walked off his own set."

The move worked not only in putting the focus on Rather and away from Bush's possible link to a major scandal, but it also opened the gate for future attacks on Rather and other mainstream journalists by candidates or right-wing media who did not like the tough questions or inquiring methods that are the basics of journalism.

"In the years since the Bush-Rather meltdown, the vilification of the news media by politicians has diminished the power of an independent press," Crawford added.

A 2003 *National Review* piece described it as "Rather roughing up Bush 41 in 1988, angrily sniping about Iran-Contra," while in 2016 the Media Research Center, the ultimate right-wing hacks masquerading as media watchdogs, described it as, "Dan Rather's attempt to verbally sucker punch George H.W. Bush."

The irony of many so-called "conservative journalists" is that they are admitting their bias in their self-description. To attach a political viewpoint to your job reveals that you are going to be slanted in your approach. Many right-wing media folks will say they are simply being more honest than the liberal press who do not reveal their bias.

Still, Bush's ability to go after Rather, and get people on the right to follow his lead, started a practice that has grown as the influence of right-wing media has grown. When an unknown Arkansas governor named Bill Clinton decide to run against Bush four years later, the conservative media found a target that they would continue to go after for decades – along with his wife.

I first heard of Bill Clinton, like a lot of people, during his much too long keynote address at the 1988 Democratic Convention, where he formally nominated Michael Dukakis and received cheers at the end of the 33-minute address when he said, "in closing ..."

Even then he was seen as a potential nominee himself with signs in the Arkansas delegation proclaiming, "Clinton in '96." That was, of course, with the hope Dukakis would win and win again in 1992.

Of course, it did not turn out that way. But for Clinton, 1992 became his year with a surprise when he toppled Bush and brought Democrats a victory they had not seen since 1976.

But his candidacy and victory gave the growing tribe of conservative media new meat to bite into and raised the attacks to a new level. Clinton didn't do much to help himself with exposed affairs, questions about avoiding the draft and admittance to smoking marijuana (which interestingly would probably not have people bat an eye today.)

But even those issues did not do enough to derail Clinton as he beat Bush, with a little help from independent Ross Perot, despite his personal issues and far right attacks.

"I shared what I considered to be the popular consensus that his private behavior was relevant only if it intruded on his public performance," veteran political columnist Jack Germond wrote about Clinton in his 1999 book, *Fat Man in the Middle Seat*, later noting "wrong again."

Germond was referring to the Monica Lewnisky scandal that broke six years later and resulted in his impeachment. But while Clinton's personal life might have been fair game in 1992, it appeared not to matter enough to voters to end in defeat.

But to the right-wing commentators, seeing Bush lose to this young, less-experienced and flawed small state governor was too much to handle. After 12 years of Republican rule, they were out of the White House. And to someone nicknamed "Slick Willie."

From Clinton's first day in office, Limbaugh, *National Review* and the even further right *American Spectator*, among others, went after Clinton with a mix of opposition to his policies – such as welfare reform, free trade and health care – as well as a clear anger that their executive dominance had ended. They found that attacking through several forms of media they could blanket coverage in a way that had not been done before.

"...the conservatives have constructed a truly intimidating media machine," FAIR's Parry wrote in 1995. "It ranges from nationwide radio talk shows by Rush Limbaugh and scores of Limbaugh-wannabes, to dozens of attack magazines, newspapers, newsletters and right-wing opinion columns, to national cable television networks propagating hardline conservative values and viewpoints, to documentary producers who specialize in slick character assassination, to mega-buck publishing houses that add footnotes to white-supremacist theories and a veneer of respectability to journalistic fabrications, and even to narrowly focused organizations that exist simply to hurt the surviving mainstream journalists who still won't toe the line."

The new president's wife angered them further. Hillary Rodham Clinton said from the start that she was going to be more involved than most of her predecessors, adding that as the governor's wife, she gladly kept working as an attorney and did not "stay home and bake cookies and have teas."

When Clinton put his wife in charge of the health care reform planning, the conservative media army went on full attack.

"With remarkable alacrity, 'Hillary-hating,' as historian Henry Louis Gates wrote in *The New Yorker*, became 'one of those national pastimes which unite both the elite and the lumpen,'" *Rolling Stone*'s Janet Reitman wrote in a 2016 retrospective piece. Reitman also noted, "...talk-show hosts like Rush Limbaugh coalesced into what Hillary would later call a 'vast right-wing conspiracy.' *The New York Times'* William Safire wrote that she was both a 'congenital liar' and a 'vindictive political power player.' Elsewhere she was derided as a selfish, untrustworthy, incompetent, ball-breaking 'bitch,' a 'closet lesbian' and a terrible mother."

In their 2001 book, *The Hunting of the President: The Ten-Year Campaign to Destroy Bill and Hillary Clinton,* authors Joe Conason and Gene Lyons describe "important journalists and news organizations succumbing to scandal fever, credulously and sometimes dishonestly promoting charges against the Clintons in heavily-biased, error-filled dispatches, columns, best-selling books and TV news specials and thus bestowing 'mainstream' prestige upon what was often little more than a poisonous mixture of half-truth and partisan malice."

Among the major early right-wing media attackers was *American Spectator,* the conservative publication that dates back nearly 100 years and was actually launched over beers at McSorley's Ale House – a Manhattan landmark known in part for not allowing women in until 1970.

In 1992, the magazine was breathing fire against the Clintons and would continue for several years. A key member of their staff was my former boss, David Brock.

Before he launched *Media Matters* in 2004, Brock had spent his early career as a conservative writer and journalist, working much of his trade at the *Spectator.* He underwent a self-described metamorphosis in the 1990s and detailed it in his informative autobiography, *Blinded by the Right.*

Before going after Clinton, Brock took on Anita Hill, the law school professor who had accused Supreme Court Justice Clarence Thomas of sexual harassment during his 1991 Senate confirmation hearings.

While Thomas was later confirmed, by a slim vote, Hill's claims had a major impact on the hearings and raised the issue of sexual harassment as never before.

Brock went after Hill first in a 1992 *American Spectator* article titled "The Real Anita Hill," and then a year later in a book of the same name.

A 1993 *New York Times* review of the book by Anna Quindlen said, in part, "Ultimately the book relies on the idea that Professor Hill was politically motivated to oppose the conservative who had been her mentor. Yet surely Mr. Brock would be affronted at the suggestion that his job at The *American Spectator*, a conservative journal – miming Mr. Brock's style, I could call it an ultraconservative journal – would provide him with the motive to slant his book. Mr. Brock received a grant from the John M. Olin Foundation, a champion of conservative causes. The book is not only steeped in ideology; it was financed by it."

The book brought Brock great fame and attention, enough that the *Spectator* assigned him to two anti-Clinton projects. First, an investigation into Clinton's use of Arkansas State Troopers to allegedly line up women for him when he was governor and other nefarious activities.

Then there was a larger effort dubbed The Arkansas Project, in which The *Spectator* received more than $2 million from a conservative foundation for a series of stories claiming everything from Clinton's alleged part in allowing the CIA to run drugs and guns through an Arkansas airport, to his unproven part in the death of former White House lawyer Vince Foster.

"The anti-Clinton scandal machine became quite a profitable business for right-wing publishers, pundits and radio talk show hosts," Brock later wrote in his book. "And we at the *Spectator* were pioneers."

Then the real anti-Clinton, and anti-respectable media organization came in: Fox News. The Rupert Murdoch creation, with the help of Roger Ailes, launched on Oct. 7, 1996, about a month before the

Election Day that gave Clinton a resounding re-election. But it also began what would become a rocky second term – due in part to his own mistakes and Fox's willingness to exploit them.

Fox, showing no shame in slanting coverage toward the right, piling up conservative voices to add commentary, and making sure little or no liberal views came in, set in motion the largest, and eventually most profitable, conservative news outlet yet.

"Things shifted with the advent of Fox News, they had their own media that claimed to be fair and balanced, but of course was not, and the rise of talk radio," David Corn the former Washington bureau chief for *The Nation*, and later *Mother Jones*, told me in an interview. "They became a double-point of the spear. With the advent of the information age it allowed other conservatives to join on with websites and hybrid organizations – think of Glenn Beck."

Murdoch got the jump on viewership early by paying cable outlets and others to carry Fox at first, reversing the long-held trend of requiring payment for such channels. This gave Fox an immediate 17 million households, according to Britannica.com.

"In the battle for viewers in the cable news market, Fox News made steady gains against CNN, which had the advantage of being viewable in several million more homes, and against MSNBC, which had been launched several months before Fox News," Britannica reported. "In the wake of the September 11 attacks, cable television viewership surged, and Fox News built on its gains to surpass CNN for the first time in January 2002 – a lead it would retain throughout the decade."

In their 2012 book, *The Fox Effect*, *Media Matters'* Brock and Ari Rabin-Havt detailed the rise of the right-leaning network and many of their unethical practices. (Full disclosure: I worked at *Media Matters* when research was being done for the book and contributed some reporting.)

Among their findings was that potential liberal staffers were weeded out of the Fox hiring process early, according to former Fox News President Joe Peyronnin, who told the authors that Ailes asked some staff "if they were liberal or not," later adding, "there was a litmus test. He was going to figure out who was liberal or conservative when he came in and try to get rid of the liberals."

Fox capitalized early on from the long-running false belief that most mainstream reporters and news outlets were biased towards the left, which was made even more ridiculous when they attempted to portray themselves as even-handed. "Fair and Balanced," and "We Report, You Decide," became the laughable slogans.

In truth, the network went after Clinton and other Democrats from the first day with less coverage and digging into Republican candidate Robert Dole and other GOP politicians.

As Clinton's presidency continued, he did give his growing conservative media enemies more and more ammunition with the Monica Lewinsky scandal in which he was forced to admit an affair with a White House intern, give a sworn deposition to congressional investigators, and become only the second president ever impeached. Although he beat the rap in the Senate trial, the entire affair put a major black eye on his administration, and on U.S. history.

Along the way, the right-wing commentators and columnists used this bad behavior to gang up even more on his actions, with a well-played plan for continuing after he left office.

When I first met George W. Bush, that was not his name. Campaigning for his father, George H.W. Bush, the younger namesake went by the moniker George Bush, Jr. during a visit to the Clark, N.J. Republican headquarters in late 1988. I ended up being the only reporter to accept the invitation to interview this unknown son of the vice-president. During the 20-minute Q&A, which occurred the day after the first Bush-Dukakis debate, Junior declared his dad the winner, claimed no third-party candidates were needed and denounced Dukakis as less-qualified.

Fast forward 12 years and it was W. himself on the ballot in 2000 against Al Gore in one of the most contested elections ever. The initial vote, of course, ended too close to call with a recount ordered for several counties in Florida. Before that decision was made, however, the national press had one of its worst Election Nights with numerous blown calls and television anchors first wrongly declaring Gore the winner, then later giving it to Bush.

The networks and news channels are often so eager to declare a winner, they can get it wrong. Here they did severely.

The New York Times the next day called it, "an embarrassment of major proportions," while former *Meet the Press* host Marvin Kalb declared it "a very major goof."

While each network and news outlet had their own "decision teams" to decide when and if they would call the race for one candidate or another, they shared data and exit polling through the Voter News Service, or VNS. It was created in 1990 by a consortium of ABC, CBS, NBC, CNN, FOX and the Associated Press under the direction of political scientist Murray Edelman to cut costs in collecting and analyzing data for congressional, Senate and presidential races in an effort to better avoid mistakes.

VNS took major blame on Election Night 2000, and two years later in the 2002 mid-terms when its data was delayed. The organization disbanded in 2003.

But while VNS and the networks and news channels were to blame in 2000, Fox News went a step beyond for Bush that night and in many ways caused the wrong early predictions of a Bush victory. John Ellis, who headed Fox's Election Night decision team – which made the prediction calls based on VNS and other analysis and data – is George Bush's cousin.

While that relationship alone should have precluded Ellis from having such a major part in the Fox coverage to begin with, it became an even more notable conflict of interest when the race became so close. But when the final choice came down to who won in Florida, where Bush's brother, Jeb, was also governor, Ellis should have had no say in the Fox's coverage of that state's voting.

Instead, it was revealed later that Fox called Florida for Bush, and essentially the presidency, after Ellis received a call from Jeb Bush at about 2:15 a.m., even though all other networks had it too close to call. Once Fox gave the state to Florida, several other networks followed on that information, according to a later review by *The Nation*.

"In fact, a separate count by the Associated Press showed Bush's margin declining precipitously, reaffirming that the election was simply too close to call," *The Nation* reported. "In that context, John Ellis— who had just taken a call from his cousin Jeb Bush – excitedly announced to his decision team, 'Jebbie says we got it! Jebbie says we got it!' A minute later, Fox projected George W. Bush the winner in Florida and the next President of the United States."

That call quickly led to similar proclamations of a Bush victory by NBC, CNN, ABC and CBS, all based on the conflicted Fox call. But, as we know, all of them turned out to be wrong and the night led to a recount that took more than a month. In the end, Bush won Florida by just 537 votes out of nearly six million cast. And even the later Florida recount did not convince everyone, as it was stopped with just four counties completed because of a U.S. Supreme Court decision to halt any further counting.

Still, the Ellis connection remained a controversial point in the years to come given what a conflict of interest it was and a sign of Fox's clear dismissal of journalistic ethics. "Ailes decision to place a candidate's cousin in charge of calling an election, regardless of his conduct on election night, reflected a lack of concern about journalistic standards," Gabriel Sherman wrote in his Ailes biography, *The Loudest Voice in the Room*.

Sherman later noted that Ellis' skills in the job had been questioned long before that night, quoting fellow Fox decision team member Cynthia Talkow as saying, "They didn't understand half the numbers on the screen ... I couldn't believe how unqualified they were."

When Election Night 2000 ended, the election did not. The Florida recount, which brought politicians, lawyers, and the press into unchartered territory, was very much a work in progress. No reporters on the story had seen something like this, and certainly weren't prepared to cover it.

The closet thing had been the 1960 presidential election, when John F. Kennedy beat Richard Nixon by the slimmest of margins. While JFK won the electoral college vote with a clear 303 to 219 count, the popular vote margin was only 113,000 out of more than 60 million votes cast. Stories have circulated ever since that Kennedy's Chicago connections through the iron-handed Mayor Richard J. Daley helped him win Illinois or that Lyndon Johnson's people in Texas threw him that state's 24 electoral votes.

But when Nixon chose not to challenge the tally, perhaps fearing his own rumored ballot-box manipulation would be reveled, the results stood. That left many unknowns, and many areas for media mistakes and right-wing "journalist" influence when the 2000 recount occurred due in part to a lack of experience covering such an event, and the growing abuse of right-wing media manipulation.

One area of conflict that was essentially unchallenged by most of the media was Florida Secretary of State Katherine Harris who had the job of overseeing the recount. The fact that she was a Republican and had been a Bush campaign state co-chair was basically ignored.

Harris had also hired a Republican-linked data company to purge the voter rolls of thousands of minority residents falsely categorized as felons, according to author Eric Alterman in his 2003 book, *What Liberal Media?* He reported that all in all, about 200,000 Florida voters were either not allowed to vote or had their votes discarded through Harris' office.

In addition, the disagreements over what counts as a vote – the so-called "hanging chads" and "dimpled chads" in the paper ballots – received little unbiased review and were, instead, under Harris' control. While the mainstream press failed in raising important questions about the recount policies, the right-wing media went full force for Bush.

Alterman also pointed out in his book what he saw as "an oddity" in the mainstream media of a push to finish the recount quickly and even show annoyance at having to wait for a complete review of the votes.

"Constitutional rule in America was frequently claimed to be in peril by one or another pundit or reporter the longer the count continued," Alterman wrote. He went on to cite examples from *Newsweek, U.S. News & World Report*, and all three network Sunday morning shows of press demands for the recount to end already.

"Another week and no more," he quoted *The New York Times'* R.W. Apple as stating in a front-page story just two days after the election. Much of that pressure was a key to Gore's unwillingness to fight the controversial Supreme Court decision that effectively ended the recount. "Al Gore could have kept on fighting, but what's the point," Alterman wrote, later adding, "the media's triumph was complete."

The right-wing voices that boosted Bush in 2000 only increased their efforts – and their impact – in 2004 when Bush, who had used influence to avoid combat in Vietnam, was somehow portrayed as more patriotic than a Vietnam veteran who had earned three Purple Hearts.

Sen. John Kerry first came to national attention as leader of the Vietnam Veterans Against the War when he testified before Congress on April 23, 1971. A five-year veteran of the U.S. Navy, part of his service was on a Patrol Craft Fast, or "Swift Boat," the shallow-water vessels that patrolled the inner waterways of Vietnam.

During his military service, Kerry received a Bronze Star, Silver Star and three Purple Hearts, which are awarded for those wounded in combat. During his testimony, he explained his change in attitude against the war stating, "In our opinion and from our experience, there is nothing in South Vietnam which could happen that realistically threatens the United States of America. And to attempt to justify the loss of one American life in Vietnam, Cambodia or Laos by linking such loss to the preservation of freedom, which those misfits supposedly abuse, is to us the height of criminal hypocrisy, and it is that kind of hypocrisy which we feel has torn this country apart."

Kerry went on to a successful career as a lawyer, then into politics, first becoming Massachusetts lieutenant governor in 1983, and later a U.S. Senator in 1985. But it was his presidential run in 2004 against George W. Bush that brought him the most attention, and likely criticism. And the press, especially on the conservative side, was there to pile it on – in most cases based on unfounded and misleading information.

That "swift boat" Kerry served on in Vietnam, which patrolled the Mekong Delta's Bay Hap River and other waterways, should have been a shining part of his military service record. But thanks to some critics who made unverified and false claims about Kerry's time on those vessels, it became something of a liability.

In mid-2004, a group called Swift Boat Veterans for Truth launched a book and ad campaign that claimed Kerry had misrepresented his record, had not earned his awards, and even questioned if he had been wounded. Interestingly, soon after that issue broke, questions about George W. Bush's National Guard Service in the late 1960s and early 1970s were raised. Among them were claims by several news outlets that he had not fulfilled his commitment and had used influence to stay out of the U.S. Military during the war.

At one point, in September 2004, CBS News aired a *60 Minutes II* segment on Bush's alleged use of influential help to avoid part of his service. It cited letters purported to be from Bush's squadron commander, the deceased Lt. Col. Jerry B. Killian, which revealed he had been given special treatment to join the guard and avoid the draft. But when it could not authenticate the letters, CBS had to withdraw part of the story and conduct its own investigation that ended with anchorman Dan Rather being forced out more than a year later.

When the claims against Kerry were made, the conservative media took the lead with many reports and hours of newscasts devoted to pushing the Swift Boat Veteran's misleading claims forward.

Fox News' Sean Hannity was among the first to give the Swift Boat Veterans a platform, with a sneak preview of their first ad on the Aug. 4, 2004, episode of *Hannity & Colmes*, the Fox News show he co-hosted with the late liberal pundit, Alan Colmes. He then went on to "feature" the group's charges 15 more times that month, according to Fair and Accuracy in Reporting (FAIR).

"The Swift Boat Vets had one crucial dynamic on their side: the right-wing pundits who championed their cause," FAIR wrote in a 2005 review of the coverage. "When the group's ads aired, its leaders became instant celebrities. Prominent conservative pundits like Sean Hannity, Rush Limbaugh and Robert Novak became staunch supporters, and leaders of the group became fixtures on right-wing talk radio and cable TV."

FAIR later noted that Novak and conservative Tucker Carlson "devoted generous amounts of airtime to the Swift Boat Vets on CNN's *Crossfire*, where the two championed the group in no less than 10 episodes during the month of August 2004 alone." But Novak "didn't mention until early September" that his son was a marketing director for the publisher of the Swift Boat Veteran's anti-Kerry book, *Unfit for Command*.

Once the right-wing voices made the issue a story, many traditional news outlets were glad to help.

"Embraced by the Republican's far right media noise machine, led by Fox News, the *Drudge Report*, Rush Limbaugh, and the *New York Post*, the mainstream media refused to stand up to those forces," Eric Boehlert wrote in his 2006 book, *Lapdogs*. "Instead, the press played along, letting the right wing set the media agenda, and pretending the media's primary duty was to accurately record the Swifty allegations, call the Kerry camp for comment, and then proclaim the story too tangled to figure out."

He cited a *USA Today* example, adding the newspaper, "threw up its hands, declaring, 'A clear picture of what John Kerry did or did not do in Vietnam 35 years ago may never emerge, given the fog of war, the passage of time and the intense partisan sentiments of the players.'"

When the dust settled, it turned out much of the Swift Boat Veterans claims were unfounded, and their own ties to the Republican Party exposed. It was apparently too late, however, as Bush won re-election and the conservative media outlets grew even more powerful, and more willing to use that power to mislead, frighten and lie.

It wasn't just the political campaigns where conservative media wielded its power. Social issues that grew to prominence with the religious right of the 1980s saw something of a rebirth when W. was elected and re-elected. A self-described born-again Christian who called Jesus his favorite philosopher and credited his faith for overcoming alcoholism, George W. Bush laid the groundwork with a strong belief system for those who took that support and used it to oppose women's rights, gay rights, women's choice, gun limitations, and science-based issues like evolution and climate change.

"...social issues tend to strike at people's most deeply held beliefs. It is hard to understand differing positions as political disagreements only. They are not the sort of issues that lend themselves to compromise or politicking. They invariably become – because they are – moral, ethical, and religious disagreements," Addison Del Mastro wrote in *The American Conservative* in 2017. "Take abortion. While many Americans are willing to make some kind of compromise – no elective abortion after 20 weeks or the first trimester, for example – millions of Americans believe that abortion is a fundamental right, and many millions more just as strongly believe it to be a barbaric act ethically indistinguishable from murder. Same for LGBT empowerment – it's not okay to give people just a few human rights. Once any question becomes understood as a matter of fundamental rights, it becomes immune to the normal political process, with little room to move on either side. It doesn't really matter who is right. What matters is that a political system based on deliberation and compromise is peculiarly ill-suited to address deep moral divides."

Perhaps that is why conservatives took up such issues as they lost White House power for eight years; to raise the hackles of the deep red voters and give them a new fight to wage.

Although the eight years of Barack Obama swung the tide for a while politically to the left, the conservative media – as it had been when

Clinton was in office – grew even angrier and more vicious, and in many cases turned to those social issues to counter the liberal leadership. Obama added fuel to the fire when he came out in favor of gay marriage, even though the Supreme Court agreed in a close 5-4 decision in 2015, which fell pretty much along its liberal/conservative lines.

But just as that case was settled, at least in the court, the movement for transgender rights arose, along with the ongoing abortion feuds and new battles over climate change. And, of course, all of this being heightened in a new era of social media, with Twitter, Facebook, and numerous other platforms that let anyone weigh in and spout counter beliefs – and often lies.

Enter Donald Trump and the 2016 election.

I won't repeat the effect Trump had on media issues that were discussed earlier. But the conservative media involved are worth noting as they reached their greatest influence, and in many cases their greatest abuses, in 2016. And they have only gotten worse.

Using the freedom made available by the web, along with increased cable access and ongoing talk radio command, right-wing commentators and so-called journalists not only helped Trump into office, but used the power gained from that success to perpetuate some of the biggest lies and misleading views ever.

A 2017 report from Harvard University's Berkman Klein Center for Internet and Society found that Trump received more favorable coverage in the 2016 election than Hillary Clinton, and that conservative partisan media played a major role.

"We document that the majority of mainstream media coverage was negative for both candidates, but largely followed Donald Trump's agenda: when reporting on Hillary Clinton, coverage primarily focused on the various scandals related to the Clinton Foundation and emails," the report stated. "When focused on Trump, major substantive issues, primarily immigration, were prominent. Indeed, immigration emerged as a central issue in the campaign and served as a defining issue for the Trump campaign."

It also noted, "The leading media on the right and left are rooted in different traditions and journalistic practices. On the conservative side, more attention was paid to pro-Trump, highly partisan media outlets. On the liberal side, by contrast, the center of gravity was made up largely of long-standing media organizations steeped in the traditions and practices of objective journalism."

No surprise there; most conservatives seek out the right-leaning news outlets, while most liberals go for the real and objective approach.

I first became aware of the major right-wing media players at *Editor & Publisher* in the 2000s when the likes of Rush Limbaugh, Sean Hannity, Ann Coulter, Bill O'Reilly and Michael Savage made noise.

Savage had actually attacked me back in 1995 when I was at the *San Francisco Independent* covering the local district attorney's race. When I wrote a three-part series on D.A. candidate Bill Fazio, a conservative prosecutor with a checkered record and misleading ads, Savage had Fazio on his then-local radio show at right-wing KSFO AM to take shots at my reporting.

Although he had no valid inaccuracy or false information claims, Savage let Fazio rip into me, but refused to let me on to defend myself. Later, after Fazio lost to eventual victor Terence Hallinan, Fazio's brother, investigator Joe Fazio, called and left a threatening message on my home voice mail. He was later fired after he admitted it.

It was no surprise when Savage, whose real name is Michael Weiner, would rise through the talk radio ranks to build a national audience that now stands at 10 million listeners in 300 markets. He fits perfectly with the Trump era right that attack real news and spout their own false or misleading views. He's made comments that are racist, anti-immigrant, called liberalism a mental disorder and told a gay caller he hoped he would die of AIDS.

Offensive comments are almost routine among many in the talk landscape – both right and left – although Savage seems to go beyond even the accepted conservative level. He plays the game of shock-value. If that's what listeners want, fine.

But where the real damage is done is in the false comments, misleading listeners and viewers with outright lies, or making up facts to fit an angry tirade. This seems to be much more prevalent on the right.

Joining *Media Matters* in 2010 threw me into the deep end where I learned about the vicious conservative media, which had not only grown larger and more influential, but had an organized structure that took full advantage of the Internet.

While Hannity and Limbaugh grew stronger under Trump, the likes of radio and web conspiracy theorist Alex Jones of *InfoWars*, who claims 9/11 was an inside job and had plenty of other offensive views; Mark Levin, who once told me to "Go to Hell" and claimed a security guard was "in on" the 2017 Las Vegas shooting; Glenn Beck, who spouted doomsday fears including that Ebola was a planned plague; and Laura Ingraham, who was recently boycotted for verbally attacking one of the surviving students of Parkland High School shooting in Florida, exploded with interest.

Talkers magazine's 2016 "Heavy Hundred" list of the most important talk radio shows indicated at least half of the top 25 were conservative voices, with Limbaugh, Hannity, Levin and Beck among the top five.

In nearly all cases, these talkers were not just spewing angry rhetoric, but false information and outright lies. And when their claims get picked up by Fox News and even more mainstream outlets – even if they are proven as false by those sources – they reach a larger audience, some of whom may seek to believe the original lie because they have been taught not to trust the mainstream press. Taught, in many cases by Donald Trump, proven to be the most untruthful president ever, and the most anti-press.

As noted earlier, Trump's record of consistently claiming "fake news" by legitimate news outlets and citing actual false reporting by those on the right as real has had a major impact on the right's ability to spread its untruths.

"The problem is there is no one invested in responsible conservative media," Jeff Jarvis, a veteran TV analyst for *TV Guide* who now teaches at the City University of New York Graduate School of Journalism, told me in an interview. "There is Fox News and it goes downhill fast from there, *Breitbart*, *InfoWars* and worse. Who is reporting on the world from a conservative viewpoint? All you have is Fox News and Fox News often doesn't report."

Breitbart is, of course, *Breitbart News*, the far-right web outlet created in 2007 by the late Andrew Breitbart, who died in 2012 after spearheading his conservative sites that were among the first to use the Internet for far-right messaging. A *New York Times* obituary called him "one of the early – and most controversial – users of blogs to disseminate political information and rumors."

While Breitbart drew credit for some scoops, such as exposing disgraced Congressman Anthony Weiner's first offensive Twitter photos, which eventually led to his resignation, he also garnered a reputation as an unethical blogger. One of his most troubling incidents involved the 2011 misreporting on then former U.S. Agriculture Department employee Shirley Sherrod. Breitbart posted an edited video that he claimed showed Sherrod making racist comments at an NAACP event, which later led to her firing.

It was eventually revealed that the tape was heavily edited, and the original full version indicated Sherrod's comments were taken out of context. She later sued him and fellow conservative commentator Larry O'Connor for defamation in a case that was settled in 2015.

Breitbart was responsive in one-on-one settings with me. I recall approaching him at the 2011 CPAC conference with a video recorder in hand to capture his response to a question about the Sherrod issue. Although he stood by a claim he had made that Sherrod was fired for a reason unrelated to his video, which was later proven false, he was cordial.

He did, however, accuse me and *Media Matters* of being unfair with no basis for his claim other than "you are at *Media Matters*, and you by default disagree with everything that I say. It's not my burden that you don't find that to be a compelling argument."

That seems to be the typical response from many of the current conservative voices – facts be damned, we are just right.

It was after his death, when the site came under the control of Steve Bannon, that *Breitbart News'* impact really increased. When Bannon became a Trump advisor, and later part of the Trump Administration, his influence helped boost Trump's and many of his readers' willingness to spew lies and disbelieve legitimate reporting.

Mediashift.org included *Breitbart News* among its most read conservative news sites in early 2018, stating, "With monthly visits in excess of 80 million, *Breitbart* recorded more audience visits in December (2017) than mainstream media sites like *Politico* (69 million), Time.com (68 million), *Newsweek* (51 million) and *Slate* (43 million). And its December audience was more than double the size of the next closest conservative website, *The Daily Caller*."

Foxnews.com had the highest traffic count among conservative websites, with 312 million monthly visits, far outpacing second-place *Breitbart*. Others in the top 10 list of conservative sites based on visits were *The Daily Caller, Conservative Tribune*, Alex Jones' *InfoWars, Washington*

Examiner, Newsmax, Glenn Beck's *The Blaze*, PJ Media and The *Washington Times. Daily Caller* founder Tucker Carlson has another outlet of influence as a Fox News host, while Alex Jones has his radio show markets and Newsmax has Newsmax TV.

"The conservative media world has been expanding because there seems to be almost a bottomless pit of demand for conservative media among conservatives," said David Corn of *Mother Jones.* "Liberals often don't mind getting information from a variety of sources and are quite happy getting news from NPR. Conservatives who want news want red meat, liberals are happy with reality."

There are many other less-trafficked sites for the right that may not get the web viewers, but are given attention from mainstream outlets including Fox, CNN and others despite their poor credibility. These include Townhall Media's Town Hall and Hot Air, both clearly partisan and misleading and World Net Daily, which has falsely claimed Planned Parenthood could not account for government funding and that California planned to register undocumented voters. Newsbusters, is a misleading news website for the Media Research Center, a wannabe media watchdog outlet for the right. On the same wavelength is the Washington Free Beacon, which launched under the conservative Center for American Freedom, which *The Atlantic* called "decadent and unethical."

Soon after I joined *Media Matters*, I would wonder why we paid so much attention to the lies and bias reporting of these lesser sites that have fewer readers than the bigger players Among the reasons why is when they put out a falsehood, it is first read by only a few million people, but also picked up by larger news outlets. Fox News seems to be the largest home for these smaller right-wing voices to get traction.

Once Fox News or Rush Limbaugh or Sean Hannity gives it attention, the word is out. Then even if it is corrected, the correction gets less attention than the lie. One example is the July 10, 2016, murder of Seth Rich, a 27-year-old Democratic National Committee (DNC) employee who was shot to death on a Washington, D.C., street and whose killer has yet to be found.

Since the murder occurred at the height of the most lie-filled presidential election in history, it was not a surprise when some right-wing outlets tried to find a related conspiracy behind it. When Wikileaks released more than 44,000 DNC emails just two weeks later, it's founder – Julian Assange – alleged that Rich, the DNC's director of voter expansion, had been behind leaking them to Wikileaks, according to Vox.com. Vox also described Rich as "a supporter of Sen. Bernie Sanders's presidential candidacy." It reported a claim that Rich released the emails once Sanders lost the nomination and was murdered for doing so.

Assange would not say if Rich was the source, according to *The Daily Mail*, which noted he had said earlier that he did not know the source's identity. But that did not stop other outlets, including *WorldNetDaily* and *InfoWars*, from speculating about Rich and running with the conspiracy about his death, and continuing to promote the flimsy information through 2018.

When Fox News picked it up from those smaller sources, with Sean Hannity among the key proponents, the story received much greater attention. This caused much greater damage to Rich's family and the DNC. So much so that Fox News retracted a major portion of their "reporting" in May 2017 after receiving a "cease and desist" letter form Rich's family. The family eventually sued Fox News and Hannity in March 2018, according to *The New York Times*.

"The suit, filed in the Federal District Court in Manhattan, accuses Fox News of 'extreme and outrageous' conduct." The *Times* wrote. "It claims that a reporter for the network, Malia Zimmerman, and a regular

Fox News guest, Ed Butowsky, intentionally fabricated a story that portrayed Mr. Rich as the person who leaked thousands of internal Democratic National Committee emails to WikiLeaks in 2016, which released them to the public in an act that proved damaging to Hillary Clinton's presidential campaign."

The *Times* in an earlier 2017 story, had noted the influence of the other right-wing sites and pundits on the spreading of the false rumor, calling it, "a conspiracy theory that had taken hold across the right-wing news media" and stating the rumor had been "seized on by Mr. Hannity and other right-wing pundits as an alternative narrative to the cascade of damaging revelations about the Trump administration's ties to Russian officials who meddled in the presidential election."

That is just one of many examples of smaller, less-honest news sites – mostly conservative – spreading rumors and lies and seeing them picked up by the likes of Fox or other slanted outlets including Rush Limbaugh and Glenn Beck who have a larger audience.

Another more recent issue saw the right-wing media spread false claims that led to a White House shake-up of personnel that some see as a detriment to international relations. Sahar Nowrouzzadeh, a Defense Department analyst who spoke Arabic, Persian, and Dari, spent almost a decade on mostly "secret programs, winning awards from the Departments of Defense and State, the Office of the Director of National Intelligence, and the F.B.I." according to *The New Yorker*.

In 2014, she was assigned to the National Security Council and part of the group that forged the Iran nuclear deal that Trump later dissolved. The daughter of Iranian immigrants, Nowrouzzadeh was credited with being "unusually able to identify, and exploit, subtle divides in Tehran" in a way that helped push Iran to give up the most concessions and agree to a better deal for the U.S. than they might have otherwise, *The New Yorker* wrote.

But when a far-right conspiracy site, The *Conservative Review*, posted a March 17, 2017, story that targeted Nowrouzzadeh with false claims she had "burrowed into the government under President Trump" and that she "sat in on high-level briefings along with President Obama, former VP Joe Biden, and former Secretary of State John Kerry, as top White House staff crafted false narratives on the Iran deal to sell to the American public," things changed.

It also mentioned her past work for the National Iranian-American Council (NIAC), a non-profit group working to improve U.S.-Iranian relations for those living in the U.S. But the *Conservative Review* described it as a "non-profit that is accused of being a lobbying group for the Iranian regime." Accused by whom? GuideStar.com, a non-partisan website that collects and provides information on non-profit organizations, describes The National Iranian American Council as "a nonpartisan, nonprofit organization dedicated to increasing Iranian American civic participation and promoting greater understanding between the American and Iranian people."

Having someone with that kind of understanding of Iran seems like it would help in negotiations for the nuclear deal. But not to the right-wing outlets seeking to disrupt her work and the Iran deal, even if they must mislead readers to do so.

Around the same time, *Breitbart News* posted a similar story meant to demean Nowrouzzadeh. It also sought to paint the NIAC as an anti-American group, calling it an "alleged pro-Tehran regime lobbying group" and claiming she had an "apparent past with the alleged pro-regime group." But of course, neither *Breitbart* or *Conservative Review* had any valid claim of any dangerous Iran relationship involving Nowrouzzadeh.

Still, these reports and some others managed to get Nowrouzzadeh kicked out of her post when they reached powerful Republican officials who seem to frighten at any mention of Middle East links, rather than appreciate the information and intelligence they can provide.

Politico revealed in an April 21, 2017, article that she was reassigned to a lesser role "amid pressure from conservative media outlets that have publicly targeted individual staffers, questioning their loyalty to the new administration."

A more recent *New Yorker* piece went on to paint a picture of the misleading conservative articles starting a chain of events that pushed the Trump Administration to make the move. Saying the *Conservative Review* story portrayed Nowrouzzadeh "as a traitorous stooge," *The New Yorker* went on to state:

"The story ... titled "Iran Deal Architect Is Running Tehran Policy at the State Dept.," derided her as a "trusted Obama aide," whose work "resulted in an agreement that has done enormous damage to the security interests of the United States." David Wurmser, who had been an adviser to Vice-President Dick Cheney, e-mailed the article to Newt Gingrich, the former Speaker of the House. "I think a cleaning is in order here," Wurmser wrote. Gingrich forwarded the message to an aide to Secretary of State Rex Tillerson, with the subject line "i thought you should be aware of this."

As the article circulated inside the Administration, Sean Doocey, a White House aide overseeing personnel, e-mailed colleagues to ask for details of Nowrouzzadeh's "appointment authority" – the rules by which a federal worker can be hired, moved, or fired. He received a reply from Julia Haller, a former Trump campaign worker, newly appointed to the State Department. Haller wrote that it would be "easy" to remove Nowrouzzadeh from the policy-planning staff. She had "worked on the Iran Deal," Haller noted, "was born in Iran, and upon my understanding cried when the President won." Nowrouzzadeh was unaware of these discussions. All she knew was that her experience at work started to change."

Among the misinformation in that exchange was her birthplace, which is Connecticut, not Iran. But the most telling part of this incident is how some lies and fear-mongering false claims by a few websites can affect American foreign policy in today's Washington, D.C. For both Nowrouzzadeh and the family of Seth Rich, such poor reporting and slanted claims did different kinds of damage.

The worst of the so-called right-wing "journalists" might be James O'Keefe, from my own home state of New Jersey. I hesitate to use the word journalist to describe this hack as he continuously breaks most parts of the Society of Professional Journalists' Code of Ethics.

O'Keefe and his Project Veritas might simply be laughed off given his amateurish and pathetic approach to undercover work that includes outright deceptions, unethical editing and criminal behavior. But some news outlets still cite his work and he has managed to have an impact for the right-wing community that promotes him. Not to mention some mainstream outlets and official entities that give him attention.

O'Keefe, a 2006 Rutgers University graduate, made his first mark while an undergraduate when he launched a mock campaign to get Lucky Charms removed from the school dining hall menus, claiming it was a slur on the Irish. He made a video and sought to make it an issue to show the overreach of political correctness. While the cereal was not removed, O'Keefe has claimed for years that it was, using the anecdote as a standard in his paid speeches. His lying started early.

He later drew national attention in 2009 when, through *Breitbart*'s BigGovernment.com site, O'Keefe released videos of himself posing as a pimp with fellow activist Hannah Giles, who pretended to be a prostitute. They entered offices of ACORN, The Association of Community Organizations for Reform Now, a collection of community-based organizations that promoted programs on neighborhood safety, voter registration, health care, affordable housing, and other social issues. The edited videos appeared to show ACORN workers helping the phony "criminals" seek ways around the law to get funding for their illegal activities.

ACORN had been a target of the right for years, with many seeking to claim it had perpetuated voter fraud with registration efforts dating back to the early 2000s. ACORN opponents also tried to undermine Barack Obama's election a year earlier with false claims about voting malfeasance.

The O'Keefe/Giles sting quickly received support from other conservative media, including Fox News, and Glenn Beck, who gave the duo airtime on several occasions. "On September 15 [2009], Giles appeared on the *Glenn Beck Program* and debuted fresh audio clips from her conversation with ACORN staffers in San Bernardino, California," Author Alexander Zaitchik wrote in his 2010 Beck biography, *Common Nonsense*. "Beck welcomed Giles as an 'American hero' and urged his audience to contact their local newspaper editors and demand coverage of the videos." Again, one right-wing outlet boosting another.

The poor publicity eventually destroyed ACORN's funding, forced it into bankruptcy, and ended its work that had helped thousands of low-income residents.

The incidents, which included ACORN offices in several California cities, prompted an investigation by the California Attorney General's Office, which later revealed in a 2010 report that it had found "a serious and glaring deficit in management, governance and accountability within the ACORN organization," but no illegal activity. The report added that "even if O'Keefe and Giles had truly intended to break the law, there is no evidence that any of the ACORN employees had the intent to aid and abet such criminal conduct or agreed to join in that illegal conduct."

The report also found that "O'Keefe and Giles violated state privacy laws" but were given immunity in exchange for their willingness to cooperate with the investigation and provide raw video footage to investigators. It went on to question O'Keefe's journalistic status, stating, "O'Keefe stated he was out to make a point and to damage ACORN and therefore did not act as a journalist objectively reporting a story. The video releases were heavily edited to feature only the worst or most inappropriate statements of the various ACORN employees and to omit some of the most salient statements by O'Keefe and Giles."

Despite the underhanded and misleading approach, O'Keefe became something of a right-wing hero and launched Project Veritas in 2011 as a registered 501©3 charity organization and donations poured in to the tune of nearly $5 million in 2015, with O'Keefe claiming a $317,691 annual salary that year. Four other employees made more than $100,000 each.

Among the group's $3.5 million in expenses were $341,000 in travel and nearly $200,000 in legal fees. A year earlier, with $3.1 million in reported expenses, the organization had $334,000 in travel and nearly $450,000 in legal fees.

No surprise given O'Keefe's legal troubles, which included a 2013 order to pay $100,000 to a former ACORN employee who was wrongly portrayed in O'Keefe's sting videos and his 2010 arrest in Louisiana after he and some of his minions posed as telephone repair workers to get into the office of Sen. Mary Landrieu and allegedly expose her staff apparently ignoring constituent calls.

I had my own run-in with O'Keefe when he spoke at a 2011 Tea Party event in New Jersey. When I approached him to ask questions about a previous incident, he said he would not do so on video. When I mentioned that seemed hypocritical given his regular use of hidden video, he conveniently found it was time to eat lunch at the event and walked away, ignoring further requests.

Still, he may have done himself irreversible damage with a failed attempt to scam the *Washington Post* in November 2017 when he hired a woman to pretend that she had been impregnated by then Alabama Senate Candidate Roy Moore, the Republican judge who lost his campaign after several claims of sexual harassment and other offensive behavior were revealed.

O'Keefe sent in the woman, Jaime T. Phillips, to tell her story to the *Post* thinking they would run with it and show their bias against Moore. But it did not take long for the reporters to do a little checking and discover Phillips had ties to O'Keefe. When they revealed the failed plot, Project Veritas received criticism from both the left and the right.

The Atlantic labeled it "his biggest backfire," while *The National Review* stated the botched sting "further degrades any reason that anyone on the Right has to treat him as a journalist, even a bad one. This looks like the work of an operative, not an activist, and his work in the future should be evaluated as such." *The American Conservative,* meanwhile, called Phillips an "utterly inept operative. It's like a junior secret agent from the People's Republic of Klutzylvania got stung by counterintelligence."

But O'Keefe did not back down and apparently is still in business.

Most recently, his misleading, deceptive videos of interviews with New Jersey teachers' union officials in May 2018 claimed to show them willing to "Cover Up Child Abuse in Schools, Protect Drug-Using, Shoplifting Teachers" according to a headline. But the very edited videos are clearly manipulated and do not include what the subjects were asked or the entirety of the footage. O'Keefe has a knack for not releasing raw footage from such scams or explaining how he or his staff misrepresented themselves to get the subjects to speak.

In a state as corrupt as New Jersey it was easy for O'Keefe to find a lawmaker willing to highlight his work and use it to further their own interests. Enter New Jersey State Senate President Stephen Sweeney, a Republican who has battled the New Jersey Education Association before when they campaigned against him. He took the weak evidence and quickly announced hearings on the matter. This, of course, gave the top media in the state, including *The Star-Ledger*, a reason to make it Page One news. Most did explain O'Keefe's shoddy and unethical background, but the information still got out there.

As bad and misleading as James O'Keefe and Breitbart are, two lesser-known conservative organizations may be doing more to infiltrate news with right-wing bias than any single person or news outlet.

Those are Sinclair Broadcasting, the largest owner of local television stations in the United States – and the purveyor of seriously unethical tactics – and the Franklin Center for Government and Public Integrity, a non-profit group that may have a hand in your state government news coverage, and with a clear right-wing bent and a history of conservative donors.

In recent years, both have sought to slant coverage in local outlets to the right, often in a way that mixes bias with poor reporting. As local and state news dwindles, both are swooping in to take it over with a clearly partisan approach.

Sinclair, which owns 192 television stations – the most of any U.S. company – was in negotiations to add to that with a large chunk of Tribune Media properties that would have brought it up to 232 local stations. But the FCC killed the deal in August 2018 after concerns that Sinclair did not "fully disclose facts" about the planned sale of three stations.

Sinclair, the Maryland-based chain, dates back to 1958 when Julian Sinclair Smith built a Baltimore radio station with partners, which eventually led to a television station there and the Chesapeake Television Corporation in 1971. It existed until 1985 when it became the Sinclair Broadcast Group, taken over by Smith's four sons, David, CEO, Fred, Duncan and Rob.

Since then, they have gobbled up television stations and put forth a clear conservative agenda. Think Koch Brothers meets The Murdochs.

"Along the way, Mr. Smith and his brothers have become active in politics," *The New York Times* reported in a May 3, 2017 article, which later noted, "In the last election cycle, the brothers donated tens of thousands of dollars to Republican causes, including at least $6,000 from Frederick Smith to a "super PAC" supporting Mr. Trump and $20,000 from David Smith to the National Republican Congressional Committee."

It also revealed that "In the days after the Sept. 11, 2001, terrorist attacks, Sinclair instructed anchors to read statements supporting Mr. Bush and his administration's efforts to fight terrorism" and "before the 2004 presidential election, Sinclair drew sharp criticism, including from Senator John McCain, Republican of Arizona, for its refusal to broadcast an episode of *Nightline* devoted to reciting the names of every member of the military killed in action in Iraq."

That followed with Sinclair's stations airing parts of a documentary critical of the past anti-war activities of Democratic nominee John Kerry days later. "While much of the station's local news broadcasts are filled with local news, Sinclair also provides commentary and syndicated reports from its Washington bureau that have generally taken stances critical of Democrats and laudatory of Republicans," the *Times* story added.

But the most partisan move may have occurred in the spring of 2018 when Sinclair ordered anchors at most of its stations to read what amounted to an attack on mainstream reporting disguised as a warning about "fake news."

"The spot includes language painting the Sinclair-owned local news stations as the heralds of real news and refers to other media outlets as publishing 'fake stories … stories that just aren't true, without checking facts first,'" *Variety* wrote in an April 1, 2018, story. "The language reflects President Donald Trump's insistence that the mainstream news media is 'fake' and that certain narratives are pushed for political reasons." At one point, the promo declared: "Unfortunately, some members of the media use their platforms to push their own personal bias and agenda to control 'exactly what people think.'"

See the entire promotional script for two anchors below:

Hi, I'm (A) _____, and I'm (B)
_____

(B) Our greatest responsibility is to serve our Northwest communities. We are extremely proud of the quality, balanced journalism that KOMO News produces.

(A) But we're concerned about the troubling trend of irresponsible, one sided news stories plaguing our country. The sharing of biased and false news has become all too common on social media.

(B) More alarming, some media outlets publish these same fake stories... stories that just aren't true, without checking facts first.

(A) Unfortunately, some members of the media use their platforms to push their own personal bias and agenda to control 'exactly what people think'...This is extremely dangerous to a democracy.

(B) At KOMO it's our responsibility to pursue and report the truth. We understand Truth is neither politically 'left nor right.' Our commitment to factual reporting is the foundation of our credibility, now more than ever.

(A) But we are human and sometimes our reporting might fall short. If you believe our coverage is unfair please reach out to us by going to KOMOnews.com and clicking on CONTENT CONCERNS. We value your comments. We will respond back to you.

(B) We work very hard to seek the truth and strive to be fair, balanced and factual... We consider it our honor, our privilege to responsibly deliver the news every day.

(A) Thank you for watching and we appreciate your feedback

Reaction was swift from all sides, with NPR declaring, "It was the latest show of the vast reach of a company that owns local TV stations across the country and has long been criticized for pushing conservative coverage and commentary onto local airwaves," while CNN compared it to propaganda and said the anchors were "echoing President Trump's dishonest attacks on the media."

In a statement issued shortly after the uproar, and still available on the Sinclair website, Sinclair's Senior Vice President of News Scott Livingston seemed to miss the point of the concern over the creepy mass message, especially since it warns about something that many on the right practice.

"We aren't sure of the motivation for the criticism, but find it curious that we would be attacked for asking our news people to remind their audiences that unsubstantiated stories exist on social media, which result in an ill-informed public with potentially dangerous consequences," Livingston wrote. "It is ironic that we would be attacked for messages promoting our journalistic initiative for fair and objective reporting, and for specifically asking the public to hold our newsrooms accountable. Our local stations keep our audiences' trust by staying focused on fact-based reporting and clearly identifying commentary."

Although most of broadcasters did not reveal that the statement being read was a corporate-ordered message.

The Shorenstein Center on Media, Politics and Public Policy at Harvard highlighted research done by two Emory University professors in a March 2018 web article that pointed to Sinclair as a chief cause of diminished news and slanted coverage on the local level.

Among its findings: "Coverage of national politics saw a rightward shift at Sinclair stations" and "the researchers found significant drops in viewership for Sinclair-acquired stations in Democratic-leaning areas and slight increases in Republican-leaning areas."

But Sinclair's power may be diminishing, according to a 2016 federal financial disclosure filing, which noted revenue and contributions had dropped from $8.7 million to $3.1 million in one year.

That brings us to the Franklin Center for Government and Public Integrity, which I first investigated for a feature story in 2012 after hearing for months how state news bureaus were shrinking and this conservative outlet was filling the gaps – for free.

A 2009 *American Journalism Review* study found that 355 newspaper reporters and editors were covering state capitols full time, a 30% decrease at the time from 524 in 2003. And it's only gotten worse since.

"The evidence suggests that, clearly, there has been a significant diminution of bodies from the legacy media outlets covering statehouses and state politics around the country," Mark Jurkowitz, then associate director of the Pew Research Center's Project for Excellence in Journalism, told me in 2012. "Even in a city like Boston, you saw the TV bodies in the statehouse diminish quite dramatically."

The Franklin Center, whose donors included The Lynne and Harry Bradley Foundation, one of the largest and most influential conservative foundations, and Dunn's Foundation for the Advancement of Right Thinking, offered up state news coverage at no charge through outlets in 48 states as of mid-2018.

Their bureaus report on state legislators and give up the content to anyone who will take it. With so little money in newsrooms for state bureaus, many grab it up. But the problem is that the Franklin Center's stories often skew right and promote the organization's agenda.

The Ohio Legislative Correspondents Association in 2010 denied credentials to The Buckeye Institute for Public Policy Solutions, a conservative site that had received funding from the Franklin Center for investigative journalism.

"They were denied because they were more of a conservative think tank than a professional news-gathering organization," Association President Jim Siegel, also a *Columbus Dispatch* reporter, told me at the time. "There were some questions about where their funding came from."

Betsy Russell, president of the Capitol Correspondents Association of Idaho and a statehouse reporter for the *Spokesman-Review* of neighboring Spokane, Washington, agreed during an interview with me in 2012: "I think it's viewed as something other than a regular news organization … They report on their own organization's activities and they reveal it, they give more play to stuff their organization is pushing."

Overall the signs are clear: right-wing media is increasing, in both power and influence. As we have seen, the constant false claims of fake news about the mainstream media, and equally false promises of fair news among the alt right, have only increased the amount of lies and hurt real investigative journalism's chances of being heard.

FALSE EQUIVALENCY IS
FALSE NEWS

One of the first things young journalists learn, (after the who, what, where, when, why and how directive) is balance and fairness. Get both sides of the story. Seek comment from the plaintiff and the defendant. Talk to both candidates. Even interview the winners and losers at the Super Bowl.

The Society of Professional Journalists (SPJ) Code of Ethics states, "support the open and civil exchange of views, even views they find repugnant," while the Online News Association ethics guide says, "In objective journalism, stories must be balanced in the sense of attempting to present all sides of a story." Then there is the Radio Television Digital News Association (RTDNA) ethics code that declares, "Practitioners of ethical journalism seek diverse and even opposing opinions in order to reach better conclusions that can be clearly explained and effectively defended or, when appropriate, revisited and revised."

Open any textbook on news ethics and the directive is clear. As Fred Brown, a communication ethics instructor at the University of Denver and former SPJ president, wrote in his 2011 book, *Journalism Ethics: A Casebook of Professional Conduct for News Media*, "Fairness means you give everyone with a stake in the story a chance to explain his or her version."

Seems simple enough, right? Wrong.

More and more news outlets and journalists are falling into the trap of "false equivalency" or "false balance." That is the practice of giving a viewpoint time or space to be heard that does not deserve it – either because the basis of that view is inaccurate, slanted or steeped in some bias, prejudicial or even racist origin.

"The problem of objectivity, when you report what everyone says, is there is limited value for that," said David Corn, Washington bureau chief for *Mother Jones* and former D.C. scribe for *The Nation*. "The goal in journalism is to report the truth. Sometimes you can get to the truth by saying what both sides say, the other times is to be more of a referee and point out what is not true. It's necessary for the media to arbitrate, when it can, factual disputes that are important to the national discourse."

We have seen it across a variety of issues, from the communist witch hunt of the 1950s to the civil rights movement, abortion coverage, immigration reporting, vaccination debates, gun rights, climate change, gay and transgender rights, and most recently the 2016 presidential election.

There is also a different kind of false equivalency – when news outlets seek to blame one side for a negative action or give the appearance of offering a full plate of viewpoints when in reality there is more focus on one side or the other. This can include disproportionate access for a source or opinion and shutting out of valid viewpoints and information.

"Even the insufficient rule of 'getting both sides' often falls by the wayside," Author Michael Parenti wrote in his book, *Inventing Reality: The Politics of News Media*. "On almost any issue official sources are heavily favored over sources that are critical of the official view." He cited a study of NPR's All Things Considered that found administration sources outnumbered non-administration sources nearly 2-to-1.

He later added, "What the press lacks in balance, it sometimes makes up for in false balance, as when it tries to create an impression of evenhandedness by placing equal blame on parties that are not equally culpable." Parenti pointed to the coverage of civil unrest in El Salvador and Guatemala in the 1980s, stating, "for years the news media ascribed the killings ... to 'extremists on both the right and the left' when in fact almost all of the killings were done by rightist death squads linked to the military and the military itself."

Among the most recent and perhaps most egregious examples of false balance was during the 2016 presidential election when Hillary Clinton's private e-mail server was often equated in the media with Donald Trump's long list of, often more heinous, sins.

On many occasions, news outlets pointed towards both candidates' high disapproval ratings at various points and tried to equalize their supposed scandals. Government investigations and journalistic scrutiny found little improper behavior in Clinton's role in the email server and Benghazi, Libya terrorist attack scandals.

That is a far cry from Trump, who made disparaging comments about immigrants, was accused by more than a dozen women of sexual harassment or other inappropriate treatment, bragged about grabbing women by their genitals, falsely accused Barack Obama of not being born in the U.S., and numerous business failures including four bankruptcies. He was also found to have lied about 70 percent of the time on the campaign, according to *PolitiFact*, compared to 26 percent for Clinton.

Eric Alterman, a long-time media columnist and author of several books, including *What Liberal Media? The Truth About BIAS and the News*, pointed to *The New York Times* as a culprit in a June 2016 piece in *The Nation*, which cited the paper's coverage of primary victories the previous March.

"*The New York Times* gave its prime spot – the top-right corner of the paper's front page – to a story headlined '2 Front-Runners, Donald Trump and Hillary Clinton, Find Their Words Can Be Weapons,'" Alterman wrote. "Readers quickly learned, if they had missed it previously, that Trump frequently used words like 'bimbo,' 'dog,' and 'fat pig' to refer to some of the women he didn't like, and this had led to disapproval ratings among women that reached historic proportions. And what 'weapons' did Clinton give her adversaries? During a recent speech in coal country, she had suggested that her support for sustainable, clean-energy jobs would 'put a lot of coal miners and coal companies out of business.'"

He then added, "Surely, you get the symmetry: Trump employs sexist school-yard taunts to denigrate roughly half the people on the planet. Clinton bravely tells her audience something they might not want to hear in support of a policy with short-term costs for some but long-term benefits for all." Alterman cited several reasons for such false balance in that election, including "old-fashioned loyalty to 'objectivity'" and "the clubbiness of Beltway culture, which is exacerbated during presidential elections."

That objectivity is a clear necessity of course, but at a time when so much political pressure from both sides is placed on reporters, they feel almost compelled to give another side to a story, even if it does not exist. And in the presidential race, making both Clinton and Trump out to be equal sinners was easier and less controversial, despite its inaccuracy.

"I think there was a lot of false equivalence in the 2016 campaign," CNN legal analyst Jeffrey Toobin admitted in January 2018 during an online podcast interview with Larry Wilmore. "Every time we said something, pointed out something about Donald Trump, whether it was his business interests, or 'grab 'em by the pussy,' we felt like, 'Oh, we gotta … say something bad about Hillary' … I think it led to a sense of false equivalence that was misleading, and I regret my role in doing that."

Huffington Post's Jeff Schweitzer offered a similar view in a September 2016 piece, but he claimed the false balance was giving both Clinton and Trump equal presidential credentials, stating in part, "Yes superficially we can claim equivalency: both are running for president, each representing a major political party after securing victories in the primary season following multiple debates with opponents. But the comparison is just that – superficial – and meaningless. And dangerously naïve." He later added, "The huge and potentially existential mistake the media have made is to include Donald Trump in that group of qualified candidates. They have erred in promoting the idea that just because he is the GOP nominee he deserves to be treated like other legitimate candidates. This may be the worst case of false equivalency ever witnessed in public life."

But is that the job of the press? To determine if a candidate is qualified or not? Or to simply present the facts of both and let voters judge?

A December 2016 study by the Shorenstein Center on Media, Politics and Public Policy at Harvard found that the tone of coverage in 2016 was overwhelmingly negative, with Clinton's alleged scandals receiving more attention: "Clinton's alleged scandals accounted for 16 percent of her coverage – four times the amount of press attention paid to Trump's treatment of women and sixteen times the amount of news coverage given to Clinton's most heavily covered policy position."

Another case occurred a few years earlier during the 2013 government shutdown debate. At the time, it seemed natural for the press to blame both Democrats and Republicans. The public has such a low opinion of Congress – a 2017 Gallup poll indicating a 19 percent approval rating – it's easy to blame both parties for most of the Capital Hill's foibles.

But when the federal government shut down most non-essential services on Oct. 1, 2013, it was clearly due to a Republican last-ditch effort to overturn Obamacare and refuse to approve certain spending legislation. "As a midnight deadline to extend Congressional spending authority ticked ever closer, Republicans staged a series of last-ditch efforts to use a once-routine budget procedure to force Democrats to abandon their efforts to extend US health insurance," *The Guardian* reported at the time.

But most U.S. press played the equal blame game with reporting that gave both parties the same responsibility, even though Republican leaders had sought to tie the funding bill passage to a delay in some of the health care initiatives implementation.

In *The New York Times* for example, the main story on Sept. 30, 2013, led with, "A flurry of last-minute moves by the House, Senate and White House late Monday failed to break a bitter budget standoff over President Obama's health care law, setting in motion the first government shutdown in nearly two decades." But no indication of who was really to blame, even though later on, the story admitted an underhanded GOP cause, reporting, "The budget confrontation — which threatened to close federal offices and facilities, idling thousands of workers around the country — stemmed from an unusual push by Republicans to undo a law that has been on the books for three years, through a presidential election, and that the Supreme Court largely upheld in 2012. A major part of the law is set to take effect Tuesday: the opening of insurance exchanges, where people without insurance will be able to obtain coverage."

Other news outlets followed suit, willing to blame both sides and ignore that one was causing the problem more than the other. "When the political leadership of this country is incapable of even keeping the government open, a political course correction is in order," veteran D.C. journalist Dan Froomkin wrote at the time for al Jazeera America. "But how can democracy self-correct if the public does not understand where the problem lies? And where will the pressure for change come from if journalists do not hold the responsible parties accountable?"

Media Matters for America compiled numerous examples of misleading reports at the time, most blaming President Obama for failing to negotiate with Republicans rather than the Republicans for sparking the shutdown. "Media outlets continue their campaign of false equivalency to misleadingly assign President Obama an equal share of the blame for not negotiating with Republicans to repeal, defund, or delay the Affordable Care Act to end the government shutdown. But polls show the American people overwhelmingly disapprove of GOP actions that led to the shutdown," the watchdog website stated.

Time and *The Atlantic* also weighed in with calls against the false equivalency that had arisen on the story. "One party (in fact, essentially one wing of the Republican party), seeking the elimination or delay of Obamacare, precipitated a government shutdown and threatened to force a default on U.S. debt. Period. There was no corresponding threat or demand on the Democratic or White House side," *Time* wrote on Oct. 7, 2013, later adding, "That's the situation. To accurately describe it, as news coverage should, is not to endorse an ideology. It's not to say that Obamacare is good or bad. It's not to say that Republicans do or don't have good reasons to oppose it. It's not to say that Democrats have or haven't sought political benefit in the aftermath. But it correctly places the impetus where it belongs."

Some of this over-emphasis on seeking balance – to the point of, well, imbalance – is due to a long history of poor journalism until about the mid-20th Century. In many cases back then some outlets purposely steered coverage a certain way or failed to address alternative views – this is among the reasons for the codes of ethics mentioned earlier, most of which did not come into place until the last few decades.

News outlets were often expected to promote news in a certain way, toward their ownership's view beyond just the editorial page. As such, names like the *Santa Rosa Press-Democrat*, or *Denver Republican* came about, as newspapers clearly revealed their viewpoints. My personal favorite newspaper name is the *Unterrified Democrat*, still publishing weekly in Linn, MO.

The first efforts to balance coverage came about in 1947 when *Time* and *Life* publisher Henry Luce commissioned a $200,000 study of press freedom by a 17-person commission headed by Robert M. Hutchins, chancellor of the University of Chicago. The group included several university professors, as well as a former assistant secretary of state and the chairman of the federal reserve – but no journalists. Perhaps this was to give it a true outsider assessment.

It's findings: The freedom of the press was in danger.

The commission cited three reasons:

○ The development of the press as a mass communication tool via technology has "greatly decreased the proportion of people who can express their opinions and ideas through the press."

○ "The few who are able to use the machinery of the press as an instrument of mass communication have not provided a service adequate to the needs of society."

○ "Those who direct the machinery of the press have engaged from time to time in practices which the society condemns and which, if continued, it will inevitably undertake to regulate or control."

In essence, Luce and others in control of news, realized that their failure to open up to alternative viewpoints and provide better, fairer coverage, would lead to their undoing – either economically as public disdain grew or legally if government entities decided to gain control.

"The press cannot and should not be expected to print everybody's ideas," the report stated, later adding that the mass media of the day "can and should assume the duty of publishing significant ideas contrary to their own, as a matter of objective reporting."

This led to, at least outwardly, a greater demand for fair and objective reporting. News outlets were expected to project a balanced standard that gave journalism the image of accuracy and unbiased coverage, and the demand that both sides in any story or issue be heard. When the necessary calls for balance and less bias occurred, many newsrooms heightened efforts to create a more equivalent approach.

This, however, opened the door to less-credible views and opinions and allowed the first hints of "false equivalency" and "false balance" as some went overboard seeking to be fair and let inaccurate or outright bias arguments and viewpoints to be legitimized.

One of the first real news stories influenced by false equivalence might have been the communist witch hunts of the 1950s led by Sen. Joe McCarthy of Wisconsin. Eventually, Edward R. Murrow and a powerful half-hour report in 1954 helped bring McCarthy down.

Before Murrow exposed McCarthy, however, the junior senator was able to manipulate much of the press into spreading his false claims that communism was infiltrating the federal government. Through the over-reaching scare tactics that included unsubstantiated claims about alleged communists in government and elsewhere, McCarthy's star rose. Many in the press helped by simply failing to challenge his clams – in part to seek that false balance.

"Under the conditions that prevailed, any politician clever enough and ruthless enough could maneuver the press into publishing such charges as his, especially when the accuser was a United States senator and for two years the chairman of a Senate committee," author Edwin Bayley wrote in his 1982 book, *Joe McCarthy and the Press*, which is considered the authority on press manipulation. "The television networks were already conditioned to be terrified of 'Communist' charges, and it was a simple matter for McCarthy to bully them into giving him free time on almost any pretext."

While McCarthy was spreading his bogus claims to a willing news media, another form of false equivalency was taking shape as the civil rights era was growing. Many point to July 26, 1948, as the unofficial beginning of the real race equality battle when President Harry S. Truman issued Executive Order 9981, which end segregation in the U.S. Armed Services.

That was followed years later by the Brown vs. Board of Education decision in 1954, when the U.S. Supreme Court ordered the desegregation of public schools, and Rosa Parks' refusal to relocate on a Montgomery, Alabama bus in 1955 – launching the first of many bus boycotts that led to protests at lunch counters and other entities.

As the civil rights movement got into full swing, so did the press – and many of their stories, in an effort to seek counterpoint views to the demands for racial equality, perhaps unwittingly let racist opinions and misleading assertions into their coverage.

In many cases, news outlets would provide valid reasons for civil rights and equal rights, but in some cases they would let opponents spew false claims about black intelligence or other unfair views and place them as equal value comments in a news story.

"What I have seen is, during the civil rights era, they had no problem rolling out religious leaders, like Billy Graham and using excerpts from the bible and then pronouncing on high their interpretation of what the biblical passage meant and allowed the continued debasement of black people," Carol Anderson, an African American studies and history professor at Emory University and author of *Eyes off the Prize: The United Nations and the African American Struggle for Human Rights*, 1944-1955, told me in an interview.

In *The Race Beat*, Gene Roberts and Hank Klibanoff's 2006 Pulitzer Prize-winning history of civil rights coverage, the authors pointed to many reporters who so vehemently supported the equality efforts – as most fair-minded people would – that they went overboard trying to be neutral and allowed false and racist claims by segregationists to be reported unchecked.

Citing a discussion between *New York Times* correspondent Claude Sitton and legendary *Atlanta Constitution* editor and Pulitzer Prize-winner Ralph McGill during the civil rights coverage, Klibanoff and Roberts wrote:

"McGill proselytized his fellow journalists with the idea that they had become mindless, robotic followers of the "cult of objectivity," at the expense of truth. Certainly, reporters had to try to be fair, McGill felt, but he did not see the point of purely objective news presentations if that meant the truth got lost in the process ... If a public figure said something that was untrue or mischaracterized a situation, McGill felt, most newspapers wouldn't report the falsity unless the reporter could get someone else to point it out. And if that someone else stretched the truth, McGill said, newspapers devoted to blind objectivity found themselves in a bind, printing two falsities."

When covering such a clear human rights violation it was a struggle between being fair and not allowing a false or clearly racist argument in to the mix. In the case of civil rights, the issue of false equivalency and even fair reporting were impacted by the racist stance many newspapers in the south took and the open advocacy many in the "black press" utilized.

It is hard to argue that the black press would be wrong to essentially advocate for a human rights stance like equal rights for all races. But in that coverage, they too needed to be complete in their reporting; does that mean providing the opposing viewpoint as long as it is clearly an opinion and not a false statement of fact?

Whether it was the segregationist *Richmond* (Va.) *Leader* or the black advocate publications such as the *Pittsburgh Courier*, it would seem important that each present both sides, even the segregationist views, as long as they are limited to opinion. In other words, if a southern sheriff, governor or KKK leader told a reporter he did not like or trust or want to eat next to a black person, that might have to be reported as a piece of fact relevant to the story – their opinion. But if he said he did not want to do so because black people were inferior, dangerous or any other false premise upon which his view was based, that either needed to be kept out or pointed out as a false premise.

"Some of the longstanding 'rules' of journalism, while seemingly rational and wise, created distorted versions of the truth," Klibanoff told *The Atlantic* in 2013. "The pursuit of journalistic 'objectivity,' for example, led many editors to reflexively demand that writers give equal and near-formulaic attention to aspects of a story, 'sides,' as it were, that were not equivalent. It is what led us to Joe McCarthy, Ross Barnett, George Wallace and the success that demagogues have had throughout history in uttering outright falsehoods that editors did not feel it was the job of reporters to challenge."

As the civil rights movement went forward and reporters struggled with the battle between fairness and falsity, other beats and issues came under similar scrutiny in the late 60s and up through today. Each case may be difficult to examine, but the basics are clear – allowing someone to present a false or misleading assertion in the guise of giving a counter argument is wrong and poor journalism.

As noted earlier, amid the continued cutbacks in resources and reduced in-depth reporting, and the increased demand for speed, viewers/readers, and often lively debates, many news outlets are willing to give two sides a chance to speak and damn the truth or accuracy.

"It's a fundamental tenant of journalism and the goal of objectivity to be fair to both sides; the words 'fair and balanced' are obviously very useful words," said author Eric Alterman, who spoke during an interview. "That's not the same thing as giving equal weight to saying the earth is flat and the earth is round. We still have journalists feeling that it is not their job to referee between truth and falsehood."

He later added, "Falsehood is given the same weight as something that approximates truth. As long as journalists feel that abstract responsibility to be fair, to quote both sides without being willing to accept the honesty and veracity of both sides, they are vulnerable to this exploitation."

In the 1970s, the abortion debate came under the false equivalency cloud. Many of those against legalized abortion claimed higher rates than usual and falsities about what fetuses can and cannot do or feel. Others, in the pro-choice movement would seek to paint the unborn child as almost non-existent and pour on unproven claims about feeling pain or showing signs of brain activity rather than focus on the rights of a mother to protect her own body – something that was done later.

Abortion could be the most divisive issue in the United States, with a 2017 Pew Research study finding 57 percent of respondents believe it should be legal in all or most cases, with 40 percent stating it should be illegal in all or most cases. That is only slightly changed from 20 years ago when 54 percent wanted it legalized and 42 percent were against legalization. While it does show a slight rise for legalization proponents, opposition groups and politicians who agree with them have not backed down.

Unlike the communist witch hunt or civil rights, where one side in those battles had no real basis for opposing the other beyond just prejudice or hype, valid arguments on each side of the abortion debate are accepted.

When the U.S. Supreme Court legalized abortion on demand on Jan. 22, 1973 in Roe v. Wade, it came about during a very newsy two-day period. First, former President Lyndon Johnson died the same day as the court's 7-2 decision, forcing *The New York Times* to offer a rare split headline on Page One that gave LBJ's death top billing, with the abortion news just below it.

The next day, the Nixon Administration announced a Vietnam peace accord. That prompted a three-line front-page header for the *Times*. But there was still space for information on Johnson's funeral and a Watergate story about testimony regarding an illegal payoff.

But the landmark decision did not stop the debates and the false assertions on both sides. Prior to the ruling, the arguments had filled news pages of broadcast programs for years, and only increased afterward as the debate still rages today.

One of the first false equivalences is that abortion became legal in 1973 and violated some long-standing religious and biblical sanctity of life. Opponents, before and after the 1973 ruling, point out the religious doctrine as a clear defense for outlawing the procedures, and news outlets did not and still don't question that assumed history.

But it isn't entirely true. In her 1996 book, *When Abortion Was a Crime*, professor Leslie Reagan reveals that abortions were common in the United States until about 1880, and "widely practiced," contrary to the argument often used by critics and repeated by reporters.

"At conception and the earliest stage of pregnancy, before quickening, no one believed that a human life existed; not even the Catholic Church took this view," Reagan wrote. "Rather, the popular ethic regarding abortion and common law were grounded in the female experience of their own bodies." She later added that until the mid-1800s, "the Catholic Church implicitly accepted early abortions prior to ensoulment ... Not until 1869, at about the same time that abortion became politicized in this country, did the church condemn abortion; in 1895, it condemned therapeutic abortion," which is abortion to save a woman's life.

Irin Carmon, writing at Billmoyers.com, agreed, stating in 2017, "Abortion is as old as antiquity. As long as people have been having sex, there have been women having abortions. The American debate over whether a woman should have the right to end her pregnancy is a relatively new phenomenon. Indeed, for America's first century, abortion wasn't even banned in a single US state." But, he added, nearly every state outlawed abortions by 1880.

Journalists have been following the abortion debate and exposing much of the hypocrisy almost as long as those restrictions have been in place. In her book, Reagan points to a major *Chicago Times* investigation in late 1888 of underground and illegal abortions, which it claimed were widespread – and favoring the rich and affluent.

"The 1888 *Times* exposé is the earliest known in-depth study of illegal abortion," Reagan writes. "The investigation showed abortion to be commercially available in the nation's second largest city despite the criminal abortion law. The reporters retold their conversations with the hundreds of practitioners whom they had approached. They made the private practice of abortion public. As the newspaper published numerous, seemingly confidential conversations with Chicago's practitioners, it described the abortion underground. Abortionists, the journalists found, were drawn from the city's physicians and midwives."

Another false view from the pro-lifers is the claim that women suffer depression after an abortion, even giving it a name – Post Abortion Stress Syndrome, or PASS. "But while this has been a staple of anti-abortion arguments since 1981, it is simply not borne out in the ample scientific literature on the topic," a recent *Irish Post* story on abortion myths stated. "A study of 365,550 Danish women found absolutely zero elevated risk of suicide or depression in the 23 per cent of the sample who'd had terminations, echoing the results of numerous other schematic reviews over decades. PASS is a myth, explicitly dismissed by numerous professional bodies, including the American Psychological Association, the American Psychiatric Association and the Royal College of Obstetricians and Gynaecologists."

But that didn't stop publications, including *Psychology Today*, from offering advice on dealing with it, even though its own article pointed out that "this is not a term that has been accepted by the American Psychiatric Association or the American Psychological Association. In fact, pro-choice advocates accuse their counterparts of making up PASS in order to further their political agendas." That's false equivalency right there – citing an alleged emotional issue in the debate, then noting that it might not be real.

A more recent false claim was that Planned Parenthood, the national non-profit women's health organization that offers health screening, support, testing and abortions, was profiting from selling baby parts of aborted infants. That inaccurate claim came from a group called the Center for Medical Progress (CMP), a right-wing non-profit organization that opposes abortion and has provided funding to ultra-right groups such as the Freedom of Conscience Defense Fund, and also supports anti-gay commerce laws and opposes teaching anti-Islamophobia lessons in school.

On the Planned Parenthood issue, the CMP conducted undercover recordings of Planned Parenthood staffers – in a very James O'Keefe way – and edited them to make it appear that the organization was negotiating to sell baby parts for medical research. In reality, the discussions were about the legal practice of donating fetuses for scientific research and recouping costs, not making a profit.

Factcheck.org investigated when several Republican candidates cited the video in comments against Planned Parenthood in 2015, finding that "the full, unedited video they cite as evidence shows a Planned Parenthood executive repeatedly saying its clinics want to cover their costs, not make money, when donating fetal tissue from abortions for scientific research … The edited video … leaves the impression that (Planned Parenthood Senior Director of Medical Services Deborah) Nucatola is talking about Planned Parenthood affiliates making money from fetal tissue. But the edited video ignores other things Nucatola said that contradict that idea."

But that did not stop the CMP and many news outlets who reported on the issue from jumping to the wrong conclusion and giving pro-lifers another false claim to promote. Many in the National Right to Life Committee still cite the videos in fundraising. I received a call in 2018 seeking donations from the group that included a reference to the video. When I told the person I was a reporter who had covered the issue and knew it was false, she continued to repeat the lie.

The anti-abortionists are not the only ones stretching the truth. Pro-choice arguments often stray into the misleading, or at least the incomplete, and the press gladly picks it up. For one thing, research has shown that press accounts offer an overwhelming focus on pro-choice views and opinions, according to the *Los Angeles Times*, which published a major study on abortion and the media in 1990 that revealed the pro-lifers often get short shrift.

"A comprehensive *Times* study of major newspaper, television and newsmagazine coverage over the last 18 months, including more than 100 interviews with journalists and with activists on both sides of the abortion debate, confirms that this bias often exists," *Times* former media writer David Shaw, among the most respected in the nation, wrote at the time. "Responsible journalists do try to be fair, and many charges of bias in abortion coverage are not valid. But careful examination of stories published and broadcast reveals scores of examples, large and small, that can only be characterized as unfair to the opponents of abortion, either in content, tone, choice of language or prominence of play."

Among his findings: "The news media consistently use language and images that frame the entire abortion debate in terms that implicitly favor abortion-rights advocates; Abortion-rights advocates are often quoted more frequently and characterized more favorably than are abortion opponents; Events and issues favorable to abortion opponents are sometimes ignored or given minimal attention by the media; and many news organizations have given more prominent play to stories on rallies and electoral and legislative victories by abortion-rights advocates than to stories on rallies and electoral and legislative victories by abortion rights opponents."

One general issue that pro-choice advocates seem to gloss over or dismiss, is the ending of a life form. Arguments and court battles continue over whether the fetus is a living human and at what stage, but the idea that an entity is being destroyed in abortion is often ignored or argued away by those who support abortion rights.

Clarke Forsythe, senior counsel for Americans United for Life and author of *Abuse of Discretion: The Inside Story of Roe v. Wade*, pointed to the often-repeated untruth that there are no long-term health effects from abortion. A 2005 study posted by WebMD, a respected online medical information site, found that "Miscarriage and abortion are both stressful events, but a study from Norway suggests that abortion may be associated with more long-term psychological distress."

Tara Murtha, a freelance writer and associate director of strategic communications at the Women's Law Project in Philadelphia, wrote in 2017 on the Poynter.org website that one of the problems with abortion coverage is it often relies on the advocacy groups of both sides rather than medical research and opinion, as well as comments from women who have had abortions. She cited a study that researched views from 31 reporters who have covered the issue.

"More than one-third of participants cited finding new voices and angles as an obstacle to covering abortion," Murtha wrote. "For all their differences, one thing that pro-choice and anti-choice communities may have in common is relying on talking points shared across coalitions, which can make for predictable stories … While it's easy enough to suggest reporters seek to interview medical professionals and women who have had abortions, the reality is that stigma and harassment can prevent such sources from going on the record."

She then stated that "reports of targeted harassment of abortion providers has risen dramatically in the past two years in the wake of discredited anti-Planned Parenthood propaganda videos … Since the videos, even scientists using fetal tissue while conducting life-saving medical research have been intimidated into silence."

Gay rights coverage contained some of the earliest false equivalency examples dating back decades to the time when anti-sodomy laws were enforced, homosexuals were banned from the U.S. military, and police would routinely harass and even arrest gay men and women.

Until gay marriage was legalized by the U.S. Supreme Court in 2015, that lack of equality not only helped support the harassment, but also the limited rights of gay couples – ranging from spousal medical insurance to serving in the military.

During the coverage of those changes, and the ongoing debates today related to transgender rights and further equality issues, the myths and false information from opponents can still seep through. The earliest claims were that gays were some sort of deviants, with a propensity toward pedophilia and other abuses of children.

When California state senator John Briggs proposed a state law banning gay teachers from working in local schools, he pushed the pedophilia claim and some in the media picked it up. The ballot measure, Proposition 6, was defeated in 1978, but only after strong opposition from gay rights supporters, including San Francisco Supervisor Harvey Milk, one of the first openly gay public officials who was assassinated just weeks later.

"Briggs' primary argument against gay teachers was his belief that gay people were more likely to be child molesters," *ThinkProgress'* Zack Ford wrote in a 2017 story that noted the same argument was being used in the more recent transgender bathroom access debate. "Often, Briggs insisted that gay people could only perpetuate their existence by 'recruiting' young people, the implication being that molestation was how that recruitment functioned. 'Safety' was the primary argument then as it is in anti-trans campaigns now."

He cited a 1978 debate between Milk and Briggs in which Milk named statistics that showed no increased deviant behavior among gay men and woman compared to non-gays, which Briggs dismissed without cause.

Another long-time claim has been biblical direction with many anti-gay voices citing scripture to claim that homosexuality was "an abomination." Opponents of that claim point to other biblical references that people do not follow, including stoning of sinners and not eating shellfish.

"There are two passages in Leviticus which are most often cited–18:22 and 20:13 – that deem a man 'lying with' another man 'detestable,' and Romans 1:26-27, which castigates men for doing 'shameful acts' with other men," Attorney Howard Ross, who is also the author of *Everyday Bias: Identifying and Navigating Unconscious Judgments in Our Daily Lives*, wrote in an online piece about false equivalency in the gay rights debate. "But, of course, if we are to consider the Bible to be the absolute law then we have to keep in mind that Deuteronomy 22:20-21 says that if a woman has sex before marriage, the men of her town must stone her to death at her father's doorstep. Judges 11:30-31 and 34-35 states that a man may sacrifice his daughter to thank God for giving him a triumph. Leviticus 25:44-45 permits the enslavement of foreigners, and Exodus 31:14 clearly states that 'Everyone who (works on the Sabbath) shall surely be put to death; for whoever does any work on it, that person shall be cut off from among his people.'"

The 2007 documentary, *For the Bible Tells Me So*, offers further rebuttal to the biblical excuse for opposing gay rights by citing both gay rights activist and theological experts, in and out of the church, who use many of Ross's same arguments to counter the false claim.

Other false claims that received media attention include arguments that marriage is for procreation only, children of gay parents are less happy, that gay marriage would lead to polygamy or bestiality, and that domestic partnerships and civil unions accomplish the same goals as marriage. All false and all at one time or another cited by gay marriage or gay rights opponents. As recently as 2015, *Politico* allowed a guest writer to cite the polygamy theory.

"The question presents itself: Where does the next advance come?" Fredrik DeBoer wrote in *Politico* in 2015, shortly after the gay marriage Supreme Court ruling. "The answer is going to make nearly everyone uncomfortable: Now that we've defined that love and devotion and family isn't driven by gender alone, why should it be limited to just two individuals? The most natural advance next for marriage lies in legalized polygamy."

Just days later in the same publication, gay rights activist Jonathan Rausch slammed the claim, writing, "The shortest answer is in some ways the best: Please stop changing the subject! When you straights give yourselves the right to marry two people or your brother or your dog or a toaster, we gay people should get that right, too. Until then, kindly be serious. If I sound exasperated, it's because the polygamy argument doesn't stand up to scrutiny. That doesn't stop it from popping up everywhere."

It also does not stop many of the other false arguments that were resurrected in recent years with the transgender debate that included laws, such as one in North Carolina, that required men and women to use the bathroom designate for their birth gender. Much of the coverage of that issue included the old pedophilia or sexual assault scares that opponents feared would increase. They have not of course.

But in such controversial issues, many of them based in ignorance or fear, it is not surprising that opponents would point to the most outlandish claims to stoke worries and drive opposition. The problem comes when the media allows these false claims and fear-based assertions to receive validation – which is the basis of false equivalency.

Many observers have compared the anti-gay rhetoric, and media support for it, to the false claims of the civil rights era, as noted earlier. The efforts to denigrate black and other minority citizens with phony arguments of lesser intelligence, dangerous behavior and even genetic limitations were all too common. Not to mention fears that integrating black and white customers, students or soldiers would cause disruption. When gays in the military or gay marriage were legalized, the same false attacks and claims of disruption were spread in the press.

"Clearly, there is definitely a parallel between gay rights and civil rights," Bill Kovarik, professor of journalism at Radford University and author of *Revolutions in Communication: Media History from Gutenberg to the Digital Age*, told me back in 2012. "People react out of fear to things they don't understand and they don't try to understand. And the media is supposed to help with that, the media is our bridge across cultures not our defense of the status quo."

But in many cases, news coverage of these stories makes the mistake of giving the opposition a chance to speak when their objection is rooted only in discrimination or incorrect facts, just as they did more than 50 years ago.

"It's absolutely our responsibility to check, to the best of our ability, to check on those who claim expertise," said James Rainey, former media writer for the *Los Angeles Times*. "And things that are repeated, like equating gay marriage or gay rights with worries about pedophiles. I don't see any reason to dignify those kinds of views, even if they claim some expertise about that. I don't think there is any proof that gay parents have not shown they have been more than adequate parents. I don't see why you need to let people roll out those arguments every time you talk about that issue."

Among the groups often sought for comment on the anti-gay rights side is the Family Research Council. During my time at *Media Matters*, we documented the group's regular appearances on major cable outlets, but often with little information on its questionable past and designation as a hate group.

In November of 2010, the Southern Poverty Law Center listed the Family Research Council as an anti-gay hate group due to its "propagation of known falsehoods" about the LGBT community. Since being listed, however, FRC spokespersons had been invited more than

50 times as of 2012 to discuss issues ranging from the repeal of "Don't Ask, Don't Tell," to the 2012 presidential campaign

Despite FRC's long history of producing anti-gay propaganda, every major news network has invited the group on national television while failing to acknowledge its hate group designation. As recently as May 2018, FRC leader Tony Perkins was still being cited as a valid commentator on gay rights and was appointed to the U.S. Commission on International Religious Freedom, giving him even more influence.

Back in 2012, at the height of the gay marriage debate, *Media Matters* collected several examples of false anti-gay views and assertions that were allowed on cable television and other outlets, and the mixed ways they were being countered – or not – by journalists.

Chris Matthews, host of MSNBC's Hardball, had Perkins on the air May 10, 2012, a day after Obama's gay marriage support announcement, and proceeded to challenge many of his claims, including Perkins' assertion that research has found that parents can influence a child's sexual orientation.

Perkins also appeared on both CNN's *State of the Union* with Candy Crowley and CBS' *Face the Nation* on Sunday without being equally challenged for incorrect and outlandish claims.

On CNN, Perkins said that denying same-sex couples the right to marry is a matter of "defending the family, the cornerstone of civilization," adding, "it's more than marriage. It's about the education of our children. It's about religious freedom. It's about public accommodations." Crowley did not cite Perkins' troubling background. On *Face the Nation*, host Bob Schieffer did not challenge Perkins' claim that parents will "lose the right to determine what their children are taught in school. Religious organizations forced to recognize or allow their facilities to be used for weddings such as this."

Aaron McQuade, director of news and field media for GLAAD (Gay and Lesbian Alliance Against Defamation), said at the time: "It's not good journalism to allow a source to give your audience incorrect facts any more than it is not good journalism to give them yourself." He later added, "They've brought them on to create some sort 'balance.' What they do is actually imbalance. There is nobody on the pro-LGBT side whose voice is as extreme as those on the anti-LGBT side."

Another past example was a May 26, 2011 appearance on Fox News by Perkins, in which he espoused several stereotypical and inaccurate claims in a discussion of a gay rights tolerance lesson plan for a California school. Perkins accused the school of trying to "indoctrinate" children "into homosexuality." Perkins then proceeded to compare teaching kids about gender diversity in nature to encouraging kids to avoid monogamy. Fox host Martha MacCallum did not challenge any of Perkins false claims or inform the viewers of FRC's designation as a hate group.

MacCallum also advanced an increasingly popular argument used to prevent children from participating in anti-bullying programs in school: that there's just not enough time to learn about reading, math, and respecting LGBT people. "I just want to interject one other thought to this. As a parent of three kids, I think I agree with you both," she said. "It's very important to teach understanding about people and to obviously warn kids against any kind of bullying that goes on in schools and it does. But when I look across the country and I see the number of children who are proficient in reading and math, okay, my question to this school system is 'have you taught these children the things that it's your job to teach them and why are we spending two days having this discussion in school?'"

Then there was a Dec. 11, 2011 Fox News segment on a Macy's employee who was fired for refusing to let a transgendered teen use a women's fitting room. The segment included Mathew Staver, founder of the anti-LGBT Liberty Counsel.

Fox host Shannon Bream allowed Staver to put forth several false claims about transgendered citizens, including referring to the transgender teen as "a man... wearing lipstick" and promoting the myth that transgender protections put women and girls "in jeopardy."

Bream also did not mention that Staver's view of transgender people has been strongly rejected by the American Psychological Association, which condemns attempts to discriminate on the basis of gender identity.

Such examples were not limited to broadcast and cable outlets. Newspapers have done their part as well to give credibility to controversial gay rights opponents, according to observers.

GLAAD has highlighted a Jan. 2, 2011, *Boston Globe* article on gay rights battles in court that quoted Peter Labarbera, president of Americans for Truth About Homosexuality, referring to gay marriage as "taxpayer-funded homosexuality" without challenging the misleading phrase. The *Globe* failed to cite ATAH and Labarbera's histories as promoters of false information about gays and lesbians, which include the Southern Poverty Law Center stating in 2010 that "AFTAH is notable for its posting of the utterly discredited work of Paul Cameron [of the Family Research Institute; see below], who has claimed that gays and lesbians live vastly shorter lives than heterosexuals. Among the Cameron propaganda published by AFTAH are 2007 claims that gays and lesbians in Norway and Denmark live 24 fewer years than heterosexuals. Reviewing that claim, Danish epidemiologist Morten Frisch found that it had no scientific basis."

For those who monitor gay rights coverage, there can be a fair approach. One moment came on June 17, 2011, with a CNN interview of former New York Giant David Tyree, who spoke out against gay marriage. CNN host Kyra Phillips countered Tyree's claim that gay marriage could cause anarchy.

"Where is the evidence though that gay marriage has any negative impact on other marriages or the sanctity of marriage or culture or children? Where is your evidence?" she asked. Tyree then declined to provide any evidence or statistics, saying "to redefine marriage changes everything." Phillips later cited a 24-year-long study from UCLA that found children of lesbian parents "gained more respect for diversity, more respect for differences." Phillips later explained her views on challenging such comments in an e-mail to *Media Matters*: "I often talk with people with strong opinions that are inflammatory. I always do what I can to shine a light on a guest's prepared talking points. Like my CNN colleagues, it's our job to expose and challenge purposefully misleading rhetoric."

MSNBC offered a similar challenge in a June 28, 2011, segment in which host Thomas Roberts oversaw a gay marriage debate between the Rev. Al Sharpton and National Organization for Marriage President Brian Brown. When Brown claimed that gay marriage was a challenge to heterosexual marriage, Roberts questioned the claim, noting that divorce is more of a challenge to marriage than gay marriage. Roberts also challenged Brown's claim that teaching gay rights in schools is not similar to teaching tolerance.

Even Fox has shown it can provide proper journalistic challenges to incorrect anti-gay claims. When Brown appeared with John Stossel on the August 18, 2011, edition of Stossel's Fox Business program, Brown claimed there were "serious consequences" caused by marriage equality, including the myth that children will be forced to learn about same-sex marriage in school. Stossel challenged Brown, asking him how teaching kids that marriage equality is "just fine" would hurt marriage. During the interview, Stossel also announced that he was just "not convinced [same-sex marriage] is a threat to marriage." He asked, "so what?" when Brown began fear mongering about the "total deconstruction of marriage."

When Brown asserted that the government should support heterosexual marriage because it is "true and good and beautiful," the audience broke out into laughter. "I don't want the state deciding what's good and beautiful," Stossel responded.

"If we're journalists who abide by the principles of truth telling and fairness, doesn't it make sense when you have advocates, no matter what side they are on, when they purport certain things and put those facts out there, we have an obligation to call them on those facts," said Kevin Smith, former president of the Society of Professional Journalists and past chair of the SPJ ethics committee. "That's Journalism 101. When you have people coming on network television and saying the things they're saying, the journalist needs to call them on it. I think a lot of these people would think twice about going on and shooting off at the hip, enforcing stereotypes and saying things that are just ludicrous."

FALSE AND DEADLY?

A recent phenomenon among the false equivalency crowd had been vaccinations. Many people have followed the fake claim for years that the annual influenza, or "flu," vaccine caused the flu. Mainstream media rarely went with this assertion during most regular related reporting. It was some of the outlandish fringe web outlets, and some conspiracy television that pushed most of it.

But it continues with outlets like the ultra-fake news site, YourNewsWire.com, reporting as recently as January 2018 that a Centers for Disease Control and Prevention doctor had said the flu shot was spreading the virus. Snopes.com, the respected fact-checking site, which labeled YourNewsWire.com a "disreputable conspiracy disseminator," quickly labeled the claim "false," noting that "the Centers for Disease Control and Prevention, in fact, urges Americans to get the flu vaccine every year. They also maintain that the shot is largely safe for most people."

While the flu vaccine falsehood has likely caused many Americans to forgo the shot, and then get sick, the worst lie revolves around other immunizations, especially those required for school-aged children to block measles, mumps, chicken pox and more dangerous afflictions such as polio and whooping cough.

With the rise in autism over the past 15 years, from one in 150 children born autistic in the U.S. in 1992, and diagnosed in 2000, to one in 59 in 2006, and diagnosed in 2014, a slow causal claim was vaccines, based in part on false rumor sites and outspoken celebrities with no valid basis whatsoever.

Among those sites is the Healthyhomeeconomist.com and quack editor Sarah Pope, whose own website reveals she has no medical, scientific or journalistic training – she holds degrees in economics and government administration. She also has ties to the Weston A. Price Foundation, another misleading organization that, among other things, promotes drinking raw milk and has been criticized by Food and Drug Administration for spreading such dangerous advice.

Pope pushed the false narrative on vaccines as recently as May 24, 2018, in a piece titled "Six Reasons to Say NO to Vaccination." Reason Number one: "Pharmaceutical companies can't be trusted (ever). Are you really going to take these companies at their word that these shots are safe when money and profits are impacted by their answer?" she asks. The remaining five are just as ridiculous, including #6, which is basically that once you are vaccinated you cannot remove the vaccine.

But that has not stopped some news outlets from giving her a voice. A 2014 *USA Today* story about the rise in childhood diseases and the spread of anti-vaccination views quoted Pope as claiming her three children contracted whooping cough and survived but failed to note her outlandish ties and lack of training.

A quick look at the Internet finds many similar sites with bogus fear-mongering articles based on nonsense claims and, likely, lots of readers. From sites like VacTruth.com to Thankyourbody.com.

An educational research article posted in 2018 by the College of Physicians of Philadelphia traces the original autistic-vaccine claim to a 1995 study by a group of British researchers published in *The Lancet*, a British-based medical journal, "showing that individuals who had been vaccinated with the measles-mumps-rubella vaccine (MMR) were more likely to have bowel disease than individuals who had not received MMR."

One of these researchers was gastroenterologist Andrew Wakefield, who in 1998 co-published a case series study in *The Lancet* claiming that in many of the 12 cases they found measles virus in the digestive systems of children who had exhibited autism symptoms after MMR vaccination.

"Though in the paper they stated that they could not demonstrate a causal relationship between MMR vaccination and autism," the Philadelphia Physicians article stated, "Wakefield suggested in a video released to coincide with the paper's publication that a causal relationship existed between the MMR and autism... Reaction to the Wakefield publication was immediate. Press outlets covered the news widely and frightened parents began to delay or completely refuse vaccination for their children, both in Britain and the United States. MMR vaccination rates in Britain plummeted."

That was all it took to get the hysteria going, and it has only seemed to grow, even though a link between MMR and autism has been "studied exhaustively and no reputable, relevant study confirmed Wakefield's findings; instead, many well-designed studies have found no link between MMR and bowel disease or MMR and autism."

As for Wakefield's research, *The Lancet* eventually discounted it, first in 2004, writing that Wakefield "should have revealed to the journal that he had been paid by attorneys seeking to file lawsuits against vaccine manufacturers" calling the data "fatally flawed." By 2010, the journal had completely retracted the paper itself.

A February 28, 2018, *Time* magazine story on the 20th anniversary of Wakefield's misleading article and the vaccine issue said it took nearly two decades for the British vaccination rates to recover from the false information, stating, "By the end, UK families had experienced more than 12,000 cases of measles, hundreds of hospitalizations – many with serious complications – and at least three deaths."

But it didn't stop a slew of celebrities, from Jenny McCarthy, the mother of an autistic child, to Oprah Winfrey, from spreading the myth, along with never-ending web sites and social media claims that keep the lie going today. Donald Trump also speculated on the dangers of immunization back in 2012. The impact is already being felt, according to the U.S. Centers for Disease Control and Prevention, which finds an alarming number of parents still holding back their kids from the shots.

"Trust in vaccinations is on the decline in the United States, even as fears of a major outbreak that the government isn't prepared to address remain high," *U.S. News & World Report* stated in a May 21, 2018, story. "Trends public health officials say have worrying implications for the prevention of deadly diseases." It cited an American Society for Microbiology and Research America survey that found the percentage of American adults who say it's "very important" to have their children vaccinated dropped 11 points in the past decade, to 71 percent in 2018 from 82 percent in 2008: "The percentage that expressed confidence in the system for evaluating the safety of vaccines to determine their proper use dropped 8 percentage points, from 85 percent in 2008 to 77 percent in 2018."

The spreading of those diseases is on the rise, according to *Time*, which wrote: "In the U.S., measles was declared eliminated in 2000. Since 2000, however, there has been a resurgence of measles, with more than 2,216 reported cases. Wakefield's anti-vaccine fanaticism contributed to the 2015 outbreak in Disneyland in California, which eventually infected more than 130 people, and to the 2017 measles outbreaks in Minnesota, where his message persuaded many parents not to vaccinate their children. The vaccine-autism myth has also prompted an alarming number of millennials – the generation that came of age in the era of

Wakefield's misinformation – in the U.S. not to vaccinate their children. Vaccine reluctance does not apply just to measles; flu kills 100 to 300 children under age 5 each year, and up to 85% of them were not vaccinated when they died."

The *Time* and *U.S. News* stories are stating the case that myths about vaccines are not only incorrect, but dangerous. They have some success in countering the Lancet-type stories and outright lies of a YourNewsWire.com or HealthyHomeEconomist.com. But with the resource cutbacks mentioned earlier and the ability for false websites to pop-up as they please, the onus is more and more on both reporters with valid credentials, and readers, to seek out the facts and weed out the lies.

The same goes for the gun debate, which is almost as divisive as the abortion question, due to the Second Amendment claims by the National Rifle Association and others and their influence in Congress. Polling, however, shows a much more lopsided view, according to Gallup, which found a steady rise in the percentage of Americans who want stricter gun laws. Its latest survey in March 2018 revealed that 67 percent of respondents wanted stricter gun laws, compared to just four percent who wanted them less strict and 28 percent wanting them kept as is. That's a slight rise from 60 percent wanting stricter laws in 2017, 55 percent in 2016 and 2015, and 47 percent in 2014.

The power of the NRA has done well to push its agenda even with so little public support. *PolitiFact* reports that between 1998 and 2018, the NRA has spent more than $200 million on political activities, including candidate and party contributions, independent expenditures and lobbying. CNN reported in February 2018 that eight members of Congress had received more than $1 million each from the NRA during their careers, and 23 had received at least $100,000 each.

It is also the misleading claim that the Second Amendment to the U.S. Constitution gives private residents the right to own any guns and as many as they wish – that may be the biggest false equivalency allowed by journalists. The Second Amendment states: "A well-regulated Militia, being necessary to the security of a free State, the right of the people to keep and bear Arms, shall not be infringed."

A simple grammatical reading of that sentence indicates it is the use of firearms for a well-regulated militia – such as an army or a military organization. Merriam-Webster defines militia as "a part of the organized armed forces of a country liable to call only in emergency; a body of citizens organized for military service; the whole body of able-bodied male citizens declared by law as being subject to call to military service." It would seem not to apply to private citizens and their ownership of firearms.

While the U.S. Supreme Court rulings on the issue have been essentially pro-gun in recent years, it is in a limited way. The Legal Information Institute at Cornell Law School writes that gun rights verdicts on the high court date back to 1939 when the justices ruled in United States v. Miller. 307 U.S. 174. The Court adopted "a collective rights approach ... determining that Congress could regulate a sawed-off shotgun that had moved in interstate commerce under the National Firearms Act of 1934 because the evidence did not suggest that the shotgun 'has some reasonable relationship to the preservation or efficiency of a well-regulated militia.'"

But since 2008, and a more conservative majority on the high court, two rulings led to the repeal of local handgun restrictions in Chicago and Washington, D.C. First in 2008 with District of Columbia v. Heller (07-290). In a 5-4 decision, the court ruled that the Second Amendment established an individual right for U.S. citizens to possess firearms and struck down the D.C. ban. Two years later, in McDonald v. City of Chicago (08-1521), the justices again ruled, 5-4, that "the intentions of the framers and ratifiers of the Fourteenth Amendment, held that the

Second Amendment applies to the states through the incorporation doctrine."

There is still disagreement over how those rulings on handguns apply to broader background checks, assault weapon bans and even limitations on ownership for convicted felons or the mentally ill. The interpretation of the Second Amendment, part of a document written more than 200 years ago, applied today with more lethal weapons and in an age when gun violence and mass shootings are exploding.

"Several questions still remain unanswered, such as whether regulations less stringent than the D.C. statute implicate the Second Amendment, whether lower courts will apply their dicta regarding permissible restrictions, and what level of scrutiny the courts should apply when analyzing a statute that infringes on the Second Amendment," the Cornell article said.

All this needs to be considered when news outlets seek to strike a balance in the gun debate, so as not to allow either side to put forth false claims. Citing the Second Amendment for gun rights, commentators can be tricky if they assume it is settled law for all guns. But opponents get caught up in the emotion of the tragic school shootings, with the Parkland, Fla., attack on Feb. 14, 2018 that left 17 dead sparking a real national student movement.

That and other shootings also brought out the misleading claims on both sides. A *PolitiFact* check found a string of false claims by gun opponents in 2018, among them:

- o **Gifford PAC, an anti-gun political committee** named for former Congresswoman Gabrielle Gifford, who was wounded in a gun attack, claiming "Paul Ryan has blocked all action to strengthen our gun laws." Not true.

o **Montana Gov. Steve Bullock**, a possible Democratic contender for president in 2020, stating, "A quarter of our guns are sold outside of the background checks." Not true.

o **Television journalist Jeff Greenfield** said: "In the rest of the world, there have been 18 school shootings in the last twenty years. In the U.S., there have been 18 school shootings since January 1." Not true.

Among the biggest misnomers allowed by news outlets is the claim that massive shootings and assault weapons are a major cause of gun-related crime. It is true the phenomenon of such massacres in the United States is like no other situation worldwide. But more shooting deaths and injuries come from other handgun and non-massacre killings each year, according to the U.S. Centers for Disease Control and Prevention, which tracks homicide causes.

CDCP reveals that an average of 13,000 annual gun-related homicides occurred in recent years, including nearly two-thirds from suicide. That rate is some 25 times higher than the average of other high-income countries and is growing – from 11 per 100,000 residents in 2015 to 12 in 2016.

A smaller percentage of those deaths are from mass shootings, which seem to get the most attention. According to Gunviolencearchive.org, a non-profit group that tracks such statistics, there were more than 15,000 gun-related deaths in 2017, but fewer than 400 from mass killings. "In contrast, deaths from ladder falls reduce life expectancy at least twice as much; choking on food lower life expectancy nearly 4 times as much and bathtub drownings are 5 times as severe as mass shootings in terms of their effect on life expectancy," Forbes.com wrote in 2017.

Another false claim is that restricting legal gun use will cut down on gun-related crimes, which are most often done with illegal guns. A 2018 *PolitiFact* item reported, "that in the 13 states with the fewest restrictions on gun ownership, 40 percent of inmates illegally obtained the gun they used ... only about 13 percent purchased the gun from a store or pawn shop. In the other 37 states, 60 percent of inmates illegally procured the gun they used."

Rather than point to illegal guns as a serious culprit, most news accounts quote anti-gun voices as seeking tighter restrictions on legal guns rather than beefed up efforts to stop the illegal gun trafficking.

"Media stories in the wake of mass shootings typically feature a laundry list of mistakes that reflect their writers' inexperience with guns and gun culture," Rachael Larimore, online managing editor of *the Weekly Standard*, wrote at *Slate* in 2016 after the Orlando shooting. "Some of them are small but telling: conflating automatic and semi-automatic weapons, assault rifle and assault weapon, caliber and gauge – all demonstrating a general lack of familiarity with firearms. Some of them are bigger. Like calling for 'common-sense gun control' and 'universal background checks' after instances in which a shooter purchased a gun legally and passed background checks. Or focusing on mass shootings involving assault weapons – and thereby ignoring statistics that show that far more people die from handguns."

That does not mean pro-gun advocates don't spew their share of fake claims that the press gladly repeats in a false equivalency mode. *PolitiFact* continuously tracks such misstatements, including the following from early 2018:

- o **New NRA president Oliver North** claiming perpetrators of school shootings "have been drugged in many cases ... many of these young boys have been on Ritalin since they were in kindergarten." False!

- o **RevolutionRadio.org**, a right-wing website, claiming "Democrats go full tyranny: now demand nationwide gun confiscation from law-abiding Americans ... at gunpoint, of course." False!

- o **Libertyheadlines.com** reporting, "Seattle Police begin gun confiscations; no laws broken, no warrant, no charges." False!

In fact, of the 509 statements or news reports on guns it has fact-checked dating back to 2007, *PolitiFact* found that 216, or 42 percent, were either false, mostly false or "pants on fire," the worst of the lies. These range from Barack Obama falsely stating in 2012 that "Operation Fast and Furious," a controversial federal gun-tracking program in Mexico, began under the Bush Administration to numerous National Rifle Association lies, among them NRA Leader Wayne LaPierre claiming New York City mayor Michael Bloomberg kept armed National Guardsman out of the city after Hurricane Sandy.

When the NRA spouts false claims, much of it is repeated on NRA TV, its popular online program, which is then often picked up by conservative media outlets, especially Fox News. That spreads the lies even further. A lengthy guide to NRA TV posted by *Media Matters* on March 2, 2018, offered a litany of misinformation examples from NRA TV hosts, from Dana Loesch claiming Women's March co-founder Linda Sarsour "believes in overthrowing U.S. government for Sharia law" to host Grant Stinchfield saying it would be "simply unacceptable" to make it more difficult for the Las Vegas gunman to get his firearms.

Loesch drew widespread attention and criticism in an NRA TV video posted in March 2018 that falsely attacked mainstream media outlets for allegedly lying and undermining the country. She said, in part, "To every lying member of the media, to every Hollywood phony, to the role model athletes who use their free speech to alter and undermine what our flag represents … to those who stain honest reporting with partisanship … your time is running out." It, of course, offered no examples or proof and any such misreporting and ignored NRA TV's own list of unethical "journalism."

But it did get picked up by other news outlets, from Fox News to *USA Today* and more. The video was the latest in a string of such online messages Loesch had posted on NRA TV dating back to 2017 that attacked media outlets and threatened unspecified opposition. An earlier one declared "they use their media to assassinate real news" and later says the only way to "fight this violence of lies is with a clenched fist."

Even *The New York Times* noted Loesch's impact, calling her a "telegenic warrior" in a January 2018 story that also referred to her as "Wonder Woman." But it detailed her troubled employment record as well, stating, "…in 2010, she joined Andrew Breitbart at his website, one of several new voices railing against establishment politics and media bias. After Mr. Breitbart died in 2012, Ms. Loesch clashed with Steve Bannon, the former Trump ally who had been named executive chair of *Breitbart News*. She sued to get out of her contract."

It later added that in 2014, she moved to Dallas to work for The Blaze. But her "particular brand of attack proved unpalatable to mainstream audiences. In 2012, CNN, which had hired her as a political commentator, distanced itself from comments she made on her radio show supporting a group of Marines who urinated on dead Taliban soldiers. She claims the reporting of her comments was 'disingenuous.'

A year later, she was banned from the now defunct "Piers Morgan Live" after getting into a Twitter fight with the host."

I've known Dana Loesch for years from my many visits to CPAC, where she often set up on radio row. She was always responsive and kind to me and willing to give a comment for a story without the anti-liberal rants of many others on the right I have encountered. We spent more time in those moments discussing our children than heated politics. She once said I was "too good for *Media Matters*" and urged me to leave on several occasions. It seems she went far right and angry in exchange for whatever the NRA is paying her and giving her a major platform to spew their message.

Even with the NRA's power and influence, it still takes more than their efforts alone to spread false claims about guns as the media battle increases. When news outlets allow the false claims to be pushed, on either side, then the false equivalency persists.

The most damaging current false balance, and the one that continues to permeate, surrounds climate change – the continued debate over whether climate change, or global warming, exists. The scientific finding that earth temperatures are rising at a higher rate than in the past, and that this is due to man-made causes such as increased fossil-fuel burning, fracking to unearth natural gas supplies, and even water vapor, is nearly universal.

"On Earth, human activities are changing the natural greenhouse," a NASA fact-page on climate change states. "Over the last century the burning of fossil fuels like coal and oil has increased the concentration of atmospheric carbon dioxide (CO_2). This happens because the coal or oil burning process combines carbon with oxygen in the air to make CO_2. To a lesser extent, the clearing of land for agriculture, industry, and other human activities has increased concentrations of greenhouse gases."

The NASA page also states that the causes of climate change, and the "greenhouse effect," stem from several areas – both natural and man-made, which include:

- **Water vapor.** The most abundant greenhouse gas acts as a feedback to the climate. Water vapor increases as the Earth's atmosphere warms, but so does the possibility of clouds and precipitation, making these some of the most important feedback mechanisms to the greenhouse effect.

- **Carbon dioxide (CO2).** A minor but very important component of the atmosphere, carbon dioxide is released through natural processes such as respiration and volcano eruptions and through human activities such as deforestation, land use changes, and burning fossil fuels. Humans have increased atmospheric CO2 concentration by more than a third since the Industrial Revolution began. This is the most important long-lived "forcing" of climate change.

- **Methane.** A hydrocarbon gas produced both through natural sources and human activities, including the decomposition of wastes in landfills, agriculture, and especially rice cultivation, as well as ruminant digestion and manure management associated with domestic livestock. On a molecule-for-molecule basis, methane is a far more active greenhouse gas than carbon dioxide, but also one which is much less abundant in the atmosphere.

o **Nitrous oxide.** A powerful greenhouse gas produced by soil cultivation practices, especially the use of commercial and organic fertilizers, fossil fuel combustion, nitric acid production, and biomass burning.

o **Chlorofluorocarbons (CFCs).** Synthetic compounds entirely of industrial origin used in a number of applications, but now largely regulated in production and release to the atmosphere by international agreement for their ability to contribute to destruction of the ozone layer. They are also greenhouse gases.

The fact-page also cites the Intergovernmental Panel on Climate Change (IPCC), which is "the international body for assessing the science related to climate change, which was created in 1988 by the World Meteorological Organization (WMO) and United Nations Environment Programme (UNEP) to provide policymakers with regular assessments of the scientific basis of climate change, its impacts and future risks, and options for adaptation and mitigation."

An IPCC 2014 report found that, "Human influence on the climate system is clear, and recent anthropogenic emissions of green-house gases are the highest in history. Recent climate changes have had widespread impacts on human and natural systems." It later added, "Warming of the climate system is unequivocal, and since the 1950s, many of the observed changes are unprecedented over decades to millennia. The atmosphere and ocean have warmed, the amounts of snow and ice have diminished, and sea level has risen."

The examples of scientific evidence backing up claims that climate change is real, temperatures are rising at an inordinate rate and that human activity is a chief cause are endless – from *National Geographic*, which published an entire edition on the issue in 2016, to Encyclopedia Britannica, which states, "Some 97 percent of scientists involved in climate research agree that it is extremely likely that much of the warming observed since the early 1900s results from human activities."

That 97 percent is repeated worldwide and backed up by research that seems to be accepted in most countries except the United States. For some reason, many news outlets here – and many politicians who speak to them – find the need to question or dismiss the science, often in a way similar to the anti-vaccination crowd. But for many, the climate change denials are more dangerous.

Why? Simply because the threat is more abundant and is seen already in increased natural disasters from hurricanes and strong storms to wild fluctuations in temperature that impact a broad swath of things.

The National Oceanic and Atmospheric Administration of the U.S. Department of Commerce detailed specific changes due to man-made climate change in an online report that stated: "Across the country, changes to water resources are of critical concern. In some regions, particularly in the western United States, drought is an important factor, conditions are critically affecting local communities. Less snow accumulation in the mountains is important in the West and Alaska where the snowpack stores water for later use. In the Midwest and northeastern states, the number of heavy downpours has substantially increased over the past few decades. In many regions, floods and water quality problems are likely to be worse because of climate change."

For some reason, many in the media have felt the need to give the anti-climate change voices space to repeat their often-misleading and outright incorrect claims. In the name of fairness and balance they commit the worst of the false equivalencies.

"There is no debate over climate change, something like 97% of scientists in the world believe in climate change so every time you do a story on climate change do you have to have a climate change denier on?" Dan Shelley, executive director of the Radio and Television News Directors Association, told me in an interview. "I don't think so. I think that newsrooms should consider that if 97% are convinced something is true, to adequately present the story one percent should be about how there isn't climate change, there is a danger and newsrooms do need to do a very serious job at trying to eliminate false equivalency. You do need to be fair and balanced, but that doesn't mean you need to seek out an opposing point of view even if it's not necessary. Some facts are facts and not alternative facts."

Media writer Eric Alterman wrote in 2013 that, "The mainstream media irresponsibly treats uncredentialled climate deniers – often funded through mechanisms such as [the conservative billionaire Koch Brothers] – with the same degree of respect as climate scientists who are qualified to make these judgments. Moreover, many U.S. meteorologists who have no particular expertise in climatology play the role of climate deniers to the general public because, according to meteorologist and writer Bob Henson, 'There is a little bit of elitist-versus-populist tensions.' He explains that, 'There are meteorologists who feel, 'Just because I have a bachelor's degree doesn't mean I don't know what's going on.'"

Among the most egregious in perpetuating the climate change lie was *The Wall Street Journal* editorial page, according to a *Media Matters* report in 2012, which found, "To forestall policy on climate change, *The Wall Street Journal* editorial board routinely downplays scientific consensus, overstates the cost of taking action, and claims that politics, not science, motivate those concerned about the climate. But an analysis of more than 100 editorials from 1976 to present shows that *The Wall Street Journal* used these same rhetorical tactics in previous decades on acid rain and ozone depletion and they did not stand the test of time."

A 2013 *Media Matters* review of CNBC coverage found that more than half of its climate change segments during the first six months of that year were misleading, stating, "The majority of CNBC's coverage in the first half of 2013 cast doubt on whether manmade climate change exists. However, denial is not prudent for the business professionals viewing CNBC, who can reduce risk and increase profits by analyzing how climate change is impacting their industries." I followed with a story in which most business journalists said such climate change denial is not good for business reporting. "I accept the evidence of climate change," *Los Angeles Times* business columnist Michael Hiltzik said in my story. "I don't think I've ever run into a legitimate business leader or business owner in the course of my reporting who doesn't. I think, for the most part, it is settled science and the debate is really over what to do about it."

More recently, Sinclair Broadcasting, the growing conservative television affiliate chain, was accused in April 2018 of forcing a reporter to add anti-climate change voices for stories and firing her when she refused. *Buzzfeed* wrote that Sinclair executives "reprimanded and ultimately ousted a local news reporter who refused to seed doubt about man-made climate change and 'balance' her stories in a more conservative direction."

That reporter was Suri Crowe, an employee of WSET-TV in Lynchburg, Virginia, who reportedly provided *Buzzfeed* with what was labeled, "company documents," detailing pressure to include climate change-deniers in her reports. "In one 2015 instance, the former news director of WSET ... Len Stevens, criticized ... Crowe because she 'clearly laid out the argument that human activities cause global warming, but had nothing from the side that questions the science behind such claims and points to more natural causes for such warming.'" She said she was also ordered to include Donald Trump's climate change opinion in the story as well.

A November 2016 piece in *The Guardian* on false equivalency and climate change coverage declared that giving the anti-climate change side equal space to spout what is unproven theory is among the most dangerous examples of the false balance approach. "When the weight of scientific evidence points incontrovertibly one direction, doggedly reporting both 'sides' equally can result in misleading coverage," the story said, later noting, "Part of the problem is that good science reporting requires a keen understanding of scientific method and the importance of evidence. In the absence of this, dubious views can perpetuate."

The Guardian story cited a 2011 independent review of the BBC and its science coverage that, among other things, singled out the state-run media outlet for their "undue attention to marginal opinion on the subject of man-made climate change, among other issues. Despite the overwhelming scientific evidence that human activity is driving climate change, the report found that several BBC shows fell victim to an 'over-rigid application of editorial guidelines on impartiality,' resulting in far too much airtime for climate change deniers."

Columbia Journalism Review in 2014 posted a lengthy investigation of climate change coverage and false balance by Robert S. Eshelman that hit hard on the political and unscientific counter-arguments that lacked evidence but made up for it with political rhetoric and outright dismissals of proven theory. Eshelman traced the first government concerns about climate change back to the Johnson Administration's Science Advisory Committee stating in 1965 of "increasing evidence that human-generated industrial emissions were impacting the atmosphere."

But Eshelman then pointed to a 1988 U.S. Senate hearing on what was then called "global warming" and the true dangers of the man-made phenomenon, according to testimony of James E. Hansen, director of NASA's Goddard Institute for Space Studies, who declared, "Number one, the earth is warmer in 1988 than at any time in the history of instrumental measurements. Number two, the global warming is already large enough that we can ascribe with a high degree of confidence a cause and effect relationship to the greenhouse effect. And number three, our computer climate simulations indicate that the greenhouse effect is large enough to begin to affect the probability of extreme events such as summer heat waves."

Eshelman stated that, "Hansen's testimony stoked front-page coverage of the issue for the first time and is widely viewed as a turning point in public understanding of human impacts on the climate. *The New York Times* ran this headline on A1: Global Warming Has Begun, Expert Tells Senate. In January 1989, PBS' *NOVA* aired Hot Enough for You? In the fall of that year, *The End of Nature*, the first book about the greenhouse effect written for a general audience, hit bookshelves, written by a 29-year-old *New Yorker* staff writer named Bill McKibben. The media had woken up."

He also noted that it did not take long for opponents, driven by everything from anti-science conspiracies to concerns about cost, to weave their false and skeptical views into coverage, most based on nothing more than fear or personal agendas.

"It wasn't long before the fossil fuel industry did a good job of turning it into a political issue, a partisan thing they could exploit," McKibbon told Eshelman. "When they started rolling out all the tools that we now understand as an effort to overcome the science. And their main target was the media."

Eshelman added, "The fossil fuel industry succeeded. In the ensuing years, the industry not only won over conservatives on the matter of climate change, but they also played into the media trope of balance and fairness … it's as if journalists are stuck in time, presenting the science as something still under debate. A notion to be evaluated, tossed around. As scientific certainty grows – 97 percent of qualified scientists agree that the planet is warming and humans are the cause – today's reporters, editors, and producers should cease with the false conceit about a debate and instead drill deeply into the political terrain."

Bobby Magill, president of the Society of Environmental Journalists and a Bloomberg energy report, points to the Trump Administration's anti-climate change views and willingness to question such facts as part of the problem for reporters. "The administration is defiantly not taking climate issues seriously, based on the actions of the EPA and their budget requests," he told me in an interview. But he does see hope, noting, "Broadly speaking, climate coverage has improved particularly from national publications and a lot of independent online news outlets have been doing an excellent job. Even at the local level several outlets have stood out."

Magill stresses that "one of the deficiencies that might still exist in climate reporting is context. If someone feels compelled to quote scientists who may not be credible or adhere to the broadly accepted scientific position, if they stray from that they need to provide a significant amount of context as to why they are skeptical, what their background is and why their contribution is important to the conversation."

These are just a few of the false equivalency examples from the most notable issues. But they can still be found daily.

WEB WOES

It's been more than 20 years since a virtual unknown website called the *Drudge Report* broke one of the biggest political scandals in history. And although *Drudge* has built up a strong history of misleading and downright false reporting – much of it from linking to stories with either questionable headlines or outright falsehoods – the site will forever be credited with that journalistic scoop.

The scandal, of course, was the Monica Lewinsky affair in which President Bill Clinton had a sexual relationship with a White House intern, later lied about it to the country and had to admit his mistake to avoid perjury. But it was not enough to avoid impeachment, which made Clinton only the second president to receive that congressional punishment and face trial – a trial he survived. But the scandal stayed with him forever.

It also gave the Internet its first real news success, showing that websites cannot only break news, but can lead the way on a big scoop and get the word out instantaneously. In addition, it did a number on mainstream media after it was revealed that *Newsweek* had known about the affair and sat on the story, allowing *Drudge* to not only break the news, but expose their reluctance. "It didn't take long, of course, for it to explode," Michael Isikoff, the *Newsweek* writer at the time who had been reporting the story wrote in 2012, according to the *Weekly Standard,* later stating he was so upset about being scooped, "I won't deny certain homicidal tendencies."

Although Matt Drudge's site was then, and still is, a very basic web page with little visual element and mostly links to other stories with typewriter-style type and numerous misleading headlines, his story was correct.

Dated Saturday, Jan. 17, 1998, at 11:32 p.m., the scoop read simply: NEWSWEEK KILLS STORY ON WHITE HOUSE INTERN BLOCKBUSTER REPORT: 23-YEAR OLD, FORMER WHITE HOUSE INTERN, SEX RELATIONSHIP WITH PRESIDENT.

"At the last minute, at 6 p.m. on Saturday evening, NEWSWEEK magazine killed a story that was destined to shake official Washington to its foundation: A White House intern carried on a sexual affair with the President of the United States! The DRUDGE REPORT has learned that reporter Michael Isikoff developed the story of his career, only to have it spiked by top NEWSWEEK suits hours before publication. A young woman, 23, sexually involved with the love of her life, the President of the United States, since she was a 21-year-old intern at the White House. She was a frequent visitor to a small study just off the Oval Office where she claims to have indulged the president's sexual preference. Reports of the relationship spread in White House quarters and she was moved to a job at the Pentagon, where she worked until last month."

DrudgeReport.com, Jan. 17, 1998

The story shook up Washington and the media establishment, cementing *Drudge*'s place in history – despite the following decades of poorly reported stories and clearly misleading posts – and delivering one of the first major blows to traditional press via the web.

While Drudge scored a blow for independent web sites two decades ago his own credibility remains crippled and weak, especially since so many other sites have popped up. Since 2008, *PolitiFact* found that eight *Drudge* stories and 20 statements quoted by Drudge were either false, mostly false or "Pants on Fire," its worst false rating. *Drudge* also was found to have helped spread *PolitiFact*'s 2012 Lie of the Year, a false claim that Jeep was moving its factory to China, which was part of a Mitt Romney presidential ad and was quickly debunked by the auto-maker, but still spread by *Drudge* and others. "...it picked up steam when the *Drudge Report* ran with it," *PolitiFact* wrote.

But even with such poor fact-checking and inaccuracy, that first big break helped *Drudge* explode in popularity – and revenue – for 20 years. And opened the door for a web revolution that has forever changed news, and not always for the better.

"As the Internet became available in the public sector, electronic publishing and chat rooms opened up forums for individuals to express their views to a large audience around the world," Oscar W. Alexander wrote in his book, *Media in the 20th Century*. "People with only a small amount of technical knowledge could air their views without the huge expense of traditional publishing."

That was Drudge to a tee. A one-time *Time/Life* telemarketer, he grew up in a D.C. suburb and began the *Drudge Report* as an email service in 1994, later jumping to the web in 1996 – the same year the Fox News Channel began. Interestingly, that was also the first year that several major newspapers – such as the *Washington Post* and the *San Jose Mercury News* – launched some of the first newspaper websites. But like most early newspaper sites, they only posted news that was already in the print product and charged no fees. News was rarely broken online by the traditional media and often had a separate editorial structure and technical base.

Social media sites were also in their early stages when Drudge made his Clinton splash. Facebook was still six years away and AOL – although in existence in one form or another since 1983 – had been operating its pay online services since 1991, and mostly in the form of email and news aggregation with little original content or space for posting views and information. Other similar services that came and went were CompuServe and Prodigy, but neither survives today.

The search engine world dates to Yahoo's 1994 launch, with Google following in 1996, both by then-students of Stanford University. "They didn't have the money to buy new computers, so they begged and borrowed Google into existence," author John Battelle wrote about Google founders Larry Page and Sergey Brin in his 2005 book, *The Search: How Google and Its Rivals Rewrote the Rules of Business and Transformed Our Culture.* "A hard drive from the network lab, an idle CPU from the computer science loading docks. Using Page's dorm room as a machine lab, they fashioned a computational Frankenstein from spare parts, then jacked the whole thing into Stanford's broadband campus network. After filling Page's room with equipment, they converted Brin's dorm room into an office and programming center."

Like most growing Internet elements of the 1990s, these innovations were as grassroots and experimental as the original personal computers that came about two decades earlier when Apple's Steve Jobs and Steve Wozniak were creating that industry's first prototypes in a garage not far from the campus where Google and Yahoo were born.

But while innovation was changing the way content, communication and ideas were being spread via computer, traditional news outlets — from print to broadcast to cable — were not taking advantage and letting others grab the opportunity in an entirely new form.

Most news outlets did not charge for content from the beginning, they did not develop their own search engines like Yahoo and Google, and they did not focus on the immediacy and limitless space on the web for longer stories and background data. News outlets also waited too long to place one of their key money-makers — classified ads — online until it was too late.

Many newspapers succumbed to the belief that the Internet must be free. Only a few major papers, such as *The Wall Street Journal*, were charging for web access from the beginning. *The New York Times* began charging for access after the first 10 articles in early 2011, but most papers remained free online. Only in recent years has that begun to change.

Gannett made a major push into pay walls in early 2012, with most of its dailies charging, while the *Los Angeles Times* also put one in place the same year. *Newspapers & Technology*, an industry publication, reported in August 2012 that at least 300 American daily papers had pay walls.

Still, the overall impact of the Internet on newspapers is also based on the progress of time and changes in society and news outlet options. Even though newspapers always battled the likes of movie theaters, radio and television, the Internet and its expanded numbers of news outlets took a lot for newspapers to fight. Many daily papers, and their owners, also did not see the demise coming until it was too late.

"What has really changed is competition that is a different type of competition," veteran newspaper financial analyst Lauren Rich Fine adds. "They did not have competition for real time news in the past. Television brought in an evening news broadcast, that was helpful and then 24-hour news and then you move to the Internet. If you are a news junkie, you can get that real time online. The Internet is a more perfect competitor than ever existed before. And it is more customizable."

Media Analyst Ken Doctor told me in a 2018 interview that, "one of the key decisions at the beginning was putting up a lot of free content, if you look at a fatal decision that was probably it," noting that major news wire services Reuters and AP both failed to charge for online content early on. "There have been a number of decisions since then, a continuing set of decisions that have placed the newspaper publishers further and further behind the curve."

He also stressed the lack of involvement in new technology by traditional news sources that brought content to the mobile age it is today, in which some 60% of online content is accessed via mobile devices: "They didn't develop search, they gave away search to Google, their mobile development is still low when the younger population uses mobile very well."

Jim Brady, former online editor of the *Washington Post* and currently CEO of Spirited Media, which runs three news sites in Pittsburgh, Denver and Philadelphia, was at the *Post* when its website began. He says the paper was handcuffed from the beginning due to limits on everything from online innovation to collecting web fees.

"We couldn't take money from people at that time, we were not set up and people were not putting credit card information online at that time," Brady told me. "It's an easy argument to make, but it's just not how the market works."

He also points out the limits of web advertising, both on effectiveness and proving success to an advertiser. Unlike print ads, which many readers see as they turn pages, online ads are limited in how much traffic they get due to the online reading habits of most readers who do not look at every headline or online story, often linking through to specific stories from other sources.

"You are comparing knowns against unknowns," he said of web revenue. "You saw that ad on A-3 every day [in print] and you knew it. Seeing that ad in the paper everyday it seemed to have value. Internet advertising is everywhere all the time, like water or oxygen. Most people who consume on the Internet, they just gloss over it."

Dale Cressman, associate chair of undergraduate studies for the Department of Communications at Brigham Young University, told me "the Internet changed the economic model" for news, in part because so much content was posted elsewhere on the web with many publishers believing ads and other subscription or paid outlets would cover the costs. "We expect to get it free and everyone is a publisher."

The first big online competition was Craigslist, the free online classified site that launched in 1995 as an email letter sent to customers, at first around San Francisco, then nationwide. But initially, as with Yahoo, AOL and Google, newspapers did not take note. Even though the website had expanded to 14 cities in 2003, many newspapers and other traditional media had still not taken owner Craig Newmark's growing assault on their classified ads seriously.

One telling moment was at the 2005 convention of the American Society of News Editors (ASNE) when, during a session about future news issues, a photo of Newmark was shown and attendees were asked who he was. Among the hundreds of those present, only a few hands went up.

"Newspapers were arrogant because there was no competition – classified ads, up until Craigslist, until the Internet, who was competing with them?" Cressman said. "They had it all to themselves and they could charge whatever they wanted to advertise."

Richard Tofel, general manager of the non-profit *ProPublica* investigative journalism site and former assistant publisher of *The Wall Street Journal*, pointed to such arrogance in a lengthy essay he wrote in February 2012, titled: "Why American Newspapers Gave Away the Future."

"The business model that had fueled the golden age of American newspapers broke somewhere around 2005," Tofel writes. "Total advertising revenues began dropping, and, at least at this writing, it seems unlikely they will rise appreciably again, at least until print newspapers have literally disappeared and been replaced by some digital future that is still emerging."

So traditional news outlets – mostly newspapers – found themselves forced online with no real way to make the kind of ad revenue they had made in print, little knowledge of the technology, and having given up the chance to charge for content, extend classified ads online in an easy way for customers, and potential income from search engines.

After Craigslist took much of the classified ad market, Monster.com and CareerBuilder also stormed in with much more sophisticated technology. News websites also found immediate competition from newer sites that did not charge for content and could do it in either a niche way or a looser news format – that led to many of the credibility problems we have discussed earlier. Along with competition, it was also the recession that stretched from 2004 until 2012, coupled with the loss of advertising, particularly classified that helped drive down newspaper revenues. In August 2012, *The New York Times* called those years "the worst economic downturn since the Great Depression."

"From a financial point of view, the true thing for newspapers has been the advertising," says Fine. "What really changed was what hit in the late 1990s, losing market share on help wanted advertising to competitive sites on the Internet. People love to say Craigslist, but it was really Monster and other sites. It was also the competitive loss of circulation."

At its peak, classified advertising was almost 50 percent of the total newspaper advertising revenue. Even though newspapers were aware they were losing share to Monster.com and Craigslist, they raised rates three times in one year because the demand was still there. Classified was close to 70 percent to 80 percent of pre-tax profit at its peak.

"The main issue is on the revenue side," Brian Tierney, former owner of the *Philadelphia Inquirer* and *Daily News* and CEO of Philadelphia Media Holdings, told me in 2012. "Dramatic changes in employment classified, which was probably the most profitable part of news advertising. The profit margin was 90 percent plus and people got fat and happy. We keep the advertiser, but they buy on the web because it is a lot cheaper. It is $300 for 30 days online with us. That was a $900 two-day print sale."

Many newspapers came too late to the technology change as well and have not done enough to keep that community feel going, while utilizing the web and other mobile technologies.

"Newspapers get sort of a bum rap on the Internet, they were doing Internet-like things such as video and using phones back when," said Mark Fitzgerald, former editor of *Editor & Publisher* magazine, which covers the newspaper industry. He added that as early as 1987 newspapers were experimenting with faxing and other technology. "If everyone had charged it might have made a difference and pretty much everyone charged at first. To get the *Los Angeles Times* online in 1988 you had to pay and you would go to a link for it. But there was a great pushback."

Fitzgerald cited an idea that got some interest in the 1990s that would have had papers be more thematic: "L.A. *Times* on Hollywood, Chicago on finance, Houston on energy, Miami on immigration and arts. Newspapers never really did that. Perhaps if they had or would go ahead and do that, it could really do some bang up journalism."

James Brady also defend newspapers' initial reaction, to a degree, saying the web was not really built for the kind of single-deadline daily product that newspapers had made a success in print.

"It's not really all [newspapers'] fault because newspapers had put out a great once-a-day general interest product," Brady told me. "The web does not reward general interest at all. It's like 'The Untouchables' – you brought a knife to a gunfight? Newspapers showed up on the Web with the wrong product, the Web rewards niche. If you're an airline are you going to buy advertising on Travelocity or are you going to buy advertising on CNN.com?"

And as Google and Yahoo grew stronger, Facebook jumped into the fray in 2004 with a whole new online service – the personal web page where customers can post comments, photos, video and connect in ways that are still being developed. Fast forward to 2018 and Google and Facebook now account for at least 60% of digital advertising. "The web is all about Google and Facebook, that is really eating up everything, it is very hard to monetize, you can't do it on scale anymore," said Lisa Granatstein, editor and vice president for content and events at *Adweek*.com.

Ken Doctor agreed, saying, "If you look at it broad brush, digital advertising is the number one advertising type in the country, that happened in 2017. It is a huge business. It's also still growing in double digits annually. Then you look at who dominates it, Google and Facebook ... none of the other top 10 are publishers, they are all platforms. Only 10% of the growth of it went to anyone other than Facebook and Google." And he also points to the controversial data collection of those sites: "All of the information they have from us – everything about profiling, demographics and tracking actual reading and buying and shopping habits."

We also know about the dangerous impact of Facebook, its collecting of data and sharing it with paying clients. That is a danger of many companies that do business online, they get your information and blanket you with spam email, annoying marketing messages and robocalls, and sell it on to others who perpetuate the cycle.

On March 17, 2018, *The New York Times* revealed Facebook's underhanded dealings with Cambridge Analytics, the British-based firm that was given access to profile information for 50 million Facebook users and used it to help Republican candidates, including Donald Trump. "The breach allowed the company to exploit the private social media activity of a huge swath of the American electorate," the *Times* reported. "Developing techniques that underpinned its work on President Trump's campaign in 2016."

Nearly three months later, the *Times* on June 3, 2018, revealed the Facebook data scam went even further, reporting that Facebook forged deals with phone and "other device makers" that allowed them access to "vast amounts of its users' personal information."

"Facebook has reached data-sharing partnerships with at least 60 device makers – including Apple, Amazon, BlackBerry, Microsoft and Samsung – over the last decade," the story said. "Starting before Facebook apps were widely available on smartphones, company officials said. The deals allowed Facebook to expand its reach and let device makers offer customers popular features of the social network, such as messaging, 'like' buttons and address books."

The *Times* noted that the secret partnerships sparked concerns about privacy protections and compliance with a 2011 Federal Trade Commission consent decree because Facebook allowed access to the data of users' friends without their consent, "even after declaring that it would no longer share such information with outsiders."

And that is just one example of how the growing online world is creeping into private lives and amassing data and information to make money and limit privacy. Still, it does not appear to be impacting the public's hunger for online and hand-held content, connections and information. But when it comes to news, that hunger is being fed in a way that is not always ethical or accurate, and pushing traditional, professional news outlets to often bend the rules to keep up with what they perceive is the need – for both profits and readers.

"As your volume of attention and traffic and audience goes down and the prices go down, desperation goes up and that's what leads to clickbait and it's not just the web, it's also cable news," said Jeff Jarvis, the former *TV Guide* columnist and current director of the Tow-Knight Center for

Entrepreneurial Journalism at the City University of New York Graduate School of Journalism. "The Internet as a whole is an abundance-based market ... Ad prices inevitably go down, you inevitably have competitors who do what you do for less, and free, and you have about a three-second control on exclusivity."

So not only did the Internet explosion cut into traditional news outlet audience and revenue, it changed the way news has to be reported. No longer could a reporter work on a story for hours and report it and refine it until 6 p.m. or 8 p.m. depending on the deadline. Even television and radio could work toward the 5 p.m., 6 p.m. or 11 p.m. newscast in the past with break-ins occurring only when needed. Except for the major news channels, news coverage had more time to confirm and develop, and more people to keep tabs and double-check before the Internet.

But once the web took over, deadlines were almost non-existent. Every story had to be up as soon as possible – disallowing more copy editing, fact-checking and even improved writing. "A lot of it has shifted to digital, you have to be ahead of your game, it is virtually impossible to be breaking news with digital, because they just plop it out there," said veteran media reporter Marc Berman, who edits *The Programming Insider* and points to the eventual effect on traditional television news as well. "What happens in 20, 30, 40 years when they are all on digital? If I am getting news online all day long do I need to watch the evening news?"

And all of this occurs with fewer people on staff as the news jobs, noted earlier, keep diminishing. "Overall revenues are down and because of that it is a continuing wave of layoffs, around the country and less announced than they used to be," Ken Doctor said in an interview. "Companies cutting the most are those that are maintaining profit levels despite declining levels. They are all still profitable. They are cutting back on the staffing of the news product and that means less content, and in addition to that fact there has been very little innovation in presentation or delivery of that content."

He later added, "If you look at the overall finances of news companies, they are down six to 10 percent in revenue year over year. Print advertising is down about 15% in 2017, digital is not growing that much, reader revenue is flat."

Some news sites are seeing beginnings of success with paywalls, which began growing in the past few years. *The New York Times*, the *Washington Post* and *The Wall Street Journal* have limited free options that require payment earlier than they used to.

"*The New Yorker* has one. *Wired* just announced they'd be building one. *The Atlantic*, too, uses a paywall if readers have an ad blocker installed," *The Atlantic* wrote in a November 2017 story noting the slow return of the paywall. "Many of these efforts have been successful. Publications have figured out how to create the right kinds of porosity for their sites, allowing enough people in to drive scale, but extracting more revenue per reader than advertising could provide."

Fast Company offered a similar view in a January 2018 piece, which noted: "Conde Nast recently announced its plans to offer more metered paywalls for magazines including *Wired* and *Vanity Fair*, *The New York Times* recently lowered the number of free reads it allows every month in an attempt to bring in even more paying customers; even digital juggernaut *Business Insider* has begun implementing a paywall for select stories. For many companies, going the digital subscription route is a somewhat new plan—an attempt to reclaim old print-era strategies to drum up revenue alternatives. This comes as publishers are faced with a digital ad crisis. Media companies have historically relied on advertising as a primary means of revenue but have seen growth sputter as Facebook and Google began sucking up the majority of the digital advertising market share."

A 2017 *Columbia Journalism Review* analysis of the 25 most-visited newspaper web sites found that 15 charged for online access, although the limits, costs and availability varied widely.

"The paywalled news sites … diverged widely in the cost of their subscriptions, the number of free articles dispensed, the specific combination of 'side door' exceptions employed, and whether they operated via one flagship website or two – one free and one for subscribers," CJR reported. "Despite what seems like widespread optimism about the prospect of digital subscriptions buttressing the industry, a full 10 sites, 40 percent of the outlets we looked at, focused on ad revenue exclusively, eschewing paywalls." Still, that is more than half of the top newspaper sites now charging.

News competition also exploded on the web when, essentially, anyone could create a website with a few keystrokes, and for little or no money. And little or no credibility, experience or reporting skills.

Notes *Adweek*'s Granatstein: "You are getting into aggregation, cheaper writers and reporters, less experience, less time on a beat than anytime, it is affecting the quality, and then what are you paying for? People don't go to sites anymore, they get their news from social media … it is hard to get eye balls to stay on the page, it is hard to get people to the page. They are not getting people to websites, they are getting people to stories through Facebook and Google."

The web hasn't been a complete killer for traditional news outlets. I call it a "necessary evil" in today's media landscape because it's where people are going to get updated information and news, and that puts old-time news sources such as newspapers and even broadcast outlets on the same playing field as instant online reporting sources. Newspapers, who had to wait until the next day's paper in the past to break news, can do it as quickly as any rival – and often better given they still have the most reporting resources, even if they are diminished.

And the reporting itself is vastly improved with online resources – information and documents that could take days and weeks to obtain and sift through in the past are often at the click of a button. Not to mention news archives that would have required trudging to the library or the newsroom "morgue" for old copies and clippings can now be brought up online in seconds. As for documentation resources, legal briefs, lawsuits, government agendas and ordinances, bills and other official items are at the touch of a button, literally.

"On the plus side, you have access to so much more than anyone would think. You can get a lot more and that is an absolute good," David Chavern, president & chief executive officer of the News Media Alliance (formerly the Newspaper Association of America) told me in an interview. But, he added, "One thing people wrestle with is the intense emphasis on speed and not thoughtfulness, which does do some damage long-term to journalism. We have to figure out the balance to that."

Chavern later noted the loss of exclusivity for newsrooms that break stories: "The other thing people didn't understand is not getting credit for being an original source. Even if you break a story, there have been statistics showing that in five or six minutes it is repackaged and on top of the Google searches by someone who has taken the content."

A 2009 poll by *The Atlantic* and *National Journal* found that "media insiders" believed about two-to-one that the Internet had hurt journalism. "The poll asked 43 media insiders whether, on balance, journalism has been helped more or hurt more by the rise of news consumption online," *The Atlantic* reported. "Sixty-five percent said journalism has been hurt more, while 34 percent said it has been helped more."

"Consensus was that the Internet has destroyed the old business model – the newspaper business model – that supported balanced, thoughtful journalism," *The Atlantic*'s Chris Good, who was a political reporter for ABC News at the time, wrote about the poll. "It promotes sensationalism and trains people to consume news in smaller, bite-sized pieces, at least two insiders said. At the same time, it has widened the audience of news consumers and put more news at people's fingertips."

But what kind of news is it when it is more rushed, less reviewed and created to desperately attract an ever-splintered audience seen more for its "clicks" than its need for real content? When the likes of CNN.com and *The Wall Street Journal* are up against *The Daily Beast*, *Buzzfeed*, and even the *Breitbarts* and *Daily Callers* of the web – not to mention outright liars like Alex Jones' *InfoWars* and *WorldNetDaily* – it can be no holds barred.

"This increased competition from media organizations like *Buzzfeed*, Vice Media and Vox have put renewed pressure on legacy media," Former NPR Vice-President Jeffrey Dvorkin wrote in a 2016 PBS.com piece. "Broadcasters especially try to entice their audiences through click-bait. This is defined as 'an [eye-catching] link on a website which encourages people to read on. It is often paid for by the advertiser ('Paid' click-bait) or generates income based on the number of clicks.' It's rarely newsworthy, but it does attract eyeballs."

One of the premiere "clickbait" sites has been *Buzzfeed*, Ben Smith's news source that is credited with breaking some significant stories – see its January 2018 Brexit internal assessment report – as well as offering a lively mix of hard news and pop. But its bread-and-butter has often been eye-grabbing heads such as "7 DIY Projects To Make with Dad," "16 Breathtaking Restaurants Around the World You Need to Try At Least Once," and "Which 'Charlie and the Chocolate Factory' Child Are You?"

"*Buzzfeed* has become popular via incoherent articles, vapid lists and heaps and heaps of cat gifs. It is the very definition of clickbait," *Adweek*'s Chris O'Shea wrote in 2014 after Smith penned an essay declaring the opposite. "If Smith was honest, he'd admit that clickbait can be many things and *Buzzfeed* indulges in all of them. All the time. The mere fact that Smith felt the need to compose an article saying 'We don't do clickbait' is because that's all *Buzzfeed* does. Smith knows it; everyone knows it. Shit is always shit. It still stinks even if you want to call it something else."

To be fair to Smith, what his site does can be misinterpreted as a negative form of clickbait, which is associated with misleading readers into going to something that is not what it claims. Most of *Buzzfeed*'s stories, as flaky as they may be topic-wise, rarely misrepresent themselves. You may not think that a link to "How Much Do You Actually Know About Polish Food?" is worthwhile. But when you go there, you enter a quiz on Polish food.

As Smith himself said in the aforementioned essay, "Different people use the term 'clickbait' differently, and it's sometimes thrown our direction to characterize entertaining web culture content that the author doesn't like. That is something different, a matter of taste. But whatever your taste, nobody likes being tricked. And whatever your goals as a publisher, there's no longer any argument for breaking promises to your readers."

Still, true clickbait, fake stories and misleading links are a growing issue online as both true news sites and those looking to just get traffic battle it out, not only for readers, but that ever splintering revenue.

"The assumption seems to be that audiences might stay for the 'serious' content after gorging on the fluff," Dvorkin added. "The public broadcaster in Canada, the CBC, seems to be particularly smitten with click-bait, even though its own journalists complain, and the public resents this waste of the public broadcaster's journalistic efforts and reputation."

Adds Jarvis: "What the Internet really killed was the mass media business model with one mass media. Yet we are trying to shoehorn our old mass media business models into this medium. That leads inevitably to cats and Kardashians and ultimately to Donald Trump. Donald Trump is clickbait. That is why CNN left the camera on him for an hour, it drives us to get the attention for attention's sake."

A look at the top 15 news websites as of May 2018, according to EbizMBA.com – which tracks such traffic data – finds some hope for genuine news online with most of the top-read sites connected to traditional legacy media outlets, including seven newspaper sites.

They include CNN.com at #4, NYTimes.com at #5, Fox News at #6, and NBC News at #7. Those are followed by; #8, *The Daily Mail Online*; #9, washingtonpost.com, #10, *The Guardian*; #11, WSJ.com; #12, ABCnews.com; #13, BBC.com; #14, USAToday.com; and at #15, LATimes.com. The disturbing trend may be that the top two sites are aggregators of other news sites – *Yahoo News* at #1 and Google News at #2. *Huffington Post*, which is a web-only site with a mix of news and opinion, ranks #3.

For newspaper websites, however, the demand for increased web traffic has impacted what they cover online, often in the area of local news, according to a 2017 *Columbia Journalism Review* examination, which also questioned using such traffic data to determine story priority.

"Several recent academic studies of online news consumers have taken a deeper, ethnographic approach to understanding reader behavior. Their findings show that counting story clicks is a misguided way to determine reader preferences," the piece by Michael Rosenwald, who also writes for the *Washington Post*, stated. "People engage in online user practices that do not necessitate clicks but do express interest in news … This behavior is seen clearly when clicks are compared to the amount of time spent on new sites. In one study, local stories represented 9 percent of story clicks by readers. But measured in time spent, those stories accounted for 20 percent of their time on the site, about the same time readers spend on local news in print."

Rosenwald then cited a study of online readers in the Netherlands that determined, "a frequent occurrence was that the participants showed interest in the news itself, but the headline was informationally complete and, consequently, they did not expect to be better informed by clicking."

While *Yahoo News* has grown with original reporting and its own White House Correspondent, a look at its top trending stories indicates the clickbait phenomenon is only growing. A random look at *Yahoo News*'s top stories on June 5, 2018, found links to three stories by *Huffington Post*, *Time* and Reuters on the North Korean summit negotiations; links to two outside stories and one *Yahoo* opinion piece on an Arizona murder spree suspect; links to two outside stories by Fox News and "The Cut," and one original story on that day's primary voting; and links to two outside stories – at *Scientific American* and Reuters on a Guatemala volcano eruption, as well as an original *Yahoo News* story on the event.

But also weaved in with those were sponsored ads for auto insurer Everquote; "The Kiwi Report," a website with paid content made to look like news stories; and other unknown sites such as "NewsD" and "New Arena," which offer no background or sourcing for their content. Those sponsored content items were placed along with real news in a way that was clearly meant to fool audiences into thinking they were as valid as the true news stories.

These "clickbait" headlines and stories are placed inevitably to draw readers to go to the link – either an eye-grabbing story, often of little real value, or an outright fake news item that is placed as a paid sponsor – and identified either with small lettering or none at all.

"Clickbait in the many forms it takes – from the intriguing to the misleading – seems to be here to stay," Ben Frampton declared on BBC.com in 2015. "So journalists and news organizations have a decision to make on what they want to offer people and where their priorities lie." Ken Doctor echoed that view in an interview, stating: "By chasing audience on the internet, click bait, and have stories that people will click on, it's first an advertising goal to have the audience that is as big as possible. Publishers are focused more on reader and reader revenue and its actual reader engagement."

And while Facebook is not listed among the top news sites, because it technically has no original reporting or news section – at least not yet – it is also a major news source for many, as is Twitter. Both have their own paid content, much of it clickbait, that can also mislead readers and send them to either fake news sites or those of limited news value that draw interest due to their celebrity, uniqueness or outrageousness.

Alexa.com, which monitors web traffic and popularity, places Google.com as the most popular U.S. site, followed by YouTube, Reddit, Facebook, Amazon, and Wikipedia. Rounding out the Top 10 are Yahoo, Twitter, Ebay.com, and Instagram. Excluding Yahoo and Google, whose news aggregation we have discussed, and eBay and Amazon – which are shopping sites – the remaining top sites are ripe for fake news or clickbait paid content.

One point of concern on Wikipedia is the free-for-all approach of the site, which can often provide general information that should always be double-checked elsewhere and often includes valuable links to news sources. But it has no standard fact-checking or editing for accuracy and is open to misleading and inaccurate information by its very nature, a fact often missed by those who sing its praises or even count on it for facts.

Facebook and Twitter, which many web surfers – mostly millennials – admit are their major news sources, rely on sponsored content, which includes links to questionable sites. And their use is only growing.

A 2017 Pew Research Center study found that at least 67 percent of respondents get at least some of their news from social media, up from 62 percent a year earlier. It also noted a "substantial increase" among older, non-white and less-educated Americans.

"For the first time in the Center's surveys, more than half (55%) of Americans ages 50 or older report getting news on social media sites," the report stated. "That is 10 percentage points higher than the 45% who said so in 2016." The survey also noted that those under 50 are even more likely to get news from these sites, with 78 percent admitting so.

The Pew study also revealed that Twitter and Facebook users are going to those sites for news more and more in recent years, with 74 percent of Twitter users saying they go to the site for news, up from 59 percent in 2016 and 53 percent in 2013. The same at Facebook, where 68 percent of users say they now go to the site for news, more than the 66 percent in 2016 and well above the 47 percent in 2013.

"Looking at the population as a whole, Facebook by far still leads every other social media site as a source of news," the Pew report said. "This is largely due to Facebook's large user base, compared with other platforms, and the fact that most of its users get news on the site." The Pew survey also found that 35 percent of respondents said they reached news stories online through a social media link, while 36 percent went directly to news sites.

But the credibility of news via social media is still very low, the report stated. Pew found that Americans have a lower trust in information from social media, noting only five percent of U.S. adults on the web "have a lot of trust in the information they get from social media, nearly identical to the 4% who said so in 2016. This level of trust is much lower than trust in national and local news organizations, and in information coming from friends and family." It referenced a separate study focusing on science news that found 52 percent of social media users distrust science posts on social media, compared to 26 percent who do trust them.

One of the dangers of relying on Facebook or Twitter for news is the potential for false and discredited sources to be spread among its members. So much of the content is based on who the reader follows on Twitter or friends on Facebook, and who those people cite as news sources. If a Twitter follower sees a link to a disreputable site such as *InfoWars* or even Fox News, which has had its share of inaccuracies as we know, and goes to that site, they are relying on that source for news.

The same with Facebook. Many valid and credible news stories are spread on that king of social media sites. But all it takes is one person to post something on Facebook, it is clicked on or "shared" by dozens of others, and eventually hundreds and perhaps millions. But, in many cases such stories are deemed false or misleading.

The fact-checking sites such as *PolitiFact*, Factcheck.org and Snopes, have been built around debunking such myths and fake news that get much of their life from Twitter and Facebook sharing.

A 2018 joint study by researchers from Princeton, Dartmouth and University of Exeter in England found that at least one out of four Americans visited a fake news website in the month prior to the 2016 presidential election, and that Facebook "was a key vector of exposure to fake news and that fact-checks of fake news almost never reached its consumers." It also found that the most conservative readers were the ones most affected by such false stories: "The 10 percent of Americans with the most conservative information diets consumed an average of 33.16 articles from pro-Trump fake news websites."

Facebook has sought to improve credibility with new algorithms and safeguards it claims will weed out the false links. In June 2018, the site also announced it would discontinue "trending" links and add in more specific news content. A note to readers posted June 1, 2018, stated:

> *We've seen that the way people consume news on Facebook is changing to be primarily on mobile and increasingly through news video. So we're exploring new ways to help people stay informed about timely, breaking news that matters to them, while making sure the news they see on Facebook is from trustworthy and quality sources. For example:*
>
> o *Breaking News Label: A test we're running with 80 publishers across North America, South America, Europe, India and Australia lets publishers put a "breaking news" indicator on their posts in News Feed. We're also testing breaking news notifications.*
>
> o *Today In: We're testing a dedicated section on Facebook called Today In that connects people to the latest breaking and important news from local publishers in their city, as well as updates from local officials and organizations.*
>
> o *News Video in Watch: We will soon have a dedicated section on Facebook Watch in the US where people can view live coverage, daily news briefings and weekly deep dives that are exclusive to Watch.*
>
> *People tell us they want to stay informed about what is happening around them. We are committed to ensuring the news that people see on Facebook is high quality, and we're investing in ways to better draw attention to breaking news when it matters most.*

It remains to be seen if such moves will improve news content and credibility.

As for Twitter, a major study from the Massachusetts Institute of Technology (MIT) and published in Science magazine in March 2018 looked at Twitter-promoted stories between 2008 and 2017 and found that the fake stories spread quicker and more often than real news: "Falsehood diffused significantly farther, faster, deeper, and more broadly than the truth in all categories of information, and the effects were more pronounced for false political news than for false news about terrorism, natural disasters, science, urban legends, or financial information."

"It seems to be pretty clear [from our study] that false information outperforms true information," Soroush Vosoughi, an MIT data scientist who co-authored the study, told *The Atlantic*. "And that is not just because of bots. It might have something to do with human nature."

But that does not take into account the sponsored content on both sites, which is often weaved in with regular Twitter postings and Facebook links. The use of such paid content, much of it clickbait, is less and less distinguishable from actual postings by Facebook friends and Twitter members. Much of the content and its links are made to look like they were placed by those the reader is following.

"As a form of media that blurs the lines between editorial content and advertising, sponsored articles have been accused of deceiving consumers, creating mistrust of brands, and damaging the editorial integrity of publications," Aaron Aders, founder and CEO of LEIF Technologies, wrote in a 2015 *Inc.* magazine piece. "Lack of industry-wide regulation from the FTC has also contributed to disparities in disclosure requirements of sponsored content, specifically regarding language and graphic separation."

Back in traditional newsrooms, meanwhile, social media, email, and the web in general have both aided and hurt news coverage. As noted before, the web is a great reporting tool, as is email that can reach a potential source or public official instantly without navigating voice mail and phone calls and allow them instant response. During my eight years at *Media Matters for America* I worked out of my suburban New Jersey home and could report on major political and journalistic issues and their ties to media events from my home office with just a PC, laptop and/or cell phone.

And I am not alone, of course. From the use of Twitter-shared photos to bypass an Internet blackout during the 2011 Egypt uprising to the continued scouring of news subject's Facebook pages and Twitter accounts for any insight in to their actions, the web is a journalistic tool like no other.

"The process that happens before a story is published has also been transformed. The web has become the go-to point for the globe when it comes to getting information; it's the same for reporters," Aleks Krotoski, an interactive and tech reporter at *The Guardian* wrote in 2011. "Online, they find a multiplicity of perspectives and a library of available knowledge that provides the context for stories. Increasingly, the stories are coming from the web."

And with a president who has taken Twitter to new heights of use, and some would say abuse, it is now a standard part of any White House reporter's day to keep an eye on @realDonaldTrump. But that is true for most any celebrity or public figure, either when they react to a major news event, their own actions, or often a famous death.

When fashion and accessory designer Kate Spade took her own life on June 5, 2018, most of the reaction comments came via Twitter. From her brother-in-law David Spade to first daughter Ivanka Trump, condolence messages were spread first online.

"Journalists are more active on social media than ever before, with a notable increase in daily activity," *Adweek* reported in 2016, citing an annual Social Journalism Study by public relations and media company Cision and Canterbury Christ Church University, "From reading posts from people they follow to monitoring the conversation around their own content and reposting on micro-blogging sites, participation from journalists is up anywhere as much as 34 percent compared with similar data from 2013."

But it later noted, "More journalists believe their job would be harder without social media, but fewer journalists are of the belief that it improves productivity. Journalists are also more worried about standards, with 54 percent agreeing that social media undermines traditional journalistic values." The Cision report also found that 42 percent of journalists and "other media professionals" reported using five or more types of social media regularly. And more than half were concerned about fake news and social media's influence on journalism.

That balance between using social media items, other web news sources and even blogs for news gathering – and making sure they are credible – is a key dilemma for today's reporters as they navigate this vital, but uncertain tool.

As with the Egyptian uprising mentioned earlier, the 2009 Iranian elections and related protests were covered in large part through tweets and personal video provided by those in country against a government blockade of other Internet and communication sources. A 2009 report from the Reuters Institute for the Study of Journalism at Oxford University cited the Iranian events as a successful example of social media use, including YouTube, in coverage.

"As in previous cases of so-called citizen journalism, it was mobile phones and other digital cameras that captured sometimes bloody street protests against election results, which the opposition said were rigged," the report said. "Dramatic footage from all over the country was uploaded to video-sharing and social media sites, as well as to mainstream media organizations like CNN and the BBC, which at one stage was receiving up to five videos a minute. For YouTube spokesman Scott Rubin, his site had become a critical platform for citizen journalism: 'Iranian citizens are having their voices heard, their faces seen, and their story gets told around the world without filtering.' But it wasn't just the scale of upload, it was the speed of distribution and way in which social media sites fed and drove the agenda which really marked out this story."

Another example was coverage of the 2014 Michael Brown story and its aftermath in Ferguson, MO., where Brown – an unarmed black teen – was killed by a white Ferguson police officer. The incident prompted several protests and some violence, and drew national attention. A number of journalists said first word of the incident and several subsequent events were discovered, and later spread, via YouTube, Instagram, Twitter and Facebook.

"Social media is what introduced me to Ferguson," Reporter Kenya Vaughn of *The St. Louis American* said in an interview with the non-profit Facing History and Ourselves project. "I was just scrolling through Instagram and there was a picture of a man who had a cardboard box that he had turned into a sign that said, 'The Ferguson Police Department just executed my unarmed son.' And it was like, I was like, 'Ferguson, Ferguson? Like, down the street Ferguson?' That's how I was made aware and this happened a mile from my house and I had no clue until I got on Instagram, so that's how I found out about it."

Yamiche Alcindor, who reported on the story for *USA Today*, said, "Social media was everything in Ferguson … I was always on Twitter looking to see what's going on, where are people protesting? I mean, I want to say 90% of the information, even from the police department, which was – to me was interesting was because the police were live tweeting in some ways. I followed #MichaelBrown, #FergusonAction, #Ferguson, #BlackLivesMatter, #BlueLivesMatter, #AllLivesMatter. And then I followed a lot of police departments and a lot of police unions on Twitter as well. So those were kind of how I followed them. I was using those same hashtags so that people could find my work and people, you know, looked for #MichaelBrown and they also found my work."

But such sourcing can sometimes backfire, as occurred in the 2009 Fort Hood, TX., shooting, in which an Army psychiatrist killed 13 people. Several outlets, including *Huffington Post* and *The New York Times*, cited Twitter postings for much of their information as the incident was ongoing with several ending up misinformed. Among the key incorrect elements was the claim that there were multiple shooters.

"...in the rush to report on events at Fort Hood, some misinformation spread quickly, most notably that there was more than one shooter in the attacks and that one was killed during the incident," a Pew Research Center review of the coverage stated. "The initial sources of the false information are still unclear, but by the time it was corrected, many in both the mainstream press and social media had reported it."

Other outlets debated the good and bad outcomes from the use of Twitter for that breaking story, which included several outlets posting "Twitter lists," with continuously updated Twitter feeds from several sources.

Megan Garber in the *Columbia Journalism Review* argued that the use of Twitter on that story was "a vast improvement over the previous means of following breaking news in real time. Lists also represent, more significantly, a new-or, more precisely, a newly facilitated-way for news organizations to collaborate: they allow news outlets essentially to co-opt others' reporting. But in a good way-to the benefit of the news organizations in question and, of course, their audiences."

But Paul Carr at *TechCrunch*, said relying on non-journalists with no verification of what they are reporting is careless: "For all the sound and fury, citizen journalism once again did nothing but spread misinformation at a time when thousands of people with family at the base would have been freaking out already, and breach the privacy of those who had been killed or wounded. We learned not a single new fact, nor was a single life saved."

Most news outlets have updated their ethics guidelines and policies to reflect this new world, but even in those cases the determination can be tricky. NPR's social media guidelines state: "When determining whether to pass along information being reported on social media sites by other news outlets or individuals, be thoughtful. When we point to what others are saying, in the eyes of many we are effectively reporting that information ourselves." The Online News Association offers a similar warning, noting that reporters should be: "Endeavoring to verify the authenticity of user-generated content before publishing or distributing it, holding it to standards that are equal or equivalent to those maintained for content acquired through other means."

Then there is the use of Facebook pages of both suspects and victims of crimes and tragedies. Almost routinely reporters will go to such pages to learn about a victim's life – background, views, schooling – or a suspect's potential incriminating thoughts or past history.

NPR's coverage of the 2017 Las Vegas shooting that killed 58 people included a lengthy story detailing information on each victim that took background, data and photos directly from several of their Facebook pages, as well as content from loved ones and relatives. One example was a description of 31-year-old Carolyn Lee 'Carrie' Parsons of Seattle, WA., who died in the hail of gunfire from the killer's barrage. The story quoted from the Facebook page of her aunt, Barbara Parsons, who wrote, "Carrie was always the life of the party and had the biggest heart, always putting others needs first. Recently engaged she had her whole life in front of her. Now it is ended." The same write-up used information from Parsons' LinkedIn account to report she had been a manager for a staffing agency.

But is that ethical? Is it an invasion of privacy to troll a Facebook page? Especially of someone who was just murdered, or attacked, or arrested? Is that the same as going through their home or desk or mail for information? The Society of Professional Journalists Code of Ethics states that journalists should: "Realize that private people have a greater right to control information about themselves than public figures and others who seek power, influence or attention. Weigh the consequences of publishing or broadcasting personal information."

The Radio Television Digital News Association offers a bit more flexibility in its social media guidelines, which argue that anything posted online in a public format is fair game, although it also warns against invading privacy: "Social networks typically offer a 'privacy' setting, so users can choose not to have their photographs or thoughts in front of the uninvited public. Capturing material from a public Facebook site is different from prying behind a password-protected wall posing as a friend."

But it also states, "When considering whether to access 'private' content, journalists should apply the same RTDNA guidelines recommended for undercover journalism. Ask: Does the poster have a 'reasonable expectation' of privacy? Is this a story of great significance? Is there any other way to get the information? Are you willing to disclose your methods and reasoning? What are your journalistic motivations?"

The most sensitive area for journalists using social media and other forms of digital communication can involve their own personal use – be it on Twitter, Facebook, email or individual blogs. Most news people today have at least one work-related Twitter account, whether on a company feed or their own, and may well blog on their own time and space. Add to that Facebook pages – either tied to their employer and/or personal pages – and there is a real web of trouble that can be formed.

Simple emails have gotten some journalist in a jam. One example I recall covering at *Editor & Publisher* back in 2004 was a personal email from *Wall Street Journal* reporter Farnaz Fassihi to friends lamenting the dangers reporters like her faced in Iraq and criticizing the Bush administration's war policy.

It is important to point out that she sent the email to about 20 friends, and apparently one of them passed it on to others (some friend). It eventually reached critical mass and widespread web attention.

The email, according to a 2004 column by the *Los Angeles Times'* Tim Rutten, states at one point, "Despite Present [sic] Bush's rosy assessments, Iraq remains a disaster. If under Saddam it was a 'potential' threat, under the Americans it has been transformed to 'imminent and active threat,' a foreign policy failure bound to haunt the United States for decades to come," later adding, "One could argue that Iraq is already lost beyond salvation. For those of us on the ground it's hard to imagine what if anything could salvage it from its violent downward spiral."

Although Fassihi had an impeccable reputation as a journalist, and the email was a private note to friends, she was still criticized, if not unfairly, for giving her views. Editors brought her back from Iraq in early October 2004, just a month before the 2004 presidential election, for what was described then as a "planned vacation." By early December 2004 she was planning to head back to the war zone, telling me at that time by email, "I'm still on the Iraq beat," adding that she had been to Ramallah to lend a hand in covering the Arafat funeral, and was currently in Amman "trying to sort out alternate housing for us…before I go back." In a later email she added that she had put the issue behind her: "I understand your interest, but once I go back and start filing next week, then hopefully the speculations will end. ... I don't know why this story doesn't die."

I got my own taste of exposed email in 2005 when I was corresponding with a source at *The Blade* of Toledo, OH, for stories I wrote for *Editor & Publisher* about some internal issues at the paper, among them concerns that a reporter might have political ties to the subject of a major Pulitzer Prize-level investigation. At one point, my source's personal emails were discovered by *Blade* editors on a newspaper-owned laptop. Although my emails revealed nothing slanted, illegal or improper on my behalf, they did help to expose the source, who was later forced out.

And *The Blade*, apparently feeling the need to show the world how they could track down the source of some legitimate concerns about its work, wrote a lengthy story on the incident as if it was some kind of Watergate mystery. Perhaps they were sore that my coverage, which also included reporting on a formal complaint letter to the Pulitzer Board about the nominated series, might have lost them the prize.

But what the entire incident did do was remind me what I had already known, any email or other Internet-related text, photo, video or other communication needed to be handled as if it will be seen by everyone. Especially when it involves work-related messages.

Later on, when I worked at *Media Matters for America*, one early policy for using Twitter and other social media while representing the organization was the same as many other outlets – "Don't be stupid." Of course, as Forrest Gump said, "stupid is as stupid does." And more clearly, one person's stupid is another person's free speech.

One of the first tightropes that journalists may walk every day is scooping themselves on Twitter or Facebook. When something newsworthy breaks, a reporter by nature wants to get the word out. But if he or she Tweets it, that hurt the news organization's chance to break the news and get the credit – and the traffic – it will bring.

"We believe in the value of using social media to provide live coverage and to offer live updates. But there may be times when we prefer that our journalists focus their first efforts on our own digital platforms," a newly updated *New York Times* social media guideline stated in late 2017. "We generally want to publish exclusives on our own platforms first, not on social media, but there may be instances when it makes sense to post first on social media. Consult your supervisors for guidance."

Again, don't be stupid.

Along with not scooping yourself, there is the appearance of bias factor, which can be raised on all forms of social media, Twitter among them.

One of the most high-profile *Times* reporters who has had an up and down relationship with Twitter is Glenn Thrush, a fellow Brooklyn College alum who walked the campus the same time I did in the late 1980s, although we never really crossed paths.

His Twitter issues took a rise in 2017, according to the recent Showtime documentary, *The Fourth Estate*, which followed the *Times* during the first year of Trump's presidency.

At one point in the four-part series, Thrush is criticized for tweeting out a response to a Trump tweet. He is seen on camera saying, "Trump just Tweeted, I am going to tweet something out about it." Fellow scribe Maggie Haberman then tells him, "No you can't, Glenn! Thrush!" He later admits on camera, "Twitter is a very, very attractive medium for me. Writing with more of an edge, I really dig it."

A quick look at his history found an interesting tweet on March 6, 2016, when Thrush tweeted: "I deleted my last tweet after realizing I didn't know what the hell I was talking about." Probably something many of us should do on occasion.

Eventually, the documentary looked at the NRA TV video from Dana Loesch mentioned earlier that attacked and threatened many news outlets, including the *Times*. A conference call involving several staffers, D.C. bureau chief Elisabeth Bumiller and executive editor Dean Baquet shows their preference to avoid any direct engagement with the NRA on the issue. "I know it's infuriating, it's infuriating for me," Baquet is heard saying during the phone meeting. "But they're baiting us to sort of make it look like we're in a fight with them. Don't do it. Tell everybody not to do it." "We'll make clear," Bumiller promises.

But several reporters tweeted out responses to the threat, which drew further NRA attacks and some criticism from Baquet on a later conference call: "Did you hear that, too Washington? We did not look good getting into a Twitter pissing match with the NRA."

The focus then returned to Thrush when he retweeted a Trump tweet promoting a clearly edited video depicting the president hitting a golf ball that then hits Hillary Clinton, with Thrush criticizing Trump for retweeting it: "Classy retweet be the leader of the free world, man with nuke codes, fella who reads TelePrompTer on national unity and respect for women."

The retweet started a Twitter storm of responses and appeared to spark a crackdown on Thrush's tweeting with Bumiller seen on the phone telling someone, "Yeah, it was Glenn. You've talked to Dean about this? 'Cause he can't control himself? Okay just take the twitter app off your phone. Okay, let's do that. Okay, I'll tell him." Later, Thrush says, "Twitter is a potential area of friction between me and management. I don't think I went over the line. But the perception is you might have. You can't do that. The stakes are too high right now.

And I'm kind of an absolutist … I need to sort of cut it off completely." And he did on Sept. 19, 2017.

But by March 16, 2018, Thrush was back on Twitter.

And he is not alone, the tweeting of either breaking news or links to stories is now a daily, almost hourly, occurrence. And both reporters and readers benefit from it. Anyone dealing with the Internet knows the mantra is "feed the beast." Whether on social media pages, websites and Twitter, more and more content is king.

And Facebook is similar, even though there is a bit more protection when Facebook pages are limited to approved "friends." Still, some public pages that are often used to promote news and journalist's work in a manner similar to Twitter can be problematic as well.

One such case involved anchorwoman Wendy Bell of WTAE-TV in Pittsburgh. She got into hot water for a Facebook post deemed racist by some that commented on a March 9, 2016, ambush shooting in nearby Wilkinsburg, PA. It left five people dead, including a pregnant woman and her unborn child, according to CBS News.

Bell, who is white, posed comments that stated, in part, "You needn't be a criminal profiler to draw a mental sketch of the killers who broke so many hearts two weeks ago Wednesday. … They are young black men, likely teens or in their early 20s. They have multiple siblings from multiple fathers and their mothers work multiple jobs. These boys have been in the system before. They've grown up there. They know the police. They've been arrested."

Critics, including the Pittsburgh Black Media Federation, said it feeds an unfair stereotype, while others offered supportive comments on the same Facebook page. Bell eventually offered contrition, stating, "I sincerely apologize for the post about the Wilkinsburg mass shooting" and admitting her comments "could be viewed as racist." But it was apparently not enough as she was let go just weeks later.

In June 2016, Bell filed a lawsuit against the station alleging she was wrongfully terminated and claiming she would not have been let go if she was black. The case was reportedly settled in February 2018 under an undisclosed agreement after both sides agree to have it dismissed.

OVERKILLED AND UNDERREPORTED

It was just after 3 p.m. on Monday, April 15, 2013, when CNN viewers first heard about the biggest news story of that day – and eventually, of that year. CNN Anchor Brianna Keilar was in the middle of an interview with attorney Carlos Warner, who was representing several Guantanamo Bay detainees involved in a hunger strike over their treatment when Keilar cut him off and announced a breaking story out of Boston.

Keilar then cut to an audio hook-up with CNN Executive Producer Matt Frucci on the scene at the Boston Marathon. Frucci announced there had been two explosions near the finish line of the annual race, stating: "It was about 15, 20 minutes ago, near the finish line on Boylston Avenue Boston when I heard two explosions, the first one I thought close to the finish line from where we were. It was big. It was booming. I saw a big mound of smoke come up. And about 10 seconds later, across the street from me, on the sidewalk, another big explosion. People are hurt. They have stopped the Boston Marathon. Everyone rushed indoors. I'm now inside the Copley Plaza Mall looking out on the scene. And I can see swarms of police officers treating people on the scene. I count at least five, six people hurt. But I have a feeling there are more."

There were more, as we sadly heard and discovered in the hours, and days, that followed; a total of three dead and 263 injured at the hands of two terrorist bombers, brothers Tamerlan Tsarnaev, 26, and Dzhokhar

Tsarnaev, 19 – one of whom later ended up dead at the hands of investigators, the other captured and sentenced to death after being convicted on 30 counts and related charges.

But also among the tragedies that day was the poor reporting and outright inaccurate coverage that followed, not only on CNN, but from the likes of *The Wall Street Journal*, MSNBC, Fox News and the *New York Post*, which was later sued for placing photos of two men at the scene on Page One with claims they were suspects. That suit was settled out of court. Not settled, however, was the litany of inaccurate reports that day on everything from other bombings around the city that turned out not to be true to one report that cell phone service had been blocked in Boston – also false.

"Whether the coverage was on television, in print or online, facts were misreported, suspects were misidentified, and presumptions were made about unknown motives," reporter Sabrina Siddiqui wrote on The *Huffington Post* a week later, even pointing a finger at her own newsroom for mistakes. "The *Huffington Post* slipped up – grappling, like many other outlets, with the sheer volume of information that was posted online and shared through social media within seconds. But cable news seemed to be the most error-prone sector, to the point that cable reporting became a story in its own right.

"The media's tendency to speculate without facts even prompted a warning from President Barack Obama late Friday night: 'In this age of instant reporting and tweets and blogs, there's a temptation to latch on to any bit of information, sometimes to jump to conclusions,' Obama said in a statement after 19-year-old suspect Dzhokhar Tsarnaev was captured. 'But when a tragedy like this happens … it's important that we do this right.' In short, it was not a banner week for the media."

But sadly, it was not a complete exception in this age of breaking news, 24-hour information and reduced checkpoints and red flags. With the demand for continued updates, especially in the face of a big, tragic breaking story, facts get misreported and, in many cases, news outlets simply fail to confirm because they want speed and forget about accuracy.

"In the early moments you do the best you can to report what you know, all the responsible journalists know that it's better to be right than first," Dan Shelley, executive director of The Radio and Television Digital News Association (RTDNA), told me in an interview. "The nature of breaking news coverage is that you learn stuff and report stuff on the fly. You often have to go fill in the gaps later."

But is that enough of an excuse? Should viewers expect that breaking news "facts" may be wrong simply because the event is still ongoing, or should news outlets be more careful; and possibly hold off on reporting something if it is not confirmed? I remain a stickler, perhaps too old-fashioned for some, that with breaking news – or early reporting – facts must be clear cut and if not, you hold off. If you need to nail down a story point or a suspect, cause, number of dead, etc., hold off. Too many times in breaking news the anchor will say "we believe" such and such happened or "it is being reported that" this person died or that was the cause. And it ends up wrong.

I can recall back to Ronald Reagan being shot in 1981 and, as a 15-year-old junior high school student, watching the false reports that his press secretary, James Brady – who was permanently disabled by a bullet to the head – had died. There is the emotional image of ABC News anchor Frank Reynolds reporting on the situation and ranting about the false report when it turned out to be wrong: "Let's get it nailed down!" he barked to his colleagues. And with good reason. Earlier in the reporting, it was originally stated that Reagan had not been hit, with Reynolds correcting that live on the air, also in a frustrated voice: "My God, the president was hit, all of this we've been telling you is incorrect."

To be fair to Reynolds and others on that point, after shots were fired, striking three other people during the incident, Reagan got into his limousine and showed no signs at the scene of having been hit. As was later revealed, he discovered on his way to the White House that he had been struck and had coughed up blood, a fact that was then relayed to the press.

Still, it was a stark lesson in verifying breaking news, but one that may not have been learned after the president's assassination attempt. Almost 30 years later, on Jan. 11, 2011, several news outlets wrongly reported that Congresswomen Gabrielle Giffords, shot in Arizona at a public event, had died. "NPR incorrectly reported her death on air and over Twitter, sending the headline to its two million followers," a *Smithsonian* magazine retrospective later that year stated. "Taking note of the NPR tweet, CNN, *The New York Times*, and Fox News carried the story."

During the initial Boston Marathon bombing coverage, the list of inaccurate news reported by at least one major news outlet – and in many cases more than one – included the following false news:

o That five additional explosive detonation devices had been found, first reported by *The Wall Street Journal's* Marketplace.com site, then spread by CNN and others. The original Marketplace.com story is still on its website five years later.

o That a third bomb had gone off at the JFK Presidential Library in Boston, repeated by both CNN and MSNBC, which turned out to be an unrelated fire.

o That cell phone service in Boston had been shutdown to prevent further cell phone-related detonations, reported by at least two Boston television stations.

o CNN and Fox News wrongly reporting the day of the bombing that an arrest had been made, with CNN indicating it was a "dark-skinned male."

o False reports on local television that suspects Tamerlan Tsarnaev and Dzhokhar Tsarnaev had robbed a 7-11 store, an incident that had reportedly killed one of them.

o False reports on at least one Boston station that a different person, a former Brown University student, was a suspect.

Shelley later cited the 2017 mass shooting in Las Vegas, in which 59 people were killed and hundreds more injured at an outdoor concert near Mandalay Bay. "Breaking news coverage was very valuable to people to tell them what is going on," he said. "Where to go and when to go and information about loved ones."

But that incident, more than four years after the Boston Marathon bombing, had its share of false claims and rumor spreading, which included:

o False claims by several outlets, including the right-wing *Gateway Pundit*, that the shooter was a man named Geary Danley, whom the *Gateway Pundit* called a "far left loon."

o False reports that the actual shooter, Stephen Paddock, had ties to ISIS after the terrorist group claimed responsibility, even though the FBI said there was no link.

o False reports spread by social media, as well as the Las Vegas NBC affiliate, that a woman also named Danley had told concert goers they were "all going to die" prior to the shooting. That woman was found to have been out of the country, police later said.

o Inaccurate reports related to which weapons are legal and illegal in Nevada.

Not all false reports were left to spread unchecked. *The New York Times* reported days after the attack that some media sites, such as *Mashable*, did a good jump of debunking social media claims as they were posted, and even reached out to a few to stop: "Several news outlets have done a fine job flagging fakes that include pranksters repurposing the photos of a German soccer player, a murder suspect in Mexico, a porn star and random social media stars," the *Times* reported. "In a telling exchange, Gianluca Mezzofiere of *Mashable* reached out to the operator of one Twitter account sharing misinformation and reported the following:

Mashable reached out to the troll to ask why he's spreading misinformation during such a critical time.

"I think you know why," he replied. "For the retweets :)"

When *Mashable* pointed out that it's unethical to spread misinformation when people are desperately looking for their missing family and friends, he just said: "You are right I'm sorry."

"Jack Sins" said he chose TheReportOfTheWeek (aka Reviewbrah) just because he's a meme and tweeted Johnny Sins because he "is a living legend."

Asked whether he's done it before and whether he'd do it again, he replied:

"Yes and maybe."

But even with those safeguards and fact-checks, the number of false reports in such breaking news episodes is higher than it should be. Most of it is simple failure to confirm information and a perceived need to get news out, even if it is incorrect.

Ted Koppel, the legendary ABC News journalist and famed host of *Nightline*, once told me that was among the biggest problems news outlets had. We spoke during the 2006 Overseas Press Club dinner, where he was honored with an award and discussed the civic responsibility of journalism at the time in his address. But during a private chat, I asked him the biggest problem for reporters of the day and he said it was the rush to be first. I recall he said most viewers and readers do not care who got the story first, they care only if it is true and informational.

"You have broadcast network newscasts, CBS, ABC, NBC, the morning franchises, the same outlets you have always had, and the news channels. With the Internet and digital and everything, it is crazy," Marc Berman, television analyst and editor of *Programming Insider*, said about the increased competition to be first. "You are getting constant updates and everyone is trying to beat up each other, it is coming out of your ears. Any telecast is in danger of fatigue … It becomes who can get this out first?"

After the Boston Marathon bombing, CBS News veteran and morning show co-host John Dickerson wrote a piece for *Slate*, in which he defended the inaccuracies of the marathon coverage, claiming today's instant news is a fact of life and thus mistakes should not be judged so harshly. He urges people to review it like baseball, where a .300 batting average – a hit every three out of 10 attempts – is considered excellent.

"If those news organizations get it wrong – as they all did in Boston – then the model for appraisal should be closer to the one we use for batters in baseball. The standards are pretty clear – we know what a ball and a strike is – but we also know how to view a strikeout in context," Dickerson wrote.

But news isn't baseball. It is an important profession that I always judged necessary to be accurate 100 percent of the time. And if not, serious corrections should be made and, perhaps, heads should roll. Instead of comparing it to baseball, compare it to another more important part of life – perhaps medicine or teaching or police work. If a surgeon failed 70 percent of the time or a teacher's class failed 70 percent of the time or seven out of every 10 arrests turned out to be bogus, would we allow that surgeon, teacher or cop to stay on the job? No.

"The speed is cable news and Internet, you try to beat somebody else, you snip it out and we are not really additive," said Jeff Jarvis, former *TV Guide* columnist and current professor at the City University of New York Graduate School of Journalism.

Dickerson appears to understand that the inaccurate breaking news is not to be ignored and notes one very important case from more than 20 years ago that still serves as a reminder: "In the fast news moments after the Boston bombing, there was a lot of stupidity on Twitter. People were sending obviously Photoshopped pictures, linking to fake Twitter accounts, and otherwise passing on bad dope – including provisional reports from media sources. But when people got out of hand, the collective started to sanction those people. When photos started being posted of young anonymous men in the crowd, people sent around

Richard Jewell's obituary to warn against early condemnation of suspects."

Jewell was a police officer and part-time security guard at Centennial Olympic Park in Atlanta during the 1996 Summer Games there who actually saved many lives when he found a knapsack with a bomb planted in the park, alerted police and began moving people away from it. Although it exploded, killing one woman and injuring more than 100 others, Jewell was credited with finding it and clearing a major part of the park so more injuries would not occur.

But that mood turned completely when *The Atlanta Journal* reported just three days later that Jewel was being investigated as a possible suspect. "The investigation by local, state and federal law enforcement officers lasted until late October 1996 and included a number of bungled tactics, including an F.B.I. agent's effort to question Mr. Jewell on camera under the pretense of making a training film," *The New York Times* recalled in Jewell's 2007 obituary (he died at just 44). The scrutiny intensified daily with news outlets swarming Jewell's home and badgering him with questions and claims, many based on no real evidence other than that the FBI was investigating."

The intense reporting, and rumor, lasted from July to October 1996 when federal investigators finally cleared him. Nearly 10 years later, another man, Eric R. Rudolph of North Carolina, who was a suspect in the bombing of an abortion clinic in Birmingham, Ala., pleaded guilty to the Olympic park attack and received a life sentence, the *Times* wrote.

Jewell ended up suing several news outlets and won undisclosed settlements from NBC, CNN, and the *New York Post*, although his libel case against *The Atlanta Journal* was dismissed when a judge determined its reporting that Jewell was a suspect to be accurate. The Georgia Supreme Court upheld the dismissal in 2012.

Still, the Jewell case stands as a testament to both checking facts and not rushing to judgement, as well as understanding that even accurate reporting can cause difficulties – and be unethical – if the context and the related aspects are not taken into account. Although the *Atlanta Journal* was correct that Jewell was a suspect, did it properly point out that there was no direct evidence tying him to the bombing? Or that he had no criminal record or apparent motive? And much of the problematic reporting came when some news outlets brought in supposed experts to paint Jewell as fitting the profile of a person seeking fame and praise by planting a bomb and then finding it.

The bombing occurred in the early hours of July 27, 1996, in enough time to make that issue of the combined *Atlanta Journal/Atlanta Constitution* Saturday edition, which spread it across Page One. Interestingly, that first edition contained an error as it reported two had been killed, when it turned out just one fatality occurred. Three days later the *Atlanta Journal* headline screamed: "FBI suspect's 'hero' guard may have planted bomb." A very misleading headline at best and perhaps inaccurate at worst.

A better headline would have been the basics of the story – that Jewell was a suspect or "being investigated" or even "a potential suspect." Saying he "may have planted" the bomb takes too many liberties with the facts and puts the image of him planting the bomb in every reader's head. That is a very hard bell to un-ring. And the story itself went even further, stating Jewell "fits the profile of the lone bomber."

A Columbia University case study of the *Atlanta Journal* reporting on the Jewell story revealed that the paper had one source for the profile claim, an anonymous voice who told a reporter "that 'there was a profile of a lone bomber' and that Jewell fit it. He didn't know who had compiled it, but he assumed it was the FBI. The information seemed solid. [Other] sources pointed in the same direction," knowing that "there was some sort of profile. And both reporters believed this was a key factor in the thinking of law enforcement officials now, and needed to be high up in the story."

Of course, Jewell had yet to be interviewed with an attorney and was never arrested or charged, or even detained. The case study also revealed that even though Jewell was not the only suspect at the time, or even the key suspect, the story's lead stated he was "the focus" of the investigation.

"Whether reporters at the *Journal/Constitution* knew it or not, by July 30 – the day of the first story naming Jewell as a suspect – law enforcement investigators were already coming to the conclusion that one of their suspicions about Jewell was unfounded," the case study said. "The investigators had all but ruled out that Jewell had placed the 911 warning call to police before the bombing. They knew the precise time of the call and where it was made. They also knew Jewell's whereabouts just before the explosion. The physical distance from the bomb site to the pay phone in question was too great for Jewell to have placed the call and returned to the scene in time to report the knapsack, police had concluded. If anyone at *the Journal/Constitution* knew this, the paper's national exclusive on July 30 made no mention of it."

In their 2016 book, *The News Media: What Everyone Needs to Know*, media professors C.W. Anderson and Michael Schudson, and former *Washington Post* executive editor Leonard Downie, Jr., grapple with several issues, including the breaking news rush to judgement pitfalls. They also cite the Boston Marathon bombing coverage, but add in two other stories that broke a year earlier – the Sandy Hook elementary school shooting that killed 20 children and six adults in Newtown, CT., and the U.S. Supreme Court's decision upholding the Affordable Care Act.

As their book notes, initial reports on many outlets misidentified the Sandy Hook killer as Ryan Lanza, when it turned out to be his brother, Adam, while the first cable television reports on the Supreme Court wrongly reported that the court had overturned the law "because CNN and Fox News reporters had not yet read the entire complex ruling."

"Digital technology has made immediacy – being first with new or breaking news on social media, news sites, and search engines – an even more important factor in the competition for news audiences," Anderson, Schudson and Downie wrote. "And it is changing how journalists and newsrooms work. Posting news fast and first, often by minimizing or bypassing editorial review and fact-checking, can attract a larger digital audience."

Once again the demand for audience, ratings and eyeballs supersedes the demand for accuracy and facts. I understand the need for revenue and traffic, that pays the bills at a time when there is less and less to pay them, and journalists. But there is a point of diminishing returns, when being first, but wrong, enough times hurts credibility, and in the end the product's worth. Anderson, Schudson and Downie do not completely bash the 24-hour news options and digital offerings, pointing out they also provide instant correction and updating that can overcome initially inaccurate reporting.

"Digital technology also gives the news media and their audience new tools to correct mistakes, check facts, provide context, update information, reveal plagiarism and fabrication, and authenticate or discredit social media posts and citizen-contributed photos and video," their book states. "It enables anyone posting news on the Internet to include hyperlinks to primary source material and other relevant information and images."

Agreed, but I would be more hopeful and flexible if it seemed that the push to correct, update and be accurate the first time was increasing and jumping to conclusions, repeating false claims and letting poorly sourced news get out in the first place was on the decline. Sadly, most anecdotal and data evidence points to the contrary. PunditFact, the news-checking arm of The Poynter Institute, and *Tampa Bay Times*' *PolitiFact*, launched in 2013, offer some worrisome trends about false news and statements on the major news channels.

As of mid-2018, *PolitiFact* found that 41 percent of statements on NBC News were either false, mostly false or "pants on fire," the worst lies. ABC is a bit better at 33 percent rating in those false categories, while CBS is a bit worse with 45 percent of its checked statements and news in the false realm. Not surprising, perhaps, are Fox and Fox News Channel, leading the false pack with 59 percent of statements on its news casts deemed false, mostly false or "pants on fire."

"Two problems immediately come to mind, one is in the rush to put something out there, but what part of the story don't you know?" asked Tom Fiedler, the former *Miami Herald* executive editor and currently dean of the College of Communication at Boston University. "Maybe what explanation did you fail to get? It's always high risk, the rush to publish or distribute, however you do it, always raises the risk that you're overlooking something."

Fiedler and Dickerson both raised the need to tell audiences that there are things you don't yet know as a way to couch some missing facts. Both noted that making clear that a story is developing and that what was just reported could be incomplete cushions the blow a bit. "What I think you've got to be able to say is this story is developing, this is what we know now," Fiedler stressed to me. "You might even say this is what we don't know now and that's important ... You need to remember that journalism has to be about facts and not speculation and not rumor."

Then there is the breaking news that's not breaking news, and the overhyping of a single story. Back in the day, breaking news meant something truly important or stunning, worth cutting into a regular television show to report. That was before CNN or MSNBC and all other online and technological news options of today. When JFK was shot, the graphic for CBS said simply – "Bulletin." When the Reagan attempted assassination discussed earlier occurred, CNN had been on less than a year, while the network news shouted: "Special Report."

When John Lennon was shot in 1980, ABC was in the unique situation of broadcasting *Monday Night Football* and learned about the killing before anyone else because one of its local New York affiliate producers, Alan Weiss, happened to be in the emergency room of St. Luke's Roosevelt Hospital in Manhattan when Lennon was brought in. Weiss had gotten into a motorcycle accident and by chance overheard doctors discussing Lennon. He phoned it into the newsroom and after some discussion, it was relayed to sportscasters Howard Cosell and Frank Gifford, who were in the last quarter of a Patriots-Dolphins game on that Monday night, Dec. 8, 1980. That was also back when *Monday Night Football* was a network event, a huge ratings grab for ABC and a major top 10 show. Cosell stated the simple news that Lennon had been shot, rushed to the hospital and was "dead on arrival." The network didn't even break in to the game to report it.

Today, breaking news can be the latest Donald Trump tweet or some minor update on a major story. On the 24-hour news channels, breaking news images are constant, even when the news is a small item, labeled "breaking" only because it just occurred. Turn on any of the three major cable news channels and a "Breaking News" graphic is likely to be in position, often related to the most common news event that's a far cry from Reagan or Lennon being shot.

"There is so much breaking news these days. The banner is almost constantly across the lower third, 'breaking news,'" RTNDA's Dan Shelley told me in an interview. "Obviously, there are big developments in major stories these days that require extra attention, but it can get to the point of exhaustion not only for the viewers but the journalists involved and consumers of other media. I'm not sure what good it does to have the breaking news banner at the lower third all the time."

Or in other cases, the news happened hours earlier, but the outlet still claims it as "breaking." "The breaking news problem is that he knows how to play squirrel with us dogs," Jarvis said about Trump and his ability to make news outlets jump anytime he tweets.

But it goes beyond Trump tweets or outrageous comments to any minor item that CNN, Fox News or MSNBC can post as "breaking," or a "Fox News Alert."

Veteran television newsman Mervin Block, a former staff writer for all three network newscasts who currently blogs about television along with being a writing coach, took the breaking news claims to task in a 2017 item that focused on CNN. He cited several examples from January 2017 of CNN overhyped "breaking news" claims and ripped them to shreds.

First, Erin Burnett's *Out Front* program that airs 7 p.m. EST. Block wrote, "On Jan. 16, she opened her program by using breaking twice, once for 'breaking news,' once for 'breaking details.' Breaking details? Never heard that one before."

Burnett then proceeded to offer an update on the deadly Orlando nightclub shooting that had occurred days earlier. During the newscast she stated, "and more breaking news, the wife of the Orlando nightclub shooter, arrested," Block wrote. "No specifics yet, but later she stated, 'And next, the breaking news, the wife of the Orlando nightclub gunman who killed 49 people, she is under arrest tonight.' Again, no details, just a teaser. Finally, 44 minutes into her newscast, Burnett said, 'Breaking news: the widow of the Orlando nightclub shooter now facing charges connected to the terror attack.'

"Finally, at 7:45 p.m., 45 minutes into her 7 p.m. newscast, she delivered the purported breaking news," Block stated. "But the story was far from breaking: the AP had run news of the arrest at 8 a.m. ET. Which means Burnett called that news breaking almost 12 hours after the AP reported it. Yes, 12 hours."

Three days later, Burnett was back again with more of her "breaking news" that was not breaking. On Jan. 19, at 7:40 p.m., she said, "Breaking news tonight, President Obama commuting 330 prison sentences, the most ever granted by a president in a single day. It comes, of course, on his last full day in office." But, again, Block notes that the news had broken hours earlier: "Although Burnett called that news breaking, the AP had tweeted news of the commutations at 11:46 a.m. EST – seven hours before Burnett called the news breaking."

Finally, on Jan. 26, 2017, there was the Burnett "breaking news" that had already been broken hours earlier by CNN itself. She opened her 7 p.m. show with: "Breaking news, Trump versus Mexico. The meeting between the two leaders canceled." But, as Block points out, it was reported by CNN itself at Noon, seven hours earlier, "and three hours before that, at 8:56 a.m., the AP tweeted word of the Mexican president's cancelation of his trip to Washington. That tweet went out 10 hours before Burnett called it 'breaking news.'"

This all may seem nit-picking and minor, but it is significant when so many news outlets perpetuate this false breaking news label on basic coverage in an effort to drum up hype or a story and give viewers a false sense of urgency on routine stories. That has brought us to a point that when real breaking and urgent news is posted or broadcast the impact is lessened.

CNN received sharp criticism three years earlier when it obsessed over the Malaysian Airlines jet that went missing on March 8, 2014, with 239 people aboard. Although little new news was occurring for weeks that followed, other than the ongoing search, CNN put a "breaking news" alert up almost daily for its news-less updates. At one point, it brought sharp rebukes from competitors.

"Another day of 'breaking news' based on finding nothing or in other words, 'not breaking news,'" future *Meet the Press* host Chuck Todd, then the NBC News political director and chief White House correspondent, tweeted on May 21, 2014, according to *Politico*. "I know it may look like I am casting stones while potentially living in a glass house. But the mistakes of one news org hurts ALL of us ... Then it becomes 'the media' is abusing 'breaking news' – no it's not 'the media' in general."

Two weeks later, when some real new news on the missing airliner occurred, then-NBC *Nightly News* anchor Brian Williams took a shot at the cable obsession when he reported the updated facts. "It's now been one month since Flight 370 has been heard from, and while the cable news coverage has called it 'breaking news' for 30-plus days, the first real break came at midday, Monday, in Australia," Williams stated at the top of the newscast, according to an NBC transcript. "With word that the underwater sound that vessels are picking up are consistent with the sounds of the submerged beacon from an underwater jet liner."

But it is not just CNN that often trips over the line. MSNBC pulled an over-hyped goof on Oct. 19, 2016, when it declared "breaking news" for a story that Joe Biden had planned to announce if he would run for president in 2016 in the next 48 hours. "Oh wow! So it's not that Vice President Joe Biden has made his decision as to whether or not he is going to run for President; the 'breaking news' element is that he will decide sometime in the next two days and someone told MSNBC," Mediaite's J.D. Durkin wrote that day in reaction to the report. "It is as if MSNBC were CNN and Joe Biden were a missing airliner."

Network news has also seen fit to break into programming more and more in recent years, often with Trump-related news about investigations into his alleged Russian ties or other events that would likely have remained just news channel fodder or a nightly news story in the past. Among the weaker breaking alerts was ABC News cutting into afternoon programming on June 1, 2018, to announce Trump had just finished a White House meeting with a North Korean envoy for Kim Jong-un. Not a meeting with Kim himself, but with his envoy.

There was also the March 23, 2018, CBS News break-in to programming to report that President Trump was set to sign a $1.3 Trillion spending bill – again, something that would have brought less special news alerts in the past. Both are clear examples of network news trying to compete with 24-hour cable, twitter and other online alerts. But with a clear lack of editorial judgment and a further deteriorating of the true nature of breaking news or special reports.

Finally, there are the all-too-common local station breaking news scams. During my nine years in California, from 1990 to 1999, I saw examples of the worst of it in Southern California. The Los Angeles and San Diego area affiliates loved to track down a stolen car chase and put their traffic helicopters on the fleeing vehicle, and still do. Although there is no real news other than a stolen vehicle – an act that happens daily around the country – producers know the mundane drama will grab eyeballs.

You can blame the infamous 1994 O.J. Simpson car chase, in which the murder suspect tried to flee in his Ford Bronco after being named a suspect in his wife's death and that of her friend Ronald Goldman. When TV crews caught up to him on a Southern California highway, it became one of the most surreal events in television history as national news outlets broke in with the feed on that Friday night; at one point several NBC affiliates in Chicago, Los Angeles and San Francisco, posted a split screen with Simpson's chase on one side and the 1994 NBC Finals Game

5 on the other. Ever since then, car chases have been local television catnip.

A recent example was a single car pursuit on May 1, 2018, broadcast by two CBS affiliates in Los Angeles, KCAL and KCBS, who remained on the 10 a.m. Tuesday morning pursuit for 40 minutes, cutting into the Price is Right on one channel and America's Court with Judge Ross on the other. It finally ended when police stopped the car and arrested the suspect without incident. Back in my home state of New Jersey, such car chases are common and often barely merit a mention on an inside page of the local paper.

Almost as bad are local weather alerts and overkill of big storms by local TV. We've all seen it. The standard approach is to "flood the zone," to borrow former *New York Times* Executive Editor Howell Raines' phrase for blanketing a story with reporters. But he was talking about real major tragedies like the Sept. 11, 2001, attacks or a mass shooting and such.

With weather stories it often takes an average storm or heavier than usual snowfall, at least in my east coast New York area market, to have local television send numerous reporters out, have them stand in the rain or snow, and tell you that it is raining or snowing. There have been times in the New York region, and I am sure others such as Boston, Toronto, or Chicago – how about Denver and Buffalo – where the regular programing is broken into and hour after hour of reporters in the snow describing the storm, with little real news, masquerades as coverage. We know that such coverage gets ratings, especially when most of the viewers are stuck inside because of the snow and for some reason want to watch it. But it's not news worthy of continuous, non-stop coverage when nothing new is happening.

In the case of hurricanes, it reaches network levels with correspondents getting blown around in the wind as they try to speak with the anchor person. A deadly hurricane barreling down on Florida or Louisiana or the eastern coast is news, but should that preclude all other coverage for hours or days? If ratings are the result, they will broadcast it – online, too. Just look at the data. The top trending news stories of 2017, according to *Business Insider*, included four hurricanes – Irma, Harvey, Maria, and Jose – along with the solar eclipse, the Dream Act immigration debate, the Las Vegas shooting, North Korea, the Bitcoin price and April the Giraffe, a 40-minute video of a giraffe giving birth in a California zoo.

But the local weather overhype does nothing in many cases other than push other news and programming off the screen – broadcast or computer – and in some cases spark concern or even fear about the pending storms that can affect everything from unnecessary school closings to other cancelled services and needs. Not to mention that mini-panics can begin as people rush to get supplies, sometimes without need.

The Weather Channel took the hype a step further in 2012 when it began naming storms, perhaps an irresponsible move given that the hurricane naming had always been done by the National Weather Service. The Weather Channel, which is owned by NBC and not connected to the federal agency, appeared to be doing so in an effort to gin up attention for storms that were not even at tropical storm level.

"Treating every storm like some fantastic aberration does a disservice to the people in harm's way," weather reporter Dennis Mersereau wrote on Forbes.com in 2017. "When every storm is the worst storm ever, the storms that deserve the strongest wording possible – say, Sandy or Harvey or a crippling blizzard – will be treated like previous storms of lesser intensity that got the same obnoxious treatment. The weather is cool enough without pretending that everything is out to maul you. Save it for the octopuses or clowns, not the storms."

Accuweather founder and president Dr. Joel N. Myers, whose organization competes with The Weather Channel, said shortly after the change, "In unilaterally deciding to name winter storms, The Weather Channel has confused media spin with science and public safety and is doing a disservice to the field of meteorology and public service."

Not long after the first storm naming occurred in 2012, the National Weather Service showed its objections in a respectful statement to outlets advising it would not refer to a Nov. 7, 2012, snowstorm as "Athena," a name The Weather Channel had given it: "The NWS does not use name storms in our products. Please refrain from using the term Athena in any of our products."

Celebrity news and gossip dates back to the Hollywood glitz and glamour of Clark Gable, Tyrone Power and – perhaps more importantly – power pens Hedda Hopper and Louella Parsons. Those lecherous ladies wielded more influence to make or break, and even destroy, careers and images than any Kardashian Tweet or Access Hollywood tidbit does today.

"Both were startlingly vindictive with major stars," author George Eels wrote in his 1972 book, *Hedda and Louella: A Dual Biography*. "Charlie Chaplin, Orson Welles, Greta Garbo, Katharine Hepburn, Laurence Olivier and Vivian Leigh all received harsh treatment. Lesser players, possibly because they received less news potential, were treated better."

Imagine if Twitter, Facebook, Instagram and the web were around in 1939 when Parsons broke the story of Clark Gable divorcing his second wife, Ria, a scoop she reportedly got by "kidnapping" Mrs. Gable and keeping her at Parson's Hollywood home until she was sure the story was "speeding across the wire" ahead of any other service, reports *Vanity Fair*.

Had that tidbit been found today, would Parsons have revealed it online or via Twitter? Certainly she would have faced steeper competition and could have broken it quicker via the web.

"Her most earth-shattering scoop during her early years in California, however, was 'the biggest divorce story in the history of Hollywood,'" according to *Vanity Fair.* "The split between the town's undisputed king and queen, Douglas Fairbanks Sr. and Mary Pickford. Pickford, who made the crucial mistake – repeated reflexively by generations of stars to come – of pouring her heart out to Louella, bitterly recalled that she had 'counted . . . upon the columnist's discretion' to safeguard her 'against sensation.' When the bombshell erupted across international headlines, Hollywood was treated to one of its first full-throttle media maelstroms."

For Hopper, her biggest and perhaps most offensive practice was during the 1950s communist witch hunts when she pounded against screenwriters like Dalton Trumbo and others who either refused to name fellow sympathizers or were found to have communist ties themselves. "When a major portion of the industry resented the scheduled ... investigation of Hollywood by the House Un-American Activities Committee, Hedda welcomed it," Eels wrote. "Her brand of Americanism was based on fear of change and made no allowances or shadings and differences of opinion."

When subpoenaed writers, actors and directors refused to testify as to their Communist membership or leanings, "Hedda was outraged," and printed a letter from one reader urging a Hollywood boycott. Hopper agreed that the industry needed a "thorough housecleaning."

Today's celebrity reporting takes pretty much the same approach. It is often said the press builds celebrities up just to tear them down. But even in Hopper's and Parsons' day, the news of the rich and famous remained pretty much in their columns and the celebrity and gossip pages. But in the desperate demand for eyeballs and readers, anything related to celebrity can get steep interest and response today.

"The belief that the news media pays too much attention to celebrity news – including Hollywood gossip and stories about individual celebrities such as Britney Spears and Paris Hilton – is widely shared," a Pew Research study found in 2007, revealing that 40% of those polled believed there was too much celebrity news, with more of them among younger respondents. "Comparable numbers of Republicans, Democrats and independents – and men and women – cite celebrity news as receiving too much news media attention." A 2014 Harris Poll found a similar view of celebrity coverage, revealing that "three-fourths of U.S. adults (76%) say celebrity gossip/scandal stories are over-covered, while half (49%) say the same about general entertainment news."

It appeared to be the one area that political affiliation played no role. The blame, in part, would go to the audience itself. Celebrity news and happenings are popular. Look at most network affiliates on weeknights, when the 7 p.m. to 8 p.m. hour – 6 p.m. to 7 p.m. central time – is chock full of pseudo entertainment news shows, such as *Access Hollywood, Extra, Inside Edition* and *Entertainment Tonight*, with the latter two ranking in the top 10 of national syndicated television shows, according to Nielsen.

"There is still a very big market for it, but there is so much competition," Longtime media analyst Marc Berman told me in an interview. "You have a network like E that built itself around the Kardashians and celebrity news. One of the reasons is that in the world of social media it resonates, and it is very strong and very appealing to the millennial generation. It is very relevant among millennials, you have networks that build their personalities around it. There is a hunger for this because it is an escape from their everyday lines."

But there is also a certain laziness and easy content creation to most celebrity news. Unlike in Hopper and Parsons day, when the viper ladies had to go out and dig up stories or get tipped off, some of today's entertainment news can simply be a celebrity tweet or leaked promotional item.

Much of what the syndicated entertainment shows "report" is merely promotion pushed by publicists and the celebrities themselves. TMZ has made a fortune off of cell phone videos of celebrities caught on the street essentially doing nothing but answering weak questions. Although that outlet did break the first word of Michael Jackson's death back in 2009, the follow-up was deemed one of the most over-covered stories of the year. A Pew Study found that about two-thirds of the public (64%) said news organizations gave too much attention to Jackson's demise. It noted that three out of 10 (29%) said the coverage was the right amount and only 3% say there had been too little coverage.

The more recent 2018 celebrity suicides of designer Kate Spade and food guru Anthony Bourdain were top stories covered heavily, but with an interesting twist in that they appeared to spark more calls to suicide hotlines. Perhaps a positive offshoot of heavy coverage that often included hotline information for viewers. "Trained counselors at more than 150 crisis centers in the United States fielded 65% more phone calls [the week after those deaths] for the National Suicide Prevention Lifeline," CNN reported, later adding, "the Crisis Text Line saw a 116% increase in volume."

But the celebrity news, on syndicated shows or the regular news outlets, is only one part of the abundance of such content. Reality shows have turned some ordinary people into celebrities and some barely famous figures into superstars. Many viewers know more about who is on the Bachelor, Bachelorette or Real Housewives than the name of their

Congressman. And the Kardashians or Paris Hilton have become household names for accomplishing nothing more than being famous.

"What ties together all the various formats of the reality TV genre is their professed abilities to more fully provide viewers an unmediated, voyeuristic, and yet often playful look into what might be called the 'entertaining real,'" Authors Laurie Ouellette and Susan Murray wrote in their 2008 book, *Reality TV: Remaking Television Culture*. "This fixation with 'authentic' personalities, situations, problems, and narratives is considered to be reality TV's primary distinction from fictional television and also its primary selling point. However, viewers have certainly been well trained in the ways of reality TV since its initial emergence and are therefore quite savvy and skeptical when it comes to how much is actually 'real' in these programs."

And they appeared to be getting tired of it as far back as 2005 when an Associated Press/*TV Guide* poll found that 80 percent of respondents said there was too much reality TV, far ahead of any other genre. More than 80% also believed that most reality shows are either "mostly distorted" or "totally made up," but more than 60 percent said they either didn't care or cared very little about that fact. So the reality shows continue, perhaps to quench the thirst for both celebrity and escape from one's own life – two factors that could explain interest in coverage of the rich and famous overall.

That leads into the most famous celebrity of the day, President Donald Trump. Aside from his political attraction for some, and the media's part in that success, Trump also serves a celebrity news role. First as he gained fame in the 1980s and 1990s as a business man who drew headlines and interest for his outspoken nature, outlandish style and self-promotion. Then he became a reality star himself on NBC's Celebrity Apprentice. But when Trump was elected president, he took to Twitter like no other politician, raising the chance for news-making comments even higher.

News outlets knew this from the start, which is why they began overcovering him on the campaign trail, as noted earlier with constant live feeds of his rallies, and later with coverage of his administration that can go wall to wall, hour after hour on some cable news outlets. "The whole fucking hour," *New Yorker* media writer Ken Auletta declares of some MSNBC and other constant Trump images. "There's no Middle East, there's no Africa, there's no Korea, and I think that's a mistake. And, I think we're walking, where the press walks into a trap, reconfirming the worst things that critics of the press say about it."

Columbia Journalism Review editor-in-chief and publisher Kyle Pope offered a frustrated view of the overkill in a January 2018 piece that urged a cutback in the hype.

"I remain astonished by the ability of this former reality TV star to be our assignment editor. He has a preternatural ability to intuit the bumps and swerves of the news cycle, enabling him to refocus attention on himself just as it is in danger of moving on," Pope wrote. "The world, finally, seems to be interested in something outside the West Wing? Zip out a late-night tweet ridiculing a senator. Congressional reporters are digging into the effects of his legislative ideas? Say something outrageous about the leader of a nuclear-armed foe. A TV anchor offers a smart analysis of the president's team? Pretend you don't watch and call him the dumbest man on TV. It's entirely within Donald Trump's rights to do what he does; the dignity of America's highest office be damned. But it is, or should be, within our rights to ignore him, or to bring him back to what we think matters."

And what matters is becoming more and more important as it gets less and less coverage. The fallout from the over-coverage of the issues noted previously is that it must be countered with under-coverage – and sometimes no coverage – of other things. Usually, those are issues that need attention the most, or at least as much as the top stories of the year.

"Cable is genetically designed to over-focus on the latest and under-focus on context," NPR media reporter David Folkenflik said in an interview. "It is just not a public service. At this point in the game if you are not shedding light you shouldn't be in the business. This is an important time."

Business Insider noted the most under-covered stories of 2017 were the Pentagon's $22 million UFO investigation; the Yemen Cholera epidemic that killed one million people; the Puerto Rico post-hurricane deaths that surpassed 1,000; a Croatia war criminal's suicide during his trial; President Obama's Iran-deal related concessions to Hezbollah; Hobby Lobby's illegal smuggling of Middle East artifacts; Egyptian terrorist attacks that killed 300; the doubling of American military militias since 2008; Bangladesh monsoons; Iraq's mini-civil war; and the continued war in Ukraine.

And as Folkenflik noted, much of the under-covered or forgotten news is in-depth reporting on major stories, as well as context. This is not a new phenomenon as the 2014 Harris Poll found the public yearning for broader coverage and more investigative efforts. "When the news never stops coming, it stands to reason that there's sufficient bandwidth to leave no topical stone unturned ... in theory," the Harris report stated. "But of course, that doesn't mean that every sort of story gets the same level of coverage."

The study found that 47 percent of respondents feel humanitarian issues in the U.S. and education were under-covered, while 45 percent pointed to science, 44 percent cited government corruption, and 42 percent corporate corruption and white-collar crimes as being diminished. About 30 percent of those polled wanted more reporting on global/international humanitarian issues and health stories.

"The thing that is so frustrating is we have so many outlets now and they trickle down on the same things. It is stressing to see," said online news veteran and former *Washington Post* web editor James Brady, who pointed to the ratings and traffic demands too often steering coverage that leads to ignored stories. "Now you have all this information about what people are reading in real time, you have to put those numbers aside and see if this is something for us to cover. If you have to worry about getting your numbers up, at some point the people consuming the site are dragged into things that drive page views. They are so wedded to that page view model, I don't know how you get out of that."

Another forgotten story is the U.S. infrastructure, which ranges from highways and public buildings to the vulnerable power grid and schools. Legendary newsman Ted Koppel has crusaded for electrical power sourcing improvements, penning an entire book on the subject in 2016, titled *Lights Out: A Cyberattack, A Nation Unprepared, Surviving the Aftermath*, which advocates for improvements and, of course, more news attention and warns that a computer hacker could wreak havoc on the power grid easily.

"Our media report daily on increasingly bold and costly acts of online piracy that are already costing the U.S. economy countless billions of dollars a year," Koppel writes, later adding, "we are unprepared, but why isn't the issue higher on our list of national priorities? It is difficult for anyone holding public office to focus attention on a problem without being able to offer any solutions."

Koppel goes on to cite the newsroom cutbacks for the lack of focus on the power issue, and other complicated subjects, stating, "attempting to alert the American public to a pending crisis becomes more difficult when the subject itself is complicated and defies easy or brief explanation."

He mentions important coverage on the power grid from the likes of NPR, *The New York Times* and *The Wall Street Journal*. Other occasional pieces from outlets such as *Time* and even Popular Mechanics in the past few years have touched on the issue, but not enough given the severity of the problem. *Time* wrote in March 2017 that the U.S. power grid was "an antiquated piece of 20th century technology struggling to power the 21st century." It then pointed to the northeast blackout 14 years earlier that left more than 50 million people in the U.S. and Canada powerless, including New York City, for several days and cost about $10 billion.

"The great Northeastern blackout of Aug. 14, 2003 wasn't caused by an attack," the story said. "When a transmission line in northern Ohio began to sag because of the intense summer heat, it tangled with the branches of a nearby tree, causing the wire to trip offline. One thing led to another in a perfect storm of equipment and human failure."

Although improvements have been made in the past decade-plus, as *Time* noted, the reliance on computers and technology has also brought about the vulnerability that Koppel fears. "Over the past several years, we have seen cyberattacks against critical infrastructures abroad, and many of our own infrastructures are as vulnerable as their foreign counterparts," Director of National Intelligence Dennis Blair said in a 2009 *Wall Street Journal* story about a Russian and China "cyberintrusion" that year. "A number of nations, including Russia and China, can disrupt elements of the U.S. information infrastructure."

But searches of power grid-related stories find few in recent years since Koppel's book, other than updates on Puerto Rico's post-hurricane issues. The same could be said of other infrastructure needs, from roads to sewers, drinking water sources, schools and public transit. But aside from news and editorials here and there in recent years, few warnings are put out in the press. "America's roads are often crowded, frequently in poor condition, chronically underfunded, and are becoming more dangerous," the American Society of Civil Engineers declared in its 2017 Infrastructure Report Card, which offered a D grade. "More than two out of every five miles of America's urban interstates are congested, and traffic delays cost the country $160 billion in wasted time and fuel in 2014. One out of every five miles of highway pavement is in poor condition and our roads have a significant and increasing backlog of rehabilitation needs."

The Council of State Governments in January 2018 described U.S. infrastructure as "precarious," citing a $926 billion backlog in needed highway and transit improvement projects; 55,710 bridges in the United States now considered structurally deficient; A series of devastating hurricanes in September causing "significant damage" in Florida, Texas and Puerto Rico and brought new warnings from engineers and urban planners about the lack of resilience in the nation's infrastructure, declaring: "the worst spike in traffic deaths in more than 50 years in 2016, with 37,461 people killed in motor vehicle crashes, a 5 percent increase over 2015." The Council also pointed to the nation's drinking water safety problem, first raised with the 2014 Flint water crisis and apparently still continuing.

"The impact of the Flint water crisis continued to be felt as testing revealed even higher lead levels in communities across the country," The Council explained. "A report released in the fall [of 2017] said outdated EPA drinking water regulations fail to regulate known carcinogens and other chemicals in our water."

Bobby Magill, president of the Society of Environmental Journalists, said covering dangerous drinking water stories is not a problem when the big, frightening initial reporting includes important information about lead or other contaminants making people sick, which occurred in Flint – as well as political ineptness and poor management by the city and state to boot.

But when you get into the details and scientific jargon, some readers – and journalists – get lost or bored, making comprehensive journalism and interest in it more difficult. And when interest goes away, so do ratings and web traffic. "One of the challenges we face, if you are working for a local newspaper or some other legacy media, they are trying to justify their reporting based on audience-gaining matrix," Magill told me in an interview. "There are multiple dimensions to audience engagement. If your story doesn't get the engagement that the editor will like it is more difficult to sell that kind of coverage to your editor."

He later added, "If you write about lead in drinking water, a lot of people care about that because it affects them directly, they want to know. But stories about what's going on down at the wastewater treatment plant or drilling on public lands, those sorts of things are incredibly important, and it is sometimes challenging to make sure those stories gain the audience they deserve."

The infrastructure story gained some steam during the 2016 presidential election when then-candidate Donald Trump vowed to spend more than $500 billion on infrastructure improvements. He said on Fox Business News in August 2016 that he would spend twice as much as Hillary Clinton, who had proposed a five-year, $275 billion plan at the time. "Well I would say at least double her numbers and you're going to really need more than that," Trump said. "We have bridges that are falling down."

Trump made more noise about it in February 2018, promising a $1.5 trillion infrastructure plan as part of his budget proposals. But on March 29, 2018, the *Washington Post* reported just $21 billion, or one percent, had been allocated by Congress. And as of May 2018, no further infrastructure improvement plan had even been proposed and White House spokeswoman Sarah Huckabee Sanders told reporters on May 9, 2018, that "I don't know that there will be one by the end of the year."

Trump is also linked to another under-covered story of recent times: his own business corruption, according to BillMoyers.com, which dubbed his personal and business conflicts of interest as its most ignored story of 2017. "The most overlooked story this year continues to be Trump's conflicts of interest and the lack of legal mechanisms to protect the executive branch of the federal government from corruption," the Moyers site wrote in December 2017. "In 2016, the press – with the exception of Kurt Eichenwald at *Newsweek* – ignored the vast web of global business interests and questionable connections that Trump and his company had and how they might conflict with American foreign policy interests.

It later stated that the press "completely failed to note that Trump was constitutionally ineligible to serve if he did not fully divest from his business, as he would be in violation of the Constitution's emoluments clause. Since the election, outlets such as *The New York Times*, the *Washington Post*, Reuters and *The New Yorker* have covered various conflicts of interest for Trump, his family members and his unpaid advisers such as Carl Icahn and Jared Kushner. But TV, the most popular medium from which Americans get their news, remains relentlessly focused on the sexier topics of the day. That's often just what Trump tweeted … the complicated connections between the personal financial interests of Trump, his White House staffers, family and associates and the policies being promulgated at the White House remains under-illuminated."

The Moyers' list of under-covered stories also included: U.S. air strikes in Iraq; placement of military personnel around the world; Trump's reductions in environmental regulations, increased right-leaning judicial appointments, and impact of his tax cut plan; and the increased appointment of federal employees that bypass Congressional approvals.

FEAR FACTOR

The weather hype can be considered a somewhat reduced version of overall fear-based reporting that has seen increases in recent decades, in which some issue – be in a health scare or a physical threat – can be blown up to both raise concern and, along with it, ratings.

We examined some of this as relates to guns and mass shootings, which as noted remain a small threat to most people, as well as the vaccine fears, although more of that is based on disinformation than hype.

Still, there are other fear-based scares the media is glad to go along with, from Ebola to terrorism, many based on the disease or infection, or more often the irresponsible reporting, of the day.

"We're so guilty of spreading it," Dr. David Marks of WNBC-TV, the NBC New York affiliate, told author Mark Siegel, also a doctor, in his book, *False Alarm: The Truth about the Epidemic of Fear*. "I don't like reporting the overhyped stories that unnecessarily scare people. But those are my assignments. I try to put things in perspective, to do my best to tone things down. But sometimes I wish we weren't covering these stories at all."

Health fears and scares are not new, and the origins are not completely surprising or always baseless. For more than a century the most feared disease, especially for children, was Polio, which could strike out of nowhere and render the victim paralyzed for life. Although some cases were mild the worries of contracting the affliction were often as crippling as the disease itself.

"Polio rapidly became every parent's worst nightmare: a horrific disease which killed and maimed children, which could break into any house without warning, and which could not be prevented or treated," Gareth Williams wrote in her 2013 book, *Paralysed With Fear: The Story of Polio*, describing the first epidemic onset of the disease in 1916, which left 27,000 people paralyzed and 6,000 dead that year. "The result was widespread fear which boiled up into panic at the approach of each year's polio season and continued to paralyse the American public for the next half-century."

The Smithsonian Institution dates the first discoveries of the Poliomyelitis, or Polio virus, back to 1789, when British physician Michael Underwood provided the first clinical description of the disease. The first outbreak did not occur for more than 100 years when it struck Vermont in 1894 with 132 cases. The virus was not identified until 1908 and no major impact occurred until the 1916 epidemic. But once that hit, the fear and panic were on, according to Williams.

"Fear of the disease was all the greater because its cause and means of spread were a mystery," Williams wrote, noting that everything from milk to fresh fruit were alleged culprits by some early on. "On the street people blamed swimming, Italian immigrants and cats – prejudices that were shared and spread by doctors."

And the press played a role in the fear spreading, according to archives of *The New York Times* and other outlets. A July 4, 1916 front page *Times* story headlined: "Bar All Children from the Movies in Paralysis War," detailed a health department order disallowing anyone 16 years of age or younger from attending movie theaters until the board of health declared the "epidemic had passed." It also listed neighborhood Independence Day events that had been canceled and repeated the New York City Health Department waning not to let children go to "parties, picnics or outings."

But, according to Williams, the danger of polio was less deadly than diphtheria, whooping cough and measles at the time. She noted that influenza later killed some 25 million people worldwide, well beyond Polio: "Yet Polio punched far above its weight in its power to terrify, because it could pick off children from inside the cleanest, most secure households." The scourge finally ended in 1953 when Dr. Jonas Salk developed the first Polio vaccine.

But health-related fears and the media's ability to promote them did not go away. About 20 years after the polio vaccine had its first real impacts in 1955, the hype around Swine Flu not only led people to be afraid of catching this virus most had never heard of, but caused a dangerous vaccine to be rushed out in 1976 and administered in a frantic, nationwide program still criticized today. The vaccination program stemmed from a small outbreak at Fort Dix in New Jersey and eventually resulted in more than 45 million Americans being vaccinated, but at least 450 developed the rare Guillain-Barré syndrome, with 30 of them dying.

"This government-led campaign was widely viewed as a debacle and put an irreparable dent in future public health initiatives, as well as negatively influenced the public's perception of both the flu and the flu shot in this country," Reporter Rebecca Kreston wrote in a 2013 *Discovery Magazine* retrospective, which also noted "while the World Health Organization adopted a cautious 'wait and see' policy to monitor the virus's pattern of disease and to track the number of emerging infections, President Gerald Ford's administration embarked on a zealous campaign to vaccinate every American with brisk efficiency." Many still blame that national goof for sparking some of the vaccine fears that still persist today.

More recently, press outlets have helped perpetuate the false fears of SARS, Ebola, Zika and the infamous Bird Flu, which *Newsweek* panicked about as recently as June 2018, with a story headlined: "What is Disease X? Deadly Bird Flu Virus Could Be Next Pandemic." But just a few graphs into the story that had warned, "A deadly new strain of bird flu threatens to become a worldwide pandemic, health officials warn," and claimed it "could cause an international health crisis," the story also made clear, "Instances of person-to-person spread are extremely rare so far" and "No cases have been reported in the United States."

We saw this before with SARS, the Severe Acute Respiratory Syndrome, which sparked unnecessary alarm in 2003 even though there were only 7,000 cases worldwide and 100 in the United States, according to Siegel. "Only a small portion of those who believe they are at risk really are, and few who become infected actually die," he wrote. "But a strange disease that only kills a few people still makes for good headlines if the story is strategically hyped."

Zika, the virus that can cause birth defects and can be transmitted by mosquitos, dates back to the 1940s. But it sparked widespread worries in 2016 after it was found to be on the rise, but mostly in Caribbean countries. With only 350 U.S. mainland infections by April 2016, mostly from "travel-related cases," according to National Institutes of Health Dr. Anthony Fauci's statements at the time, it was not a major threat. Still, the U.S. media made it the health scare of the year for a while, with more focus on the unlikely mosquito-related cause than sexually transmitted infections and other sources.

Then there's Ebola, the deadly virus that had been on scientific radar since 1976, which saw a major African outbreak in 2014 when the infection data jumped from 80 cases at the beginning of the year to more than 20,000 by the end of 2014. And when many of the doctors who went to Sierra Leone, Iberia and Guinea to treat patients returned to the

United States, panic set in that they might spread the disease, even though the few who had it were not infecting others and some with similar symptoms who were targeted for unnecessary quarantine turned out not to be infected.

The low point was Dr. Craig Spencer, who had returned from treating Ebola patients in Guinea and later was diagnosed with Ebola. When it was discovered he had bowled at a Brooklyn alley prior to showing symptoms, panic ensued, and the alley was actually closed and disinfected for two days. Even though some stories at the time, such as *Time* magazine, made clear that "the virus only survives inside bodily fluid of an infected person – meaning their blood, sweat, vomit or feces – that then comes into contact with an open sore or the mucus membranes of another person," others let the fear spread, and the related ratings and clicks increase.

"After my diagnosis, the media and politicians could have educated the public about Ebola. Instead, they spent hours retracing my steps through New York and debating whether Ebola can be transmitted through a bowling ball. Little attention was devoted to the fact that the science of disease transmission and the experience in previous Ebola outbreaks suggested that it was nearly impossible for me to have transmitted the virus before I had a fever," Spencer later wrote in the *New England Journal of Medicine*. "The media sold hype with flashy headlines – 'Ebola: The ISIS of Biological Agents?'; 'Nurses in safety gear got Ebola, why wouldn't you?'; 'Ebola in the air? A nightmare that could happen' – and fabricated stories about my personal life and the threat I posed to public health, abdicating their responsibility for informing public opinion and influencing public policy."

But things got out of control when both then-New Jersey Gov. Chris Christie and New York Governor Andrew Cuomo set tight restrictions on people entering airports from Ebola-infected countries, even if they showed no symptoms. The official joint announcement stated, in part: "Each State Department of Health ... will, as permitted under applicable law, make its own determination as to hospitalization, quarantine, and other public health interventions for up to 21 days. There will also be a mandatory quarantine for any individual who had direct contact with an individual infected with the Ebola virus while in one of the three West African nations (Liberia, Sierra Leone, or Guinea), including any medical personnel having performed medical services to individuals infected with the Ebola virus. Additionally, all individuals with travel history to the affected regions of West Africa, with no direct contact with an infected person, will be actively monitored by public health officials and, if necessary, quarantined, depending on the facts and circumstances of their particular situation."

Is this public health safety or Big Brother watching you?

Some media outlets such as *Slate* and *The New Yorker* raised objections to the overreaching approach, while the *New England Journal of Medicine* stated it was "not scientifically based, is unfair and unwise, and will impede essential efforts to stop these awful outbreaks of Ebola disease at their source, which is the only satisfactory goal. The governors' action is like driving a carpet tack with a sledgehammer: it gets the job done but overall is more destructive than beneficial."

One infamous effect was the story of Kaci Hickox, a nurse who helped treat Ebola patients in West Africa in 2014 and found herself detained when she returned home to Newark Airport just in time for the new quarantine regulations. Although she tested negative for the virus and displayed no symptoms, she was forced to spend three days in a tent behind University Hospital in Newark, initially with no visitors or contact with a lawyer. She was allowed to return to her home in Maine, but only with an escort and a promise of isolation. Hickox later sued the state, settling in 2017 with an agreement that provided her with no monetary settlement, but created a quarantined patients' bill of rights.

"The periods of outbreak were met with frenzied reporting and saw a series of coordinated international efforts in response," Forbes.com health writer Tim Chen wrote about the Ebola and Zika coverage in 2017. "They were also accompanied by surges in public alarm ... Yet, globally more people died from HIV in a week than the entire period of the Ebola outbreak."

Siegel also noted in *False Alarm* that millions more are infected each year from tuberculosis, AIDS, malaria and influenza – resulting in hundreds of thousands of deaths – than those who catch Zika, Ebola, SARS or most other panic illnesses. Still, those continue to get the attention, and cause unnecessary worry, because they also drive up ratings, clicks and circulation.

"Fear-based news stories prey on the anxieties we all have and then hold us hostage," Psychologist Deborah Serani wrote in a 2011 *Psychology Today* piece. "Being glued to the television, reading the paper or surfing the Internet increases ratings and market shares – but it also raises the probability of depression relapse. In previous decades, the journalistic mission was to report the news as it actually happened, with fairness, balance, and integrity. However, capitalistic motives associated with journalism have forced much of today's television news to look to the spectacular, the stirring, and the controversial as news stories. It's no longer a race to break the story first or get the facts right. Instead, it's to acquire good ratings in order to get advertisers, so that profits soar."

And the effect on the audience is being seen more and more, with what a 2018 Pew Research Study labeled "news fatigue." Its survey found that nearly 70 percent of respondents felt overwhelmed by news today. "Almost seven-in-ten Americans (68%) feel worn out by the amount of news there is these days, compared with only three-in-ten who say they like the amount of news they get," the Pew study said. "The portion expressing feelings of information overload is in line with how Americans felt during the 2016 presidential election, when a majority expressed feelings of exhaustion from election coverage."

AFFORDING THE FIRST
AMENDMENT

Ali Watkins may not be the gold standard for news ethics, but her ethical faux paus – and the way it sparked a major government attack on her rights – has already made her something of a press freedom martyr. And it reminded many in the industry how the recent anti-press fervor of Washington, D.C., and many in the public, is sparking new legal issues for reporters every day.

A young *New York Times* reporter, Watkins managed to climb the journalistic ladder of success quickly through McClatchy, *Buzzfeed*, The *Huffington Post* and *Politico* before reaching the *Times* in late 2017 at the ripe old age of 26. On her way up, she earned a reputation as a dogged reporter who worked sources and files on the competitive national security and intelligence beat, scooping more experienced rivals and landing a Pulitzer Prize finalist nod in 2015, just one year out of college.

But along the way she also sparked a romance with James Wolfe, the former security director of the Senate Select Committee on Intelligence, the very group her Pulitzer coverage focused on. When Wolfe was arrested in the spring of 2018 for allegedly lying to the FBI about knowing Watkins and three other journalists, she was dragged into the proceedings when it was revealed the FBI had seized her email and phone records.

While her romance with a person involved in a story she was covering drew ethical rebukes among the journalism community – and an internal *Times* investigation – the heavy-handed government information grab drew even greater outrage, as it should. It also heightened worries about press freedom and access in the age of Trump – and a time of declining revenues – which limit the financial support for most journalistic legal defense efforts.

In the case of Watkins, who has said Wolfe was never a source for her coverage, supporters contend it is another sign that a federal shield law is needed. A shield law, which exists in 36 states and the District of Columbia, protects reporters from having to reveal their sources in court proceedings, although 25 of those states offer some exceptions for prosecutors seeking the information. Thirteen states, including Virginia where *USA Today* and several other news outlets are based, have no shield law.

And there is no federal shield law, which could very well protect Watkins and many other national reporters facing subpoenas and contempt of court charges stemming from coverage of federal court actions or related news. Several versions of such a statute have been introduced and even passed one house of Congress, but none have been given approval by both or any presidential support. Many media advocates have claimed that reporters deserve the same privileges as a doctor or lawyer, who can cite doctor-patient, or attorney-client privileges. Such views have led to the state-level shield laws.

But on the federal level, the 1972 Branzburg ruling by the U.S. Supreme Court, a 5-4 vote that found reporters cannot withhold sources related to a criminal act, has been the ultimate ruling for many. But even in that case, which involved a Kentucky newspaper reporter who had written about local drug dealers he observed and refused to divulge their identity to investigators, had a complicated ruling.

Although the court affirmed the demand for the reporter to reveal his sources, Justice Lewis F. Powell Jr. added a stipulation in his concurring opinion, writing, "the Court does not hold that newsmen, subpoenaed to testify before a grand jury, are without constitutional rights with respect to the gathering of news or in safeguarding their sources," later noting "the courts will be available to newsmen under circumstances where legitimate First Amendment interests require protection."

Constitution Law Reporter points out that, "Justice Powell then went on to describe a balancing test that is still used in most federal courts when determining the existence of the reporters' privilege. '[I]f the newsman is called upon to give information bearing only a remote and tenuous relationship to the subject of the investigation, or if he has some other reason to believe that his testimony implicates confidential source relationships without a legitimate need of law enforcement, he will have access to the court on a motion to quash, and an appropriate protective order may be entered. The asserted claim to privilege should be judged on its facts by the striking of a proper balance between freedom of the press and the obligation of all citizens to give relevant testimony with respect to criminal conduct. The balance of these vital constitutional and societal interests on a case-by-case basis accords with the tried and traditional way of adjudicating such questions,' Justice Powell explained."

Many contend that left open a large hole for a shield law or other expanded press source protection at the federal level. When the Watkins records seizure occurred, many in the press used that idea to push for the nationwide protection.

"What is to be done?" *Chicago Tribune* syndicated columnist and Pulitzer Prize-winner Clarence Page wrote days after the Watkins incident. "The Watkins case and the strong possibility of more like it underscore the need for a federal 'shield law' like those in various forms in most states. Reasonable safeguards are needed to prevent government from indiscriminately seizing confidential records or forcing reporters to disclose anonymous sources. At a time when one party controls the White House, Congress and appointments to the Supreme Court, it is particularly important to strengthen the independent voice of a free press."

He also pointed out that anti-press actions by the federal government did not begin with Trump but have slowly been creeping up for years. Most recently with President Obama: "Obama, a former teacher of constitutional law at the University of Chicago, alarmed CPJ (Committee to Protect Journalists) and other press freedom advocates with the worst record on press freedom of any president since Richard Nixon put reporters on his "enemies list" – or perhaps since Abraham Lincoln suspended the writ of habeas corpus during the Civil War."

Indeed, a 2013 CPJ report on Obama's press treatment, co-authored by former *Washington Post* Executive Editor Leonard Downie, Jr., stated that, "CPJ is disturbed by the pattern of actions by the Obama administration that have chilled the flow of information on issues of great public interest, including matters of national security. The administration's war on leaks to the press through the use of secret subpoenas against news organizations, its assertion through prosecution that leaking classified documents to the press is espionage or aiding the enemy, and its increased limitations on access to information that is in the public interest – all thwart a free and open discussion necessary to a democracy."

"I think we have a real problem," *New York Times* national security reporter Scott Shane told Downie in the report. "Most people are deterred by those leaks prosecutions. They're scared to death. There's a gray zone between classified and unclassified information, and most sources were in that gray zone. Sources are now afraid to enter that gray zone. It's having a deterrent effect. If we consider aggressive press coverage of government activities being at the core of American democracy, this tips the balance heavily in favor of the government."

One of Obama's notable actions occurred in 2009, the year he took office, when he declared a defacto war on Fox News, stating they would not be treated like other news outlets. The salvos quickly drew opposition from other White House reporters and the short-lived anti-Fox stance ended. While Obama was credited with backing down on some of the press restrictions and hostile policies, he left office with a poor legacy of press treatment that some say has fueled Trump's continued and accelerated abuse of journalists' rights.

"The record is clear," former *New York Times* reporter James Risen wrote in a December 2016 column just weeks before Obama left office. "Over the past eight years, the administration has prosecuted nine cases involving whistle-blowers and leakers, compared with only three by all previous administrations combined. It has repeatedly used the Espionage Act, a relic of World War I-era red-baiting, not to prosecute spies but to go after government officials who talked to journalists. Under Mr. Obama, the Justice Department and the F.B.I. have spied on reporters by monitoring their phone records, labeled one journalist an unindicted co-conspirator in a criminal case for simply doing reporting and issued subpoenas to other reporters to try to force them to reveal their sources and testify in criminal cases."

Risen, who now reports for *The Intercept,* knows Obama's anti-press moves first-hand, having been targeted in a seven-year court battle to reveal his source for a story on a CIA plot to disrupt Iran's nuclear program. Although Risen lost his Supreme Court appeal, Obama Attorney General Eric Holder chose not to prosecute Risen.

Still, the Obama policies remained mostly in place and have helped Trump's administration and Justice Department to continue and even expand the efforts. "That the government sought records from a reporter, any reporter, in this case is troubling," Gabe Rottman, Technology and Press Freedom Project Director at the Reporters Committee for Freedom of the Press, wrote after the Watkins records seizure. "Internal guidelines at the Justice Department prohibit investigators from targeting a reporter unless they cannot get the relevant information from a non-media source and the information is truly essential to the case ... Those principles – that journalists should be subject to investigation only when absolutely necessary – implicate both sound public policy concerns and the First Amendment. Journalism doesn't work in a democracy if reporters can't protect the identity of their sources."

George Freeman, former assistant general counsel for *The New York Times* Company and current executive director of the Media Law Resource Center, feared Trump's approach could begin to target reporters more than leakers in court. "So far Trump on the one hand is basically all rhetoric and not much action, the libel law hasn't changed even though he's talked about it. The thing I am most scared about that would be a real game changer is actually prosecuting not only the government leaker but prosecuting the publication that it is leaked to. No one has gone after the *Washington Post* or *The New York Times* or NBC for publishing or reporting the leaks. If Trump does that it is really a game changer."

Protecting news sources and journalists' personal records is just one of many legal issues facing today's reporters and their employers both due to Trump's policies and the state of the industry. From source protection to increased libel and slander claims to fewer resources for challenging access to public information, fighting anti-press attacks and even diminished access to credentials, the legal battles for news outlets and their staff are at a peak not seen in many decades, attorneys and press rights groups say. And much of the opposition is coming as resources are diminishing, as we've noted, reducing the time and money available to both fight legal challenges and demand press rights.

"I've been seeing a higher rate of cases being brought against the press," Jeff Hermes, former director of the Digital Media Law Project at Harvard University and now a deputy director of the Media Law Resource Center, said in an interview. "There is certainly some [anti-press] encouragement in our society, emanating from the White House, chasing down the press with allegations of fake news, suggesting that the press is somehow vulnerable and should be held to a higher level."

Citing specific data on libel and slander and other anti-press lawsuits is difficult, attorneys contend, because the actions are brought in both state and federal courts and no clearinghouse exists. However, anecdotal findings and some examples of large-judgement verdicts and settlements reveal an alarming trend.

"There's no question there has been a rise in the number of libel lawsuits being filed, and the tone in those lawsuits has become much more shrill," Charles Tobin, a partner at Ballard Spahr in Washington, D.C., one of the country's top media law firms, said in an interview. "The courts are still grappling with the First Amendment and applying it to the new technologies." He said the verdicts and settlements are still mostly going the press' way, but with more cases filed and a longer process to adjudicate them, the cost in time and money is huge.

"More cases are going to discovery, which is the real expensive part of it," Tobin said. "Judges have more tendency to let plaintiffs get some evidence and letting cases go on a little longer, and too long, and that is costing a lot of money and bleeding more resources."

Among the most impactful recent cases involves the Hulk Hogan sex tape and *Gawker*. Celebrity wrestler Hulk Hogan, whose legal name is Terry Bollea, was videotaped in 2006 having sex with the wife of a friend,

Radio host Bubba "the Love Sponge" Clem. The video, shot by Clem himself, was eventually obtained by the news site *Gawker*, which posted excerpts of it online in 2012. Bollea, who had claimed the video was made without his knowledge, sued *Gawker* for invasion of privacy and won a $140 million jury judgement in 2016, including $115 million in compensatory damages and $25 million in punitive damages.

The initial award prompted *Gawker* to file for bankruptcy, and eventually shut down. In the end, *Gawker* was sold to Univision and agreed to a $31 million settlement with Bollea in late 2016. But the case also had another twist when it was learned that Billionaire entrepreneur Peter Thiel had supported Bollea's cause with up to $10 million in financial assistance that helped him put the pressure on *Gawker* and settle the case before it could be appealed.

Thiel's interest stemmed from a 2007 *Gawker* story that revealed Thiel is gay. A fact not disputed, but also not something Thiel wanted to be reported. As the founder of PayPal and an early Facebook investor, Thiel has amassed a large fortune, and a prominent reputation in Silicon Valley. So when Bollea took on *Gawker* years later, Thiel was glad to step in and help with a clear revenge move. "It's less about revenge and more about specific deterrence," he told *The New York Times* in 2016. "I saw *Gawker* pioneer a unique and incredibly damaging way of getting attention by bullying people even when there was no connection with the public interest."

Outing gay people, especially celebrities and other public figures, has been a controversial move for decades, especially years ago when gay rights were still in their infancy and anti-gay laws, and fervor, were much worse. While today's gay rights are much stronger, and public support greater, some still contend it is an unfair move. But also a concern is the ability of Thiel and others with deep pockets to take on a media outlet they do not like and overwhelm them with legal battles to the point of destruction.

"The settlement leaves many questions unanswered," a Forbes.com analysis stated after the settlement. "They range from First Amendment implications to the extent of billionaire investor Peter Thiel's involvement and the fate of two of *Gawker*'s most recognizable faces, [*Gawker* founder Nick] Denton and ex-editor A.J. Daulerio. Observers of the case are now left wondering what would have happened if it continued with its appeal of Hogan's $140 million judgment. Those left asking 'what if' may be wondering of the private details behind the financing of Hogan's lawsuit, which was secretly funded by billionaire investor Peter Thiel, or the First Amendment boundaries that could have been tested on appeal. Given the content of the 2012 article on Hogan's sex tape that prompted the landmark lawsuit, a new trial would have allowed an appeals court to re-examine just how far a publication can go in defining what is newsworthy."

As for the case itself, Hermes contends it was badly handled by the judge and the Florida court where it occurred and could have been reversed on appeal. "This is bad acts and a judge who made some poor decisions," Hermes said in an interview. "We never had an appellate court look at the case. A preliminary injunction was denied on appeal and determined it was a case of public concern, so the video could have continued." He added that, "The size of the verdict was so large that it had an effect on the ability to appeal the case … Sex tapes are always tricky because they evoke all kinds of reactions, but did it relate to a matter of public importance, yeah."

Katie Townsend, litigation director at Reporters Committee for Freedom of the Press, also cited the lack of an appeal that could have changed things, telling *Forbes*: "The claims that Hulk Hogan prevailed on, we're not going to see those tested on appeal. I think it does set some precedent, not in a legal way, but in a very real way, for future plaintiffs who may be emboldened to do this kind of thing, because we know juries can have a different reaction to privacy claims than a court would necessarily support."

A lengthy 2016 *New York Times* Magazine analysis of the *Gawker* case and other similar legal challenges by Emily Bazelon, an attorney and author of *Sticks and Stones: Defeating the Culture of Bullying and Rediscovering the Power of Character and Empathy*, points out that Hogan had bragged about his active sex life on TMZ and the Howard Stern Show. She claims that led the Florida Court of Appeals in a preliminary ruling to determine the video posting was part of an "ongoing public discussion" – another aspect that an appeal could have helped prove, but the cost was too high.

"*Gawker* is out of business because one wealthy person maliciously set out to destroy it, spending millions of dollars in secret, and succeeded," former *Gawker* Editor Tom Scocca wrote in 2016. "That is the only reason … It is true that *Gawker* was always a publication that took risks. It had bad manners and sometimes bad judgment … But every publication gives itself room to make mistakes and is prepared to absorb the damage when it does make a mistake."

But, Scocca added, "what Thiel's covert campaign against *Gawker* did was to invisibly change the terms of the risk calculation. The change begins with the post about Thiel's sexual identity in a homophobic investor culture, the post Thiel now cites as the inspiration for his decision to destroy *Gawker*. It was solidly protected by media law and the First Amendment, as were the other posts that, as Thiel wrote, 'attacked and mocked people' – specifically, his cohort of rising plutocrats in Silicon Valley. Hurting rich people's feelings is, in principle, not a punishable offense."

Freeman said the intimidation impact on future reporting could be strong: "Psychologically, it certainly has scared people to see what kind of numbers juries can throw around, that a pretty well-respected publication can go down the tubes is pretty chilling. The amount of money involved has become so high in terms of legal fees and potential damages it is hard not to take that into account in whatever calculation you make about publication."

And Thiel's bankrolling of anti-press legal action is not unique, according to Bazelon, who stated, "Superrich plaintiffs … aren't subject to the same market forces. They can treat suing the press as an investment, with the payoff being, at a minimum, the expense and time required for the other side to produce documents and sit for depositions."

Another such example involved *Mother Jones*, which published a 2012 story about Idaho billionaire Frank VanderSloot and his support for GOP presidential nominee Mitt Romney. The story noted that in 1999, in response to a documentary about teaching homosexuality in the classroom, VanderSloot sponsored billboards that asked, "Should public television promote the homosexual lifestyle to your children?" The magazine also claimed VanderSloot "outed" a local gay reporter, Peter Zuckerman, and attacked his reporting that broke the story of local pedophile Boy Scout counselor.

VanderSloot sued for libel, racking up $2.5 million in legal fees, Bazelon wrote. But the case was thrown out in 2015. "If VanderSloot had prevailed, he would have proven that with enough money to throw at lawyers, you can wipe the slate," *Mother Jones* wrote in a follow-up piece. "You can go after those who document the past and the present, and if you can't make them cry 'uncle' you can at least append a legal asterisk to their work forevermore."

The other recent case of note is the 2014 *Rolling Stone* expose on an alleged rape at a University of Virginia fraternity house that resulted in three different legal claims against the magazine, one of which is still being litigated. "A Rape on Campus: A Brutal Assault and Struggle for Justice at UVA" went to press on Nov. 19, 2014 and described the alleged gang rape of a female student identified only as "Jackie," who had claimed she was gang raped by seven men at the Phi Kappa Psi fraternity in 2012.

Sabrina Rubin Erdely, the reporter, had reached out to UVA rape crisis counselors in June 2014 looking for a good example to profile about rape on campus and was referred to "Jackie." At the time, campus rape was a major story. NPR had reported in April 2014 that "The number of 'forcible rapes' that get reported at four-year colleges increased 49 percent between 2008 and 2012," while a *Huffington Post* story that year revealed that students found responsible for sexual assaults were expelled only 30 percent of the time and suspended 47 percent of the time.

In addition, high-profile sexual assault cases at five college campuses – University of Kansas, Michigan State University, University of Toledo, University of California, Santa Barbara, and James Madison University – were scrutinized in the press and prompted outcry. Then there was the case of Emma Sulkowicz, the Columbia University student who accused an acquaintance of turning a consensual sex at into an abusive anal rape. She drew attention in 2014 when she began carrying a mattress around campus to protest the incident after police and the university chose not to take any action against the alleged rapist. She vowed to continue until her alleged attacker was expelled. He never was and actually sued the university in a case that was settled out of court in 2017.

There was more backlash related to campus assaults in 2014 when conservative columnist George Will drew fire for a column that suggested attempts to curb campus assaults had made "victimhood a coveted status that confers privileges." When he was invited to speak at Michigan State University later that year, it prompted major protests on the campus that would later be wracked by a major sex assault scandal involving sports doctor Larry Nasser and up to 150 women accusing him of molestation in 2017.

So for *Rolling Stone*'s Erdely to be in search of a valid campus rape case to profile was not unusual in 2014. And when she was first in touch with "Jackie," the story seemed credible. "Jackie" told her that during her freshman year in 2012, she had worked at the campus aquatic center and gotten to know a fellow lifeguard who was an upperclassman. This unnamed student invited her to the fraternity house for a party and had allegedly led the rape in a dark upper floor bedroom.

But the reporting did not note certain red flags. For one thing, the alleged victim would not identify the lead suspect, the lifeguard, saying she feared that he would retaliate. The story also did not name any of the other accused rapists, likely because "Jackie" might not have known their names. This gave the magazine no other sourcing and also left open accusations that any of the fraternity members or guests at the party could be assumed to be potential suspects.

According to a follow-up independent investigation of the story led by Columbia University Graduate School of Journalism Dean Steve Coll – prompted after the story's credibility was later questioned – "Jackie" was seen as credible because her recollections were vivid and precise and rarely changed upon later review. "Jackie proved to be a challenging source. At times, she did not respond to Erdely's calls, texts and emails. At two points, the reporter feared Jackie might withdraw her cooperation," Coll's report said, later adding that her refusal to reveal the alleged lead rapists' name, "led to tense exchanges between Erdely and Jackie, but the confrontation ended when *Rolling Stone*'s editors decided to go ahead without knowing the lifeguard's name or verifying his existence. After that concession, Jackie cooperated fully until publication."

But after the story ran and Erdely again asked "Jackie," about the lifeguard's identity, she still refused to name him, even though Erdely promised not to report it. When she finally agreed, she was unsure how to spell the name, which immediately set off a worry in Erdely. Coll wrote: "Over the next few days, worried about the integrity of her story, the reporter investigated the name Jackie had provided, but she was unable to confirm that he worked at the pool, was a member of the fraternity Jackie had identified or had other connections to Jackie or her description of her assault. She discussed her concerns with her editors. Her work faced new pressures."

By Dec. 4, 2014, less than three weeks after the story was first posted, Erdely and *Rolling Stone* knew they had a problem and printed a retraction. They quickly sought out Coll and others to do an outside investigation, which was completed by April 2015. Its overall findings: "*Rolling Stone*'s repudiation of the main narrative in 'A Rape on Campus' is a story of journalistic failure that was avoidable. The failure encompassed reporting, editing, editorial supervision and fact-checking. The magazine set aside or rationalized as unnecessary essential practices of reporting that, if pursued, would likely have led the magazine's editors to reconsider publishing Jackie's narrative so prominently, if at all. The published story glossed over the gaps in the magazine's reporting by using pseudonyms and by failing to state where important information had come from."

But the review made another interesting point, noting that both cutbacks in reporting resources and the current news media drive for quick breaking news – and perhaps seeking to take advantage of the heightened interest that year in campus sexual assault news – had likely added to the mistakes and poor reporting.

"As at other once-robust print magazines and newspapers, *Rolling Stone*'s editorial staff has shrunk in recent years as print advertising revenue has fallen and shifted online. The magazine's full-time editorial ranks, not including art or photo staff, have contracted by about 25 percent since 2008," the review said, although it later pointed out that "*Rolling Stone* continues to invest in professional fact-checkers and to fund time-consuming investigations like Erdely's ... The problem was methodology, compounded by an environment where several journalists with decades of collective experience failed to surface and debate problems about their reporting or to heed the questions they did receive from a fact-checking colleague."

When the police in Charlottesville, where the alleged rapes occurred, completed their investigation in March 2015, and found "no substantive basis to support the account alleged in the *Rolling Stone* article" the damage was done. And the legal actions soon followed.

In all there were three lawsuits filed against *Rolling Stone* related to the article: a suit by the Phi Kappa Psi chapter settled in July 2017 for about $1.65 million, which claimed the entire chapter was damaged by the false allegations; another from University of Virginia administrator Nicole Eramo, who claimed the article portrayed her unfairly as dismissive of the allegations, which was settled in April 2017 for an undisclosed amount after a jury ruled in her favor; and a third suit from three fraternity brothers who claimed the story implicated them even though their names were not used.

The third suit, which is still unresolved, had been dismissed by a lower court judge, but reinstated in September 2017 by a federal appeals court to allow two of the three fraternity brothers to keep the suit alive. The lawsuit contends that the two fraternity brothers still involved in the legal action faced negative attention because it could be inferred that they were among the men accused due to descriptions in the article, in one instance because one of their bedrooms in the house was similar in location to the alleged rape location in the article. The final lawsuit also cited comments Erdely made during a Nov. 27, 2017, podcast interview with *Slate* about the article.

Hermes said the *Rolling Stone* case can have an effect both on news outlets willingness to go after big stories like rape, as well as the appeals court decision to allow individual members to sue on a claim of damages simply because they are part of the overall group: "The second circuit's ruling in the *Rolling Stone* case that the members of the fraternity may sue could have some impact. In future cases when we're talking about reports about small groups, we might have to think about if the group itself is likely to bring a case, will the individuals do so?"

The robust reporting around the #MeToo movement has shown news outlets are willing to go after the issue, although in most of those cases – as well as the recent Brett Kavanaugh Supreme Court hearings – news coverage that revealed alleged sexual harassment or assault by Harvey Weinstein, Charlie Rose, Matt Lauer and others has involved multiple alleged victims that provide a greater defense for journalists and major news outlets such as *The New York Times*, the *Washington Post* and *The New Yorker* who can afford to face legal challenges better than smaller outlets if needed.

Finally, there is the ABC News "pink slime case," which was settled in 2017 after a five-year battle that reportedly cost the network at least $177 million. That case relates to a 2012 ABC News report on Beef Products Inc. of South Dakota that claimed the company "misled consumers about the safety of low-cost processed beef trimmings, which are officially known as 'lean finely textured beef' but are more commonly known as 'pink slime' because of the appearance," *The New York Times* wrote.

During the proceedings, ABC News stood by its reporting and never retracted anything, pointing out that the phrase "pink slime," had come from industry veterans, not its reporters. "Throughout this case, we have maintained that our reports accurately presented the facts and views of knowledgeable people about this product," ABC said in a statement, according to Reuters, saying that it agreed to the settlement because "continued litigation of this case is not in the company's interests."

Media law observers said the settlement was another example of an expensive case setting a precedent that could discourage other investigative reporting. All of these outcomes and others put an understandable burden on already cash-strapped newsrooms to think twice about taking on a big issue. "There is a sensitivity and worry about spending oodles of money defending yourself," Freeman of the Media Law Resource Center said in an interview. "Many papers and broadcasters kind of changed their policies to make sure that before spending millions of dollars defending reporters, they will make sure that what is being agreed to will result in a legal fight that might not be worthy fighting to stay out of jail. Is the risk of a subpoena and fighting a subpoena battle worth the risk of spending a million dollars keeping a reporter from jail?"

Lucy Dalglish, former executive director of Reporters Committee for Freedom of the Press and current dean of the Phillip Merrill College of Journalism at the University of Maryland, pointed out that most newsrooms have insurance to handle the costs of large damage awards. But she said that has not stopped all of the fallout from big lawsuit payoffs, which are sparking new hesitations. "They are as courageous as they've always been, but they are making choices whether to go after high-impact stories and packages of stories. They may not be doing as many investigations as they had in the past," she said in an interview. "Newsrooms are making tough choices."

Libel cases are getting more heated and nasty, says Tobin, who also said there is "a very heavy diet" of such cases in recent years. He noted that "the tone is more acerbic ... the coarseness of political discourse and you are seeing it in the courtroom. The litigation has become more unpleasant, it is much more antagonistic." Tobin added that the court actions are more involved, perhaps in part to cause more disruption to the defendant journalists and make things more difficult, even in simple cases: "The demands in discovery are a lot wider and broader and unnecessarily so. The arguments to judges are a lot angrier. The issues are usually for very good journalism but the plaintiffs are just angrier, [there is a] general deterioration in the discourse of society."

Robert Balin, a 30-year media law attorney and chairman of the Media Law Committee of the International Bar Association, has represented numerous news outlets, including *The New York Times*, ABC News and CNN. He said it's the smaller newsrooms that face the most impact from costly legal fights and may end up holding back on coverage out of concern for their bottom line. "Larger news organizations are much more willing to go to bat for their reporters than others," he said in an interview. "The real problem is in the small, local newsrooms who really have a limited budget. It's a real problem for smaller news organizations and one could argue that it could affect your reporting when you are steering clear of controversy."

Balin said some news outlets are beginning to share the costs of FOIA and other filings for access to information and events, as well as the formal lawsuits. "One of the things we have found … is more joint press applications so news organizations can share the cost and the burden," he said, noting "the press bands together to do a lot of amicus briefs, a lot of times we will do it pro bono or at a drastically reduced billing rate."

Hagit Limor, chair of the Society of Professional Journalists Legal Defense Fund, said his organization had been called in to help much more in the past two years on legal defense and advisory cases than in the recent past. After averaging 12 to 15 requests per year to either provide funding or support to media-related legal cases during the previous 10 years, the SPJ fund received 29 such requests in 2017 and 22 in the first six months of 2018.

"There are quite a few different kinds of cases bubbling up now, prior restraint comes up, but most of them are involving public records requests, FOI, and some of them are at universities," Limor said in an interview. "Cases involving public records that journalists are unable to get." She said there had been an unusual rise in "student newspapers fighting universities that do not want to give information. A lot more universities these days are refusing to give out information and using student privacy for a reason not to release information that has nothing to do with privacy."

On a positive front, the SPJ Legal Defense Fund has also seen an increase in individual donations, which rose from 79 contributions totaling $4,600 in 2016 to 526 contributions totaling $21,423 in 2017. Although they make up a small portion of the fund's $100,000 annual budget, the increased interest and wider support base is telling.

"A lot of it is because people are concerned about some of the challenges that have come up in covering news as well as addressing some of the animosity toward the press," Limor said. "A lot of people have signed up to give monthly."

The increased support also prompted the organization to create a separate fund for more active legal efforts to seek better access to records and information, as well as legislation. Dubbed the "First Amendment Forever" fund, it was launched in 2015 "to basically fight for press freedom and be offensive about it, not wait for someone to come to us."

That kind of proactive campaign appears to be needed, media law veterans say, given that news outlets and journalists are seeing increased opposition to public records access, information, crime and other news scenes, and even credentials. And, once again, fewer resources and less money to wage the battle.

"They are still bringing those challenges, but there aren't as many reporters in newsrooms to engage in self-help as there used to be, that makes things busier and tougher to make those requests," Lucy Dalglish said about the access fights. "Newsrooms have to make tougher choices in bringing those affirmative lawsuits or challenges to public meetings or public record laws that they would have been more willing to bring in the past."

She later stated, "big media companies ... are being very competitive, setting very strict budgets, they are capping fees ... There are probably fewer lawyers doing it pro bono." Dalglish also pointed out that there are simply fewer lawyers in practice overall: "Over the last 10 years or so there has been a dramatic reduction in the number of law students and law school graduates. Law firms are shrinking."

Jeff Hermes echoed that view: "When it comes to freedom of information and access fights, I think it's true that we've seen a reduction in the resources devoted to hunting down documents and information, particularly at the state level."

Daniel Bevarly, executive director of the non-profit National Freedom of Information Coalition, said some of the biggest barriers in recent years have been at the state level, where individual legislatures are trying to chip away at open government laws with numerous exemptions to access. With more news outlets cutting back on state reporting in recent years, this widespread effort to block information is another way that statehouse news is being affected.

"There is that type of trickle-down effect that you see in the challenges of journalism to be able to do their work, that is something we have noted," Bevarly said in an interview. "We are seeing more exemptions, information available five or ten years ago is now exempt."

He mentioned several states trying to tighten press access to police body camera videos, which are becoming standard law enforcement equipment. "Some consider it a training video, so it is exempt, or [not available if] a crime is being investigated," Bevarly said. "Another one is a couple of states trying to exempt the names of law enforcement officers from any kind of public record. Where is the evidence-based research that shows a need for that kind of restriction?"

One example is a 2018 attempt in Washington State to exempt the state legislature from all state open government laws. Senate Bill 6617 exempted both state houses from the state Public Records Act. To add to the sleaziness of it, the bill was approved just one month after a judge ruled that the state legislature was subject to the act. "Even more disturbing was the process that was used to ram through the bill – no committee process, no meaningful public hearing and no debate on the Senate or House floors," *The Seattle Times* wrote in a rare front-page editorial on Feb. 27, 2018. "Yes, and lawmakers defending their vote called it a transparency bill. The public will have more access than it did, more than one lawmaker said. Well, a little more than nothing is not very much."

Ten news media organizations including The Associated Press and the *Times* filed suit against the bill, while six other daily papers also published Page One editorials slamming the secrecy effort. Those included *The News Tribune of Tacoma, The Spokesman-Review in Spokane, The Olympian, The Columbian of Vancouver, The Bellingham Herald, The Tri-City Herald, The Yakima Herald-Republic* and *the Walla Walla Union-Bulletin.*

One of the bulls in this fight was *Times* Publisher Frank Blethen, who has been among the newspaper industries top battlers for decades. Top dog of the Blethen family, which has run the *Times* and a handful of other outlets for years, Blethen has angered many in the news world with a brash style that sought to protect his interests, but also shake up the business that as we have seen can often get stuck in a rut.

I first came across him in 2001 when he was leading the fight against the estate tax, even convening a gathering in Washington, DC, to lobby congress. Later that year he also caused an uproar when he gave me the first word of his threat to move the *Times* out of Seattle if city officials did not improve conditions for local businesses. It was also a slight jab at Seattle officials for refusing to speak with replacement reporters during a 2000 newspaper strike. The leak to a trade publication like *Editor & Publisher* likely annoyed his rival news outlets in Seattle, who ended up seeking details from me in the following days.

Eventually, Washington Gov. Jay Inslee vetoed the 2018 exemption bill. But press freedom advocates said it is just one of many anti-access moves still being made at the state level. Another such attempt was in Kentucky, where state leaders tried in March 2018 to tack on an amendment to a routine reorganization bill that would have exempted personal communication devices of any government official from FOIA requests. After opposition similar to those who opposed the Washington law, the amendment was dismissed at the last minute.

"It's a combination of fewer watchdogs out there and an increase in the technology that's being used in the public sector to allow people to get around laws and policies," Bevarly said about the increased opposition to access. "You also see a lot of special interests that are involved in this process."

Former *Washington Post* Executive Editor Leonard Downie, Jr., who now teaches journalism at Arizona State University, said the need for news outlets to have effective legal support is more crucial than ever: "It's important to have lawyers who can help you file public information request suits when you don't get your public information request," he said in an interview. "To help you to get really aggressive investigative reporting published with the minimum amount of problems, to fend off people that are trying to stop you from publishing."

Hermes also cited the impact of more freelancers on press freedom. With staff cuts, more news outlets are using part-timers and freelancers who often face stronger opposition to access and even credentials. "That's where I think you see more of an effect with reduced budgets, and a rise in the use of freelancers," Hermes said. "They can run into access issues that employees don't. You are more likely to be denied a reporting credential as a freelancer than as an employee."

He pointed to a 2014 study by the Berkman Center for Internet and Society at Harvard University and Harvard's Shorenstein Center on Media, Politics and Public Policy that found freelancers and newer digital journalists are facing greater scrutiny in credential access. "Certain categories of applicants are more likely to be denied than others: freelance journalists were significantly less likely to receive media credentials than employed journalists; photographers were more likely to be denied than non-photographers; and respondents who identified themselves as activists were more likely to be denied than those respondents who did not," the report said.

The study found that only 14 percent of full-time employed journalists surveyed were denied credentials at least once, while 32 percent of freelancers were denied, and 36 percent of contributors. "This is particularly troubling given an apparent trend among institutional newsrooms to turn to freelance journalism to help meet economic challenges," the report said. "For example, in May 2013, the *Chicago Sun-Times* laid off its entire staff of employed photographers, with plans to rely upon its freelancer staff for professional photography. The Society of Environmental Journalists has reported more freelance members, while the Committee to Protect Journalists has said it has seen more cases involving freelancers. If the pattern of denying access to freelancers continues, the greater use of freelancers by media organizations could affect newsgathering ability."

Press access to information has also been diminished, even with the Freedom of Information Act (FOIA) – the federal law passed in 1967 that guarantees certain access to official documents and information for the press and the public. But the time and money needed to file requests, and lawsuits when denied access, is a problem in the 24-hour news cycle and with the limited financial resources.

A 2016 Duke Law School report on FOIA use and effectiveness found that fewer journalists are using it than previously believed, and facing more difficulties. "Contrary to the intent of Congress and widespread expectations at the time FOIA was passed, the news media has failed to find FOIA the great government-transparency tool it was promised to be, and, in fact, constitutes a tiny fraction of FOIA users," the report said, later adding, "Members of the news media also represent a tiny – and declining – proportion of the requesters who file lawsuits to challenge FOIA denials, ranging between 1 and 2 percent of all FOIA plaintiffs."

Mark Feldstein, an award-winning investigative journalist formerly at CNN and ABC, told researchers: "I found FOIA to be occasionally, but not frequently useful, when I was an investigative reporter … There are many exemptions in the law that allow agencies to avoid turning over information, and it can be a slow process under tight news deadlines, especially if you have to file an appeal … The FOIA law is great on paper, but in reality, it has many loopholes." The Duke Law School report then stated, "Delay is one of the biggest problems cited by the media, and it is indeed a very real problem."

Researchers cited an example from Associated Press CEO Gary Pruitt, who recounted how, after Malaysia Airlines Flight 370 went missing in 2014, the AP filed a FOIA request regarding the U.S. efforts to help locate the plane: "Despite a twenty-business-day statutory deadline for a response, the only response the AP ever received – a full year later – was a notice that the agency has too many requests to meet the deadline. Another AP request to the Treasury Department remained unfilled for nine full years."

The report revealed that the average processing time for "complex FOIA requests" was 118 days, noting that the oldest pending request at the end of 2014 dated back to 1993. "The difficulties encountered by the news media demonstrate some of the prerequisites to effectively make use of FOIA," the report stated. "For instance, the requester has to have time to wait for what may be a much-delayed response. The requester also has to have some degree of specialized knowledge about the agency and the industry it regulates sufficient to know what to ask for."

The results can vary widely. In 2016 when I covered my hometown school district in Maplewood, N.J. for a website I operated, I had to sue for access to legal invoices the district had accumulated for outside legal counsel related to bullying complaints and lawsuits. After they denied the FOIA request, my lawyer filed the suit, we won, and they had to pay him about $4,000 in legal costs in addition to releasing the documents.

But more than 10 years earlier, the opposite happened in another case. Reporting for *Editor & Publisher* on the tragic suicide of legendary environmental reporter Kevin Carmody of the *Austin American-Statesman*, I filed a FOIA with Austin, TX., police and received every related police record, autopsy report and even gruesome photos of his tragic hanging in a local park (We did not publish that image.)

A 2017 analysis by investigative reporter Jason Leopold for the Committee to Protect Journalists found many challenges, costs among them, in today's FOIA requests. "A common FOIA complaint among journalists, especially freelancers whose funds are limited, is that agencies also often charge astronomical fees in an effort to deter requesters from filing requests and obtaining records. This practice is rampant on the state level and very difficult to overcome," he wrote.

Leopold mentioned a 2014 request he made for emails from officials with the City of Ferguson, Missouri, which had been wracked by protests and complaints following the police shooting death of unarmed African-American teenager Michael Brown. "The city clerk told me that I would have to pay $2,000 in advance for a search to be conducted and to pay the city attorney to review and redact any responsive emails," he recalled. "Clearly, this was an attempt to discourage me from accessing public records. I told the clerk that these records were in the public interest, given the widespread media attention surrounding Brown's case, and that I, as a journalist, should be granted a fee waiver." He said he filed an appeal, but it was denied.

"Even when a journalist acts with the utmost diligence in filing a FOIA request, agency foot-dragging can and often frustrates their attempt to obtain records at the time when they are needed most," Leopold later wrote. "In most cases, filing a lawsuit moves the request to the top of the pile and catalyzes the release of documents. That's certainly been my experience over the past six years. However, not all investigative journalists are in a position to expend the substantial resources necessary to bring FOIA lawsuits, and even large media outlets may conclude that the cost of litigation outweighs the benefits."

A 2018 U.S. Government Accountability Office review of FOIA requests found things had gotten better at 18 federal agencies in terms of access, but also stated backlogged requests had increased tremendously at four of the most important federal agencies for public information. The review found that between 2012 and 2016, backlogged FOIA requests had jumped from 5,196 to 10,644 at the Department of Justice; from 28,553 to 46,788 at the Department of Homeland Security – with a huge boost to more than 100,000 briefly in 2014 – and from 10,464 to 22,664 at the Department of State.

"Specifically, all agencies had updated response letters to inform requesters of the right to seek assistance from FOIA public liaisons, implemented request tracking systems, and provided training to FOIA personnel," the GAO review stated about the improvements, but it later stressed, "Until these agencies address all of the requirements, they increase the risk that the public will lack information that ensures transparency and accountability in government operations ... Until agencies develop such plans, they will likely continue to struggle to reduce backlogs to a manageable level."

Then there are the legal demands and challenges related to simple coverage of events, often resulting in physical and even violent barriers to the press. Whether journalists are simply barred access to news events and locations or actually arrested or physically harmed the incidents are on the rise and the court fights don't come cheap.

"Press advocates see an increasing climate of anger, disrespect and hostility aimed at the media from the public and elected officials," Paul Farhi of the *Washington Post* wrote in May 2017. "And they generally blame President Trump for rhetoric that has made attacks, verbal and otherwise, more common and even acceptable."

Trump began his assault on the press years before he took office, but has continued it aggressively ever since, as noted in earlier chapters. On several occasions since his inauguration, most recently at a June 25, 2018 rally, he referred to the press as the "enemy of the people." He's also referred to coverage of his North Korean summit of 2018 as "almost treasonous."

Farhi's story cited four incidents that had occurred in one month, May 2017, involving the abuse of reporters or the serious barring of access and press rights. They included:

○ Reporter Nathaniel Herz of the *Alaska Dispatch News* accusing Republican state Sen. David Wilson, of Wasilla (Sarah Palin's hometown) of slapping him in the capitol building in Juneau on May 2, 2017.

○ Republican congressional candidate Greg Gianforte "body-slamming" and breaking the glasses of reporter Ben Jacobs of *The Guardian* on May 24, 2017, when he continued to ask questions. Gianforte later apologized and was charged with misdemeanor assault.

○ On May 18, 2017, reporter John M. Donnelly of *CQ Roll Call* being pinned against a wall by security guards inside a hallway at the Federal Communications Commission in Washington, D.C., after he tried to question a commissioner after a hearing on net neutrality. He later said they followed him to the lobby and threw him out of the building.

○ *Public News Service* journalist Dan Heyman arrested and handcuffed on May 9, 2017, after he tried to question Health and Human Services Secretary Tom Price as he walked with Trump special counsel Kelly Anne Conway in the West Virginia state capitol. Heyman was charged with willful disruption of state government process and later released on $5,000 bail.

More recently, in May 2018, an Associated Press reporter was "grabbed by the shoulders and shoved out of an Environmental Protection Agency building by a security guard … for trying to cover a meeting on water contaminants in which some reporters were welcomed and others were not," AP revealed. The incident occurred when reporter Ellen Knickmeyer was attempting to cover the meeting described as a "national summit on dangerous chemicals that have been found in some water systems."

AP said the reporter had been told by the EPA that it was invitation-only and there was no room for her. She showed up anyway and sought entry but was denied. Knickmeyer said she was grabbed and removed when she asked to speak to a representative. AP also said the announcement of EPA Administrator Scott Pruitt's appearance at the meeting indicated it would be open to all press. Knickmeyer was later allowed into the meeting and received an apology from Pruitt's office.

"The Environmental Protection Agency's selective barring of news organizations, including the AP, from covering today's meeting is alarming and a direct threat to the public's right to know about what is happening inside their government," AP Executive Editor Sally Buzbee said at the time.

The deadliest and most frightening example of such revenge or abuse of the press was on June 28, 2018, when five employees of the *Capital Gazette* in Annapolis, MD., were gunned down by a disgruntled man who had sued the paper falsely for defamation after it reported on his conviction for stalking-related crimes. Although the case was tossed by a judge, gunman Jarrod Ramos kept up a grudge that included threats and eventually the murders of five staffers, four of them journalists. Although there is no sign he was a Trump follower, it is clear the anti-press hatred of his administration and many in his White House has created an atmosphere where violence against journalists is more acceptable to many.

Trump's most recent "enemy of the people" press claim occurred just three days before the attack, while right-wing commentator Milo Yiannopoulos – who has a history of offensive and hateful speech – said in a text message to a reporter days earlier that he "can't wait for vigilante squads to start gunning journalists down on sight."

The Committee to Protect Journalists reveals 1,310 journalists have been killed worldwide since 1992, with an average of 48 per year. The most occurred less than 10 years ago in 2009 when 76 died, with the lowest total just seven years before that, in 2002, when 21 were killed. Three of the last six years, 2012, 2013 and 2015 were among the deadliest ever with at least 73 news people murdered each of those years, with 2018 on pace to be a deadly year with 33 killed by June.

The U.S. has had only 11 journalists killed since 1992, although more than half of them – six – occurred in just the past four years, including four who died in the *Capital Gazette* shooting.

Incidents such as those above showed a need for more monitoring of anti-press efforts, which sparked The Reporters Committee for Freedom of the Press to launch its new U.S. Press Freedom Tracker in 2017 to help tabulate the increased anti-press actions. The Tracker's first report on March 27, 2018, described a "rising tide of hostility toward the press" and declared that "journalists have become targets." Among its findings: There were 45 "physical attacks" on journalists in 2017, with nearly 70 percent of them taking place as reporters sought to cover protests. Among those, nearly 30 percent involved police implicated in the incidents. It also counted at least 15 cases in which "law enforcement seized and in some cases even searched a journalist's equipment, such as cellphones and cameras."

In addition, there were 34 arrests of journalists in 2017, according to the Tracker, with 18 of those involving freelancers. They ranged from reporter Jordan Chariton and cameraman Ty Bayliss of online news outlet *The Young Turks*, who were arrested after covering a St. Louis protest on October 3, 2017 (one of 11 journalists arrested in related protests in that city), to David Clarey, editor of the University of

Minnesota's student newspaper, Minnesota Daily, arrested on June 17, 2017 while recording a mass protest of the acquittal of a former police officer in the shooting death of motorist. His chargers were later dropped.

The report also indicated threats against reporters were on the rise in 2017, noting that Reporters Committee for Freedom of the Press had seen an "uptick" in calls seeking help with threats and harassment.

The Press Freedom Tracker cited the case of a man arrested in January 2018 after making 22 threatening calls to CNN's headquarters, in which he called CNN "fake news" and threatened to murder its employees. There was also American Urban Radio Network White House correspondent April Ryan reporting that she and other journalists received death threats after asking questions of the administration, while *Washington Post* syndicated columnist Kathleen Parker reported receiving death threats when she "wrote critically of Trump."

Former Fox News host and NBC News morning talk host Megyn Kelly wrote in her book, *Settle for More*, that she received rape and death threats whenever Trump targeted her: "'Every time, he wrote about me, it was like he flipped a switch, instantly causing a flood of intense nastiness.'"

I experienced my first attempted intimidation during my first job at *The Daily Journal* in 1990 when I covered the campaign of former mayor John T. Gregorio. First elected mayor of Linden, N.J. – a political hotbed if there ever was one – in 1967, Gregorio had reached the level of state assemblyman in 1973 and then state senator five years later. But he was forced out in 1983 after being convicted of conspiracy for hiding his interest in two Linden go-go bars run by his son, John Jr. The charges didn't stop him from being re-elected as mayor in 1982 while still under indictment. The following year, however, under the terms of his sentence, he was placed on probation, fined $10,000, and forced to vacate both the mayor's office and his Senate seat. "It was probably the most embarrassing thing I ever went through," he said years later.

But his exile lasted only seven years as he ran for re-election in 1990 after an unusual move by former Republican Governor Thomas Kean, who quietly pardoned Gregorio on his last day in office before handing the governorship to Democrat James Florio. Kean told me at the time he was asked by Florio's office to provide the odd pardon to a political rival, a claim that Florio later denied. Years later, State Senator Raymond Lesniak said it was his plea to Kean that drew the still puzzling pardon.

So when Gregorio ran again in 1990, the battle was on as he took on incumbent Paul Werkmeister, a popular moderate, but hardly one with the political influence or hardball approach of Gregorio. Those who don't know New Jersey politics learn quickly it is among the most corrupt and mudslinging in the nation. The fact that Gregorio and others could then effectively hold two elected seats – in his case mayor of Linden and state Senator – was just one of the ways that power was and is still waged and income rewarded.

Lucky me, I was promoted to cover Linden and neighboring Rahway in 1989, just as Gregorio's return began. For the next few months I reported on his possible improper voter registration as a convicted felon, his threats against a firefighter union chief and his verbal attack on another driver after a car accident. He indicated he had people following me at one point and noted where I had been seen having lunch. After a candidate debate, which ended early due to crowd issues, several of his supporters surrounded me and launched verbal assaults. Then on Election Night, after he won the Democratic primary – which made his general election automatic in such a Democratic community – I joined other reporters at his victory party, where his son came after me with fists flying.

Since then, the harassment of me has come and gone as it has with many reporters. I earlier noted the phone threat from the brother of a San Francisco D.A. candidate in 1995 who disliked my coverage of the campaign. And recently at *Media Matters for America*, it surfaced in 2016 that Fox News had hacked my phone records in an attempt to track down my sources for a 2010 story on Fox staffers critical of the network. That required at least some legal action by my former employers, who initially issued a request to require Fox News to "retain any information in their possession or control that would be relevant to allegations of surveilling *Media Matters* employees."

But in the end the legal demands were seen as too great financially and otherwise to file a full lawsuit against the network for essentially invading my privacy.

Private attorneys told me later that the chances of coming out with anything worthwhile or finding proof of Fox's hacking were minimal. Still, that kind of underhanded attempt to thwart coverage is unacceptable at any level, and sadly increasing.

The *Capital Gazette* editorial board said it best in an editorial published three days after that horrible shooting, when they said they would not forget: "Death threats and emails from people we don't know celebrating our loss, or the people who called for one of our reporters to get fired because she got angry and cursed on national television after witnessing her friends getting shot. We won't forget being called an enemy of the people. No, we won't forget that. Because exposing evil, shining light on wrongs and fighting injustice is what we do."

But if the legal costs of doing it continue to rise, that task becomes ever more difficult.

WHO IS WATCHING?

When one thinks of Louisville, Kentucky, thoughts of bourbon whiskey, championship college basketball and Muhammad Ali come to mind. And, of course, the most famous horse race in America, the Kentucky Derby at legendary Churchill Downs, can't be ignored. Rarely, however, is it thought of as the site of important journalistic history.

But a significant newspaper moment occurred there in 1967 when the *Courier-Journal*, still the mainstay newspaper of the River City, took a bold step in newspaper ethics and quality that led to a decades-long era in news accountability: it hired the first American daily newspaper ombudsman.

Sadly, that era has ended and the downfall effect on today's journalism has followed. But for a time, when these "public editors" and "reader representatives" were at nearly every major daily paper and other news outlets, quality and critique were at least on the minds of one editor in the newsroom. The loss of such independent observers of news practices and decisions at a time when the press is being inundated with criticism and outside attacks – some warranted, many not – is detrimental as it cuts out what is a clear middle man (or woman) of reason, explanation and even mediation in many cases.

"I firmly believe, when everyone talks about transparency, I absolutely believe in having someone who is independent, but knows the business and the particular institutions and asks the right questions," said

Esther Enkin, past president of the Organization of News Ombudsmen and Standards Editors (ONO) and the ombudsman at the Canadian Broadcasting Corporation. "It seems to me an absolute no brainer. It makes a tremendous difference. It's quite a popular tool in emerging democracies who understand the need."

But not in the United States, where Enkin confirmed that ombudsmen number in the low single digits, with current positions only at National Public Radio, Public Broadcasting System and the Corporation for Public Broadcasting. "Except for public broadcasting there are virtually none left in the United States," she said. "Some newsrooms have standards editors, but it's not quite the same thing. At least they are maintaining journalistic standards."

But are they?

The ONO website offers a grim picture as it points out the few ombudsmen still on staff full time at U.S. news outlets, and none among the top 25 newspapers or major broadcast outlets. The purge began in the early 2000s, one of the many news cutbacks from the ad recession and lost readership to the Internet of that era. *The St. Louis Post-Dispatch*, which dropped its "reader advocate" in 2001, reported in 2008 that similar positions were cut that same year at the *Baltimore Sun, Fort Worth Star-Telegraph, Orlando Sentinel, Minneapolis Star-Tribune, Hartford Courant* and the *Palm Beach Post*.

A 2014 report at the University of Nebraska College of Journalism and Communications revealed that there were as many as 50 news ombudsmen or reader representatives in the United States at one time, but that it had dropped to less than a dozen. The report, titled "The Diminishing Role of The Ombudsman in American Journalism," declared, "coincidentally, the declining ombudsmen numbers in the U.S. come at a time when opinion polls indicate the American people have growing trust issues with the news media, and are a sharp contrast to news ombudsmen positions internationally which are growing in number and popularity."

The report also tallied another handful of lost ombudsman jobs at major newspapers in the previous decade or so, including *The Boston Globe, The Washington Post, Raleigh News and Observer, The Oregonian of Portland, The Miami Herald, The Sacramento Bee, Jacksonville Times-Union, Atlanta Journal/Constitution, Akron Beacon-Journal, Seattle Post-Intelligencer, Chicago Tribune, Philadelphia Daily News, Detroit Free Press, The Virginian-Pilot, San Diego Union-Tribune, San Francisco Chronicle, USA Today, Arizona Republic, Salt Lake Tribune, Arizona Daily Star, St. Paul Pioneer Press,* and *Fort Myers News Press.*

"It's understandable why ombudsmen are so vulnerable in the current climate. Newsroom after newsroom has slashed its staff in the punishing era of digital transformation," Rem Reider, the former editor of the *American Journalism Review* wrote in 2013. "As the roster shrinks, tough choices have to be made. You've got to cover city hall and the police beat." He later added, "But it's a big mistake to look upon the position as a frill. The credibility of the news media is low. Mistrust on the part of the public is high. Having someone dedicated to listening to readers or listeners or viewers and dealing with their concerns can be a major plus."

By 2018, there were still some ombudsmen in media, but mostly in broadcast and cable with National Public Radio (NPR) and the Public Broadcasting System (PBS) still staffing the job, but few others.

Several broadcast and cable operations, such as CNN and CBS, have a "standards" or "standards and practices" editor. But they mostly review material before it is reported and have no mechanism for responding to viewer complaints. None appear to go by the traditional independent approach in which ombudsmen had been engaged.

That process usually involved a news outlet appointing an ombudsman under a set contracted time, often two years, during which the person would have autonomy to review and investigate any issue related to the news organization's practices he or she chose and write about it. Such a procedure would guarantee independence because the person would not worry about keeping their job, would have no interference, and would know they will be replaced after their term. But these days, having such an internal watchdog is the exception, not the rule. And the effects are troubling.

"The bottom line is there is no amount of reader criticism that can replace the role of the internal ombudsman," said Andy Alexander, a former *Washington Post* ombudsman and past D.C. bureau chief for Cox Media. "Who can roam the newsroom and ask reporters and editors uncomfortable questions that they couldn't ignore if they wanted to."

Ombudsman, which comes from Sweden, technically means "representative." The first institutional use of the word, according to historians, was in 1809 for a Swedish government officer appointed to handle citizen complaints.

The first U.S. newspaper ombudsman-like process dates back to 1913 at the *New York World,* which created a "Bureau of Accuracy and Fair Play," with the goal to "promote accuracy and fair play; to correct carelessness and to stamp out fakes and fakers," according to author Neil Nemeth's 2003 book, *News Ombudsmen in North America.* He wrote that the first such bureau included a director and two associates who "investigated complaints, prepared corrections, and coordinated the correspondence with readers who lodged complaints." Other such committees arose in later years at newspapers in Des Moines, Minneapolis, Philadelphia and Sacramento.

The Organization of News Ombudsmen and Standards Editors based in Toronto notes the first international use of the term at the *Asahi*

Shimbun in Tokyo, which established a committee in 1922 to "receive and investigate reader complaints." It reports another Japanese paper, The *Yomiuri Shimbun* made a similar move in 1938, later naming the group an "ombudsman committee" in 1951 that still hears reader complaints today and meets daily with editors.

But in the United States, it was Louisville and the *Courier-Journal* that first created the individual ombudsman position, appointing John Herchenroeder in July 1967 to handle concerns for that paper and the sister *Louisville Times*. Both were owned by the Bingham Family, which prided itself on honesty and journalistic integrity for decades but had its own tragic downfall of power struggles and family in-fighting that led to its 1986 sale to Gannett after the internal disputes could not be resolved.

"For large families struggling with the problems of multi-generational ownership of a business, the saga of the Binghams and their failure to hold together was particularly poignant," Alex S. Jones, former media writer for *The New York Times* wrote in his 1986 Pulitzer Prize-winning account of the family downfall, which he compared to the Kennedys, and later led to a 1991 book on the subject, *The Patriarch*. "And for the dwindling number of families still operating their own newspapers, the news from Louisville was chilling."

But before the ownership change, the Binghams and their news pages were seen as a prominent and professional accounting of local and national events that led to eight Pulitzer Prizes and great respect. Part of that image and determination was the first ombudsman creation that is still seen as historic today. "They took themselves very seriously, the Binghams did, and they wanted to engage the journalism issues of the day and the journalism issue of people complaining has been there all along," Jones, who more recently served as the executive director of the Shorenstein Center on Media, Politics and Public Policy at Harvard University, told me in an interview. He also credits the newspaper's editor at the time, Noman Isaacs, with sparking the ombudsman idea and pushing it through.

"He also had the idea of a National News Council," Jones said, noting such a council would be made up of journalism leaders around the country who would review complaints from readers and others, then render a non-monetary judgement. "To get something before the news council you had to give up the idea of seeking monetary reward, but you would get a judgement. The idea was to get things out of the courts and reward justice for people who had complaints."

But the council never got off the ground, Jones said, pointing to *The New York Times* and then-editor Abe Rosenthal's objections: "The main reason it didn't work was because the *Times* declined to participate, and Abe Rosenthal said they do their own investigation and admit if they did it wrong."

Still, the ombudsman position was born in that Louisville newsroom on a hot July day in 1967 and lived on for more than 40 years until the last person in the role, Pam Platt, saw it cut in 2008. During its time, however, the *Courier-Journal* ombudsman faced many issues and broke its share of journalistic ground. Soon after taking the job in 1967, Herchenroeder instituted daily correction columns in both papers and eventually fielded up to 3,000 reader calls and letters a year in the pre-Internet age.

"He did it as a newsman, he did not come into it with pre-conceived notions, he listened to every person who called him, he took notes and was extremely polite," recalls Keith Runyon, who worked at the *Courier-Journal* from 1969 to 2012, first as an obit writer, then editorial page editor and book editor. "In those days, we got a lot of calls talking about us being a communist rag, as well as descriptions that began with the letter N, and Hersch would just listen."

Runyon points out that he did not write any kind of column for the paper and worked strictly in-house, but as a conduit for readers with concerns. His name and number were listed daily on the masthead and when readers or sources and story subjects called to complain, Herchenroeder responded, took notes on each call, and wrote up a daily report for staffers, Runyon recalls.

"He was the fairest newsman I ever knew," Runyon, who is something of a *Courier-Journal* historian, said. "He was very reticent about public comments, he viewed himself as an editor and a defender of the truth, not necessarily a defender of the staff." Herchenroeder's previous time as city editor made staffers trust him. "Let's say a reader called to complain that they misspelled their niece's name," Runyon said. "He could approach you if you were the reporter, ask you if you asked how to spell it, did you spell it back? And if you did not, he would call you on it."

Herchenroeder also held the job longer than most, from 1967 to 1979, and during some of the most tumultuous times for Louisville. One of the first was when a young reporter named Paul Branzburg wrote a 1969 front-page expose on drug sales in the city, which included details on two hashish dealers that featured photos of men making the product, but no names or faces. Investigators later demanded to know the identity of the subjects, but Branzburg and the paper refused, sparking threats of jail for the journalist.

The case eventually went to the U.S. Supreme Court and ended with landmark Branzburg vs. Hayes ruling in 1972 that rejected the paper's claim and set a precedent that reporters cannot protect sources that break the law or refuse to testify about them. But it also set standards that reporters be used to unmask sources only as a last resort. Runyon said the coverage and court case sparked numerous complaints and inquiries to Herchenroeder, who handled them like a pro.

"He took all of the complaints about Branzburg and kept reporting to the staff what the calls were and what the issues were," Runyon recalls. "But he was totally informed about it and I never knew what he thought about the case."

Several years later came one of the greatest tests for the paper and its ombudsman when Jefferson County, Kentucky, ordered integration and busing of white and black students to other schools in September 1975. When the *Courier-Journal* editorialized in favor of the move, the paper took heat that ranged from cancelled subscriptions to violent protests outside the building. "There was uniform support for it in the black community and pretty broad support in the white community," Runyon remembers, but says the opposition was fierce. "The *Courier-Journal* was an aggressive advocate and we had demonstrators in the street, reporters who were assaulted, people who broke windows and massive cancellations of the paper."

He said Herchenroeder was flooded with letters and calls, many angry that the paper would support such a move. But Runyon says he helped keep the angry elements calm, while keeping the newsroom updated on the public reaction. "Hersch helped to keep the community from bursting wide-open," he said. "He would listen to people who didn't like the news, who didn't like the editorials, he would take notes and hear them and write up a report that circulated to all of the news desks."

While Herchenroeder was the first newspaper ombudsman, the *Washington Post* and its first ombudsman, Richard Harwood, get the attention by most for bringing the position into the big time in 1970, and utilizing it strongly and soundly in sometimes historic ways. Former *Post* foreign editor Philip Foise, who would later become the first ombudsman for *Stars and Stripes* in 1989, is credited with launching the *Post*'s ombudsman effort in 1969 with a memo to then editors Ben Bradlee and Gene Patterson.

The memo stated, in part, "The ombudsman would be under contract to serve for a set period of time – perhaps a year or a little longer – and his pay would be guaranteed for the entire period. His contract would be non-renewable. At the end of that time, the panel, or a panel similarly selected, would employ another ombudsman under the same conditions."

When the job was later created, that general approach was the basis for its existence, and also for other news outlets that eventually created such positions: Hire an independent editor, give them a set time for the job so they would not have to worry about being fired or re-hired, and give them autonomy.

But Foise also saw the pitfalls, adding in the memo: "…we must have an ombudsman who was mature, tolerant, understood the limitations and the problems of the newspaper industry. But there would be a risk, even with such a man."

Harwood, himself a veteran newsman who had actually started at the *Louisville Times* and later served as its political correspondent in Washington, had joined the *Post* in 1966 and risen to national reporter. His son, veteran newsman John Harwood – who spent many years at *The Wall Street Journal* and is now an editor-at-large for CNBC – said the senior Harwood was such a news ethics proponent that he took himself off coverage of the 1968 presidential campaign because he had become a huge fan of then candidate Robert F. Kennedy.

"By the end of the '68 campaign, he fell in love with the guy and asked to be taken off of the Kennedy campaign, he made the request," John Harwood said in an interview about his father. He later added, "Dad was very concerned that journalism be fair … He had a sensibility rooted in the middle of the country and someone who had not grown up with a lot of advantages, he was orphaned as kid."

Richard Harwood, who died in 2001, left his ombudsman mark in several ways, among them convincing the paper's sports section to stop referring to Muhammad Ali as Cassius Clay after the boxer changed his name and religion. He also "helped eliminate potentially divisive terms like 'hippie' and 'hard hat' from the paper's news columns," according to his *Los Angeles Times* obituary. On another occasion, his investigation of a reader complaint sparked a front-page apology.

John Harwood cited one of his father's pieces about an intern at the *Post* during the Vietnam War who went up to a construction worker and said, "why do you beat up kids?" "Dad said this person made assumptions about someone she didn't even known," the younger Harwood told me. "He crusaded against clichés, false assumptions, against prejudice. I think he thought it was an important role." As for the elimination of the role today in so many newsrooms, John Harwood said, "I think he also would be practical about the financial challenges the paper is facing ... I think he would understand but exhort everyone to try to uphold the principals that ombudsman promote."

After Richard Harwood's ombudsman term ended in 1972, he had a string of successors who continued the position with similar ethical demands, clear explanations and oversight of tough issues. Among those were Ben Bagdikian, the former *Post* national editor who obtained the first copies of the original Pentagon Papers and later served as dean of the University of California Graduate School of Journalism; and Robert C. Maynard, who became the first black editor of a major newspaper at the *Oakland Tribune*, and then the first black publisher. *The New York Times* called him "journalism's Jackie Robinson."

But the *Post* ombudsman position, and perhaps the paper itself, faced its greatest test in 1981 when the front-page feature story on an eight-year old heroin addict, dubbed "Jimmy's World," won the Pulitzer Prize.

The ombudsman at that time was Bill Greene, who had taken the job in September 1980 on a one-year term.

Greene, a former World War II pilot and small-town North Carolina newspaper editor, did not have the big-time newspaper or national reporting chops of his predecessors. He actually came to the *Post* from Duke University, where he served as director of university relations and later taught journalism.

But he became the most historic *Post* ombudsman ever, and perhaps of all such internal newspaper watchdogs to come, after it was revealed that "Jimmy's World" was fabricated. The entire tale of the "third-generation heroin addict, a precocious little boy with sandy hair, velvety brown eyes and needle marks freckling the baby-smooth skin of his thin brown arms" had been made up by reporter Janet Cooke.

Although it was published on Sept. 28, 1980, not long after Greene joined the paper, the fallout did not hit until Monday, April 13, 1981, when the Pulitzer Prize for feature writing was announced, naming Cooke the winner. The *Post* story on her prize eerily quotes the Pulitzer Board announcement as saying her article "was met by a wave of shock and disbelief." It also noted, perhaps in a sign of foreshadowing, that "the story also led to a fruitless search for the boy by District of Columbia officials, who once threatened to subpoena Cooke for his identity."

Within less than a day, however, concerns began to crop up not from the story itself, but from Cooke's official Pulitzer biography that accompanies every winning announcement. Within days Cooke admitted her fabrication, lost her job, prompted Bradlee to offer his resignation (it wasn't accepted) and sparked what remains the worst *Post* scandal ever. Enter Bill Greene, who was tasked with researching the facts and presenting a complete account, while also creating an atmosphere where public trust could be rebuilt.

His final product was the textbook approach to how an ombudsman should handle a crisis of confidence, and a reminder of how valuable such a position is. The keys: get the facts, tell the whole story, and make it easy to read.

Greene's nearly 14,000-word front-page report ran on Sunday, April 19, 1981, with a prominent Page One placement and several inside pages. It included Cooke's work and career, beginning with her first job-seeking letter to Bradlee and even included an interview with her father about her childhood.

Other background elements ranged from comments of a fellow reporter she roomed with about Cooke "being hard to live with" and "high strung" to word of her bouncing a rent check to her goal of winning a Pulitzer Prize within three years. (She beat it by nearly two years). But it also did not let editors off the hook, explaining how several of her supervisors ignored initial doubts and let her assurance guide their fact-checking in many cases.

The lynchpin of the investigation was the play-by-play account of how her story came about, the first sniffs of doubt about its accuracy, and the somewhat dramatic way that editors drove Cooke around the slums of D.C. at one point to look for the young "Jimmy" before she later broke down and confessed while under heavy pressure from editors. Some passages read like a Mickey Spillane novel as Greene recreates the detective-like interrogation of Cooke by top editors.

Greene described how Cooke first told bosses she had come across the eight-year-old boy during extensive interviews with sources and other addicts about the growing heroin epidemic in Washington at the time, visited his home and he even had dinner with his mother. But he also disclosed how no one pushed Cooke for the subject's identity or demanded more proof, such as a photo, that he existed.

Cooke managed to cover that as well with lies about the mother's boyfriend, whom she claimed had threatened Cooke with a knife if she revealed anything about them. "The threat was taken so seriously by Coleman and others at the *Post* that when Richard Cohen wrote a column after 'Jimmy's World' appeared, Coleman insisted that Cohen's reference to the knife be deleted," Greene wrote. "It was. [Managing Editor Howard] Simons, whose concern for the staff is nearly parental, wouldn't let Cooke go home for two nights after her story was published. He arranged for her to stay with another *Post* employee."

In the days that followed, as Greene wrote, the story landed like a bombshell on the city and on journalism, with more than 300 news outlets reprinting it, city officials launching a search for the boy and even new first lady Nancy Reagan opining that the story was "terribly sad." At one point, 11 *Post* reporters were assigned to follow up on the story, help find "Jimmy" and seek others in the same situation for potential stories as well.

But Greene wrote that editors began to feel uneasy about the story just weeks after it ran, mostly due to the fact that Cooke could not lead them to "Jimmy's" house, where she supposedly spent time and was allegedly threatened, and appeared not to know the area well. Greene's report also walked the delicate line of race in newsrooms and how the lack of diversity and ongoing push for more minorities might have caused editors to hold back questions about Cooke's work given that she was a bright, energetic young black woman who could write well, too.

Greene pointed out how new doubts arose when the editorial staff considered Pulitzer nominations in late 1980, with some fearing that if "Jimmy's World" won, the scrutiny that had died down a bit would grow even louder and open the paper up to eventual problems. As someone who covered the Pulitzer Prizes for more than 10 years, I saw annually the fierce competition for the coveted awards, which still remain the top journalism prize and likely always will. And when they were announced, it was jubilation in newsrooms and the knowledge that the winner's lives would be forever changed. They are the Oscars, Emmys, and Tony's of news.

The 19-member Pulitzer Board makes the decision each year, and with strict secrecy, although word often leaks out. In the case of the 1981 awards that included Cooke's prize, the Pulitzer Board actually had a descendent of founder Joseph Pulitzer – his grandson and then-St. Louis *Post-Dispatch* publisher Joseph Pulitzer III. But there was also a *Washington Post* employee on the board, columnist William Raspberry. When the board chose the winners on April 3, 1981, word soon leaked to the *Post* newsroom, according to Greene.

Ten days later, the official announcement went out and that's when the real collapse began. Greene wrote that it was *The Blade* of Toledo, OH, where Cooke had previously worked, that raised concerns first when, during preparation of its own story on the prize won by its former reporter, editors found a discrepancy in her background. *Blade* editors said there were elements of her official Pulitzer bio that claimed she had received educational degrees and previous news awards that her *Blade* resume never included. Among the false claims were the number of languages she spoke.

When *Post* editors were contacted on April 14, less than 24 hours after the awards were announced, it turned out the Pulitzer resume also differed from the original version Cooke had submitted back when she applied to be a *Post* reporter. When the Associated Press' national story on the Pulitzer winners was released, *Blade* editors noticed it include some of the false information and contacted the wire service, which did its own background rechecking.

That same day, one editor took Cooke across the street from the *Post* to the bar at The Capital Hilton and began quizzing her on her resume, eventually finding out she had fabricated portions of it, but defended her award-winning story, Greene wrote. Soon after, Cooke, the editor and other editors met with Bradlee in an empty office at the *Post* where she broke into tears but remained adamant the story was real. She revealed for the first time the supposed identity of "Jimmy" and his parents, as well as his home street. Several editors, including Watergate legend Bob Woodward – then an assistant managing editor and a top supervisor on the story – said they no longer believed the story was true.

Bradlee's response: "You've got 24 hours to prove the 'Jimmy' story is true."

With that, Cooke and City Editor Milton Coleman again went out to find "Jimmy" and his home. But again, Cooke could not lead him to the location. Later during more meetings with top editors, among them Deputy Metropolitan Editor and Maryland Editor David Maraniss – who would go on to be a top historian and biographer – the high-pressure tactics continued, according to Greene. In the end, Cooke confessed to Maraniss, the editor she had been closest to, that, "There is no Jimmy and no family. It was a fabrication. I did so much work on it, but it's a composite. I want to give the prize back." So, the *Post* did. The next day, April 15, 1981, Cooke submitted a written resignation.

But her confession and departure, while cleansing and contrite, left the *Post* with a huge image problem and credibility void. Anti-press advocates who had attacked the paper for years dating back to the Nixon presidency, Watergate and the Pentagon Papers, had a field day with the Cooke story. Some demanded Bradlee resign, others said the paper could never recover. One of the solutions would have to be Greene.

Greene's lengthy review and report was clearly a key part of the *Post* recovery. Along with detailing the facts and process that went awry in the Cooke case, it also included a 15-point plan for recovery that recommended more background checks on reporters, increased scrutiny of facts, less demand on young reporters, and no more use of anonymous sources without editors knowing their identity. But Greene's final point said simply, "The *Post* is one of the very few great enterprises in journalism, and everybody associated with it ought to be proud of it."

In his 1995 biography, *A Good Life*, Bradlee praised Greene's assessment, describing him as "one wise and fair sumbitch, as the locals say" and called his report "a no-holds-barred, meticulously reported account of what went wrong." When Greene died in 2016, the rival *New York Times* declared in an obituary that his Cooke report was "a blistering verdict on journalistic lapses." Greene lived long enough to see his former job eliminated in 2013 in the recent wave of cuts.

Greene and Herchenroeder were not the only ombudsmen who proved the position worthwhile. From *the Boston Globe* to *the Rocky Mountain News* to *the Hartford Courant* – and others who have eliminated the position – many examples of ombudsmen weighing in and diffusing disputes or explaining controversial issues span the history of ombudsmen.

At the *Globe*, for instance, former ombudsman Christine Chinlund, who now serves as managing editor, helped shield the paper from a tidal wave of angry backlash during its 2002 Pulitzer Prize-winning expose of child abuse in the Catholic Church, which sparked hundreds of such examples worldwide and received acknowledgement in the 2016 Oscar-winning film, *Spotlight*.

In one column on April 29, 2002, Chinlund deftly defended the coverage, but also noted the impact it had had on loyal Catholics who might find uncertainty in their reaction. She wrote that the series was understandably "a source of considerable pain for many Catholics in the Boston area. Some have responded by faulting the *Globe*'s aggressive coverage. It's just fresh proof, they say, that the *Globe* is 'anti-Catholic.'

From others, the critique is more nuanced, suggesting [among other things] a *Globe* attempt to impose a liberal agenda on the church."

She went on to add, "It was through the eyes of these critics that I went back and reread the 80-plus stories on the topic that have appeared on page one since Jan. 6. I looked hard for signs of bias – or at least journalistic insensitivity – to support the 'anti-Catholic' charge. I could not find it ... More often I found careful, restrained use of language and an attempt to balance the coverage of deviant priests with stories about dedicated church servants harmed by the revelations."

In June 2005, *Hartford Courant* reader representative Karen Hunter took on the issue of the paper identifying two minor children, ages 12 and 14, in a story about the tragic killing of their mother by their father outside a courthouse where a divorce proceeding was set to take place. The father, Michael Bochicchio, then turned the gun on himself and took his own life.

Hunter wrote that many readers found the identification of the children unacceptable. But even as she defended the move, her column explained the process for the decision and noted the paper's awareness of the sensitivity of such actions: "In the flurry of gathering the details of a such a tragic event and crafting a well-written story for the next day's newspaper, reporters and editors constantly weigh what details the public needs to know, what details contribute to a well-reported story and what details are unnecessarily intrusive. When a story achieves the right balance, I've seen the community of support for those touched by violence grow far wider than family, friends and acquaintances."

In many cases, that simple effort to explain an editorial approach or let readers and story subjects know that their concerns are heard is a key asset of the ombudsman position, which is all but gone these days.

Among the most telling ombudsman tales, almost a classic "rise and fall" story of the position and its value, occurred at *The New York Times.*

Some 22 years after the Cooke scandal, the *Times* would find itself in a similar controversy with a deceptive young black reporter who had gotten by in part on efforts to integrate a newsroom and editors' dismissal of early warning signs. The difference at the *Times*, however, was they did not have an ombudsman at the time, although the fallout would spark its decision to hire one. Unfortunately, that decision would be reversed less than 15 years later.

Given its reputation as the paper of record and considered by many the best daily paper in America, it was always surprising *The New York Times* did not have an ombudsman, someone like Greene, Enkin or Harwood who could respond to public concerns with an independent, investigative toolbox and the freedom to tell it like it is. But as Jones noted earlier, previous executive editor Abe Rosenthal dismissed the idea, a view that carried on for decades as the paper collected Pulitzer Prizes (the most of any paper at 125 as of 2018), dug up scoop after scoop, and dazzled the industry with great stories, writing and broad reporting.

Who needed some outside critic to raise issues and problems, take editors and reporters away from their news pursuits, and perhaps show that the paper is not perfect? They could do it in-house with great oversight, experienced editors and "All the News That's Fit to Print" behind them.

Then Jayson Blair happened.

Blair, a 27-year-old *Times* reporter, had a similar situation to Cooke. He was young, black, an excellent writer and a charming employee. But he was also a liar. The story of his fabrications, which spanned more than a year and included numerous articles, came out on Mother's Day 2003 in a 7,200-page investigative report that started on Page One, included four bylines and spanned four inside pages. It caused an avalanche of fallout for the paper, in some ways worse than Cooke's damage to the *Post*.

The investigative piece, titled "CORRECTING THE RECORD; *Times* Reporter Who Resigned Leaves Long Trail of Deception," landed with a thud on the newspaper world, offering detailed accounts of how this junior reporter managed to make up stories, lie about being at locations when events occurred, and regularly plagiarize. Similar to Greene's Cooke report, the investigation mixed detailed facts with novel-like descriptions and insider accounts of newsroom meetings, frantic phone calls and even specific editor concerns.

But unlike Cooke, Blair's sins went beyond just one story. As the review revealed, the paper found problems with at least 36 of the 72 stories Blair had written for the national desk between October 2002 and May 2003, with numerous other problems in many of the previous 600 articles he wrote during his nearly four years at the *Times*.

Blair "misled readers and *Times* colleagues with dispatches that purported to be from Maryland, Texas and other states, when often he was far away, in New York. He fabricated comments. He concocted scenes. He lifted material from other newspapers and wire services. He selected details from photographs to create the impression he had been somewhere or seen someone, when he had not. And he used these techniques to write falsely about emotionally charged moments in recent history, from the deadly sniper attacks in suburban Washington to the anguish of families grieving for loved ones killed in Iraq," the investigative report stated.

The internal review also detailed how early concerns from some editors about Blair's work and potential problems were ignored, similar to the Cooke case. Most of the red flags related to sloppy work and mistakes more than outright fabrication or plagiarism. "His mistakes became so routine, his behavior so unprofessional, that by April 2002,

Jonathan Landman, the metropolitan editor, dashed off a two-sentence e-mail message to newsroom administrators that read: 'We have to stop Jayson from writing for the *Times*. Right now,'" the report stated.

But, as the investigation further revealed, those warnings were only partially heard as Blair was promoted months later, in October 2003, to the coveted national desk "after taking a leave for personal problems and being sternly warned, both orally and in writing, that his job was in peril." Two of the most prestigious beats in the *Times* newsroom are the Washington bureau and the national desk. National reporters get the cream of assignments outside the nation's capital, and sometimes inside. Many a Pulitzer is won there.

It is surprising that the paper would trust such a prestigious and monitored beat to a less-experienced reporter who had had so many problems. As the investigation report put it: "Mr. Blair improved his performance. By last October, the newspaper's top two editors – who said they believed that Mr. Blair had turned his life and work around – had guided him to the understaffed national desk, where he was assigned to help cover the Washington sniper case."

The review also noted how Blair's charisma and friendliness charmed co-workers, and likely some editors, making them reluctant to come down too hard on him. "…many at The *Times* grew fond of the affable Mr. Blair, who seemed especially gifted at office politics. He made a point of getting to know many of the newsroom support workers, for example. His distinctive laugh became a familiar sound," the report stated.

But it didn't take long for new cracks to appear, the report later added, "By the end of that month, public officials and colleagues were beginning to challenge his reporting. By November, the investigation has found, he was fabricating quotations and scenes, undetected. By March, he was lying in his articles and to his editors about being at a court hearing in Virginia, in a police chief's home in Maryland and in front of a soldier's home in West Virginia. By the end of April another newspaper was raising questions about plagiarism. And by the first of May, his career at the *Times* was over."

That other newspaper was the *San Antonio Express-News*, which, like *The Blade* of Toledo in the Cooke case, notice something questionable in Blair's work. While it was Cooke's resume that raised first suspicions of her, Blair was caught plagiarizing portions of a story that had run in the *Express-News*. At issue was a front-page story Blair wrote on April 26, 2003, about a U.S. Army mechanic from Texas missing in Iraq. The story was published just months after the U.S. invasion of Iraq that year.

Three days after the story appeared, *Express-News* editor Robert Rivard e-mailed *Times* editors with concerns that Blair's piece was "disturbingly similar" to an earlier *Express-News* story on the same subject that was published April 18, 2003. After conducting its own internal review, the *Times* forced Blair to resign and announced his departure in a May 2, 2003, story that indicated further reviews of his work were ongoing. Nine days later, on May 11, 2003, the lengthy investigative report was published.

One wonders how the situation might have been handled better or the damage prevented if an ombudsman or public editor had been involved early on. And instead of taking four journalists away from reporting time to work on the eventual report, a public editor could have at least done the majority of the work as Greene did.

Instead, the *Times* took a major hit that some believe may still be reverberating, especially as the "fake news" claims of Donald Trump and others add a new attack on the press. When the dust settled, Blair was forced to resign, Executive Editor Howell Raines and Managing Editor Gerald Boyd were fired, and the paper created its first ombudsman position, with the title "Public Editor."

In the announcement of the new editor post in late July 2003, Bill Keller, who had been appointed to replace Raines as executive editor, stated, "…we can profit from the scrutiny of an independent reader representative. A pair of professional eyes, familiar with us but independent of the day-to-day production of the paper, can make us more sensitive on matters of fairness and accuracy and enhance our credibility."

Too bad they did not stick to that belief. And what followed showed why they should have.

WHO IS
NO LONGER WATCHING?

For the next 14 years, *The New York Times* public editor did just what Executive Editor Bill Keller promised when he announced the new position in 2003 after the Jayson Blair scandal. Six people held that post, from the first public editor, Daniel Okrent, to the last, Liz Spayd. In between those two, there was Byron (Barney) Calame, Arthur Brisbane, Margaret Sullivan and Clark Hoyt. Each took the job seriously and ruffled their share of feathers, as well as raising important issues.

Okrent's first column landed in the paper and online on Dec. 7, 2003, nearly seven months after the Jayson Blair scandal was revealed. The new position attacked some of the paper's sacred cows and offered the first real counterattack to journalistic actions at the most celebrated, and sometimes arrogant, U.S. newspaper. A veteran book editor and author, Okrent is also among the group that created the modern fantasy baseball, originally known as rotisserie baseball for the fact it was started at La Rotisserie Française, a New York restaurant.

In that first piece, Okrent did not hold back on his plans to take on the issues and work for the reader, not the newspaper as he braced for the worst as well almost predicting he would be ousted: "Reporters and editors (the thickness of their skin measurable in microns, the length of their memories in elephant years) will resent the public second-guessing. The people who run the newspaper may find themselves wondering how they might get away with firing me before my 18-month term is up. Too many combatants in the culture wars, loath to tolerate interpretations other than their own, will dismiss what I say except when it serves their ideological interests. But those are their problems, not mine. My only concern in this adventure is dispassionate evaluation; my only colleagues are readers who turn to the *Times* for their news, expect it to be fair, honest and complete, and are willing to trust another such reader – me – as their surrogate."

Okrent went on to tackle issues ranging from using full quotes in stories to coverage of a sex slave ring in New Jersey. He also took issue with the paper's failure to question the White House claims of weapons of mass destruction leading up to the 2003 U.S. invasion of Iraq, which turned out to be false. "I began to look into a question arising from the past that weighs heavily on the present: Why had the *Times* failed to revisit its own coverage of Iraqi weapons of mass destruction?" he wrote on May 30, 2004. "To anyone who read the paper between September 2002 and June 2003, the impression that Saddam Hussein possessed, or was acquiring, a frightening arsenal of W.M.D. seemed unmistakable. Except, of course, it appears to have been mistaken."

One theme he recalled that arose often was how news consumers will "approve of journalism they agree with and object to journalism they do not agree with." He cited a phone call he received during the 2004 presidential campaign from a reader who objected to a front-page photo of George W. Bush that showed him "smiling toward the crowd with flags, blue skies and a positive image. She said that showed the paper's favoritism toward the president." But when he pointed out that a similar photo of challenger John Kerry had appear a day earlier in the same place, she said she had not seen it.

Okrent might have caused the biggest stir when he admitted that the *Times* is a liberal newspaper. "Of course it is," his column began on July

25, 2004, later stating that when it comes to social issues such as gay rights, gun control, abortion and environmental regulation, "if you think the *Times* plays it down the middle on any of them, you've been reading the paper with your eyes closed."

But one of the top issues for Okrent and most of those who followed him in the job was anonymous sourcing. In many cases, such anonymity is necessary to protect a source from legal action, loss of employment and even physical harm. But as Okrent and others pointed out for more than a decade the *Times* and other news outlets use it too often, a practice that diminishes its value and increases untrustworthiness.

"It's one of those things that executive editors say, 'we have a problem with,' they put in a new policy, and within a year it reverts to the old, it continues to be a major, major problem," Okrent told me. "What the editors don't understand is how readers really don't trust it." He cited the issue as among the most prevalent in one of his final public editor columns on May 8, 2005, writing, "Since I've been in this job, use of anonymous sources has been the substantive issue raised most often by readers. They challenge the authenticity of quotations. They question the accuracy of the information in the quotations. They believe reporters who invoke unidentified sources are lazy or, far worse, dishonest ... Reporters bristle when they hear this sort of thing, just as you would if your integrity were challenged. But I don't think it matters if it's fair or not. If readers perceive deception or dishonesty, the *Times* has a problem."

And that issue did not end with Okrent. A review of *Times* public editor columns found that anonymous sourcing was an issue in 102 of the 915 public editor columns between 2003 and 2017 – more than one out of every 10 – with each public editor addressing the issue at least once.

Margaret Sullivan, who served in the position from 2012 to 2016 – the longest tenure of any such editor – visited the subject the most, with 64 of her columns at least referencing anonymous sourcing, most often with a critical eye. She was also on the job in 2016 when the *Times* instituted yet another revised anonymous sourcing policy after two major Page One errors in a six-month period involving unnamed attribution. That policy would require one of three top editors to review and sign off on articles that depend "primarily on information from unnamed sources – particularly those that 'hinge on a central fact' from such a source."

"I'm not in favor of banning anonymous sources, although I've written repeatedly about their overuse," Sullivan wrote at the time. "Many important stories – some of the most important, in fact – could never have been written if their sources had not been kept confidential. Reporters risk a lot to protect those sources, and they need to be able to do so. But there's a big difference between, for example, a national security article that simply can't be written with on-the-record sources and the other kinds of anonymity one often sees. That latter category includes allowing unnamed government officials to use the press as a megaphone, to float politically sensitive trial balloons, or to disparage their enemies without accountability."

The issue had appeared to have gotten better in recent years with word in late 2017 from Washington reporter Peter Baker that the *Times*' D.C. newsroom had stopped using "blind quotes," according to Sullivan, who is now a media writer for the *Washington Post* and noted the change in a *Times* article.

But anonymous sourcing has not diminished in all cases as coverage of the White House under Trump shows. The *Times* and other outlets have taken advantage of the increased leaks from staffers during Trump's first term at levels unseen in many decades.

One recent example was a Sept. 21, 2018 front-page *Times* story that claimed Deputy Attorney General Rod J. Rosenstein had suggested in 2018 that he secretly record Trump "to expose the chaos consuming the administration" and using it to invoke the 25th Amendment to remove Trump from office. The juicy story was credited to "Several people [who] described the episodes in interviews over the past several months, insisting on anonymity to discuss internal deliberations." It received such harsh criticism from several news outlets that the paper posted online a very Public Editor-style column with answers to reader questions about the article.

It is likely the Rosenstein story and its fallout would have been handled more completely and with better transparency if a traditional public editor had been involved.

Another past concern of note was conflict of interest, visited several times by public editors, including Clark Hoyt, who held the post for the second-longest period of time – from 2007 to 2010. In February 2010, he raised the issue of *Times* Jerusalem bureau chief Ethan Bronner, whose son had joined the Israeli military, wondering if it created a conflict of interest for the elder Bronner. Hoyt wrote that Keller found no issue with the arrangement, but Hoyt also referenced the *Times* own ethical guidelines: "They say that if a family member's activities create even the appearance of a conflict of interest, it should be disclosed to editors, who must then decide whether the staffer should avoid certain stories or even be reassigned to a different beat."

Hoyt eventually came down on the side of caution and urged that Bronner be reassigned. "I have enormous respect for Bronner and his work, and he has done nothing wrong. But this is not about punishment; it is simply a difficult reality," Hoyt wrote. "I would find a plum assignment for him somewhere else, at least for the duration of his son's service in the I.D.F." But that suggestion was ignored and Bronner stayed on the beat.

Interestingly, Bronner came under attack again about 18 months later for a different conflict of interest, in September 2011, when the *Columbia Journalism Review* criticized his financial ties to an Israeli public relations firm that also represented entities seeking *Times* coverage. It revealed that the firm, Lone Star Communications, arranged paid speaking appearances for Bronner, while also pitching him story ideas for its other clients.

"Complicating the arrangement is the fact that Lone Star has a fairly clear ideological bent, and that Bronner has reported on a handful of the firm's PR clients – this in a bureau where every nuance is scrutinized," the CJR story said. By late 2011, Hoyt had left the public editor post, replaced by Arthur Brisbane, who served until 2012. Brisbane weighed in with his own take on Sept. 24, 2011, writing that the conflict was wrong and that Bronner had agreed to cut ties with Lone Star.

"A close examination of the facts leads me to conclude that the case for an actual conflict of interest is slender. But the appearance of a conflict clearly exists, and that is a problem in and of itself," Brisbane wrote. "The *Times*'s 'Ethical Journalism' guidelines state that staff members 'may not accept anything that could be construed as a payment for favorable coverage or as an inducement to alter or forgo unfavorable coverage.' Mr. Bronner has now severed his ties to the public relations firm. 'In my view, it is all about appearances,' he told me. 'I am not denying they matter. There is nothing of an actual conflict.'"

Byron Calame, a former *Wall Street Journal* veteran, had one of the shortest tenures – from May 2005 to May 2007 – but also had to work during a difficult time at the paper and throughout journalism as severe cutbacks occurred and removed some necessary levels of scrutiny and fact-checking from the news process. In addition, the growing demands of 24-hour news via the web and exploding online competition dealt more pressures.

As he wrote in his final column, "Editing lapses, among both the so-called backfield editors who shepherd and shape stories and the copy editors who pore over articles detail by detail, have been a recurring theme in my columns. Often the problem was that, even on non-deadline stories, editors didn't have enough time to spot problems and ask questions ... Doing more with the same size staff of reporters also has implications for the quality of the reporting."

Finally, the position endured Liz Spayd, the final public editor whose work received more criticism than any of her predecessors, and perhaps helped bring about the end of the position. Appointed in July 2016, Spayd was gone in less than a year, posting her last column on June 2, 2017. She came to the job with a lengthy resume, having spent more than two decades at the *Washington Post* in various roles, then editing the prestigious *Columbia Journalism Review*. A perfect fit, right? Wrong.

During her short term in the job, Spayd defended false equivalency in stories, prompting one critic to call it "disastrous"; supported narrow-minded reader complaints that the *Times* sports page should stick to the basic sports and ignore interesting tales of unique fishing expeditions and foreign soccer players; backed a false, far-right "fringe campaign" aimed at a *Times* writer, and criticized some *Times'* reporters' tweets as "over the line" in an interview with right-wing host Tucker Carlson.

When the *Times* hired climate change-denier Bret Stephens to be an Op-Ed columnist in April 2017, Spayd defended the move, opining that Stephens views should be heard since he is an alternative, conservative voice, something she believed might be lacking in the "mostly liberal echo chamber around here." That comment was in response to Stephens' first column, on April 28, 2017, which questioned the scientific findings of man-made climate change that are nearly universal, and also trying to tie that view to some kind of political leaning stemming from the failed Hillary Clinton campaign. Stephens wrote, "...history is littered with the human wreckage of scientific errors married to political power."

Stephens and Spayd's views received critical response from several journalistic corners, among them *The New Republic*, where staff writer Emily Atkin wrote: "Spayd never grapples with the complaint that Stephens pushes falsehoods. She never says whether it was within the *Times'* standards to allow Stephens to incongruously compare the reliability of polling data with the reliability of climatology."

One example was the Jan. 20, 2017, Spayd column ripping the *Times'* coverage of the federal investigation into Donald Trump and possible ties to Russian interference. She wrote, in part, "Was there a way to write about some of these allegations using sound journalistic principles but still surfacing the investigation and important leads? Eventually, the *Times* did just that, but only after other news outlets had gone first." She also slammed the paper for agreeing to an FBI request to delay publication of some information, stating, "In this cat-and-mouse game between government and press, the government won."

It did not go over well. The next day, *Times* Executive Editor Dean Baquet slammed the column in emails to the *Washington Post's* Erik Wemple, calling it a "bad column" with "fairly ridiculous" conclusions. What Spayd appeared to get wrong according to Baquet and Wemple were her claims that the paper held off information on the Trump-Russia story, at one point due to government requests, and let other outlets beat them to the punch.

"The newspaper made some key contributions to this coverage area, particularly with its August story uncovering some smelly documents relating to then-Trump campaign chief Paul Manafort – specifically, 'handwritten ledgers' indicating '$12.7 million in undisclosed cash payments designated for [Paul] Manafort from [Viktor F.] Yanukovych's pro-Russian political party from 2007 to 2012, according to Ukraine's newly formed National Anti-Corruption Bureau,'" Wemple wrote. "It also produced a probing look at Manafort's influence and business dealings involving Ukraine. The *Times* in late July also reported that the two Russian intelligence agencies were behind the hacking of the Democratic National Committee."

Added Baquet, "She doesn't understand what happened. We reported the hell out of this, as did other news organizations, and we could prove nothing more than that there was some packets of information from a bank to Trump Tower … Sorry, Liz is just wrong. That is not journalism. It is typing." Ouch! But it wasn't just Wemple and Baquet who went after Spayd during her short stint. Hits came from *The Atlantic*, *Politico*, *Slate*, and my old friends at *Media Matters*.

"But if we've learned one big lesson from Spayd's work so far, it's this: Readers are quite often wrong," wrote *Slate*'s Will Oremus. "Of course the public editor should listen to them and take them seriously. The real challenge, though, is to distinguish between their wishes and their true interests, to understand not only where those overlap but where they diverge, and to recognize which should influence the paper's editorial decisions and which should not. At that difficult task, Spayd has repeatedly failed."

While the *Times* might not have ended the position because of Spayd's weak performance, it surely did not help the cause for independent criticism of the newspaper. In announcing the public editor's demise in 2017, both Baquet and then Publisher Arthur Sulzberger Jr. came up with weak reasoning. "I think it's like one of those cases when governments create big bureaucracies to fix a scandal – one particular scandal," Baquet told *the Daily Beast*. "They should ask themselves after the passage of 20 years or whatever, 'Is this what we need now?' And I would argue that now we need something different." In a memo to staff, Sulzberger claimed, "The responsibility of the public editor — to serve as the reader's representative — has outgrown that one office. There is nothing more important to our mission, or our business, than strengthening our connection with our readers. A relationship that fundamental cannot be outsourced to a single intermediary."

So now it is outsourced to the Twittersphere and other social media hounds who likely do not have the experience, the access to internal information or the respected audience to make clear, valid critiques. I am sure Baquet and Sulzberger meant well, but the reasoning still does not hold up. The *Times* could have used a public editor in late 2017 and early 2018 when two internal embarrassments hit the newsroom and sparked outcries for correction.

The most recent was the strange case of Ali Watkin, the *Times* reporter and subject of a lengthy report on June 24, 2018, detailed in an earlier chapter for her apparent conflict of interest with a government official. And her confusing lack of disclosure to some bosses on some of the details.

The triple bylined piece, which also cited work from five more staffers, read like some kind of bad D.C. soap opera with anonymous sources, personal details and even cutesy descriptions of Watkins' home life: "In recent years she has zipped around Washington on a motorcycle, taken boxing lessons, and doted on her Husky, Kellan, whom she outfitted with a Putin chew toy."

To be fair, it is also an example of the *Times* seeking to tell the entire, open story of an embarrassing internal issue, very similar to the Blair scandal. Ali Watkins is no Jayson Blair, far from it. But feeling the need to expose all of the details about her issue mirrors the paper's reaction to Blair's sins. But instead of showing editors the need for a public editor,

Watkins' situation forced the paper to deal with such an issue without one.

The June 24 *Times* report, which began on Page One and filled an entire inside page, said Watkins had long claimed that her former lover, Senate Intelligence Committee aide James Wolfe was never a source on her reporting, but also revealed she did not tell all of her editors who he was when disclosing that she was involved in a relationship with a committee official. "People at *Buzzfeed* say they had a general sense of her personal life," The *Times* wrote. "During a job interview, Ms. Watkins told Miriam Elder, an editor, that she was dating a man who did intelligence work on Capitol Hill. She said he was not a source, but did not volunteer Mr. Wolfe's name or title, and the discussion went no further. (Ms. Elder declined to comment but did not dispute the account.)"

It later added, "Ms. Watkins made another move in May 2017, to *Politico*, while she and Mr. Wolfe were still together. She has told friends that when she was hired, she informed a *Politico* editor, Paul Volpe, that she was dating a man in the intelligence community, though she again did not volunteer Mr. Wolfe's name or his position. A spokesman for *Politico*, Brad Dayspring, said only that she "did not disclose the personal nature of her relationship early on in her tenure." Watkins' and Wolfe's romance first became public after Wolfe was arrested June 7, 2018, for allegedly lying to investigators about his contacts with Watkins and three other journalists, according to the *Times*. In a bizarre twist that prompted serious backlash among journalists, Watkins' phone and email records were seized, a serious violation of journalistic rights.

But that story also forced the *Times* and Watkins to reveal her relationship, which the lengthy article expanded upon, detailing when the two first met in 2013, first kissed in 2014, and later broke up in late 2017.

The *Times* also revealed that Watkins had been approached by two FBI agents asking about Wolfe just days before she began working at the paper in December 2017, a fact she told editors about at the time, although it is unclear if she revealed the entire Wolfe relationship then. The paper also disclosed that, "In February, however, Ms. Watkins received a letter that she did not tell her editors about: a notice from the Justice Department, informing her that investigators had seized some of her email and phone records."

The *Times* said Watkins was advised by her lawyer not to disclose the letter to her employers. Asked about that decision, *Times* spokesperson Eileen Murphy said that editors "obviously would have preferred to know." And editors perhaps would have preferred that such a relationship did not exist at all. To make clear, it appears Watkins' romance with Wolfe had ended before she joined the *Times*, where she had not reported on stories related to him or the Senate Intelligence Committee. But her past actions with a potential conflict of interest relationship clearly raised concerns.

The *Times'* own Ethical Journalism handbook, which was not even mentioned in the report, states: Clearly, romantic involvement with a news source would foster an appearance of partiality. Therefore, staff members who develop close relationships with people who might figure in coverage they provide, edit, package or supervise must disclose those relationships to the standards editor, the associate managing editor for news administration or the deputy editorial page editor. In some cases, no further action may be needed. But in other instances, staff members may have to recuse themselves from certain coverage. And in still other cases, assignments may have to be modified or beats changed. In a few instances, a staff member may have to move to a different department – from business and financial news, say, to the culture desk – to avoid the appearance of conflict.

Watkins had said Wolfe was not a source on her reporting, but wouldn't her relationship with him be at least a perceived conflict of interest? In the end, the paper quietly kept Watkins on staff, but announced on July 3, 2018, that she would be reassigned to the paper's New York headquarters.

A few months earlier a different *Times* issue worthy of a public editor review had arisen when reporter Glenn Thrush was suspended and later reassigned after allegations of mistreatment of women. He was kept on the job, but not until *Times* editors went through their own investigations and decided to allow him to remain after a two-month suspension.

The 2018 Showtimes series *The Fourth Estate*, which chronicled the paper's first year covering Donald Trump's presidency, included a segment devoted to the Thrush incident. Executive Editor Dean Baquet said during a conference call with editors about Thrush, "I think that kind of behavior has got to end." When someone on the call asked why Thrush would not then be fired, Baquet answered, "What I said in the statement is that we're in a moment where there is a huge debate about how to deal with this stuff. But that in my view these things have to be taken as individuals, and individual circumstances. That there can't be blanket rules or blanket punishments."

It would have been interesting to see what part a public editor would have played in that situation, or in the Watkins debates, and in any future internal issues that would benefit from some real independent assessment.

A public editor could clear a lot of the air on these and other such internal issues, and without requiring so many staff members to take time away from covering other important news. It also would remove an obvious conflict of interest the *Times* faces when having its staff report on itself.

"I think there's a real negative," Okrent said about the loss of the public editor and other newspaper ombudsman positions. "It's a bad thing, it's an inevitable thing in the sense that those institutions and the people running those institutions have a cover story – we are running out of money and cutting staff and is it more important to have someone covering city hall?" He said even when the affected papers, such as the *Times*, claim there will still be scrutiny of coverage and response to readers, the independent outside voice with special inside access cannot be replaced: "...there is no one to hold their feet to the fire." He also stressed that "a good ombudsman would distinguish between" valid attacks on the paper and those that need defending, calling it "an independent arbitrator who would make the case for whether the paper is right or wrong."

Okrent then went on to accuse the *Times'* former publisher, Arthur Sulzberger Jr., of removing the public editor position because his son, current publisher Arthur G. Sulzberger (who took over in early 2018), did not want it in place. "There was a time when the editor wanted to get rid of it and Arthur said no, and then there was a time when he wanted to get rid of it and the editor said no," Okrent said. "I had a feeling that Arthur G. Sulzberger didn't like the position and his father took the hit so he wouldn't have to."

He also said Spayd's poor performance made it easier: "I think there was an internal wish to get rid of it, but they would take a public relations hit. But they did not have a person in the position who had the support inside the institution or outside the institution for an outcry when she was fired. They took advantage of the opportunity to get rid of her to get rid of the position. It's disappointing to think that would possibly be a replacement for what a good critic could do."

Even more recently than the *Times* public editor cutback was ESPN's removal of an ombudsman position in March 2018 that had played an important part in several issues at the nation's oldest cable sports network. The network's cutback might have been a bit more understandable since it occurred just months after two different rounds of layoffs affecting more than 200 staffers. James Brady, the former *Washington Post* web editor who served as the last ESPN ombudsman – from 2015 to 2018 – said he did not like the move, but also believed it was a practical decision.

"I think if you are at ESPN, you have *Deadspin* and *The New York Times* and other people out there [who can critique the network]," he said in an interview. "The public is the ombudsman now ... I think it is a good role to have, but I understand if you cut two-thirds of your newsroom you cannot afford it."

ESPN's ombudsman dated back to 2005 and included a string of issues that Brady and his predecessors helped guide through the public ridicule and debate that followed. One instance had the network hearing calls for the firing of writer Jemele Hill after she tweeted in late 2017 that Donald Trump was "a white supremacist who has surrounded himself with other white supremacists." It did not help that detractors dug up a column she wrote years earlier, in 2008, that said "rooting for the Celtics is like saying Hitler was a victim. It's like hoping Gorbachev would get to the blinking red button before Reagan."

That got Hill a week's suspension and prompted a written apology for ESPN's Page 2.

When an avalanche of complaints called for her head after the Trump tweet, the network suspended her again and again accepted an apology. Brady helped ease some of the demands with a column that agreed Hill was wrong for what she had done, but also explained the internal review process and why he stopped short of calling for her to be fired.

"But in defense of Hill, she and all of ESPN's public-facing employees have been put in a tough situation," Brady wrote. "ESPN, like all media companies, is grappling with new issues: Objectivity seems to be a dying ideal, and, in a crowded media environment, keeping your editorial volume at a moderate level isn't always good for business. And, as I've written before, media companies are simultaneously asking many of their personalities to be active and engaging on social media but not partisan or opinionated. It's a line that is, at best, blurry and, at worst, nonexistent."

No doubt Brady's outreach and explanation did a lot to cool the animosity and answer many questions. Interestingly, he came to Hill's defense a month later when, in October 2017, she was again suspended after she tweeted support for Dallas Cowboys players who had been directed by owner Jerry Jones to stand for the national anthem at a time when many players were kneeling to protest police abuse of some black citizens. Among her tweets: "This play always work. Change happens when advertisers are impacted. If you feel strongly about JJ's statement, boycott his advertisers."

ESPN announced her suspension with a statement that said her tweets violated the network's social media policy and hinted it would "reflect negatively on ESPN." But unlike his past view that Hill had made a mistake worthy of punishment, Brady in an Oct. 11, 2017, column disagreed with the latest suspension, stating, "Don't get me wrong, I understand exactly what it is that upset ESPN about Hill's actions: One of its highest-profile personalities suggested an advertiser boycott that would impact an important network partner, and she did so on Twitter, the same platform she used to call out Trump … But it's not the job of Hill – or any other ESPN journalist, for that matter – to concern herself with the network's business relationships. In fact, the separation of 'church and state' is a longstanding core concept in any news organization worth its salt. So, it shouldn't matter whether Hill's comments put ESPN in a bad position with the NFL, any more than with the network's excellent reporting on concussions that has done the same."

But ESPN soon joined the long list of news outlets lacking true independent, internal reviews and watchdogs. In many cases, those who dropped the ombudsman-type editors claimed that weaker reader representatives or standards editors could fill the void, or the journalists themselves. Others pointed to the Internet and involved social media followers, as well as outside media critics, claiming they could take the place of a dedicated staff watchdog.

"We know that media writers inside and outside the *Post* will continue to hold us accountable for what we write," *Washington Post* Publisher Katharine Weymouth said in a 2013 note to readers after announcing that paper's ombudsman position had been eliminated and replaced by a less-independent reader representative. "As will our readers, in letters to the editor and online comments on *Post* articles."

But many detractors and veterans of the news watchdog positions saw through the sales pitch. They know that relying on outside critics who do not have the experience of a newsroom ombudsman – or social media voices lacking the inside access to ask real questions and demand real answers – will not do enough to properly hold the news outlets accountable and help explain inner policies and practices to readers and viewers.

"I don't buy any of those arguments," said Clark Hoyt, who served as *Times'* public editor from 2007-2010 and spent more than 30 years covering Washington as a reporter and editor. "What is lost is having the in-house, independent voice that has the authority to look into complaints and then the independence to register judgments about how something was handled, and also has the standing to explain to readers news values, the way news works and the way it should work, and point out when it does and call it out when it fails to do so."

Geneva Overholser, a former *Des Moines Register* editor who served as *Post* ombudsman from 1995 to 1998, agreed. "It's exactly wrong for this moment," she said about the recent ombudsmen cutbacks at various outlets. "A lot of people are also saying we need to really worry about listening to readers, readers need to be seen and heard in our publications. Reaching you is one thing, listening to readers is another entirely. I see what happens in newsrooms where someone is responsible for listening to readers, but not necessarily getting word back to reporters and editors. Are they really thoughtfully considering it?"

She said one of the issues she wrote about at the *Post* was the paper's local coverage, which she said did two things: let readers know their concerns were heard and made the paper's staff listen and make improvements. "I think it was discussed more. I know I brought attention to the question of anonymous sources. At least ombudsmen take it seriously and write about it," she said in an interview. "You receive it and if it is valid you really reach the journalist. It is a very unfortunate time to do away with these important positions."

Jeffrey Dvorkin, who served as ombudsman from 2000 to 2006 for National Public Radio – one of the few U.S. outlets that still has such a position – recalled the necessity of the job when he had to respond to reader concerns about NPR's Middle East coverage after the Sept. 11, 2001 attacks.

"I saw first-hand that it had a lot of usefulness," he said of the position at NPR and elsewhere. "I think the media organizations have confused the role of the Internet and have felt that somehow the invisible hand of the Internet will keep the news organization on the straight and narrow. But in fact, what we are seeing is the social media seems to be rather unsocial media, the coarseness of public engagement has logically pushed publishers to believe that not only do they not need an ombudsman but do not need to engage with the public."

He recalled the backlash NPR received after 9/11 when it sought to explain the Taliban philosophy and Middle East culture, which some claimed was unpatriotic. "I tried to engage the audience with the idea that more information is better than less information," he remembered. "And that it is very easy to have a government have its way with you if there isn't a journalistic organization prepared to say this is not a proper approach."

Dvorkin, who currently teaches journalism at the University of Toronto, also pointed to research that indicates more self-criticism and correction by news organizations improves its believability: "Studies show that a news organization with an ombudsman has more credibility with the public than one without. It gives the audience a sense that there's someone there looking after their interest."

He later added about the reliance on social media and Internet critics, "This is another down side of this digital culture that was supposed to be a way we are bound together but it has pushed us further and further apart. We need to be more skeptical about the role of the Internet, especially when it comes to news organizations who have found it is really a double-edged sword. It is valuable, but the fact that the captains of industry in media organizations have grabbed on to the digital culture makes me suspicious that there is a kind of desire for big journo that sees this as some kind of salvation."

Alicia Shepard, another former NPR ombudsman who served from 2007 to 2011, said simply: "The position I think is more important than ever today, to hold the news organizations accountable in a way that it can't do for itself with any credibility … That public accountability is important."

She recalled an issue that came before her in January 2011 when NPR wrongly reported that Congresswoman Gabby Giffords, who was shot in a horrific attack in Arizona that drew international attention, had died.

The situation worsened when the false report was picked up and reported by many others, including CNN, Fox News, *The New York Post*, ABC, CBS, NBC, and Reuters.

Some of the blame for the mistake, which occurred over a weekend, was placed on NPR's weekend management structure, which did not have the source confirmation demands of a weekday approach. It also was due to the network relying on anonymous sources. As Shepard explained in her column on the incident days after it happened, "NPR had two sources, though neither was identified in any way, and should have been. And the newscast should have put the news in context, explaining that a tragedy had just occurred, the story was changing quickly, and this was what NPR knew at that moment ... It turns out that neither source had accurate, first-hand information. The congressional source had heard it in a meeting on Capitol Hill, where undoubtedly rumors and half-truths were flying around."

Shepard said NPR source confirmation policies were changed after her review and other reactions. She also stressed how that example and others show an ombudsman's ability to explain inner workings of newsrooms and help the public understand the news process.

"The other reason [an ombudsman] is so important is the public has no idea in general how a story is reported, edited, the level of review and then hand-wringing inside a newsroom," Shepard added. "An ombudsman can explain the decision-making process, and he or she can then criticize the decision-making process."

NON-PROFIT IS THE FUTURE

The grim facts and figures from this book paint a bleak picture, as they should. The news industry is in big trouble and may have already lost the chance to regain the respect, impact and proper journalism that have been robbed from it during the recent decades of cutbacks and greed.

But there is hope. The answer may well be in a simple, growing approach to newsgathering: non-profit. As we have seen, many of the problems and cutbacks in today's news operations stem from demands for profits and satisfying shareholders, larger and larger media companies leveraged to the hilt, and a focus more on making money that committing journalism.

"It's now as clear as 56-point type that newspapers are responding to the continued upheaval by shattering the very foundation of what news and newspapering have meant since the days of the penny press," The *Columbia Journalism Review* declared in 2017. And it's not just newspapers, of course, but all the outlets we have discussed – from print to cable television to the Internet and social media.

I'm not saying the non-profit mode will save everyone. And, of course, not all the problems relate to the profit demands and revenue streams. But for the issues revolving around cutbacks for revenue increases, a non-profit structure is a key answer.

And it's not entirely new. Several daily papers have continued to operate as essentially non-profits for decades, among them the *Tampa*

Bay Times, The Day in New London, CT., and the respected Manchester, NH, *Union-Leader*. Each has a unique ownership structure that either funnels profits back into the paper or into a connected non-profit organization – or both.

In the magazine world, *Mother Jones, National Geographic* and *Consumer Reports* have similar models, while NPR and PBS remain stalwarts of news quality under a non-profit umbrella. In addition, *PBS Newshour*, which launched in 1975 as the *McNeil/Lehrer Report*, continues as a respected and quality daily news program helped in large part by its non-reliance on advertising or profit goals.

In the case of the *Tampa Bay Times*, formerly the *St. Petersburg Times*, its ownership is the Poynter Institute, the renowned journalism educational institution that shares in the profits; while *The Day* provides its net revenues back into the paper, *The Day* Trust and the related Bodenwein Public Benevolent Foundation, which funds local charities and programs. The arrangement dates to the directive from former publisher Theodore Bodenwein, who died in 1939 and left specific instructions for the paper's operation after his death.

"Bodenwein's will created *The Day* Trust," the paper's online history states. "The trust was to pay most of the stock dividends to Bodenwein's three heirs: his wife, Edna; daughter, Elizabeth; and son, Gordon, as long as they were alive. After the last heir died, all the earnings would be distributed to the communities in *The Day*'s circulation area. The trust was to ensure that the newspaper operated in the public interest according to standards of journalism Bodenwein spelled out in the will. The New London and Waterford Probate Court is responsible for holding the trust accountable to the will."

Since then, the paper has stayed in local hands and provided the freedom of non-profit financing that promotes journalism, not corporate bottom lines. "Without stockholders, *The Day* is insulated from customary stockholder pressures to hold expenses down," its website states. "*The Day* must make a profit like any other business, but it is at greater liberty to spend more of its revenue on newsgathering operations than other newspapers its size. The newspaper historically has paid higher salaries and maintained a larger staff than comparable newspapers. It occasionally has paid for major capital improvements out of cash reserves rather than through borrowing."

In Manchester, the *Union Leader*, which remains an influential news source in the first-in-the-nation presidential primary state, provides much of its profits to the Nackey S. Loeb School of Communications, named for the former publisher, with the rest to the William Loeb *Union Leader* Trust, which in turn provides dividends to employees. Such a structure has not stopped the *Union Leader* from being a major news force in the Granite State, as well as a major influence on policy. Many have credited (or blamed) the newspaper's editorial page for New Hampshire remaining the only state with no sales tax and no income tax. (Although it does have a high property tax.)

Similar arrangements that provide a portion of profits for a local charity and reinvestment into the newspaper are in place at the *Northwest Mississippi Daily Journal* in Tupelo and the *News-Gazette* of Champaign, IL. *The Christian Science Monitor*, one of the most respected news outlets, is also a non-profit, owned by the First Church of Christ, Scientist, but with a respected non-secular basic news approach.

But the largest non-profit news outlet is also the largest news outlet in the world, and one of the oldest: The Associated Press, which dates back to 1846 when five New York newspapers shared the cost of a reporter to cover the Mexican-American War so they could save money. Since then, AP has remained the king of the news trade and essentially a non-profit.

"We are not a charity, we have to be viable, we pay taxes, but we don't have owners, so we can't be bought or sold and, most importantly, no one can take money out of the AP, it's illegal," AP CEO Gary Pruitt told me in an interview.

AP is technically a news cooperative, which is not the same as a 501(c)3 non-profit that avoids taxes and can accept tax-deductible contributions, said Pruitt, who has been at the helm since 2012 and previously served as McClatchy CEO for 16 years. But it also means that there are no shareholders or single owners who take a dividend or profit cut. "Everything we generate has to go back into the organization," he said. "It goes to either taxes or capital spending, investing in the organization."

The success shows as AP remains the leading source for most election night data, according to Pruitt, who said the cooperative calls thousands of races on election nights every November. It was the first to call the race for Donald Trump in 2016. And AP was among the few not to call the 2000 presidential race for either George W. Bush or Al Gore on that fateful night when so many newsrooms made the wrong early call. That race, of course, was not decided until about a month later and after recounts and a U.S. Supreme Court ruling.

Along the way, AP has also managed to win 52 Pulitzer Prizes, with 31 for photography. The most recent was in 2016 for an investigation into slavery in the fishing industry in Southeast Asia. I'm not here to give a commercial for the news organization, just to point out that a non-profit approach can be successful and provide quality news.

With 3,500 employees, plus many contractors and stringers in 110 countries, AP is in the unique position of providing content to news outlets who then serve the public at large. "We're business to business, it is kind of like a news wholesaler in a way," Pruitt explained. "We gather news and largely license that news to other media and they take it to consumers. We have not had to invest and maintain a platform for reaching consumers."

He also points out that AP's focus on basic news, without opinions, editorials or agenda-driven columnists, is a growing commodity in the current news atmosphere: "It's totally news, focused on news, it's desire is always to be objective, we don't take editorial opinions, and we don't endorse candidates, the goal is objectivity. That's part of our business model because our customers span the ideological spectrum. If we were skewing one way or another we would pay for it, that is what our customers want."

That's not to say that AP is unaffected by the same money pressures and competition that the rest of the journalism industry is feeling. Pruitt said staffing has been cut through attrition by several hundred since he took over in 2012, and from its highest employment of about 4,000 around 2006.

"AP has felt the effects of the decline in the advertising market place because we feel the ripple effect of that," Pruitt said. "AP got hit hard in 2008 and 2009 when the newspaper industry got hit hard and demanded cuts in the AP assessment ... We've tackled that by diversifying our revenue stream more." He pointed out that U.S. newspapers only represent 18 to 19 percent of revenue, with the rest from television, digital, academics, and video and digital archives. About 40 percent of AP revenue now comes from outside of the United States.

"I talk to investment bankers here in New York sometimes and they'll say, 'you know what you should do, you should go public,'" Pruitt told me. "They just think that way and I say to them, 'your exactly right and for the next five years that would be the best structure for AP, but the next time there is a financial crisis, the next time there is a panic, then we'd be sold, or we'd go bankrupt and we'd be lost forever.' And the media companies today are not going to get together and say, 'hey, let's start a non-profit news organization we can all share in.' So, I feel like AP is this different breed of cat that needs to be preserved and protected and nurtured. Because it is different."

But while AP and the *Union Leader*s and *Tampa Bay Times* of newspapering have shown the way for non-profit success in some areas, the newest and perhaps most important approach has been the independent, non-profit news shops that are popping up annually using donations and subsidies to create journalism that is made available free online and in print to anyone who wants it. Unlike AP, which charges for content and counts on the revenue stream, these pioneering news organizations are structured to give away the news with the goal of getting important journalism out there and helping shore up what many mainstream news outlets have lost in the economic downturn.

"The moment is ripe for bold innovation on a national and global scale," Journalist Charles Lewis wrote in a 2006 paper on non-profit journalism for the Shorenstein Center at Harvard University. "Whether or not it will happen is unclear: But there is an unmistakable, momentous opportunity and a profound societal need for national leadership to solve a finite, discernible problem: How to regularly generate high quality, investigative and international reporting news content in an unprecedented, broadly accessible, multimedia way. This is a problem that is eminently solvable, with various possible solutions."

Titled "The Growing Importance of Non-Profit Journalism," the paper added: "This would seem to be a natural, large-scale, nonprofit journalism situation – doing not what makes 20 percent or higher annual profits but what is important and serves the broad public interest. There are reasonably realistic opportunities for significant future annual income and shrewd efficiencies which could plausibly be achieved through partnerships, over time as an institutional presence and relationships are cemented."

Since Lewis' examination of the non-profit approach, and even before, hundreds of such profitless sites – most with private fundraising and little or no fees for content – have popped up, with many doing Pulitzer Prize-winning work. "The reporting conducted by nonprofit news ventures has triggered meaningful actions and outcomes," a 2015 report on such outlets from The Knight Foundation concluded, later noting, "Nonprofits leading the way when it comes to capturing and communicating impact identify clear reporting objectives and ways they will measure those objectives from the outset."

The Institute for Non-Profit News, which launched in 2009, boasts at least 180 members nationwide, from the *Adirondack Explorer* of Saranac Lake, N.Y., to *Youth Today* of Kennesaw, GA. "Their high-impact stories have exposed corruption and inspired legal and policy reforms; alerted the public to environmental perils, financial scams and faulty products; and informed communities about the issues of business and government that affect daily life," the INN website states. "The INN members do this work at a time of tectonic shifts in media technology, culture and economy. They do it because journalism's mission of public service demands nothing less from them. They do it because a viable, sustainable Fourth Estate is essential for a healthy democracy."

Sue Cross, INN CEO and executive director since 2015, sees non-profit news as a key solution to the current news problems.

"It's definitely one of the answers and you are seeing that in the tremendous growth," said Cross, a former AP staffer and senior vice-president. "They have gone from 27 to almost 180 in under 10 years. And you are seeing that growth accelerate."

While Cross agrees they are not the only answer, she says the dwindling commercial base leaves plenty of room for the profitless news sources. "There will always be commercial and profit news organizations, but what doesn't do well in the commercial model are things that have been cut – investigative reporting, accountability, truly expert beat reporting and a level of community engagement," she said. "They are formed to their communities. There are a lot of variations and not one set model."

Cross says the news outlets use eight funding sources – grants and foundations, major donors, philanthropists, individual donors, members, sponsorship and underwriting, and even events. "It is born out of need, people will see a vacuum in coverage or they will see a type of coverage go away, or they see that coverage is not happening in their community. The biggest plus is that they are nimble, they are able to shape themselves to the community's needs and focus on really strong journalism, the biggest negative is the economics supporting that kind of reporting are definitely in flux."

Much of the success of these news outlets is their ability to collaborate with mainstream news outlets or others to spread the work beyond their base websites or publications. Like Pruitt's view that the AP distributes its work through member newspapers and organizations, the non-profit sites often use mainstream outlets to get the word around as well.

"Those are all good developments and the collaboration is good. You can't afford anymore to stand alone and cover as much as you might have before, particularly due to the kind of investigative and enterprise journalism that you would've done all by yourself before," said Leonard Downie Jr., the former executive editor of the *Washington Post*, who is board chairman of *Kaiser Health News*, one of the top profitless news sites in the U.S.

The rock stars of such non-profits may be *ProPublica*, the New York-based organization launched in 2008 by former *Wall Street Journal* managing editor Paul Steiger, which focuses on investigative news and has already garnered four Pulitzer Prizes, along with a handful of Pulitzer finalist honors and numerous other awards. The site drew attention from the start with big names like Steiger and current Editor-in-Chief Stephen Engelberg, who has been on board since day one after defecting from *The Oregonian* in Portland.

In describing its mission, Engelberg said in an interview: "Can we invest in ... journalism that has the potential to make change? That is the metric. Are we writing about something that, if new facts are brought to light, change is at least possible? We don't do a lot of feature writing or ... off-the-news brights. We are very focused on what is it we can tell readers that would potentially prompt something to be better in the world?"

Since its launch, *ProPublica* attracted top journalists from *The New York Times*, the *Washington Post* and elsewhere. And it quickly showed its stuff with a strong report in October 2008 on California's trend of licensing nurses with serious criminal histories, among them convicted murderers. As with many of its projects, the report ran in the *Los Angeles Times* and on the *ProPublica* site. Two months later, a bombshell report on New Orleans police using deadly force in the aftermath of Hurricane Katrina – done with the *Times-Picayune* and PBS *Frontline* – appeared on the site and later resulted in indictments and convictions of police for unjustified shootings.

"It was a fine piece of work and had enormous impact," Engelberg said.

ProPublica has kept a healthy bank account as well with a budget that averaged about $24 million in 2018, up from $13.7 million in 2016, and $10 million in 2014, according to federal records. And they are not alone.

Similar investigative-minded outlets span the nation, from The Center for Investigative Reporting (CIR) in California to the New England Center for Investigative Reporting (NCIR) in Boston to The Marshall Project in New York. Each outlet targets in-depth reporting and often collaborates with mainstream outlets to promote their work.

"The amount of money that is going into this sector is way up, the sense that we had 10 years ago that there was a capacity for Americans to give to journalism, that's true," Engelberg said about the contribution flow. "How big is that capacity and what does it extend to is an interesting question. National readers and people who care about the direction of our country … certainly are willing to step up and fund a good size news organization." But, he added, "people are still grasping the notion that journalism is not something that you just kind of get."

And that journalism has appeared from a variety of non-profit outlets, who have been named Pulitzer Prize winners and finalists 15 times between 2008 and 2018 for work ranging from *InsideClimate News'* revelations of "flawed" pipeline regulations to the Center for Investigative Reporting's expose on prison work camp abuse across several states.

INN honors such work each year with awards that point out which projects had the most impact. Those winners for 2017 and the judge's comments on them are below:

- The Wisconsin Center for Investigative Journalism's exploration of "how hostility towards immigrants following the election of President Donald Trump has affected Wisconsin's dairy industry, which is reliant on foreign workers. The story had a companion piece on Wisconsin Public Radio, was turned into a 21-minute video documentary and a story for Reveal by the Center for Investigative Reporting."

- *Pine Tree Watch*'s investigation that "prompted a legislative inquiry into the spending of hundreds of millions of dollars by Maine PowerOptions, a state-sponsored consortium that helps municipalities and school districts buy electricity."

o *NJ Spotlight* reporting "how local governments let their employees accumulate so many unused sick days that taxpayers are liable for about $2 billion in payouts, detailed on an interactive map and searchable database. Bills were introduced in the New Jersey legislature to halt the practice."

o *Oklahoma Watch* disclosing "campaign donations from oil and gas interests to every state legislator, with searchable data, and every gift and meal purchased for lawmakers during their latest session. The ongoing 'Inside Democracy' series has intensified debate about whether corporate lobbying and money are distorting the democratic process in a state facing a severe budget crisis and serious social-welfare issues."

o Months of reporting by InvestigateWest showing "Washington State's foster care program under strain and in disarray. The series helped prompt six new laws and $48 million in funding to keep children from being shuttled around to hotels or sleeping on the floors of caseworkers' offices."

o *The Hummel Report* investigating "how much the part-time [Rhode Island] legislature spends on itself – more than $42 million and rising, compared with $18 million in neighboring New Hampshire. The findings launched a discussion about benefits across state government."

Local news, which as discussed earlier has taken a terrible hit in recent newsroom cutbacks, is also benefitting from profitless coverage. A 2015 Knight Foundation report stated: "The digital age has drastically and forever altered the landscape of local news. Faced with traditional media organizations that continue to reduce their resources committed to local news coverage, it's imperative to support approaches to safeguarding the supply and quality of local information and reporting. Nonprofit news organizations offer the potential to become part of the bedrock of a strong local news and information ecosystem."

One of those successful outlets is *Investigative News Source*, or *inewsource*, of San Diego. Launched in 2009 by 25-year *San Diego Union-Tribune* veteran Lori Hearn, this outlet puts a local spin on many investigative issues.

"We mainly do data-driven investigative work," she said about the organization, which launched after *Union-Tribune* layoffs and buyouts forced several staffers out in 2008. "The newspaper was sold and a lot of people I knew were taking buyouts and getting laid off and we were talking about what are we going to do. I have always been passionate about investigative work and wanted to continue doing this kind of journalism."

The first version of *inewsource* began at San Diego State University's journalism program as The Watchdog Institute. Eventually Hearn and company worked with the *Union-Tribune* to take over its investigative reporting through a two-year contract. But she said the newspaper pulled out after nine months. The effort continued, however, in 2010 with a $100,000 grant from the Ethics and Excellence in Journalism Foundation. By 2011, they had worked a deal with nearby public broadcaster KPBS to move into their newsroom and provided content. Their work also goes to the local CBS affiliate and Internet partners, as well as NPR.

"I still take the greatest pride in our narrative text story-telling, we always do really in-depth stories for the web," Hearn said. "I realized the importance of precision reporting and data is one way that you can really feel confident that you have the facts. And someone can see how you really crunch the numbers. Data is everything."

The annual budget runs about $1.1 million, half from individual donations and the rest from foundations and organizations. "Everything we do has a San Diego regional component," she said. "That's what stands out!"

Among its work is an August 2016 investigation exposing San Diego city officials' regularly ignoring open government laws; a 2017 investigation that revealed toxic vapors under two local mobile home parks; and another 2017 report that indicated a new power plant was built without competitive bidding and spewed more pollutants than first thought.

In New Orleans, the local news gap created by cutbacks at the *Times-Picayune* and other traditional outlets is being filled, in part, by *The Lens*, a targeted local investigative non-profit news site that focuses primarily on a few areas: criminal justice, government accountability, environment coastal restoration, and land use. "We focus on a few issues," said Editor Steve Myers, a former Poynter.org journalist and veteran of several daily papers who joined in 2012. "We try to pick our targets and go narrow and deep."

Launched in 2009, the news outlet has just six full-time staffers and an annual budget of about $400,000. But in their time, they have managed to pick up a slew of awards and spark reforms and improvements in a variety of government entities. All *Lens* work is posted free, with the option for free email alerts of new stories. "We are not writing about most votes at city hall, we are writing about issues we are interested in," Myers declared. "We have to say 'no' to a lot of things."

But areas where they said 'yes' included exposing a scandal involving three local district attorneys issuing fake subpoenas to trick witnesses into being questioned and testifying. *The Lens* broke the story in April 2017 that revealed the Orleans Parish D.A. and those in two neighboring parishes were failing to get judicial approval for such subpoenas. "We had a tip that led us to it," Myers said in 2018. "There is a state agency looking into it and a federal lawsuit and a criminal complaint filed with the state Attorney General."

Other examples of *The Lens'* investigations include a May 2018 report revealing that paid actors were used by local power utility Entergy to shore up support at public hearings for a proposed power plant and several 2017 stories about the effect of growing Airbnb expansion in the city where tourism is a major industry. "The issue here is that it's so lucrative to run Airbnbs that some investors were buying homes and running Airbnbs out of them," Myers said. "How does it affect housing prices and dynamics of a neighborhood when you just have tourists living there?" It also included a map of data, done with *Huffington Post*, showing where new Airbnbs were being licensed and operating.

"It seems like a lot of times when you break a story these days there is not a lot of effort to compete on it," Myers said about the growing need for such non-profit sites in New Orleans and elsewhere. "There is a lot of follow and people doing things around the edges. But [news] people don't want to dive into a story if they don't know what the return will be."

He said *The Lens* has joined with other news outlets on some projects as most non-profit newsrooms do. He pointed to a 2014 partnership with *ProPublica* for a report on coastal erosion, as well as similar team investigations with *PolitFact*, *The Nation*, Weather.com, and *Huffington Post*.

"We've done a couple of those a year and that is good because we can do something we wouldn't have been able to do," Myers said, adding that *The Advocate* of Baton Rouge, which also circulates in New Orleans, regularly buys his site's content. "And they get our expertise on those issues."

Along with local press needs, state-level coverage is also in trouble and a place where non-profits like *CalMatters* of Sacramento are making a difference. The 20-person outlet that launched in 2015 has beat reporters on health care, education, environmental, fiscal issues, and politics, as well as columnists, data reporters, videographers, and social media staff, according to co-founder David Lesher. His annual budget is about $3 million – most from individual donors, with about 25% from foundations.

"The state level of coverage is the most impacted, and especially in a state as big as California," said Lesher, a former *Los Angeles Times* statehouse reporter. "I would argue that the quality of life in California is more impacted by the state level than the federal level. The decisions in Sacramento are how to spend $290 billion a year."

One such project was a 2017 investigation of school funding formulas and how they affect performance, which also ran in several newspapers. "We did a report card on how it is doing, and we did a deep dive on data and where it is working," Lesher said. "It stirred up a conversation about whether it is working or not."

And similar efforts are at work in many state capitols, where news has been diluted by cutbacks and government efforts left unchecked in many areas. State news-focused non-profits have sprung up from New Jersey, where NJSpotlight.com reports on Trenton happenings, to

MinnPost.com in Minneapolis, which targets capital doings in St. Paul and elsewhere in the Gopher State.

"Our design was we did not want to duplicate what was still being done by [traditional] media and we did not want to compete," Lesher said. "We wanted to collaborate with them. We have increased substantially the amount of content." He said *CalMatters* runs 10 to 12 stories weekly, along with major projects. Among those was the "What Happened to the California Dream" project, a two-year collaboration with four public radio stations and the Corporation for Public Broadcasting.

"It's a lot of different areas, the shrinking capacity of government to deliver services, the cost of living and what it means for decisions people have to make and what does it mean for the future of the state?" Lesher explained. He also cited a one-year project with the *Los Angeles Times* and Capital Public Radio on public pension debt that won a California Newspaper Publishers Association honor.

"I think there is no question it is the answer for the foreseeable future," he said about non-profit news. "There isn't a way for earned revenue to pay for some of the quality and experts and time it takes to do some of these stories. There is a substantial part of media that is becoming philanthropic."

Another state-level news success in the non-profit realm is Texas Tribune, the Austin-based site that launched in 2009 with 11 staffers under the direction of veteran journalist Evan Smith. By 2018, the news outlet boasted 70 journalists and other staff, according to editor-in-chief Emily Ramshaw. "We are all things Texas politics and policy, some have described us as a hybrid of *ProPublica* and *Politico*," Ramshaw said in an interview. "The best part of working at the Texas Tribune is we feel freed from a lot of those for-profit, marketing pressures."

Part of that freedom is a revenue plan that draws from several sources – private donors, funding grants, corporate underwriting, membership dues, and an events business that includes forums, conferences and reader gatherings. The budget is about $8 million, with at least $2 million annually from events.

"Our business model has turned out to be extraordinarily effective," Ramshaw said. "*The Tribune*'s commitment to a diverse set of revenue streams. We are not solely dependent on a single big donor or a single foundation. When we have a rough year in one particular bucket, it does not mean we cannot turn to other buckets. We are constantly trying to work with new and effective revenue streams."

But it's still the news focus that remains first priority and the website has a long list of accomplishments to bolster that belief. Among those projects:

○ A 2016 collaboration with *ProPublica* that produced a detailed, interactive data map and report on how a major flooding hurricane would affect Houston, published more than a year before hurricane Harvey struck and proved much of the information correct. It won a 2017 Peabody award.

○ A 2017 report on sex trafficking in Texas and how efforts to fight it have ignored helping the child victims.

○ A 2015 interactive report on religion in state politics, dubbed "God & Governing," which also resulted in a half-hour PBS special.

"Coming to *The Tribune* was a no-brainer because I wanted to try something different," said Ramshaw, who joined in 2016 after many years at the *Dallas Morning News*. "There are a lot of unique circumstances we have been able to learn from. We have a super, charismatic and entrepreneurial leader who is not afraid to take risks. Texas has an extreme and outsized sense of place, people like to have news that is just for them."

The website also has a Washington, D.C., bureau and a Dallas office. Along with *ProPublica, Texas Tribune* has also partnered with *the Dallas Morning News, Texas Monthly* and several local newspapers.

But while the non-profit sites are doing a great job in many cases filling the void of investigative, local news and national coverage, their continued success is unclear given the limits of donations and the uncertainty of future sustainability. A 2015 Knight Foundation report declared that, "as a cohort the nonprofit news sites grew revenue quickly, but sustainability remains a distant goal."

It later noted: "Between 2011 to 2013, organizations grew revenue on average by 73 percent and average growth in 2013 was 30 percent. About a quarter of the sites experienced flat or declining revenues over the period of the study, suggesting growth has been uneven in this field. Nonprofit news sites still rely heavily on foundation funding, albeit slightly less so than in the past. Grant funding represented 58 percent of total revenue for the average organization in 2013, down from 63 percent in 2011. In turn, organizations have continued to increase earned revenue over time, which now represents 23 percent of total revenue."

But the Knight report also stressed, "Although progress has been slow, it is encouraging to see steady growth in this area. We still found relatively little experimentation with earned revenue sources among the cohort and hope sites will continue to pilot new approaches to generating income that leave them less dependent on philanthropic funding. The findings also emphasize the importance of shifting from a startup to scale-up mentality by planning for growth."

Several of those operating the profitless newsrooms also say they are not the entire answer.

"I don't know that they're the savior, I think the non-profit ecosystem is still pretty fragile," *inewsource*'s Hearn said. "There are more than 130 non-profit news outlets, from really local to organizations that cover the state house and single topic organizations. They are one of the answers." Engelberg of *ProPublica* agreed: "People joked with me that 'you are going to a job to save journalism?' and I said there is no chance that an organization the size of *ProPublica* is going to save journalism. We can make a small contribution and maybe fill some holes, but the larger problems of journalism related to sort of these fundamental tides of the business model and how advertising is sold, that is something we are not able to address ... The problems of the industry are clearly bigger than anything a single non-profit can address."

Ramshaw offered a similar view: "Non-profit news is one piece of the equation, I think it is disingenuous to think there is any one solution to the demise of local news across the United States. Each community needs that entrepreneur we are lucky enough to have. The key to sustainability is to use a diverse set of revenue streams. I would be very nervous if we were dependent on a single philanthropist."

Still, the non-profit effort is making a difference and can continue simply by its economic approach that removes the drive for profit – in some cases greedy profit by traditional news outlets – and puts the funding demand on contributors and philanthropists whose goal is making important journalism, not making more money.

ACKNOWLEDGMENTS

I must thank many people for their time, support and contributions that made this book possible.

First, to my wonderful editor and publisher Susan Brady Konig, who helped guide me from the first proposal to the final product with energy, smarts and kind suggestions that made this longtime goal of mine a reality; David Brock, Matt Gertz, Ben Dimiero and all of my former editors at *Media Matters for America* who gave me eight years of space and assignments that helped inform me about the good and bad of today's media; Greg Mitchell, Shawn Moynihan and all of the hard-working staff at *Editor & Publisher,* where I spent 11 years learning and earning as we dug into the ups and downs of the news industry; the South Orange and Maplewood public libraries, the Pew Research Center, Harvard University's Shorenstein Center on Media, Politics and Public Policy and Nieman Lab, as well as the Knight Foundation, all of whom offered great data and statistical information; former bosses Dave Levine, Jack Robinson, Ted Fang, Howard Saltz, Steve Liebman, Jack Lyness, Isabel Spencer, Ana Gonzalez, and everyone else I wrote for who chose not to fire me; and colleagues, long-time sources and friends Marc Berman, David Zurawik, Tom Fiedler, Margaret Sullivan, Steve Scully, Ken Auletta, Ed Wasserman, Clark Hoyt, Alex S. Jones, David Folkenflik, Frank Sesno, Bill Moyers, Michael Harrison, Michael Medved, Marvin Kalb, Jim Lehrer and Clarence Page, among others. For their continued support and friendship during the research, writing and editing thanks to

Steve Seeman, Sam Delson, Lou De Rossi, Tina Kelley, Fred Smith, Tony and Jen Thomas, and Rick's front porch. Also, my nurturing and loving parents, Jim and Margo Strupp, who fed my journalism addiction from day one.

But most importantly I thank my wonderful wife, Claire, who has spent more than 20 years understanding about late deadlines and phone calls, hours and days spent at the computer, and spilled coffee; and my amazing children, Cloey and Cole, who lost dad to the computer keyboard during some field hockey, baseball and soccer games, day trips and family dinners, and who usually knocked before coming into my office.

ABOUT THE AUTHOR

Joe Strupp is a 30-year, award-winning journalist with experience in newspapers, magazines, television, radio, and the Internet. He has spent nearly two decades covering media and news issues for several outlets, including *Editor & Publisher* and *Media Matters for America*.

He's interviewed Rupert Murdoch, George W. Bush, Ben Bradlee and O.J. Simpson, and spoken about media issues on Fox News, MSNBC, NPR, Voice of America, Current TV, and Sirius XM Radio. His writing has appeared in *MediaWeek, San Francisco* magazine, *NJ Biz, New Jersey Monthly, Salon.com* and *Poynter.org*.

Joe has received honors from the New Jersey Press Association, The Jesse H. Neal Business Journalism Awards, Syracuse University's Mirror Awards, the Society of Professional Journalists and Folio.

He also serves as an adjunct professor at Fairleigh Dickinson University and Rutgers University, hosts a podcast called "Joe's Media Corner," and wrote *The City and County: A Novel of San Francisco Newsmakers*.

More Advance Praise for Killing Journalism

Edward Wasserman, University of California Graduate School of Journalism dean and veteran *Miami Herald* columnist

Joe Strupp has been giving us tough and penetrating coverage of the news media since the '90s, and he has now shaken off the constraints of quick-turn analysis to produce a sweeping and sobering look at these decades of decline, along with a thoughtful look at the civic harm that decline continues to cause. If you want a thoroughly reported, one-stop chronicle of why we don't have the news media we need, this is it.

Clark Hoyt, Pulitzer Prize-winning former Knight Ridder Washington editor, former *New York Times* public editor

Joe Strupp, a respected reporter on the nation's news media, has produced a fascinating look at the landscape today. It's sobering — chronicling partisan attacks on the credibility of mainstream media and the economic forces that have led to smaller newsrooms and less coverage of important issues. But it also offers hope, particularly from the rise of strong non-profit outlets.

Clarence Page, Pulitzer Prize-winning columnist and editorial board member at the *Chicago Tribune*

If you wonder, as I often do, why news media diversity in the age of Donald Trump morphed into a contest of competing realities, *Killing Journalism* will help you to make sense of the nonsense. Award-winning media watchdog Joe Strupp has pulled years of research into a chilling explanation of what went wrong and, more important, useful suggestions for how we news workers and news consumers can make things right.

Steve Scully, C-SPAN political editor, host, *Washington Journal*

Donald Trump has been a media ringmaster since his early days as a New York businessman. In *Killing Journalism*, Joe Strupp offers a keen eye and sharp perspective on the cascade of changes in America's media landscape since Trump first made his mark with the New York tabloids. From legacy newspapers to upstate social media sites, he offers a compelling narrative on the state of journalism today, with lessons for all of us in the media moving ahead.

Michael Harrison, *Talkers* magazine editor

An important new book about the precarious state of journalism in the modern era of audience-targeted corporate media.

SOURCES

Introduction

Southern Poverty Law Center website declaration of Family Research council as a hate group.
10 Facts about the Family Research Council –*Human Rights Campaign website*
Trump to Media Matters on When He'll Return to Fox: "They Have to Treat Me Fairly and I'm Sure They Will" – *Media Matters for America, 9/25/15*
U.S. Department of Labor statistics – 2005-2015

Chapter 1

"Trump Sued by Casino Bondholders"- *New York Times, July 6, 1990*
"I wrote 'The Art of the Deal' with Trump. His self-sabotage is rooted in his past" – *The Washington Post, May 16, 2017*
"Little Guy Comes to Trump's Aid' – *The Daily Journal, June 1990*
NBC Nightly News, June 1990
Wayne Barrett interview – 2016
Rona Barrett interview with Donald Trump – ABC TV – 10/6/80
"Born in the USA" – *Factcheck.org, 4/27/2011*
"Donald Trump says people who went to school with Obama never saw him" – *PolitiFact, 2/14/2011*
"14 of Trump's most outrageous 'birther' claims - half from after 2011" – *CNN.com 9/16/2016*
The View, ABC TV, 3/23/2011
The Laura Ingraham Show – 3/30/2011
Flashback: How Fox News Promoted Trump's Birtherism – Media Matters for America, 9/16/2016
Where's the Birth Certificate? The Case That Barack Obama is Not Eligible to Be President - Jerome Corsi, 2011.
"Corsi: We Are Still Asking 'Where's the Birth Certificate?'" – *Media Matters for America, 5/19/2011*
Public Policy Polling – 2/15/2011
"US election: Trump accepts Barack Obama was born in US" – *BBC.com, 9/16/2016*
"Trump Once Said the 'Access Hollywood' Tape Was Real. Now He's Not Sure" – *The New York Times, 11/28/2017*
"How Donald Trump Bent Television to His Will" – *Buzzfeednews.com, 3/18/2016*

"Pre-Primary News Coverage of the 2016 Presidential Race: Trump's Rise, Sanders' Emergence, Clinton's Struggle" – Shorensteincenter.org, 6/13/2016

"$2 Billion Worth of Free Media for Donald Trump" – The New York Times, 3/15/2016

"Crossing the Line: How Donald Trump Behaved with Women in Private" – The New Yok Times, 5/14/2016

Pulitzer.org – Washington Post stories, 2016

"Trump Has Lost the Support of Morning Joe, and That's Saying Something" – Fortune.com, 6/6/2016

"An awkward Joe Scarborough protests that he's not, in fact, a 'supporter' of Donald Trump" – The Washington Post, 2/10/2016

"Trump asked 'Morning Joe' hosts for softball questions on hot mic" – New York Post, 2/23/2016

"Joe Scarborough-Donald Trump friendship increasing source of discomfort at NBC" – CNN.com, 2/12/2016

"How Morning Joe Morphed into Mean Girls" – National Review, 5/3/2016

"Matt Lauer's Fact-Challenged Moderation Is A Cautionary Tale for Debate Moderators" – Media Matters for America, 9/8/2016

"Will Presidential Debate Moderators Really Not Challenge Lies?" – Huffington Post, 9/5/2016

PolitiFact.org, Donald Trump file, 7/6/2016

"Trump's Week of Errors, Exaggerations and Flat-out Falsehoods" – Politico.com, 3/13/2016

"Those fact-checking chyrons can't be just an anti-Trump gimmick" – Poynter.org, 8/13/2016

"How Donald Trump made fact-checking great again" – CNN.com, 11/7/2016

Shattered: Inside Hillary Clinton's Doomed Campaign, Jonathan Allen and Amie Parnes, 2017

"But Her Emails" – U.S. News & World Report, 9/11/2017

Berkman Klein Center at Harvard University, 2017 study

"Hillary Clinton Assails James Comey, Calling Email Decision 'Deeply Troubling'" – New York Times, 10/29/2016

"Republicans' $7 Million Benghazi Report is Another Dud" – Vanity Fair, 6/28/2016

"REPORT: Fox's Benghazi Obsession by The Numbers" – Media Matters for America, 9/16/2014

James Rainey interview, 2018

Unbelievable: My Front-Row Seat to the Craziest Campaign in American History, Katy Tur, 2017

WHCA board member interview, 2018

Andy Alexander interview, 2018

"Poll: 46 percent think media make up stories about Trump" – Politico.com, 10/18/2017

"Democrats see most news outlets as unbiased. Republicans think they're almost all biased" – Niemanlab.org, 6/22/2018

*"Questioned by Media Matters, Roger Stone 'Vehemently' Denies His "Negro" And "C*nt" Tweets Were Racist and Sexist"* – Media Matters for America, 4/19/2016

"The Breitbart Team Turned an Anti-Clinton Smear Book into a Terrible Documentary" – Media Matters for America, 5/13/2016

"Clinton Cash's Peter Schweizer Pushes Stat That Even Fox News Calls 'Incredibly Misleading'" – Media Matters for America, 5/8/2015

Ken Auletta interview, 2018
"The Trump Administration's War on The Press" – Media Matters for America, 2/1/2017
Daniel Okrent interview, 2018
Michael Harrison interview 2018
Dana Priest interview, 2018
"The Overlooked, Under-Reported and Ignored Stories of 2017" – Billmoyers.com, 12/19/2017
Eric Boehlert interview, 2018
Marc Berman interview, 2018
"New York Times has record subscriber growth – and some bad news too" – CNN.com, 5/3/2017
"The Fourth Estate" – Showtime, 2018

Chapter 2

State of the News Media 2017 – Pew Research Center, 6/13/2018
U.S. Labor Department
Pew Research Center report – 7/23/2018
"Tronc cuts dozens of employees, including former Times Editor Lewis D'Vorkin" – Los Angeles Times, 4/12/2018
Leonard Downie, Jr. interview 2018
Rick Edmonds, Poynter Institute, interview 2018
"Twenty Years of Media Consolidation Has Not Been Good for Our Democracy" – Billmoyers.com, 3/30/2016
David Chavern, President & Chief Executive Officer of the News Media Alliance and American Press Institute – interview 2018
"Another big round of layoffs set to hit The Record" – NJ.com, 1/23/2017
"Media conglomerates: The Big6" - Webfix.com
"NAFTA's Impact on U.S. Workers" – Economic Policy Institute, 12/9/2013
"How Bill Clinton's Welfare 'Reform' Created a System Rife with Racial Biases" – Truthout.org, 5/13/2014
Gannett.com corporate page
Michael Barthel, Pew Research, interview 2018
Clark Hoyt interview 2018
David Folkenflik interview 2018
Tom Fiedler interview 2-18
Crime Coverage Study, Center on Media Crime and Justice at the John Jay College of Criminal Justice, 2/14/2018
"Mexican heroin is flooding the US, and the Sinaloa cartel is steering the flow" – Business Insider, 11/18/2017
"Drug firms poured 780M painkillers into WV amid rise of overdoses" – Charleston Daily Mail, 12/17/2016
"Gazette-Mail declaring bankruptcy; Wheeling Newspapers is planned buyer" – 1/29/2018

"Great local reporting stands between you and wrongdoing. And it needs saving" – The Washington Post, 4/16/201

"How local news sounded the alarm over the GOP's defeated health plan" – Columbia Journalism Review, 3/24/2017

The State of Health Journalism in the U.S., Kaiser Family Foundation, March 2009

FCC Report – The Information Needs of Communities, July 2011

"Cuts to local newspapers hurt all local news" – The Denver Post, 4/6/2018

"Small digital news sites: young, lean and local" – Pewresearch.org, 4/10/2014

Local Independent Online News Publishers, mission statement.

"The Fight for the Future of Local News" – The Ringer, 1/10/2018

"AOL is hiring hundreds of journalists" – Bizjournals.com, 8/17/2010

"You've Got News" – The New Yorker, 1/24/2011

"The Emerging Threat of News Deserts" – Savingcommunityjournalism.com

"Last Call at the ASNE Saloon" – Journalism.org, 4/26/2006

Bell Scandal series – Los Angeles Times, July-December 2010

"Trump thrives in areas that lack traditional news outlets" – Politico.com, 4/8/2018

"The 2016 Presidential Campaign – a News Event That's Hard to Miss" – Pew Research Center, 2/4/2016

"We Have Reached Peak Punditry" – The Washington Post, 6/2/2016

<u>Bad News: The Decline of Reporting, the Business of News, and the Danger to Us All</u> - Tom Fenton, 2005

"Fox News Primetime Completely Ignores Resignation of Rob Porter, the Trump Aide Accused of Abuse" – The Daily Beast, 2/8/2018

"Fox News Ignored Manafort, Covered Hillary Clinton and Russia Dossier for Trump" – Newsweek, 10/230/2017

"Local TV News Fact Sheet" – Pew Research Center, 7/12/2018

"Local TV News and the New Media Landscape" – Knight Foundation report, 4/5/2018

"Reinventing Local TV News" – Nieman Reports, 4/18/2018

"Buying spree brings more local TV stations to fewer big companies" – Pew Research.org, 5/11/2017

"Video Reveals Power of Sinclair, As Local News Anchors Recite Script in Unison" – NPR, 4/2/2018

Chapter 3

"American views: Trust, media and democracy" – Knight Foundation.org, 1/16/2018

Dana Priest interview 2018

James Rainey interview 2018

"THE 1992 CAMPAIGN: Personal Finances; Clintons Joined S.& L. Operator in an Ozark Real-Estate Venture" – The New York Times, 3/8/1992

"Newspapers a Hot Commodity After Obama's Win" – The New York Times, Nov. 5, 2008

Michael Schudson interview 2013

Dale Cressman interview 2013

Douglass Brinkley interview 2013

Hank Klibinoff interview 2018
"Text of Unabomber Manifesto" – *New York Times, 5/26/96*
Zay N. Smith interview, 2013
Mark Fitzgerald interview 2013
Bill Kovarik interview 2013
"Aug. 31, 1920: News Radio Makes News" – *Wired.com, 8/31/2010*
Encyclopedia Britannica: Broadcasting entry – *2018*
History of Radio News, 1920-1950 – *Indiana University of Pennsylvania*
"The Trial of Richard 'Bruno' Hauptmann: An Account" – *Famous-Trials.com.*
"Journalists Discuss Coverage of Movement: Media Role in Civil Rights Era Reviewed" – *Los Angeles Times, 4/5/1987*
<u>*"Television and the Civil Rights Movement: An Interview with Aniko Bodroghkozy (Part Three)"*</u>
– *Henryjenkins.org, 9/27/2012*
"The First Televised War" – *The New York Times, 4/7/2017*
Morley Safer C-SPAN interview, 4/25/1990
David Halberstam interview, YouTube, 2009
"Vietnam on Television" essay, Museum of Broadcasting, David Hallin,
"How TV Changed America's Mind" By Edward Wakin, 1996
Walter Cronkite Editorial, CBS News, Feb. 27, 1968.
"When Walter Cronkite Pronounced the War a 'Stalemate'" – *The New York Times, 2/26/2018*
"Walter Cronkite: A Witness to History" – *PBS.org, 7/26/2006*
"40 Years Ago, TVs Tuned to Watergate Hearings" – *WETA.org, 5/17/2013*
"Watergate Revisited" – *American Journalism Review, Aug.-Sept. 2004*
"Don Bolles murder: A look back at the Arizona Project" – *The Arizona Republic, 6/2/2016*
"Pulitzer Prize Board Meets to Pick 2006 Winners" – *Editor & Publisher, 4/11/2006*
"Pulitzer Winners Not the Best-Kept Secret" – *Editor & Publisher, 4/8/2004*
"The New York Times prematurely announces its Pulitzer Prize win by mistake"- *Poynter.org, 4/10/2017*
Pulitzer.org
"Survival First, Then Needed Newsroom Adjustments" – *Nieman Reports, Fall 2007*
"Media Talk; Abrupt Departure by Executive Editor of The Oklahoman" – *The New York Times, 1/17/2000*

Chapter 4

"Hannity Urges Fellow Broadcasters to 'Protect Freedom of Speech' by Opposing Politicized Boycotts" – *CNSNews.com,* June 8, 2012
"Rush Limbaugh Still Toxic for Advertisers One Year After Fluke Attacks" – *Media Matters for America, March 1, 2013*
"How Far Will Sean Hannity Go?" – *The New York Times, 11/28/2017*
"The Rise of the Right-Wing Media Machine" – *Fair and Accuracy in Reporting, March 1995*
"All the President's Men" – *Bob Woodward, Carl Bernstein*
"A forgotten lesson of Watergate: conservatives may rally around Trump" – *Vox.com, 5/17/2017*

The Loudest Voice in the Room, Gabriel Sherman

Fact Sheet, TVhistory.tv

The Selling of the President, Joe McGinnis

The Age of Evangelicalism: The Born-Again Years, Steven P. Miller

Call Me Ted, Ted Turner

Media in the 20th Century, Oscar W. Anderson

"Whatever Happened to Air America?" – *Vanity Fair*, March 2009

"Host: Deep into the Mercenary World of Take-No Prisoners Political Talk Radio" – *The Atlantic*, April 2005

"The Talk Radio Effect" – *Politico.com*, 6/17/2014

"Rather Walked Off Set of CBS News" – *The New York Times*, 9/13/1987

The Quest for the Presidency 1992, Newsweek reporters

Attack the Messenger, How Politicians Turn You Against the Media, Craig Crawford

"Dan Rather's Soft Serve" – *National Review*, 2/27/2003

"CNN Showcases Dan Rather's Famous 'Assault,' George Bush's Retort" – Newsbusters.org, 3/2/2016

Fat Man in the Middle Seat, Jack Germond

"Hillary vs. the Hate Machine: How Clinton Became a Vessel for America's Fury" – *Rolling Stone*, 9/20/2016

The Hunting of the President: The Ten-Year Campaign to Destroy Bill and Hillary Clinton, Joe Conason and Gene Lyons

"The First Woman Let into McSorley's Reminisces (Over an Ale, of Course)" – *The New York Times*, 1/22/2015

Blinded by the Right, David Brock

"Public & Private; The Real Anita Hill?" – *The New York Times*, 4/25/1993

David Corn interview 2018

Encyclopedia Britannica

The Fox Effect, Media Matters' David Brock and Ari Rabin-Havt

"THE 2000 ELECTIONS: THE MEDIA; A Flawed Call Adds to High Drama" – *The New York Times*, 11/8/2000

"Election Night from Hell" – *The Nation*, 11/6/2006

What Liberal Media? Eric Alterman

"Burgher Rebellion: GOP Turns Up Miami Heat" – *The Wall Street Journal*, 11/24/2000

"A President by Judicial Fiat" – the *Weekly Standard*, 12/18/2000

"The Right's Too Nice" – *National Review*, 12/16/2000

Vietnam Veterans Against the War Statement by John Kerry to the Senate Committee of Foreign Relations

April 23, 1971, University of Virginia

Hannity & Colmes, Fox News Channel, Aug. 4, 2004

"Judgment Reserved to Judgment Reversed" – FAIR, December 2005

Lapdogs, Eric Boehlert

"Submerging the truth about Swift Boat Vets on Hannity & Colmes, Scarborough Country" – Media Matters for America, 8/5/2004

"Social Issues Are Destroying American Politics" – *The American Spectator*, 10/18/2017

"Supreme Court Ruling Makes Same-Sex Marriage a Right Nationwide" – *The New York Times, 6/26/2015*

Report, Harvard University's Berkman Klein Center for Internet and Society, 2017

"DA targets Fazio's brother for phone call to reporter" – *San Francisco Examiner, 1/4/1996*

TALKERS *magazine's 2016 "Heavy Hundred"*

Jeff Jarvis interview 2018

"Andrew Breitbart, Conservative Blogger, Dies at 43" – *The New York Times, 3/1/2012*

"Shirley Sherrod, Andrew Breitbart's widow reach settlement" – *AL.com, 9/15/2015*

"Who Gets the Most Traffic Among Conservative Websites?" – *Mediashift.org*

"The Ascendant 'Smear Wing' of the Conservative Movement" – *The Atlantic, 1/8/2013*

"Did murdered DNC staffer leak 20,000 party emails?" – *Daily Mail, 8/9/2016*

"Everything you want to know about Seth Rich story" – *World Net Daily, 5/15/2017*

"Statement on coverage of Seth Rich murder investigation" – *FoxNews.com, 5/23/2017*

"Fox News continues to push Seth Rich conspiracy after Rich family sent cease and desist to Fox contributor, demanded apology" – *Media Matters for America, 5/22/2017*

"Family of Seth Rich Sues Fox News Over Retracted Article" – *The New York Times, 3/13/2018*

"Fox News Retracts Seth Rich Story That Stirred Controversy" – *The New York Times, 5/23/2017*

"Trump vs. The Deep State" – *The New Yorker, 5/21/2018*

"The Aspiring Novelist Who Became Obama's Foreign-Policy Guru" – *The New York Times, 5/5/2016*

"Iran deal architect is running Tehran policy at the State Dept" - *The Conservative Review, 3/17/2017*

Guidestar.com

"Obama Adviser on Iran Worked for Pro-Regime Lobby" – *Breitbart News, 3/14/2017*

"State Dept. official reassigned amid conservative media attacks" – *Politico, 4/21/2017*

"The ACORN Videos: Did NPR Ignore Them?" – *NPR, 9/23/2009*

"Attorney General's Report on ACORN Activities in California" – *4/1/2010*

Ballotpedia.com

"Who is Jaime T. Phillips? Woman falsely claimed Roy Moore impregnated her" – *AL.com, 11/27/2017*

"How James O'Keefe Made Himself Irrelevant" – *The Atlantic, 11/28/2017*

"James O'Keefe Shoots at the Washington Post and Misses" – *11/28/2017*

"WaPo Badly Burns James O'Keefe" – *The American Conservative, 11/27/2017*

"NJ Senate investigating whether union tried to protect teachers accused of sex abuse" – *Northjersey.com, 5/7/2018*

"Sinclair Broadcasting's Hostile Takeover" – *Rolling Stone, 4/24/2018*

"Fox's Unfamiliar but Powerful Television Rival: Sinclair" – *The New York Times, 5/3/2017*

"THE STRUGGLE FOR IRAQ: THE MEDIA; Debate Over 'Nightline' Tribute to War Dead Grows, as McCain Weighs In" – *The New York Times, 5/1/2004*

"Sinclair Broadcast Group Faces Backlash Over Scripted Promos: 'This Is Extremely Dangerous to Our Democracy'" – *Variety, 4/1/2018*

"Video Reveals Power of Sinclair, As Local News Anchors Recite Script in Unison" – NPR, 4/2/2018

"Sinclair-Owned Station Refused to Air 'Fake News' Mandatory Promo" – Newsweek, 4/3/2018

"Sinclair Responds to Unfounded Media Criticism" – Sinclair statement, SBGI.net

"How A Right-Wing Group Is Infiltrating State News Coverage" – Media Matters for America 7/11/2012

"AJR's 2009 Count of Statehouse Reporters" – AJR, April/May 2009

Watchdog.org

"Local news hurt by broadcast media conglomerate" – Shorenstein Center, 3/29/2018

Chapter 5

SPJ.com code of ethics

Online News Association ethics guide

Radio Television Digital News Association (RTDNA) ethics code

Journalism Ethics: A Casebook of Professional Conduct for News Media, Fred Brown

David Corn interview 2018

Inventing Reality: The Politics of News Media, Michael Parenti

PolitiFact.org, Donald Trump data

"How False Equivalence Is Distorting the 2016 Election Coverage," The Nation, 6/2/2016

Jeffrey Toobin interview, The Larry Wilborn podcast, 2018

"The Curse of False Equivalency" – Huffington Post, 9/18/2017

"News Coverage of the 2016 Election: How the Press Failed the Voters" – Shorenstein center, 12/7/ 2017

Gallup poll 2017

"US government begins shutdown after Congress debates end in stalemate" – The Guardian, 10/1/2013

"Government Shuts Down in Budget Impasse" – New York Times, 9/30/2013

"Shutdown coverage fails Americans" – Al Jazeera, 10/1/2013

"Media Keeps Up False Equivalency Reporting on Government Shutdown" – Media Matters for America, 10/9/2013

'"We Need to Get This Right': Obamacare Turns Five" – Time, 3/23/2015

'Not 'Both Sides,' Now: Why False Equivalence Matters in the Shutdown Showdown" – Time, 10/7/2013

"Commission on Freedom of the Press Report" – University of Chicago, 1947

Joe McCarthy and the Press, Edwin Bayley

Carol Anderson, author of Eyes off the Prize: The United Nations and the African American Struggle for Human Rights, 1944-1955, interview 2018

The Race Beat, Gene Roberts and Hank Klibanoff

"What Today's Journalists Can Learn from MLK Coverage" – The Atlantic, 8/28/2013

Eric Alterman, 2018 interview

"Public Opinion on Abortion" – Pew Research Center, July 2017

An Overview of Abortion Laws" – Guttmacher Institute, May 2018

When Abortion Was a Crime, Leslie Reagan
"A Brief History of Abortion Law in America" – Billmoyers.org, 11/14/2017
"Myths and lies about abortion must be debunked" – The Irish Times, 4/3/2018
"Post Abortion Stress Syndrome (PASS) –Does It Exist?" – 10/25/2010
"Unspinning the Planned Parenthood Video" – Factcheck.org, 7/21/2015
"Planned Parenthood's Trafficking of Baby Body Parts is 'Reprehensible'" – National Right to Life website, 7/28/2015
"Abortion Bias Seeps into News" – Los Angeles Times, 7/1/1990
Abuse of Discretion: The Inside Story of Roe v. Wade, Clarke Forsythe
"Abortion Impact: Long-Term Stress?" – Webmd.com, 12/12/2005
"New study shows why it's so hard to get abortion coverage right" – Poynter.org, 10/17/2017
"If gay people can safely be teachers, then trans people can safely use bathrooms" – ThinkProgress.com, 3/31/2017
"A False Equivalency" – Cookross.com,
For the Bible Tells Me So, 2017 documentary
"It's Time to Legalize Polygamy" – Politico, 6/26/2015
"No, Polygamy Isn't the Next Gay Marriage" – Politico, 6/30/2013
Bill Kovarik interview, 2012
James Rainey interview, 2018
Southern Poverty Law Center
"Tony Perkins appointed to US panel on international religious freedom" – Religionnews.com, 5/15/2015
"MSNBC's Chris Matthews Demonstrates How to Handle Tony Perkins On Television" – Media Matters for America, 5/10/2012
"Fox Host MacCallum, Tony Perkins Rail Against LGBT Tolerance Lesson" – Equality Matters.org, 5/26/2011
"Tucker Carlson Wants Kids to Know The 'Unhappy Facts' About Gay People" – Equalitymatters.org, 4/19/2011
Fox News Channel, Dec. 11, 2011
"The Boston Globe, Peter LaBarbera, and the 'Other Side'" – GLASSD.org, 1/3/2011
"18 Anti-Gay Groups and their Propaganda" – SPLC.org 11/4/2010
CNN interview, former New York Giant David Tyree, 6/17/2011
"Lesbian parents are really good parents" – UCLA study, 11/23/2010
MSNBC Gay Marriage Debate, 6/28/2011
John Stossel, Fox Business, 8/18/2011
"National Organization for Marriage says Massachusetts public schools teach kindergartners about gay marriage" – Politifact.com, 2/10/2011

Chapter 6

"Did a CDC Doctor Say the Flu Shot Is Causing a Deadly Outbreak?" – Snopes.com, 1/18/2018
Autism Spectrum Disorders, Centers for Disease Control and Prevention
"Six Reasons to Say NO to Vaccination" – The Healthy Home Economist, 6/5/2018

"Anti-vaccine movement is giving diseases a 2nd life" – USA Today, 4/18/2014

"Do Vaccines Cause Autism?" – Philadelphia College of Physicians, 1/25/2018

"The Vaccine-Autism Myth Started 20 Years Ago. Here's Why It Still Endures Today" – Time, 1/28/2018

"How Oprah Helped Spread Anti-Vaccine Pseudoscience" - Mother Jones, 1/10/2018

"Donald Trump Enters Anti-Vaccine Quack Territory" – Slate, 1/3/2012

"Public Confidence in Vaccines Sags, New Report Finds" – U.S. News & World Report, 5/21/2018

"Minnesota measles outbreak exceeds last year's nationwide numbers" – CNN, 6/2/2017

"Growing Number of Young Children Dying from Flu" – NBC News, 1/25/2018

Gallup Gun Survey, March 2018

Eric Alterman interview 2018

"Counting up how much the NRA spends on campaigns and lobbying" – PolitiFact.org, 10/11/2017

"Why the NRA is so powerful on Capitol Hill, by the numbers" – CNN, 2/23/2018

Merriam-Webster Dictionary

Second Amendment, Cornell Law School Legal Information Institute

District of Columbia v. Heller

McDonald v. City of Chicago

PolitiFact.org, gun false statements.

Centers for Disease Control and Prevention, gun homicide statistics

Gunviolencearchive.org

"The Puzzling Media Obsession with Mass Shootings" – Forbes.com, 11/22/2017

"Bullet Points" – Slate, 6/16/2016

"A guide to NRATV: NRA's news outlet is a hybrid of Breitbart and InfoWars" – Media Matters for America, 3/2/2018

NRATV.com

"The National Rifle Association's Telegenic Warrior" The New York Times, 1/20/2018

"Dana Loesch sues Breitbart.com LLC" – Politico.com, 12/21/2012

"Dana Loesch, CNN Contributor, Says She'd Urinate on Taliban Soldiers Too (AUDIO)" – Huffington Post, 1/13/2012

"Morgan: Loesch banned from show" – Politico, 5/22/2013

Nasa.gov fact page: climate change

Intergovernmental Panel on Climate Change – Climate change report 2014

National Geographic climate change issue 2016

Encyclopedia Britannica

National Oceanic and Atmospheric Administration – climate change impacts

Dan Shelley interview, 2018

"The Mainstream Media and the Slowly Boiling Frog" – Americanprogress.org, 8/29/2013

"The Wall Street Journal: Dismissing Environmental Threats Since 1976" – Media Matters for America, 8/2/2012

"REPORT: CNBC's Climate Denial Is Bad for Business" – Media Matters for America, 6/18/2013

"Business Journalists: Climate Change Deniers Have No Place in Our Reporting" - Media Matters for America, 7/3/2013

"She Tried to Report on Climate Change. Sinclair Told Her to Be More 'Balanced.'" – Buzzfeed, 4/22/2018

"Impartial journalism is laudable. But false balance is dangerous" – The Guardian, 11/8/2016

"The danger of fair and balanced" – CJR.org, 1/17/2017

"Global Warming Has Begun, Expert Tells Senate" – The New York Times, 6/24/1988

"Hot Enough for You" – PBS Nova 1989

Bobby Magill, president of the Society of Environmental Journalists and a Bloomberg reporter, interview 2018

Chapter 7

"Newsweek Kills Story on White House Intern" - The Drudge Report, 1/17/1998

"Isikoff: I Had 'Certain Homicidal Tendencies' After Drudge Scooped the Lewinsky Story" – Weeklystandard.com, 12/24/2012

PolitiFact.org, Drudge Report review

"Lie of the Year: the Romney campaign's ad on Jeeps made in China" – PolitiFact.org, 12/12/12

Media in the 20th Century, Oscar W. Alexander

The Search: How Google and Its Rivals Rewrote the Rules of Business and Transformed Our Culture, John Battelle

"History of Apple: The story of Steve Jobs and the company he founded" – MacWorld, 4/25/2017

Lauren Rich Fine interview 2012

Ken Doctor interview 2018

Jim Brady interview 2018

Dale Cressman interview 2018

"Why American Newspapers Gave Away the Future" – Richard Tofel, 2012

Lisa Granatstein interview 2018

Brian Tierney interview 2012

Mark Fitzgerald interview 2012

"How Trump Consultants Exploited the Facebook Data of Millions" – The New York Times, 3/17/2018

"Facebook Gave Device Makers Deep Access to Data on Users and Friends" – The New York Times, 6/3/2018

Jeff Jarvis interview, 2018

"Prepare for the New Paywall Era" – The Atlantic, 11/30/2017

"You Say Paywalls Are Back? For The FT, They Never Went Away" – Fast Company, 1/12/2018

"In paywall age, free content remains king for newspaper sites" – CJR.org, 9/22/2017

"Media Insiders Say Internet Hurts Journalism" – The Atlantic, April 2009

"Why click-bait will be the death of journalism" – PBS.org, 4/27/2016

"Buzzfeed: We Don't Do Clickbait" – Adweek, 11/7/2014

Ebizmba.com

"Is the quest for profits and clicks killing local news?" – CJR.org, Spring 2017

"Clickbait: The changing face of online journalism" – BBC.com 9/14/2015

Alexa.com

"News Use Across Social Media Platforms 2017" – Pew Research Center, 9/7/2017

"Science News and Information Today" – Pew Research Center, 9/20/2017

"Selective Exposure to Misinformation: Evidence from the consumption of fake news during the 2016 U.S. presidential campaign" – Dartmouth College, 1/9/2018

"Removing Trending from Facebook" – Facebook.com, 6/1/2018

"The spread of true and false news online" – Science, 3/9/2018

"The Grim Conclusions of the Largest-Ever Study of Fake News" – The Atlantic, 3/8/2018

"The 2015 State of Sponsored Content" – Inc. magazine

"What effect has the internet had on journalism?" – The Guardian, 2/19/2011

"How Are Journalists Using Social Media? (Report)" – Adweek, 8/23/2016

"Report: How journalists use social media in 2017" – PR Daily, 9/18/2017

"The rise of social media and its impact on mainstream journalism" – Reuters Institute, September 2009

"Journalists and Social Media" – Facing History and Ourselves Report

"The Fort Hood Tragedy Highlights the Reporting Role of Social Media" – Pew Research Center, 11/12/2009

"Fort Hood: A First Test for Twitter Lists" – CJR.org, 11/6/2009

"After Fort Hood, another example of how 'citizen journalists' can't handle the truth" – Techcrunch, 11/7/2009

NPR Social Media Guidelines

Online News Association guidelines

"58 Killed In Las Vegas: How the Victims Are Being Remembered" – 10/4/2017

Society of Professional Journalists Code of Ethics

The Radio Television Digital News social media guidelines

"Private e-mail is public" – Los Angeles Times, 10/02/2004

"'WSJ' Reporter Farnaz Fassihi Going Back to Baghdad" – Editor & Publisher, 12/3/2004

"Anonymous letter to Pulitzer Board spurs investigation by The Blade" – The Blade, 5/28/2006

New York Times social media guideline

"The Fourth Estate" – Showtime, 2018

"TV anchor admits post about fatal shooting "could be viewed as racist"" – CBS News.com, 3/24/2016

"Fired WTAE anchor Bell files suit for reinstatement" – Pittsburgh Post-Gazette, 6/20/2016

"Wendy Bell, WTAE apparently reach settlement in discrimination lawsuit" - Pittsburgh Post-Gazette, 7/8/2018

Chapter 8

Boston Marathon breaking coverage, CNN, 4/15/2013

"Boston Marathon Terror Attack Fast Facts" – CNN, 3/25/2018

"President Obama Praises Capture of Boston Marathon Bombing Suspect" – Huffington Post, 4/19/2013

Dan Shelley interview
ABC News coverage, Reagan shooting, 3/30/81
"Five more explosive devices found in Boston: WSJ" – Marketwatch.com, 4/15/2013
"False ISIS Connections, Nonexistent Victims and Other Misinformation in the Wake of Las Vegas Shooting" – The New York Times, 10/2/2017
Marc Berman interview
"Why We Should Judge Breaking News Like Baseball" – Slate, 4/22/2013
Jeff Jarvis interview
"Richard Jewell, 44, Hero of Atlanta Attack, Dies" – The New York Times, 8/30/2007
"Ga. Court Upholds Ruling in Jewell Suit" – AJC.com, 1/10/2012
Atlanta Journal, July 27, 1996, July 30, 1996
"Richard Jewell Case Study" – Columbia University, 6/13/2000
The News Media: What Everyone Needs to Know, C.W. Anderson, Michael Schudson, and Leonard Downie
"Fact-checking Fox, MSNBC and CNN: PunditFact's network scorecards" – PolitiFact.org, 9/16/2014
Tom Fiedler interview
"The man who broke the news that John Lennon had died" – NY Post, 10/7/2016
"When 'Breaking News' Is Neither Breaking nor News" – Mervinblock.com, 2017
"NBC's Chuck Todd takes aim at CNN" – Politico, 3/21/2014
NBC Nightly News, 4/7/2014
"Note To MSNBC: This Is Not Breaking News" – Mediaite, 10/19/2015
ABC News special report, 6/1/2018
CBS News special report, 3/23/2018
NBC Sports 1994 NBA Finals coverage, June 17, 1994
KCAL and KCBS car chase, May 1, 2018
"The Top 10 Trending News Stories of 2017, according to Google" – Business Insider, 12/13/2017
"Calling Every Bad Storm a 'Superstorm' or 'Weather Bomb' Is Why People Tune Out Weather Forecasts" – Forbes.com, 10/31/2017
"Weather Channel Decision to Name Winter Storms Will Increase Confusion in Delivering Critical Safety Information to Public" – Accuweather.com, 10/3/2012

Chapter 9

False Alarm: The Truth about the Epidemic of Fear, Mark Siegel
Paralysed With Fear: The Story of Polio, Gareth Williams
The Smithsonian Institution, Polio History
"Bar All Children from the Movies in Paralysis War" – The New York Times, 7/4/1916
"The Public Health Legacy of the 1976 Swine Flu Outbreak" – Discover magazine, 9/30/2013
"What is Disease X? Deadly Bird Flu Virus Could Be Next Pandemic" – Newsweek, 6/15/2018
"The Irony of Fear" – The Washington Post, 8/30/2005
"NIH doctor explains U.S efforts to combat Zika virus" – CBS News, 4/17/2016

"Can You Get Ebola From Subway Poles and Bowling Balls?" – Time, 10/24/2014

"Having and Fighting Ebola – Public Health Lessons from a Clinician Turned Patient" – 3/19/2015

"Ebola and Quarantine" – New England Journal of Medicine, 11/20/2014

"New Jersey Accepts Rights for People in Quarantine to End Ebola Suit" – The New York Times, 7/27/2017

"The Ebola Effect: How Media Hype Distracts from Silent Epidemics" – Forbes.com, 4/6/2017

"If It Bleeds, It Leads: Understanding Fear-Based Media" – Psychology Today, 6/7/2011

"Almost seven-in-ten Americans have news fatigue, more among Republicans" – Pew Research Center, 6/5/2018

"Most Americans already feel election coverage fatigue" – Pew Research Center, 7/14/2016

Hedda and Louella: A Dual Biography, George Eels

The Powerful Rivalry of Hedda Hopper and Louella Parsons" – Vanity Fair, April 1997

"Too Much Celebrity News, Too Little Good News" – Pew Research Center, 10/12/2007

"Lots of Sizzle, Not Enough Steak in U.S. News Media" – Harris Poll, 10/21/2014

Nielsen.com ratings

"Michael Jackson Dies" – TMZ.com, 6/25/2009

"Coverage of Jackson's Death Seen as Excessive" – Pew Research Center, 7/1/2009

"Calls to suicide prevention hotline spiked after celebrity deaths, but what's the next step?" – CNN.com, 6/13/2018

Reality TV: Remaking Television Culture, Laurie Ouellette and Susan Murray

AP/TV Guide Viewer Study, September 2005

Ken Auletta interview 2018

"It's time to rethink how we cover Trump" – CJR.org, 1/22/2018

David Folkenflik interview 2018

"Overlooked News Stories 2017" – Business Insider, 1/2/018

James Brady interview 2018

Lights Out: A Cyberattack, A Nation Unprepared, Surviving the Aftermath, Ted Koppel

"How Vulnerable is U.S. Infrastructure to a Major Cyber Attack?" – Popular Mechanics, 9/30/2009

"Why America's Power Grid Is Susceptible to Cyberattacks" – Time, 3/30/2017

"Electricity Grid in U.S. Penetrated by Spies" – The Wall Street Journal, 7/27/2017

American Society of Civil Engineers 2017 Infrastructure Report Card

"Rethinking the 'Infrastructure' Discussion Amid a Blitz of Hurricanes" – ProPublica, 9/13/2017

"Flint Water Crisis Fast Facts" – CNN.com, 4/8/2018

Bobby Magill, president of the Society of Environmental Journalists, interview 2018

"Trump Promises to Double Clinton Infrastructure Spending Plan" – Fox Business News, 8/2/2016

"Building a Stronger America: President Donald J. Trump's American Infrastructure Initiative" – Whitehouse.gov, 2/12/208

"Trump promised $1.5 trillion in infrastructure spending. He's 1 percent of the way there" – The Washington Post, 3/29/2018

"White House Admits Trump's Infrastructure Promise Isn't Happening" – New York,
5/9/2018
"The Overlooked, Under-Reported and Ignored Stories of 2017" – Billmoyers.org, 12/19/2017

Chapter 10

Pulitzer.org 2015 finalists and winners
Pulitzer.org 2015 finalists and winners
"How an Affair Between a Reporter and a Security Aide Has Rattled Washington Media" – The
New York Times, 6/24/2018
RCFP.org, Shield Law Data
"Branzburg vs. Hayes: The Evolution of Reporter's Privilege" – Constitution Law Reporter
"Trump's War Against Leakers Shows Why We Need a Shield Law" – Chicago Tribune,
6/12/2018
"CPJ's Recommendations to the Obama Administration" - Committee to Protect Journalists,
10/7/2013
"If Donald Trump Targets Journalists, Thank Obama" – The New York Times, 12/30/2016
"The Trump Administration's Pursuit of Ali Watkins Proves We Need Federal Shield Law
Now" – The Daily Beast, 6/9/18
Attorney George Freeman interview 2018
Jeff Hermes, former director of the Digital Media Law Project at Harvard University and now a
deputy director of the Media Law Resource Center, interview 2018
Charles Tobin, a partner at Ballard Spahr, interview 2018
"Peter Thiel is Totally Gay, People" – Gawker, 12/19/2007
"Peter Thiel, Tech Billionaire, Reveals Secret War with Gawker" – The New York Times,
5/25/2016
"Sorting Through the Fallout from Gawker's Hulk Hogan Settlement" – Forbes.com,
11/4/2016
"Billionaires vs. The Press in the Era of Trump" – The New York Times, 11/22/2016
"Gawker was Murdered by Gaslight" – Gawker, 8/22/2016
"Pyramid-Like Company Ponies Up $1 Million for Mitt Romney" – Mother Jones, 2/6/2012
"School-Yard Rumble" – The Advocate, 9/14/1999
"We Were Sued by a Billionaire Political Donor. We Won. Here's What Happened." – Mother
Jones, 10/8/2015
"Campus Rape Reports Are Up, And Assaults Aren't the Only Reason" – NPR.org,
4/30/2014
Multiple Huffington Post campus rape stories, 2014
"It's High Time Columbia's Mattress Girl Was Discredited" – National Review, 8/4/2017
"George Will's Michigan State University Commencement Speech Sparks Protests, Outrage" –
Media Matters for America, 12/9/2014
"The sex abuse scandal is far from over at Michigan State" – AP, Chicago Tribune, 1/25/2018
"Rolling Stone and UVA: The Columbia University Graduate School of Journalism Report" –
Rolling Stone, 4/5/2015

"Rolling Stone settles Rape on Campus lawsuit" – *imediaethics.org, 4/16/2017*

"University of Virginia grads can sue Rolling Stone for defamation over fake story about fraternity gang rape" – *N.Y. Daily News, 9/19/2017*

Elias IV vs. Rolling Stone LLC.

"ABC Settles with Meat Producer in 'Pink Slime' Defamation Case" – *The New York Times, 6/28/2017*

"ABC TV settles with beef product maker in 'pink slime' defamation case" – *Reuters.com, 6/28/2017*

Lucy Dalglish interview 2018

Robert Balin, chairman of the Media Law Committee of the International Bar Association, interview 2018

Hagit Limor, chair of the Society of Professional Journalists Legal Defense Fund, interview 2018

Daniel Bevarly, executive director of the non-profit National Freedom of Information Coalition, interview 2018

"Our historic decision to counter violation of public trust" – *The Seattle Times, 2/27/2018*

"You did it Washingtonians! SB 6617 vetoed!" – *Washingtonpolicy.org, 3/1/2018*

"Top Senators lecture press then remove House Bill 302 from consideration" – *Kentucky Press Association, 3/23/2018*

Former Washington Post Executive Editor Leonard Downie, Jr. interview 2018

"Who Gets a Press Pass? Media Credentialing Practices in the United States" – *Berkman/Shorenstein Center report, June 2014*

FOIA, INC. report, Duke University Law School, 2016

"Deadly Silence" – *Editor & Publisher, 6/1/205*

"Thwarting Freedom of Information" – *CPJ.org, 4/25/2017*

"FREEDOM OF INFORMATION ACT: Agencies Are Implementing Requirements but Additional Actions Are Needed" – *U.S. Government Accountability Office, 6/25/2018*

"Press Advocates See Trump's Words Behind Physical Attacks on Reporters" – *The Washington Post, 5/25/2017*

"Enemies and anthems" – *National Review, 6/26/2018*

"Donald trump Says North Korea Summit Media coverage Was 'Almost Treasonous'" – *Newsweek, 6/21/2018*

"EPA blocks some media from summit, then reverses course" – *AP, 5/22/2018*

"11 Journalists Killed in USA" CPJ.org, 2018

U.S. Press Freedom Tracker, Reporters Committee for Freedom of the Press, rcfp.org

Settle for More, Megyn Kelly

"Our Say: Thank you. We will not forget" – *Capital Gazette, 7/1/2018*

Chapter 11

Esther Enkin, past president of the Organization of News Ombudsmen and Standards Editors (ONO) and the ombudsman at the Canadian Broadcasting Corporation, interview 2018

"Miss the readers' advocate?" – *St. Louis Post-Dispatch, 8/5/2008*

"The Diminishing Role of the Ombudsman in American Journalism" – *University of Nebraska, December 2014*

"Ombudsman role still has a place in newsroom" – USA Today, 2/21/2013
Andy Alexander interview, 2018
"What Does the Word Ombudsman Mean?" – Ombudsman.com, 2/18/2014
News Ombudsmen in North America, Neil Nemeth
The Organization of News Ombudsmen and Standards Editors Website
The Patriarch, Alex S. Jones and Susan Tifft
Alex S. Jones interview, 2018
"First US news org with an ombudsman eliminates the position" – Poynter.org, 8/4/2008
Keith Runyon, former Courier-Journal employee 1969 to 2012, interview 2018
Branzburg vs. Hayes decision
"Philip M. Foisie's memos to the management of The Washington Post" – Newsombudsmen.org, 11/9/1995
John Harwood, interview 2018
"Richard Harwood; Editor, First Ombudsman at Washington Post" – Los Angeles Times, 5/22/2001
"THE PLAYERS: It Wasn't a Game" – The Washington Post, 4/19/1981
"Post Writer Wins Pulitzer for Story on Child Addict" – The Washington Post, 4/14/1981
A Good Life, Ben Bradlee
"Bill Green, Who Dissected Washington Post Scandal, Dies at 91" – The New York Times, 4/2/2016
"Washington Post Eliminates Ombudsman Position" – The Wrap, 3/1/2013
"Bias on the church scandal?" – The Boston Globe, 4/29/2002
"Did Paper Add to Kids' Pain in Shooting Case?" – Hartford Courant, 6/26/2005
"A Deadly Ambush: Ex-Trooper Kills Wife, Himself; Injured Lawyer in Stable Condition" – Hartford Courant, 6/16/2005
"CORRECTING THE RECORD; Times Reporter Who Resigned Leaves Long Trail of Deception" – The New York Times, 5/11/2003
"Times Reporter Resigns After Questions on Article" – The New York Times, 5/2/2003
"NY Times to Appoint First Ombudsman" – Editor & Publisher, 7/30/2003

Chapter 12

"THE PUBLIC EDITOR; An Advocate for Times Readers Introduces Himself" – The New York Times, 12/7/2003
"The Public Editor; What Do You Know, and How Do You Know It?" – The New York Times, 2/29/2004
"THE PUBLIC EDITOR; Weapons of Mass Destruction? Or Mass Distraction?" – The New York Times, 5/30/2004
"THE PUBLIC EDITOR; Is The New York Times a Liberal Newspaper?" – The New York Times, 7/25/2004
Daniel Okrent interview, 2018
"THE PUBLIC EDITOR; Briefers and Leakers and the Newspapers Who Enable Them" – The New York times, 5/8/2005

"*A Clinton Story Fraught with Inaccuracies: How It Happened and What Next?*" – *The New York Times, 7/27/2015*

"*Systemic Change Needed After Faulty Times Article*" – *The New York Times, 12/18/2015*

"*How Do You Use an Anonymous Source?*" – *The Washington Post, 12/10/2017*

"*Too Close to Home*" – *The New York Times, 2/6/2010*

"*Conflict in Israel?*" – *CJR.org, 9/14/2011*

"*Tangled Relationships in Jerusalem*" – *The New York Times, 9/24/2011*

"*Final Thoughts About My Tenure and The Times's Future*" – *The New York Times, 5/6/2007*

"*New York Times Public Editor Liz Spayd Writes Disastrous Defense of False Equivalence*" – *New York, 9/12/2016*

"*Covering Sports. Including Smelt Fishing. And Bighorn-Sheep Hunting.*" – *The New York Times, 4/8/2017*

"*NY Times Public Editor Helps Out An 'Alt-Right' Harassment Campaign*" – *Media Matters for America, 3/17/2017*

"*New York Times Public Editor: Some tweets from our politics reporters 'outrageous' and there 'ought to be some kind of consequences'*" – *BusinessInsider.com, 12/5/2016*

"*Bret Stephens Takes on Climate Change. Readers Unleash Their Fury*" – *The New York Times, 5/3/2017*

"*Climate of Complete Certainty*" – *The New York Times, 4/28/2017*

"*FAIL*" – *The New Republic, 2017*

"*Trump, Russia, and the News Story That Wasn't*" – *The New York Times, 1/20/2017*

"*NYT's Dean Baquet rips 'fairly ridiculous conclusion' in public editor's column on Russia coverage*" – *The Washington Post, 1/21/2017*

"*A Conversation with Liz Spayd, the Controversial Public Editor of The New York Times*" – *The Atlantic, 5/16/2017*

"*Good Riddance to The New York Times' Public Editor*" – *Politico, 5/31/2017*

"*Dear Public Editor: What Are You Doing?*" – *Slate, 4/14/2017*

"*Liz Spayd's final NY Times column shows why she failed as public editor*" – *Media Matters for America, 6/2/2017*

"*Why The New York Times Fired Its Public Editor in Favor of a 'Reader Center'*" – *The Daily Beast, 5/31/2017*

"*New York Times eliminates its public editor*" – *Politico, 5/31/2017*

"*How an Affair Between a Reporter and a Security Aide Has Rattled Washington Media*" – *The New York Times, 6/24/2018*

"*Ex-Senate Aide Charged in Leak Case Where Times Reporter's Records Were Seized*" – *The New York Times, 6/7/2018*

"*Ethical Journalism: A Handbook of Values and Practices for the News and Editorial Departments*" – *NYTimes.com*

"*New York Times Reassigns Reporter in Leak Case*" – *7/3/2018*

"*Glenn Thrush, Suspended Times Reporter, to Resume Work but Won't Cover White House*" – *The New York Times, 12/20/2017*

"*The Fourth Estate*" – *Showtime 2018*

"*ESPN laying off 150 staffers Wednesday*" – *The Sporting News, 11/29/2017*

James Brady interview 2018
"ESPN awash in rising political tide" – ESPN.com, 12/16/2017
"Apologizing for an error in judgment" – ESPN.com, 6/23/2008
"ESPN navigating uncharted political, social and controversial waters" – ESPN.com, 10/11/2017
"A reader representative for The Washington Post" – The Washington Post, 3/1/2013
Geneva Overholser, former Des Moines Register editor and Washington Post ombudsman from 1995 to 1998, interview, 2018
Jeffrey Dvorkin, NPR ombudsman from 2000 to 2006, interview, 2018
Alicia Shepard, NPR ombudsman from 2007 to 2011, interview, 2018
"NPR's Giffords Mistake: Re-Learning the Lesson of Checking Sources" – NPR.com, 1/11/11

Chapter 13

"Is the quest for profits and clicks killing local news?" – CJR.org, Spring 2017
PBS NewsHour History – PBS.org
"Theodore Bodenwein's will" – The Day
Media Management in the Age of Giants, Dennis F. Herrick
"Journal Publishing Company, CREATE Foundation boost region" – Mississippi Business Journal, 5/9/2005
"History of the News-Gazette" - News-Gazette of Champaign, IL.
"What is The Christian Science Monitor?" – CSMonitor.com
AP CEO Gary Pruitt, interview 2018
"The Growing Importance of Non-Profit Journalism" – Shorenstein Center at Harvard University, April 2007
"Gaining Ground: How Nonprofit News Ventures Seek Sustainability " – Knight Foundation, 2015
The Institute for Non-Profit News
Sue Cross, INN CEO and executive director, interview, 2018
Leonard Downie, Jr. interview, 2018
ProPublica.org Editor-in-Chief Stephen Engelberg, interview, 2018
"Criminal Past Is No Bar to Nursing in California" – Propublica.org, 10/4/2008
"Five New Orleans Cops Convicted for Their Role in Post-Katrina Shootings" – Propublica.org, 8/5/2011
"Lisa Song, Elizabeth McGowan and David Hasemyer of InsideClimate News, Brooklyn, NY Win Pulitzer" – Pulitzer.org, 2013
"Finalist: Amy Julia Harris and Shoshana Walter of Reveal from The Center for Investigative Reporting" – Pulitzer.org, 2018
"The Best Nonprofit Journalism of 2017" - The Institute for Non-Profit News
Lori Hearn, creator, inewsource of San Diego, interview, 2018
Steve Myers, editor, The Lens of New Orleans, interview, 2018
"Orleans Parish prosecutors are using fake subpoenas to pressure witnesses to talk to them" – The Lens, 4/26/2017

"Actors were paid to support Entergy's power plant at New Orleans City Council meetings" – The Lens, 5/4/2018

"Losing Ground" – The Lens/Propublica, 8/28/2014

CalMatters co-founder David Lesher, interview, 2018

"Learn about districts we studied to understand how well California's school funding system is working" – CalMatters, 6/18/2017

Texas Tribune Editor-in-chief Emily Ramshaw, interview, 2018

"Hell and High Water" – Texas Tribune/Propublica, 3/3/2016

"Sold Out" - Texas Tribune, 2017

"God and Government" - Texas Tribune, 10/24/2015

CPSIA information can be obtained
at www.ICGtesting.com
Printed in the USA
LVHW092307210319
611506LV00001B/170/P